IOLO MORGANWG AND THE ROMANTIC TRADITION IN WALES

General Editor: Geraint H. Jenkins

Iolo Morganwg by William Owen Pughe

The Truth Against the World

Iolo Morganwg and Romantic Forgery

MARY-ANN CONSTANTINE

UNIVERSITY OF WALES PRESS
CARDIFF
2007

www.wales.ac.uk/press

British Library Cataloguing-in-Publication Data
A catalogue record for this book is available from the British Library

ISBN 978-0-7083-2062-4

Printed in Wales by Dinefwr Press, Llandybïe

I David, Tom a Gwyn – gyda chariad

Truth walks a circle. A system formed by rule and square
touches tangentially that circle but in a few points.

Iolo Morganwg (NLW 13120B, p. 193)

IOLO MORGANWG AND THE ROMANTIC TRADITION IN WALES

Other volumes already published in the series:

A Rattleskull Genius: The Many Faces of Iolo Morganwg, edited by Geraint H. Jenkins (University of Wales Press, 2005)

Bardic Circles: Personal, Regional and National Identity in the Bardic Vision of Iolo Morganwg, by Cathryn A. Charnell-White (University of Wales Press, 2007)

Contents

Figures

(between pages 142 and 143)

Preface

This book owes much to other people and institutions, and it is a pleasure to acknowledge their help here.I have received a great deal of support from all those directly involved in our AHRC-funded project 'Iolo Morganwg and the Romantic Tradition in Wales' at the University of Wales Centre for Advanced Welsh and Celtic Studies in Aberystwyth. Both permanent and temporary members of the research team have been generous with advice and material: for this, and for their company, I would like to thank Cathryn Charnell-White, Marian Beech Hughes, Andrew Davies, Glenys Howells, Bethan Jenkins, David Ceri Jones, Eluned Jones, Ffion Mair Jones, Marion Löffler and Hywel Gethin Rhys. I am grateful, too, to all the members of our Advisory Panel for their ideas and suggestions at various points. The project itself is the brainchild of Geraint H. Jenkins, who has directed operations with an energy and thoroughness born of a positively eighteenth-century enthusiasm for his subject: I am extremely grateful to him for giving me the opportunity to discover the riches of the Iolo Morganwg archive. The staff of the National Library of Wales have been unfailingly helpful in providing access to that archive and much more: it has been a real pleasure to work there, to feel part of its daily activity. I am especially indebted to Geraint Phillips and Huw Walters for sharing their knowledge of the library's resources and of the period in general.

The British Academy enabled me to attend a conference in Latvia, and funded a period of research in Brittany. I am grateful to Jean-François Simon, the director of the Centre de Recherche Bretonne et Celtique at the Université de Bretagne Occidentale, Brest, and to the library staff for making me feel welcome during my research period there; also to Fañch Postic and Donatien Laurent, who provided invaluable help with the La Villemarqué archive. One of the most stimulating aspects of writing this book has been the opportunity to approach English/British romantic literature, as it were, from a Welsh perspective, and I have learned a great deal from attending various conferences on different aspects of Romanticism: among many friends and colleagues who have given specific help and advice I should like to thank Damian Walford Davies, Gavin Edwards, Howard Gaskill, John Goodridge, Nick Groom, Ronald Hutton, Bridget Keegan, Joep Leerssen, Jon Mee, Dafydd Moore and Sarah Prescott.

I am very grateful to Gwyneth Lewis for her kind encouragement at the start of this project, and for permission to reprint and translate her poem 'Iolo

Morganwg' (originally published by Gomer in *Sonedau Redsa a Cherddi Eraill* (Llandysul, 1990)). Some sections of the chapters on Chatterton appeared in an article published in Alistair Heys (ed.), *From Gothic to Romantic: Thomas Chatterton's Bristol* (Bristol, 2005): I am grateful to John Sansome of Redcliffe Press for allowing them to be reprinted here. Likewise, some sections of the *Ossian* chapters and the Epilogue appeared earlier in Peter Knight and Jonathan Long (eds.), *Fakes and Forgeries* (Cambridge, 2005), while the first part of the introduction borrows from a short piece written for *Planet* 172 (2005): again, I am indebted to the editors for permission to use this material.

My parents have been, as ever, interested and involved in my work, and I continue to be more than grateful for all their encouragement. My greatest debt is to David Parsons for his constant support, emotional, practical and editorial. My eldest son, Thomas Huw, has kept me laughing, while my youngest, Gwyn, gave a new urgency to the word 'deadline' by arriving as this book was in its very final stages – and with a timing Iolo would have approved of – on Alban Hefin, Midsummer Day.

February 2007 Mary-Ann Constantine

Acknowledgements

http:www.blakearchive.org: Fig. 7

Musée départemental breton, Quimper / P. Sicard: Fig. 8

The National Library of Wales: Frontispiece, Figs. 1, 3, 4, 6, 9, 10

Scottish National Portrait Gallery: Fig. 5

Tate Britain: Fig. 2

Abbreviations

BB	Th. Hersart de la Villemarqué, *Barzaz-Breiz: chants populaires de la Bretagne* (Paris). The three substantive editions of 1839 (2 vols.), 1845 (2 vols.), and 1867, are distinguished by the year of publication.
BBCS	*Bulletin of the Board of Celtic Studies*
BL	British Library
BL Add	British Library Additional Manuscripts
BSAF	*Bulletin de la Société Archéologique du Finistère*
Cardiff	Cardiff Central Library
GPC	*Geiriadur Prifysgol Cymru* (4 vols., Caerdydd, 1950–2002)
IMChY	G. J. Williams, *Iolo Morganwg a Chywyddau'r Ychwanegiad* (Llundain, 1926)
LlC	*Llên Cymru*
MAW	Owen Jones, Iolo Morganwg and William Owen Pughe, *The Myvyrian Archaiology of Wales* (3 vols., London, 1801–7)
NLW	National Library of Wales
NLWJ	*National Library of Wales Journal*
ODNB	*Oxford Dictionary of National Biography* (60 vols., Oxford, 2004)
PBA	*Proceedings of the British Academy*
PO	Howard Gaskill (ed.), *James Macpherson: The Poems of Ossian and Related Works* (Edinburgh, 1996)
RAEW	Elijah Waring, *Recollections and Anecdotes of Edward Williams* (London, 1850)
Rattleskull Genius	Geraint H. Jenkins (ed.), *A Rattleskull Genius: The Many Faces of Iolo Morganwg* (Cardiff, 2005)
THSC	*Transactions of the Honourable Society of Cymmrodorion*
TLlM	G. J. Williams, *Traddodiad Llenyddol Morgannwg* (Caerdydd, 1948)
WHR	*Welsh History Review*
Williams: *IM*	G. J. Williams, *Iolo Morganwg – Y Gyfrol Gyntaf* (Caerdydd, 1956)
Williams: *PLP*	Edward Williams, *Poems, Lyric and Pastoral* (2 vols., London, 1794)

Iolo Morganwg

Gwyneth Lewis

Fe wyddai'n iawn mai anwar oedd ei awen ef
yr hawliai ganddo, hwyr neu hwyrach, lawer mwy
na rhoddion ei amserau.
Meistrolodd foesau Llundain, crefftau'r oes,
pamffledu ei freuddwydion, ennill ei ail blwyf
mewn sgyrsiau ffraeth tafarndai, lle'r oedd dawn yn ach,
a dysgodd gario'r dyddiau byr â'i ddeall chwim.

Gwrthododd hi cyn hir ei ysgolheictod bro.
Ysgolor hiraeth, gyrrodd ef o'i go'
a'i droi yn wyddon hanes.

Haelionus oedd ei dwyllo, llawen, rhydd
o grintach beirdd gwangalon a'u gonestrwydd tlawd.
Heb air wrth neb, gweithiodd yn oes gorffwylledd,
colli'i bwyll, a mynd yn hen, hen, cyn ei amser.

Ond chwarddai nerth ei ben fel bachgen ambell nos
wrth weled amser yn ei ufuddhau
a'r byd yn gwireddu ei eiriau.

[He knew full well his muse was wild,
that sooner or later she would demand
more than the usual tributes.
He mastered London manners, the crafts of his age,
the pamphlets of his dreams, and won his place
in the wit of taverns, where skill was his patrimony,
carrying the short days with his darting thought.

But parochial learning soon left her cold:
she drove him, the scholar of longing, out of his mind,
and turned him into history's wizard.

His deceptions were generous, joyful, free
of the meanness of weakhearted poets and their poor honesty.
Without telling a soul, he worked in a mad age,
lost his reason and grew old, old, before his time.

But some nights he'd be laughing like a boy
to see time bend to his bidding
and the world make his words come true.]

1

Introduction: 'Seeing daylight all the way': Iolo Morganwg and Romantic Forgery

The winter of 1775–6 was bitter. In Kent, where the Welsh stonecutter Edward Williams had gone to find work, the river Medway froze over and ships were wrecked in the harbour at Chatham; snow settled '40 or 50 feet deep . . . and they have been oblidged to dig ways under the snow, like the ways under ground in coal mines to go out to the country for necessaries'.[1] He worked in Faversham and in Sandwich, initially pleased with his new responsibilities, but soon complaining to his father and brothers that this was 'the most disagreable Situation I ever was in, the Englishmen are damn Mad (to use their own phrase) that a Taffy Should rule them, whilst on the other hand my master will lay all their errors to my charge'.[2] He was overworked, frustrated, wanting time to himself to write poetry in Welsh and English, and to pursue his antiquarian interests in the language and history of early Britain. He asked his father, also a stonecutter, though a less literate one, to send down his precious copy of Edward Lhuyd's *Archaeologia Britannica* ('a pretty large Book almost as large as a church prayer book'): the thought of its precarious journey 'by James's waggon to the Three Cups in Breadstreet, London, from thence to be sent by the Faversham Hoy lying at Custom House Quay' is terrifying.[3]

An odd episode from this period captures something of the strain he must have been under. A version of it was included in the *Recollections* published by Elijah Waring in 1850; but a pencilled manuscript note in his own hand, perhaps written out for Waring's benefit, tells the story rather better:

> E.W. about 1774 worked at his Trade as a Marble and Freestone mason with Mr Davison [*sic* Deveson] of Sandwich in Kent to whom he was foreman. Mr Davison being in a fever confined to his Bed sent for EW up to him and desired him to go very early next morning to Mr Minter of Ash, a village about 2 or 3 Miles distant

[1] NLW 21285E, Letter no. 782, Iolo Morganwg to Edward William(s) [his father], 1 February 1776.

[2] Ibid., Letter no. 773, Iolo Morganwg to Edward William(s), 13 September 1775.

[3] Ibid., Letter no. 782, Iolo Morganwg to Edward William(s), 1 February 1776.

> from Sandwich and to draw out an Account of freestone done on Ash Church and to measure a freestone coping that had been laid on a wall round a very large Church Yard, and to add it to the other acct. and also to request of Mr Minter (who was Church Warden) to pay £10 on acct. – E.W. went according, but he got up at Midnight dressed himself, to[ok] his pocket book and the acct. with him, rule for measuring, &c and went towards Ash seeing daylight all the way. When he came to the Church Yard he measured the coping, having daylight, apparently, all the while. Having measured the whole of the coping he took out his Pocket book and a piece of paper whereon to enter the number of feet which the coping measured. Just as he had done this the clock struck One, he awoke, and found himself in the middle or dead of night and that all that he had done had been done in sleep, in which he had seen daylight all the while. Having been thus awakened from his sleep he was surprized, but not frightened he staid untill it was day. And then measured the work and found that he had in his [sleep] measured it with the greatest exactness.[4]

There is something compelling in the thought of that three-mile walk and the careful manual work performed inside sleep, a sleep lit up by a wholly imaginary daylight. The stonecutter Edward Williams would become far better known as the Welsh bard Iolo Morganwg (Edward of Glamorgan), whose vision of the Welsh past also combined the meticulousness and craftsmanship of the dedicated scholar with the dazzling illumination of powerful personal conviction. Iolo is no great user of metaphors, but in his essays and notes he often uses terms of light and darkness to think with, and they produce some of his best images. The Welsh literary tradition is itself constantly figured as a kind of beacon, 'long and luminous', handed down the centuries by a succession of bards. And light, of course, is at the very heart of his Gorsedd ceremony of bardic initiation, which must take place in the open air in a circle of stones, 'yn wyneb haul a llygad goleuni' (in the face of the sun and the eye of light), at the significant calendrical moments of the solstices and equinoxes. 'I was born', he wrote in one autobiographical draft, with poetic if not historical exactness, 'on the 21st day of March (New Stile) 1747 at six o'clock in the morning at the same instant as I have been told that the rising sun appeared.'[5] The internal daylight of Iolo's midnight walk can be read as a precursor of what would become his bardic vision, the 'truth' that in his most famous motto he set 'against the world' ('Y Gwir yn erbyn y Byd').

The complicated nature of that truth is the subject of this book, which in effect puts Iolo into a series of dialogues with other figures from the period whose writings, one way or another, caused people to think about, and occasionally to rethink, notions of what might constitute the genuine, the real, the authentic. The term 'Romantic forgery' of the title is not intended to

[4] NLW 21387E, no. 4. Cf. *RAEW*, pp. 69–71.
[5] NLW 21387E, no. 10.

be provocative, merely reflective of the period's own controversy-ridden attitude to the question; as Iolo himself put it, with typical indignation:

> Forgeries of this nature are very recent things. So is the taste, or more properly rage, for antiquities of all kinds, ancient Poetry, ancient Castles, ancient Taylor's bodkins etc etc. Booksellers have of late years given large sums for ancient mss and translations from them, as Macpherson very well knew.[6]

Romantic literary forgery is, thanks to the revived fortunes of 'Ossian' Macpherson and Thomas Chatterton, currently the focus of lively critical interest. New explorations of textual authenticity, of how it is defined and by whom, have brought previously marginal literary figures into the heart of British Romanticism. There are now several general studies, from Anthony Grafton's broad-ranging account of literary fraud through time (which has helped to define and contextualize what often seems to be an eighteenth-century obsession, showing parallels and continuities in practice which stretch back into the ancient world) to the work of Ken Ruthven, for whom literary forgery ultimately reveals the 'fakeness' of all literature.[7] Within the Romantic period, Ian Haywood has argued that the controversies raised by specific texts helped the late eighteenth century to distinguish historical from fictional modes of writing about the past, while Paul Baines has tied literary forgeries into their legal and criminal context, showing in particular how the concept of fraud developed with the growing complexity of the economy.[8] Recent work has concentrated on rescuing literary forgery from the scrappy edges of literary history to play its part in the ushering-in of Romanticism itself, with both Nick Groom and Margaret Russett arguing for its status as a formative strand – if not *the* formative strand – in what could be considered 'Romantic' notions of self, authorship and the nature of poetic inspiration.[9] Further monographs are expected.[10] Alongside these general surveys there has grown up an increasing body of detailed work on the lives and the writings of the major figures of the era – Macpherson, Chatterton and William Henry Ireland most prominently among them, with a critical Samuel Johnson invariably looming nearby – to add ballast to what tends to be a rather

[6] NLW 13112B, p. 21.

[7] Anthony Grafton, *Forgers and Critics: Creativity and Duplicity in Western Scholarship* (Princeton, NJ, 1990); K. K. Ruthven, *Faking Literature* (Cambridge, 2001).

[8] Ian Haywood, *The Making of History: A Study of the Literary Forgeries of James Macpherson and Thomas Chatterton in Relation to Eighteenth-Century Ideas of History and Fiction* (Rutherford, 1986); idem, *Faking It: Art and the Politics of Forgery* (Brighton, 1987); Paul Baines, *The House of Forgery in Eighteenth-Century Britain* (Aldershot, 1999).

[9] Margaret Russett, *Fictions and Fakes: Forging Romantic Authenticity, 1760–1845* (Cambridge, 2006); Nick Groom, *The Forger's Shadow* (London, 2002); Groom has a useful list of further works on literary and other types of forgery on p. 307.

[10] Jack Lynch is currently working on a book provisionally entitled *Deceits and Deceptions*.

excitable subject.[11] Behind these more fully contextualized lives stands a growing chorus of fraudulent eccentrics, from the Frenchman George Psalmanazar who, early in the eighteenth century, claimed to be a native of the island of Formosa and arrived in London complete with mysterious language and alphabet, to, a century later, the servant girl Mary Baker, who spent ten glorious weeks as the black-turbaned Princess Caraboo, abducted by pirates from an island near Sumatra.[12] The prevailing interest in deception and authenticity has also affected studies of autobiography and authorial identity, with some particularly interesting results in work on the period's labouring-class poets; discussions of eighteenth-century canon formation and the development of notions of textual authority likewise cannot avoid the implications of the various contemporary controversies. And yet the word 'forgery' remains, in spite of or because of this attention, a slippery one to pin down. Ultimately, perhaps, the only legitimate argument for its continued use in literary criticism is its prevalence in the terminology of a period which Iolo (still righteously indignant) called 'the present age of forgery'.[13] Our own present age of forgery-criticism has dissected the word to reconfigure it a little differently every time, and while it has been understandably rejected altogether in some quarters (it is not now generally considered helpful to refer to Macpherson as a 'forger'), others have insisted on reclaiming the more positive origins of the word, giving the verb 'to forge' renewed glamour as the original creative act. In my own use of the word in this book, these inherent complexities should be taken as read, and, following Groom, will be 'henceforth written without "scare-marks"'.[14]

The figure of Iolo Morganwg has been strikingly absent from this recent debate; if mentioned at all, he is an off-stage presence, referred to in footnotes

[11] The major revisionist texts for *Ossian* are Fiona J. Stafford, *The Sublime Savage: A Study of James Macpherson and the Poems of Ossian* (Edinburgh, 1988); Howard Gaskill (ed.), *Ossian Revisited* (Edinburgh, 1991); Fiona J. Stafford and Howard Gaskill (eds.), *From Gaelic to Romantic: Ossianic Translations* (Amsterdam, 1998); and Howard Gaskill (ed.), *The Reception of Ossian in Europe* (London, 2004). For a useful summary of recent approaches, see James Porter, 'Bring me the Head of James Macpherson: The Execution of Ossian and the Wellsprings of Folkloristic Discourse', *Journal of American Folklore*, 114 (2001), 396–435. For Chatterton, see Nick Groom (ed.), *Thomas Chatterton and Romantic Culture* (Basingstoke, 1999); Alistair Heys (ed.), *From Gothic to Romantic: Chatterton's Bristol* (Bristol, 2005). For a biography of Ireland, see Patricia Pierce, *The Great Shakespeare Fraud: The Strange, True Story of William-Henry Ireland* (Stroud, 2004).

[12] For Psalmanazar, see Michael Keevak, *The Pretended Asian: George Psalmanazar's Eighteenth-Century Formosan Hoax* (Detroit, MI, 2004) and Jack Lynch, 'Forgery as Performance Art: The Strange Case of George Psalmanazar', *1650–1850: Ideas, Aesthetics and Inquiries in the Early Modern Era*, 11 (2005), 21–35; for Caraboo, see Russett, *Fictions and Fakes*, pp. 113–36.

[13] NLW 13104B, p. 124.

[14] See Groom, *The Forger's Shadow*, p. 14. There is a stimulating discussion of the term and its many relations (counterfeit, copy, plagiarism etc.) on pp.16–50.

or gestured at in brusque parallels.[15] It is hard to see why. To borrow Nick Groom's image, Iolo may not have cast as dramatic a shadow on the British Romantic poets as Macpherson or Chatterton, but he was not, at the time, as invisible as he has now become to most critics outside Wales. He participated intensely in the literary life of the period, in London as well as Wales; his ideas, often disseminated through the works of others, influenced the likes of Blake and Southey, while the work he did in creatively editing early medieval Welsh manuscripts affected – and continues to affect – perceptions of Welsh literature, if not the culture as a whole. Indeed, even if viewed from a purely English-Romantic perspective, the life and works of this man as they are revealed in over a hundred volumes of manuscript papers and letters held in the National Library of Wales, are alive with directly relevant material – much of it in English. Iolo was by turns a struggling provincial poet in London, a manipulator and victim of the world of literary patronage, an opium eater, a political and religious radical, an agriculturalist, a medievalist, a prime source of bardic and druidic knowledge, and a sharp and opinionated critic of the literary controversies of his day. Through it all, almost from the beginning, he was a forger, an inventor of selves, texts and traditions. The Iolo archive is a gold mine for those interested in the late eighteenth century and the early decades of the nineteenth century. He merits more than footnotes.

But this book is also a plea for a non-English-Romantic perspective, for starting from another cultural standpoint. The Ossian material is a case in point: for the last fifteen years or so, an increasingly subtle and sympathetic understanding of the social and political background to James Macpherson's life has informed discussions of the nature of his controversial adaptation of native Gaelic tradition. Biographies and studies have teased out his shifting allegiances and relations with the cultures, languages and identities available to a writer in eighteenth-century Scotland: Gaelic, Scottish, English, British and European (and, in Macpherson's case, Transatlantic). By contrast, outside knowledge of, and interest in, the Welsh culture and society of this period is poor indeed. Much so-called 'four nations' criticism in both historical and literary fields is heavily biased towards Scotland and Ireland, and studies of the development of 'Britishness' in this period are marred by poor knowledge of Welsh archives; post-colonial readings of England's complex relations with her Celtic neighbours have tended to assume that because the Acts of Union came early (1536–43), eighteenth-century Wales had been unproblematically

[15] Of the five monograph studies of romantic period literary forgery mentioned above, only one gives him as much as a page, another has two sentences and one reference (in three different parts of the book) and three do not mention him at all.

assumed into a greater English/British identity.[16] Literary studies show little awareness of the Welsh literary canon, while knowledge of the Welsh language (which remained the first language for the majority of the population in Wales until the end of the nineteenth century)[17] is abysmal, with otherwise sympathetic and intelligent readings marred by simple errors and spelling mistakes.[18] There are exceptions, of course, and with a growing body of work explicitly devoted to the Welsh presence in British Romanticism, it is to be hoped that these attitudes will change.[19]

Within Wales, Iolo Morganwg still has a powerful reputation (and not just in academic or literary circles) as a pivotal figure in a period of national revival, a bringer of a potent blend of inspiration and confusion to almost every branch of cultural life. Most scholars of Welsh literature, and of the medieval period in particular, encounter his works sooner or later. The question of forgery, of what exactly he did and why, will not go away; and yet in Welsh criticism, until recently, the subject has not been treated especially well: for earlier writers it was essentially a character failing or a moral problem – what G. J. Williams, Iolo's most thorough biographer, called 'yr hen ysfa' ('the old

[16] For recent 'four nations' or 'archipelagic' approaches to questions of British national identity in this period, see Hugh Kearney, *The British Isles: A History of Four Nations* (Cambridge, 1989); Murray G. H. Pittock, *Inventing and Resisting Britain: Cultural Identities in Britain and Ireland, 1685–1789* (New York, 1997); idem, *Celtic Identity and the British Image* (Manchester, 1999). Much of the historical work is a response to the thesis of Protestant unity presented by Linda Colley in *Britons: Forging the Nation, 1707–1837* (Yale, 1992), but, as Murray Pittock has noted, 'four nations' literary criticism is currently less developed than its historical counterpart: 'Robert Burns and British Poetry', *PBA*, 121 (2002, published 2003), 196. Wales is particularly under-represented: Katie Trumpener's otherwise stimulating study of *Bardic Nationalism: The Romantic Novel and the British Empire* (Princeton, NJ, 1997) wavers uneasily from the outset, with the book's first sentence announcing a study of 'England, Scotland, Ireland, and Britain's overseas colonies during the late eighteenth and early nineteenth centuries'; Wales quietly tags along in the third paragraph, and is given some prominence in the opening pages, but is otherwise seriously neglected. For a response, see Sarah Prescott, '"Gray's Pale Spectre": Evan Evans, Thomas Gray and the Rise of Welsh Bardic Nationalism', *Modern Philology*, 104, no. 1 (2006), 72–95. For various interpretations of the (admittedly difficult) post-colonial question, see Jane Aaron and Chris Williams (eds.), *Postcolonial Wales* (Cardiff, 2005).

[17] Before 1801 'nine of every ten of the population spoke Welsh and seven of every ten were monoglot'; the picture changed dramatically following the huge demographic rises of the nineteenth century: Geraint H. Jenkins (ed.), *Language and Community in the Nineteenth Century* (Cardiff, 1998), p. 2, and idem (ed.), *The Welsh Language before the Industrial Revolution* (Cardiff, 1997).

[18] See e.g., Trumpener, *Bardic Nationalism*, p. 295, n. 20; Nick Groom, *The Making of Percy's 'Reliques'* (Oxford, 1999), pp. 71–2; several 'grotesque' misspellings of Iolo's name are noted by Geraint H. Jenkins in 'On the Trail of a "Rattleskull Genius"' in *Rattleskull Genius*, pp. 4–5.

[19] See, e.g., Damian Walford Davies, *Presences that Disturb: Models of Romantic Identity in the Literature and Culture of the 1790s* (Cardiff, 2002); Gerard Carruthers and Alan Rawes (eds.), *English Romanticism and the Celtic World* (Cambridge, 2003) has a relatively high proportion of Welsh contributions. Damian Walford Davies and Lynda Pratt are currently editing a collection of essays on *Wales and the Romantic Imagination* (Cardiff, forthcoming).

itch').[20] Gwyneth Lewis is one of the few critics to take a different approach, seeing the forgeries rather as a coherent response to the political repression of the 1790s, and comparing the context of Iolo's writings to those of Macpherson, Chatterton and William Henry Ireland. Her lucid doctoral dissertation of 1991 is the best work in English on the subject: had it been published, there would, arguably, have been less need to write this book.[21] But Lewis's work has barely been noticed by those in the wider field, and since then the 'authenticity debate' has taken some new and unexpected turns. In 1956, G. J. Williams suggested that there was no need for the English to worry too much about their literary forgers, since, unlike Iolo Morganwg, they had only a 'minimal' impact on the literary tradition:[22] this picture has changed dramatically, and English literary criticism is currently taking its forgers very seriously indeed. It will be to the benefit of both sides – from a 'four nations' angle, all sides – if Wales joins this discussion.

And so the aim of this book is to place Iolo in various perspectives, to define the quality of his writings, and in particular the style and nature of his forgery, through comparison, dialogue, shifting context; to this end, it quotes extensively from the unpublished manuscripts which, more than his publications, best represent the variety of his life's work. As a comparative study, it builds on the work already done by Gwyneth Lewis, but with the emphasis on tracing direct connections and influences between Iolo and the literary forgers of the Romantic period, as well as on Iolo's own readings and opinions on various aspects of forgery. The book is shaped around three other writers and their cultural contexts, beginning with Chatterton, and Iolo's relations with England and English literary society, and moving then to consider Macpherson, the Ossian debate, and Iolo's attitude towards Scotland. A posthumous connection links him to the young Breton aristocrat, Hersart de La Villemarqué, whose experiences at a Gorsedd in Wales in 1838 would have far-reaching implications for the cultural revival in Brittany. While other characters and cases do make their presence felt (books on literary forgery tend to be extremely crowded), I have tried to keep the focus firmly on Iolo's works and ideas, these being new material to the wider debate: what is lost in thickness of detail should, I hope, be gained in narrative clarity.

The subject sits at the intersection of two currently popular critical domains: British Romantic literary forgery, and 'Celticism', which, neatly defined by Joep Leerssen, is 'more than the sum of the peripheries' relations with their respective centres: it is also the story of these regions' sense of ethnic inter-relatedness as "Celts", and of the contacts between these peripheries mutually'.[23]

[20] Williams: *IM*, p. 16.

[21] Gwyneth Lewis, 'Eighteenth-Century Literary Forgeries, with Special Reference to the Work of Iolo Morganwg' (unpublished University of Oxford D.Phil. thesis, 1991).

[22] Williams: *IM*, p. xxxvii.

[23] Joep Leerssen, 'Celticism' in Terence Brown (ed.), *Celticism* (Amsterdam, 1990), p. 18.

The relations of this self-consciously Welsh writer with Scotland and England, and the use made of his legacy in Brittany, offer ample opportunities to explore the notion of an 'inter-Celtic' allegiance based on resistance to English (or French) hegemony (there is, perhaps surprisingly, very little in the way of serious engagement with Ireland in Iolo's work). As should become clear, the situation was not only shifting and contradictory during Iolo's lifetime, but remained so after his death. Instrumental as his work was in encouraging a sense of 'Brythonic' fraternity between Wales and Brittany in the middle of the nineteenth century, the translation of bardism to a new cultural context was not without its ironies and strains. Iolo's relations with England are even more complicated, ranging as they do (often in the space of a page or two) from an aggressive proto-nationalism to a full and delighted participation in English/British literary and political life. The man who invested so much in the beauty and endurance of the Welsh language was entirely in favour of opening up the Gorsedd ceremony to English.[24] Such contradictions are not unusual (Macpherson and La Villemarqué also have their cake and eat it), but they are hard to convey. A perennial difficulty in writing across cultures is the danger of explaining too much or too little: it is hard to keep the reader aware, without cluttering one side or the other, that a writer who can place himself in a tradition running Chaucer – Shakespeare – Milton – Thomson – Cowper is at the same time highly aware of his position in a tradition running Aneirin – Taliesin – Dafydd ap Gwilym – Guto'r Glyn – Huw Morys – Evan Evans; that the 'manuscript culture' of eighteenth-century Wales is not the same as that in England; that the concept of the 'self-taught labouring-class poet' does not have quite the same resonance in a Welsh context. The dual inheritance becomes in itself an issue of authenticity: Iolo puzzled over his true poetic voice during those cold months down in Kent when, in the brief respites from Mr Deveson and his recalcitrant labourers, he found himself simultaneously crafting *cywyddau* for the appreciation of the London Welsh, and expressing his longing for Glamorgan in neat stanzas of English verse. 'I always', he wrote to Owain Myfyr (Owen Jones) in 1776, 'thought myself more successful in my British than my English Poetry.'[25] But the only collection of poems he ever published under his own name was in English.

The relationship with England is fundamental, and highly typical of a process repeated across Europe during Iolo's lifetime and beyond, as similar complex relations between cultural or linguistic minorities and their larger hegemonic neighbours conjured up a whole host of literary and historical versions of the past – translations, 'scholarly' editions and outright forgeries – in which the

[24] See the account of the Gorsedd held on Primrose Hill in September 1792 in *Gentleman's Magazine*, LXII, part 2 (1792), 956–7.

[25] NLW 21285E, Letter no. 783, Iolo Morganwg to Owain Myfyr, 25 January 1776. Owen Jones will be referred to by his bardic name throughout.

outlines of newly discovered sources blended imperceptibly with visions of the longed-for and the politically expedient.[26] Rooted though each case is in a specific historical milieu, the patterns are often strikingly alike; indeed at times it seems as if authenticity debates, like folk dramas, can only be expressed through a certain number of fixed roles. Thus in the controversy that followed the discovery of the Czech manuscripts of Dvůr Králové and Zelená Hora in the first decades of the nineteenth century, the vested political interests of the various supporters and detractors of their genuineness can be readily paralleled from Wales to Finland; the resurrection of the past is inextricably bound up with a developing cultural self-consciousness among peoples previously excluded from official versions of history – the provision, in the words of Robert Evans, of 'channels and themes for national self-expression'.[27]

The three sections of the book roughly follow the contours of his long life (he died in his eightieth year), but much has necessarily been left out. A select bibliography offers suggestions for further reading from a growing body of monographs, articles and pamphlets; my specific debts to these are made evident at relevant points. The core of the work, however, has involved picking a trail through the Iolo manuscripts at the National Library of Wales. The bulk and chaos of the archive has been vividly described elsewhere,[28] but the papers run to over a hundred different-sized volumes, bound in no particular order, and with few or no chronological anchors. The correspondence, well over a thousand letters, provides a detailed biographical framework and is the most useful tool for dating. But Iolo revised and recopied endlessly; he lost material and began it again, and he had great difficulty in completing any of the myriad projects he sketched out in what he calls a 'mixon of papers' piled up over decades in the little cottage at Flemingston.[29] This study dips liberally into the manuscripts, but it is hard not to be conscious of what has been left out: somewhere in the archive there will be more examples, different versions of events, or flat contradictions that should have been chased down and included. But to do that would run the risk of never getting started at all.

[26] Anne-Marie Thiesse, *La création des identités nationales* (Paris, 1999); Benedict Anderson, *Imagined Communities: Reflections on the Origin and Spread of Nationalism* (London, 1983).

[27] R. J. W. Evans, '"The Manuscripts": The Culture and Politics of Forgery in Central Europe' in *Rattleskull Genius*, p. 51. See also Eric Hobsbawm and Terence Ranger (eds.), *The Invention of Tradition* (Cambridge, 1983).

[28] See Jenkins, 'On the Trail' in *Rattleskull Genius*, p. 7.

[29] NLW 13221E, pp. 99–106, Iolo Morganwg to William Owen Pughe, 7 June 1803.

Part I: CHATTERTON

2

Proximities

Stay curyous Traveller and pass not bye
Until this fetive Pile astounde thine Eye
Whole Rocks on Rocks with Yron joynd surveie
And Okes with Okes entremed disponed lie
This mighty pile that keeps the Wyndes at Baie
Fyre Levin and the mokie Storme defie
That shootes aloofe into the Reaulmes of daie
Shall be the Record of the Buylders Fame for aie.[1]

Thomas Chatterton's medieval Bristol is a remarkable fusion of antiquarianism, history, poetry and invention: it is, as Donald Taylor puts it, 'an imaginary construct from books, local monuments, and local topography'.[2] Those attempting to describe the nature of this creation have reached for parallels in other literary genres, such as fantasy (Tolkien) or the historical romance (Scott, even Hardy). Others have claimed that Chatterton's creation is unique.[3] Few people have noticed that the best parallel can be found much closer to home, a short boat-trip across the water, in Glamorgan.[4]

Iolo Morganwg was born five years before Chatterton. But when Chatterton died in 1770, Iolo, at twenty-four, was just beginning a long literary life, much of it devoted to summoning up a vision of medieval Glamorgan as intricate and passionate as Chatterton's Bristol; it was described by his biographer in 1956 as 'one of the great creations of the Romantic period in Wales'.[5] The parallels in the lives and works of the two men are striking: poets, collectors and coiners of medieval words, both were shrewd manipulators of historical sources and of historically minded contemporaries searching for light on dark ages. Like Chatterton, but over decades rather than months, Iolo constructed elaborate genealogies, rewrote the histories of local families, wove connections between them, and gave life and poetic *oeuvres* to dozens of characters who were bare names in the sources. And

[1] 'Stay Curyous Traveller' from 'A Discorse on Brystowe' in Donald S. Taylor (ed.), *The Complete Works of Thomas Chatterton: A Bicentenary Edition* (2 vols., Oxford, 1971), I, p. 99.

[2] Taylor (ed.), *Complete Works*, I, p. xliv.

[3] Cf. Ian Haywood's claim (*Faking It*, p. 54) that 'this convoluted art form was totally *original*, and has not been attempted since'.

[4] The fullest discussions of Iolo and Chatterton to date are Gwyneth Lewis, 'Eighteenth-Century Literary Forgeries' and Geraint Phillips, 'Math o Wallgofrwydd: Iolo Morganwg, Opiwm a Thomas Chatterton', *NLWJ*, XXIX, no. 4 (1996), 391–410.

[5] 'un o greadigaethau mawr y cyfnod rhamantaidd yng Nghymru': Williams: *IM*, p. 320.

although Iolo's Bardic Order was envisaged as (and indeed became) a national institution for all of Wales, its centre of gravity was always Glamorgan: what Claude Rawson says about Chatterton's 'local pride' giving his work a 'mythologizing radiance' is also exactly right for Iolo.[6]

The Rowley controversy was played out during some of Iolo's most productive years as a poet and as a forger of literary texts. And yet Chatterton's presence in his writings is intriguingly faint: in thousands of manuscript pages in Welsh and English, Iolo rarely mentions him at length. But he was well aware of the debate and he had certainly read at least some of the poems: at one particularly difficult period in his life (like so many poverty-stricken authors before and after him) he was dangerously haunted by the thought of Chatterton's death. The most obvious connection between the two men, of course, is that of place. Over much of Iolo's lifetime the fate of south Wales, and indeed much of Iolo's own ideological positioning, was intimately (and often ambiguously) bound up with the economic and cultural dominance of Bristol.[7] Iolo came to know Bristol as a stonemason, a tradesman, a radical abolitionist, a Unitarian and an aspiring poet. He walked the city's streets from the late 1760s, when Chatterton walked them too, until the second decade of the nineteenth century, when illness and old age kept him closer to home. In that time both 'old Iolo' and the 'marvellous Boy' had become numinous literary characters in their own right. Another strand that binds them to each other and to Bristol is their appearance as inspirational figures in the work of the most Bristolian of the Romantics, Coleridge and Southey.

St Mary Redcliffe is the best place to start. There is no hard proof that Iolo ever visited the church, but there are compelling reasons to take him there, especially once Chatterton's death had magnetized it with literary significance. Even before then, there are tempting possibilities for an evocative near-miss. In one autobiographical draft Iolo claims that he first visited Bristol in 1765: he would have been eighteen, working as a mason for his father.[8] At any point between then and Chatterton's departure for London in 1770 they could have passed each other in an aisle, absorbed in their different worlds. There is perhaps a greater likelihood, however, that Iolo visited the church when he left Wales in 1773 to work as a mason in London and then Kent. In another draft he says:

[6] Claude Rawson, 'Unparodying and Forgery: The Augustan Chatterton' in Groom (ed.), *Thomas Chatterton and Romantic Culture*, pp. 25–6.

[7] See Caroline Franklin, 'The Welsh American Dream: Iolo Morganwg, Robert Southey and the Madoc Legend' in Carruthers and Rawes (eds.), *English Romanticism and the Celtic World*, pp. 69–84; Geraint H. Jenkins, 'The Urban Experiences of Iolo Morganwg', *WHR*, 22, no. 3 (2005), 463–98. For the connections between Bristol and south Wales, see Philip Jenkins, *The Making of a Ruling Class* (Cambridge, 1983).

[8] NLW 21319A, p. 12.

> Soon after my mother died I went to Bristol and London, and other places in England. My chief study during these rambles was Architecture. I have particularly studied the Gothic and am surprized to find that hardly a man living knows any thing of its true principles.[9]

To any one even mildly interested in gothic architecture, St Mary Redcliffe is an important site; to a stonemason with a passion for the medieval, it would have been a revelation. Iolo's manuscripts contain numerous sketches and designs, usually connected with his work: urns and drapery, flourishes for headstones and chimney pieces. These, work undertaken for patrons, tend to be in the best classical style, but a genuine interest in the gothic appears in word-lists of gothic terms, in sketches of arches and windows, and in more extravagant fantasy-designs (notably a 'Gothic summerhouse . . . for a Gentleman in Canada 40 miles higher up than Quebec on the River St Lawrence').[10] There are no dates to any of these (and it may be wrong to suppose that Iolo would have been much aware of Chatterton before the Tyrwhitt edition of Rowley sparked the debate in 1777), but it is not inherently unlikely that one of his many journeys through Bristol could have taken him to Rowley's church.

The first datable mention of Chatterton, however, is in 1782, a peak year in the controversy, when the elaborate Rowleyan citadels constructed by Jeremiah Milles and Jacob Bryant were comprehensively attacked by Thomas Warton, Edmond Malone and Thomas Tyrwhitt;[11] it was also the year in which George Hardinge, a judge on the Welsh circuit with whom Iolo would eventually cross swords, published his anonymous and witty *Rowley and Chatterton in the Shades*. Iolo was by now in his mid-thirties, back in Glamorgan, married and trying to make a living at various trades. The letter containing his thoughts has apparently not survived, but his correspondent is gratifyingly informative: he is Daniel Walters, son of the lexicographer John Walters, a likeable young man somewhat intoxicated by the older 'Bard Williams'. In the first letter, proposing 'a little literary correspondence between Yourself, my Brother, and me' which 'might be productive of mutual gratification, if not improvement', he asks:

[9] NLW 21387E, no. 10.

[10] NLW 21416E, no. 60; for Gothic mouldings and arches, see NLW 21417E. See also Richard Suggett, 'Iolo Morganwg: Stonecutter, Builder, and Antiquary' in *Rattleskull Genius*, pp. 197–226.

[11] Jacob Bryant, *Observations upon the Poems of Thomas Rowley: in which the authenticity of those Poems is ascertained* (London, 1781); Jeremiah Milles, *Poems . . . by Thomas Rowley* (London, 1782); Thomas Warton, *An Enquiry into the Authenticity of the Poems attributed to Thomas Rowley* (Oxford, 1782); Edmond Malone, *Cursory Observations on the Poems attributed to Thomas Rowley* (London, 1782); Thomas Tyrwhitt, *A Vindication of the Appendix to the Poems, called Rowley's* (London, 1782).

> Have You ever read Rowley's (or Chatterton's) Poems? If You have not, I will send my Father and You some extracts. Be sure to say something about this in your Letter that I may not tell You what You already know.[12]

Iolo's reply (which has not survived) is conveniently summarized in the next letter:

> Your Remarks upon the Chattertonian Controversy are shrewd and ingenious; but yet, I confess, my sentiments do not perfectly coincide with yours on that subject. I cannot admit your idea of a Third Person. I argue thus: What could have induced any Third Person to usher those Poems into the world through the hands of Chatterton? For, if he supposed they would pass for the real Production of the ancient Poet to whom they were ascribed, why not put them off himself? But You will say, perhaps, that he fixed upon Chatterton, as a more proper person, from the access which he had to the recesses of Redcliffe-church. In opposition to which I will ask You whether You think it probable that the well-known pride of Chatterton, and the Jealousy which must have arisen in a breast like his on such an occasion, would have [su]b[m]itted to act so low a part in this grand Imposture? – If, on the other hand, this third person, whoever he might be, thought that the world would suspect the originality of these Poems, he might be assured that all the credit of them would be given to Chatterton – in which the Mind that could produce such exquisite pieces would hardly acquiesce. – And where is this ingenious Person? What has he written besides? Has so great a Genius laid dormant ever since? – In short, I see no reason for supposing a third person to have had any concern in the matter. – I have been a Rowleyist, but am now rather inclined to Chatterton's side of the Question. – Dr Milles, Dean of Exeter, has lately published a very splendid Edition of these Poems in Quarto, with a multiplicity of Notes, the purport of which, together with a long Introductory Essay, and an Appendix, is to endeavour to prove that Rowley was the Author of them. – As You say You have transcribed only a few lines, I shall send you a passage or two, with this letter, and more another time, if you desire it.[13]

The passages included were the Chorus from 'Goddwyn, A Tragedie', and stanzas from the 'Balade of Charitie': interesting and appropriate choices since both could have been read as critiques of social inequality, a topic close to Iolo's heart (the Goddwyn chorus was apparently anthologized as 'Ode to Freedom').[14] However, since, according to this letter, Iolo had 'transcribed only a few lines', he clearly did not own a copy of the poems: one may perhaps deduce that in 1782 he was not especially in thrall either to Chatterton or

[12] NLW 21283E, Letter no. 512, Daniel Walters to Iolo Morganwg, 27 June 1782.

[13] Ibid., Letter no. 513, Daniel Walters to Iolo Morganwg, 1 October 1782.

[14] See David Fairer, 'Chatterton's Poetic Afterlife, 1770–1794: A Context for Coleridge's *Monody*' in Groom (ed.), *Thomas Chatterton and Romantic Culture*, pp. 236, 251 n. 28.

Rowley. We do learn though that he advocated the idea of a 'Third Person', a position that seems to have been held (at least briefly) by Dr Johnson at almost the same period, and which is teasingly trailed as a 'way out' of the debate in Hardinge's *Rowley and Chatterton in the Shades*.[15] As Nick Groom and others have shown, the authenticity debate rapidly succumbed to the lure of biography, with speculation built on the analysis of the slender (and often specious) psychological data:[16] Daniel Walters's reply here shows one version of the Chatterton myth fully in action, with the poet's 'well-known pride' and 'jealousy' forming a key part of his refutation. By a typical irony, his earnest argument that the poet who could turn out such pieces would hardly let someone else bask in their glory was later used by Iolo himself when arguing for the authenticity of one of his own forged medieval works:

> A beautiful piece of this kind or on any similar subject would never, we may fairly infer, have been given by any Poet to another, he would not have had the useless self-denial to deprive himself of the just fame to which his genius would be entitled. We can not perceive an adequate motive for such a conduct. But I leave to every man his opinion, mine is that the poem under consideration of Bardd Glas is authentic for of such Poetry it does not appear that we have any spurious pieces in our Language.[17]

When Chatterton's name appears elsewhere in Iolo's work it is usually in the context of his own discussions of authenticity, a topic on which he has a good deal to say, much of it alarmingly perceptive. Here (probably in the early 1800s), he is defending the honour of the Welsh manuscript tradition:

> If a great number of copies of any old MS exist it is a sufficient proof that the work has long been extant for nothing but a considerable length of time can give existence to such a number of copies, more especially if these are obviously of different ages, evinced to be so by the writing, and other appearances of colour, decay etc which art can never give, at least has not been hitherto successful in attempting to do so. Witness Chatterton and Ireland.[18]

[15] For Johnson, see Pat Rogers, 'Chatterton and the Club' in Groom (ed.), *Thomas Chatterton and Romantic Culture*, p. 128. Hardinge concludes his preface with the words: 'This may be the opinion of those who consider a third, fourth, fifth, sixth &c person or persons as the author or authors of them, for when this hypothesis is formed, the number of them may be limited or multiplied at pleasure, with a glorious uncertainty, and a high probability of settling the question.' See George Hardinge, *Rowley and Chatterton in the Shades* (London, 1782), p. vi.

[16] See especially Groom, *The Forger's Shadow*.

[17] NLW 13138A, pp. 88–9. For the 'Bardd Glas', see p. 25 below.

[18] NLW 13104B, p. 123.

Chatterton (Iolo has by now clearly abandoned the idea of the Third Person) and the equally youthful William Ireland are dismissed as *failed* forgers. Iolo's own forgeries rely on the assumption that they are faithful copies of lost originals: he was never, with one intriguing exception,[19] tempted by the messier side, the ink-and-vellum physical re-creation of the past. Elsewhere, linked dismissively with James Macpherson or John Pinkerton, the Bristol poet becomes a mere shorthand for imposture: 'it is no difficult thing to manufacture very fine Poems, and impose them on the Public for works of great Antiquity. Macpherson & Chatterton, and others of very inferior Abilities, as Pinkerton, have done this'.[20] In all Iolo's writings and letters there is to my knowledge no more detailed consideration of the Chatterton controversy; nor is there any further sign of close engagement with the poetry. When one considers the many similarities in technique, execution and intention between the work of the two men, that silence is somewhat unnerving.

'Experiments in Imagined History'

Chatterton's Bristol grew out of hints and traces in the material world around him; he made it from ruins and foundations, inscriptions, coins and documents. Favourite buildings were invested with narratives of the past that twisted together fragmentary facts, informed speculation and personal fantasy. St Mary Redcliffe was doubtless the richest blend of all these: the tombstone of William Canynge, 'five times Mayor of Bristol', is the solid centrepoint of his most famous imaginative work, the poems and documents which explore the relationship between the rich fifteenth-century merchant and the poet-priest Thomas Rowley. Chatterton grew up in the shadow of the church. His father, who died shortly before Chatterton was born, had been sexton there, and had come into possession of various manuscripts, scraps of which were still being used by Chatterton's mother and sister for household purposes as he grew up. These documents and the church itself were the basis of his reinventions, but his world extended beyond St Mary Redcliffe to whole streets and areas, reconstructed in his imagination as he walked them. His first published forgery, which crucially hooked the interest of the eccentric antiquaries George Catcott and William Barrett, was an account, in proto-Rowleyan English, of a splendid pageant held to celebrate the opening of the first stone bridge, built in 1247, and sent to the editor of *Felix Farley's Bristol Journal* to coincide with the opening of the new Georgian bridge in 1769. As outside interest developed in the potential value of the charity-school boy's

[19] See pp. 208–10.
[20] NLW 13104B, p. 124.

manuscript finds, other areas of Bristol – Clifton, the Avon Gorge – were endowed with precious scraps of annals, poetry and legendary accounts, all pointing to a civic glory traceable from the earliest times. And this extraordinary work of antiquarian creativity was packed into a mere two or three years, with most of the Rowley material composed in a matter of months in 1768–9, when Chatterton was sixteen.[21]

Donald Taylor, characterizing in the 1970s the unsettling blend of fact and fiction in Chatterton's work, attempted to differentiate it from conventional historical research and from the novelist's historical realism, in which fictional characters inhabit carefully researched historical environments. The distinction, which grows harder and harder to maintain the deeper one gets into more recent debates about the 'constructed' nature of conventional history and the many examples of historical sources presented as fiction, relies on an indefinable (and perhaps old-fashioned) common-sense perception of where the boundaries sit most naturally, and when they have been transgressed. But Taylor is surely not far from the truth in describing Chatterton's creations as 'experiments in imagined history'; it would be difficult to find a better phrase for Iolo's Glamorgan. As with Chatterton, the *oeuvre* is multigeneric, the product of obsessive (and often highly perceptive) scholarship and intense local pride; it expresses an ability and determination to give a beloved place the past it deserves. And it is 'thickened' (Taylor's term) with a bewitching mixture of evidence, the varied nature of which was, in Chatterton's case, beautifully summed up (and manfully resisted) by a sceptical Thomas Warton in his 1782 *Enquiry*:

> It is not from the complexion of ink or of parchment, from the information of contemporaries, the tales of relations, the recollection of apprentices, and the prejudices of friends, nor even from doomsday-book, pedigrees in the herald's office, armorial bearings, parliamentary rolls, inquisitions, indentures, episcopal registers, epitaphs, tomb-stones, and brass-plates, that this controversy is to be finally and effectually adjusted.[22]

Or, as Ian Haywood puts it, 'diverse fabricated historical sources interconnect and intermesh to form a living past'.[23] In Iolo's case the process took not months but decades, and the results, overwhelmingly greater in volume, are even more enmeshed and contradictory than is the case with Chatterton, complex as his work is. In spite of a lifetime's labour by the scholar G. J. Williams

[21] The standard biography is still E. H. W. Meyerstein, *A Life of Thomas Chatterton* (London, 1930); for a detailed analysis of the works, see Donald S. Taylor, *Thomas Chatterton's Art: Experiments in Imagined History* (Princeton, NJ, 1978) .

[22] Warton, *An Enquiry into the Authenticity of the Poems*, p. 124.

[23] Haywood, *Faking It*, p. 54.

and the contributions of many others since, we are still a long way from understanding the development of Iolo's literary and historical forgeries in anything like the painstaking chronological detail of Donald Taylor's critical edition. But we do know enough, as the following examples show, for the similarities in their work to be demonstrated.

Buildings, ruined and otherwise, are a vital element of Iolo's inspiration. A good instance of Iolo's Chattertonized history can be found in his account of the elegant carved porch at Beaupre (locally 'Bewper') Castle. Iolo originally had noted Beaupre in his list of buildings in the region which could be attributed to the architect Inigo Jones, but some time after 1789 it appears that he developed a more localized and personal story.[24] In a letter to the Wiltshire antiquarian Sir Richard Colt Hoare in 1797, he gave a minutely detailed account of the porch: '3 stories high, in the three Greek orders, the Doric, above it the Ionic, and uppermost the Corinthian: the workmanship is masterly, the sculpture elegant and uncommonly delicate. The trigliphs in the Doric frieze are executed in a very singular and very neat manner, such as I have not yet observed elsewhere'.[25] The accompanying origin story is an affecting tale of two stonemason brothers, Richard and William Twrch, who fell in love with the same beautiful girl and vowed never to speak to each other again. Richard left the country and travelled abroad, coming under the tutorship of an Italian master in London and eventually travelling to Italy. Upon returning to Glamorgan, where his brother had meanwhile died, he began to practise his new Continental skills and was soon employed by local gentry. He built the chapel at Beaupre in 1586 and the porch in 1600:

> When we consider the dates of these pieces (i.e. the chapel and porch) we must allow them to be amongst the very first samples of Greek architecture in this Kingdom; perhaps the very first by a Native, supposing that the tradition of its having been executed by Richard Twrch is true. For Somerset House, the oldest sample in London, (before it was, some years ago taken down) of Grecian architecture was probably by Italian architects and workmen. Inigo Jones is generally supposed to have been the first that introduced into this Kingdom the Greek and Roman architecture, but he did nothing in England before the year 1620 when King James the first brought him to London, and employed him to build White Hall Palace (see an acct of Inigo Jones in Walpole's *Anecdotes of Painting*). He died in 1651.[26]

[24] 'Inigo Jones' is credited with the work in a list of buildings in NLW 13115B, p. 285, but in a similar list in NLW 13129A, p. 528, 'Bewper Porch' has been struck out. See Williams: *IM*, pp. 272–3 and Suggett, 'Iolo Morganwg: Stonecutter', pp. 222–3.

[25] NLW 13116B, p. 135, Iolo Morganwg to Sir Richard Colt Hoare, 17 August 1797 (a draft).

[26] Ibid., p. 136.

Having established Glamorgan's claim to architectural history, Iolo then moves on to authenticate it, with various sub-clauses sounding a typically disarming note of caution:

> This tradition is pretty common amongst the Glamorgan masons and stonecutters, of which last trade I am myself. But I took it more particularly, as I fancied it the most correct, consistent and circumstantial, from the mouth of Richard Roberts, who with his brother William and son Thomas, worked the Bridgend quarries till between the years 1780 and 1785, when they all died. They were, or at least pretended to be, lineally descended from Richard Twrch, and had, hereditarily ever since its having been first opened, worked the Bridgend freestone quarries. Richard Twrch is also upon the same traditional authority said to have been a lineal descendant of Iorwerth Fynglwyd a famous Welsh bard, who wrote about the year 1450. His works are numerously extant, in manuscript, by which it appears that he was (according to what tradition says of him) a stonecutter or carver in stone, and that he was a native and an inhabitant of St Brides Major, in which parish Seaton quarries are.
>
> Of what authority these traditions are must be left to judgements greatly superior to mine, but that we may sometimes depend considerably upon tradition will be tolerably well evinced by an anecdote of one of the monumental stones at Lantwit Major, which you will receive Sir in a letter that accompanies this.[27]

Authenticity (with flattering due deference to 'superior' judgements) is here subtly reinforced by what amounts to a genealogy of craftsmen, whose testimony, as 'insiders', buttresses the main narrative event from either side; Iolo the stonemason takes his information ('correct, consistent and circumstantial') from the lineal descendants (also stonemasons) of Richard Twrch, whose artistic credentials are further extended to the fifteenth-century poet (another stonemason). The story, like Chatterton's poem on St Mary Redcliffe, becomes 'a record of the Buylders Fame for aie'. Iolo's claim on behalf of Glamorgan is also in many ways comparable to the two Rowleyan pieces on early English art which Chatterton sent to Horace Walpole in March 1769.[28] 'The Ryse of Peyncteynge, yn Englande' was offered as a source for any future edition of Walpole's *Anecdotes of Painting*,[29] providing evidence for artistic practice in a more distant past than Walpole had been able to trace, and making sure that imaginary Bristol artists – such as the twelfth- to thirteenth-century Abbot John of St Austin's Minster, 'the fyrste Englyshe Paynctere yn Oyles' – had a prominent place in the narrative. Walpole responded with interest to this document, and was soon provided with another, the 'Historie of Payncters yn

[27] Ibid., p. 137.

[28] Taylor (ed.), *Complete Works*, I, pp. 259–66.

[29] Horace Walpole, *Anecdotes of Painting in England: with some Account of the Principal Artists, and Incidental Notes on other Arts* (4 vols., Strawberry Hill, 1762–71).

England bie T. Rowley', which also included some strategically placed information about various poets whose work Chatterton hoped to persuade a suitable patron to publish. It is doubtless a coincidence that, a generation later, Iolo should also have been stimulated to expand on a piece of local history after perusing Walpole's *Anecdotes*, but the parallels – including the rather gratuitous mention of the poet Iorwerth Fynglwyd, whose work Iolo sometimes forged – are striking (although Iolo does not go so far as to slip a specimen of his poetry into his account).[30] Where Chatterton offered Walpole a transcript of a faux-medieval document, however, Iolo sent his prospective patron a less tangible blend of oral tradition, authenticated by informants' names and personal testimony, and 'thickened' with scholarly references. After the second letter Walpole consulted Thomas Gray, grew suspicious of the language of the texts, and pulled back from Chatterton's overtures, thereby earning himself the undying scorn of a whole generation of struggling poets who came to identify intensely with that moment of rejection. Colt Hoare, somewhat less dramatically, seems likewise to have resisted becoming another of many unsuspecting conduits for Iolo's ideas about bardism and the druidic past.

As with Chatterton, a great deal of Iolo's basic material was genuine, and he may well have based his story of the Twrch brothers on a now-lost hint of a tradition among local workers in stone; he may equally well have made it all up. What most aligns Iolo with Chatterton, and distinguishes his work as a literary forger from other zealously interpretative antiquarian writings of his period, is the peculiarly close weave of his creations, and their alchemy of suggestion. Here, poetry, prose, material remains and (something Chatterton did not use) oral tradition are so inextricably plaited together, and presented with such careful diffidence, that rejection cannot be merely a matter of verifying, or suspecting, a single text. Individual elements that would be frail evidence on their own (the identification of Iorwerth Fynglwyd as a stonemason comes, apparently, from Iolo's mistaken interpretation of some lines in his work)[31] take heart, as it were, from being collected and woven together. In several cases, it appears, these hunches and suggestions yielded concrete results: the extraordinary case of the discovery of the 'Samson' Cross at Llantwit Major, hinted at in the final lines of the letter to Colt Hoare above, is a good example of this type.[32] The religious foundation at Llantwit was Iolo's answer to St

[30] Iorwerth Fynglwyd (fl.1485–1527) was born at St Brides Major; most of his poetry was addressed to various Glamorgan patrons. See Howel Llewellyn Jones and Eurys Rolant (eds.), *Gwaith Iorwerth Fynglwyd* (Caerdydd, 1975).

[31] *TLIM*, pp. 52–3.

[32] Brian Davies, 'Archaeology and Ideology, or How Wales was Robbed of its Early History', *New Welsh Review*, 37 (1997), 38–51; H. J. Thomas, 'Iolo Morganwg Vindicated: Glamorgan's First Field Archaeologist', *Glamorgan–Gwent Archaeological Trust Annual Report*, 1983–4 (Swansea, 1985), pp. 149–57, and Suggett, 'Iolo Morganwg: Stonecutter'. For more on Iolo and oral tradition, see below, chapters 8 and 9.

Mary Redcliffe, a many-layered testimony to the past, from the crumbling remains of Roman walls in neighbouring fields to the ruins of the precinct and the church with its inscribed stones and evocative tombstone effigies. What inspired him above all were the hints, which could be fleshed out from saints' lives and charters, of its former glory as an early monastic settlement. Into the Llantwit orbit Iolo brought not only local saints like Illtyd and Cadog, but names from other manuscript sources – including heroes of the Old North such as Urien, or the poets Aneirin and Taliesin – to give Glamorgan the privilege of being the first foothold of Christianity in Wales, with Llantwit providing a continuous 'university' of saints and scholars through the Middle Ages.[33] His rough sketch of the place is not unlike the map of the Redcliffe area which Chatterton included in a letter penned by Rowley to accompany his 'Discorse on Brystowe'.[34]

Inspiration for the forgeries was, however, textual as much as material and hugely diverse in subject matter, with a wide chronological sweep. Inevitably, Iolo and Chatterton ended up digging many of their raw materials from the same antiquarian sources: just as Chatterton's 'Discorse on Brystowe' was an indignant response to the dismissive page given the city in Camden's *Britannia* ('it is not taken notice of before . . . 1063'),[35] so Iolo, in his 'Cursory remarks on Camden', expands and improves on the orginal.[36] Mentors and acquaintances such as Lewis Hopkin and John Bradford had given him access to various antiquarian works early on in his career, and it seems likely that he had read works by Speed, Stillingfleet and Leland before his first extended visit to London in the early 1770s.

But it was his extraordinary knowledge and subtle manipulation of early Welsh texts that would prove his most lasting (and for future scholars most frustrating) legacy. One document which he copied over a dozen times from several sources was the sixteenth-century 'Statud Gruffudd ap Cynan' (The Statute of Gruffudd ap Cynan), a codification of the rules and regulations governing the Welsh bards, which outlined their duties and rights, as well as defining their status through different ranks: it was drawn up at an eisteddfod in Caerwys (north Wales) in 1523. As recent work has shown, Iolo's copies of

[33] NLW 13158A, pp. 147–60, 243–85, and Suggett, 'Iolo Morganwg: Stonecutter', p. 221; for Iolo's appropriation of the Northern heroic past, see Williams: *IM*, pp. 314–18.

[34] NLW 13089E, pp. 87–8; NLW 21413E, no. 2b. For Rowley's map of Redcliffe, see Taylor (ed.), *Complete Works*, II, frontispiece; the letter it accompanies is in vol. I, p. 136. A Rowleyan map of Bristol appeared in William Barrett, *The History and Antiquities of the City of Bristol* (Bristol, 1789), p. 51.

[35] See Taylor (ed.), *Complete Works*, II, p. 866. For the centrality of Camden to eighteenth-century antiquarian research, see Rosemary Sweet, *Antiquaries: The Discovery of the Past in Eighteenth-Century Britain* (London, 2004).

[36] NLW 13089E, pp. 128–31. Jonathan Barry has shown that Camden's silence on the city's early history motivated many eighteenth-century Bristol historians besides Chatterton: 'The History and Antiquities of the City of Bristol: Chatterton in Bristol', *Angelaki*, 1, no. 2 (1994), 61–3.

this text, although largely in line with other extant versions, contain additional sections connecting it to a much earlier (and southern) eisteddfod in Carmarthen, at which Iorwerth Fynglwyd and other Glamorgan poets played a prominent role.[37] The portentous style of the 'Statud' was also thoroughly absorbed, and woven into Iolo's own bardic rules and regulations, which would be promulgated through his invented institution, the Gorsedd.

Again, the process of 'thickening' his medieval world can be seen in the attention he gave to documents relating to medieval medical practice. He collected (and improved upon) a series of recipes attributed to a famous family of Carmarthenshire doctors known as Meddygon Myddfai (The Physicians of Myddfai), and claimed to be distantly related to one of their descendants.[38] The manuscripts also contain more recent recipes and proverbs from a variety of sources, some clearly derived from local oral tradition, others copied from journals. Iolo's interest in medicine went beyond the need for depth or colour in his own creations: he always described himself as having been extremely sickly from birth, and a tradition of healing was clearly part of the family romance. In one autobiographical sketch he claims that his mother, brought up by her aunt, had 'no despicable knowledge of surgery and physic':

> My father when single had his hand shatter most terribly by the crush of a large stone every bone tore to pieces in every one of his fingers. Amputation of the hand was deemed absolutely necessary by all the faculty, in the sore distress of mind which he felt on this occasion he recollected what he had heard of the remarkable cures performed by Mrs Seys. He applied to her, and my mother assisted by her aunts advice set the bones and in time performed a successful cure so as to restore to my father the full use of his hand. This was the occasion that brought them first an acquaintance that in about a twelvemonth ended in marriage.[39]

Related to the medical proverbs are hundreds of other proverbs encapsulating traditional wisdom, often attributed to local Glamorgan characters or saints. In one particularly subtle case, Middle Welsh versions of the widespread medieval school text, the 'Disticha Catonis' (a series of didactic maxims attributed to a

[37] Einir Gwenllian Thomas, 'Astudiaeth Destunol o Statud Gruffudd Ap Cynan' (unpublished University of Wales Ph.D. thesis, 2001), pp. 320–2.

[38] Williams: *IM*, pp. 85–6. In 'Meddygon Myddfai', *LlC*, I, no. 3 (1951), 169–73, Williams shows that Iolo systematically purified the rather motley Welsh of a later text based on an English original and ascribed it to the famous medical family. Compare Chatterton/ Rowley's brief excursus on various medieval diseases in 'The Rolle of Seyncte Bartlemeweis Priorie' in Taylor (ed.), *Complete Works*, I, pp. 143–51 (which first appeared in Barrett's *History and Antiquities*, p. 48). Taylor's commentary is once more highly apt: 'In this piece, particularly in his notes, Chatterton emerges as an antiquary of the broadest competence, expert in medicine, books, and plays, and in popular, ecclesiastical, architectural, and artistic antiquities' (II, p. 903).

[39] NLW 21387E, no. 10.

third-century Latin author) were, with almost minimal interference on Iolo's part, transferred to the shadowy figure of the Bardd Glas, or Blue Bard, and published in the third volume of *The Myvyrian Archaiology of Wales* (1807) as 'Athrawiaeth Geraint Vardd Glas' (The Teachings of Geraint the Blue Bard).[40] As Diana Luft has shown, a complex transmission history had done most of Iolo's work for him, muddling Cato with the figure of the wise man Catwn Ddoeth, and linking his name with an elusive 'Bardd Glas'. Iolo (and possibly earlier writers) promptly conflated Catwn with the sixth-century St Catoc, to whom he attributes many other forms of wisdom literature, copiously illustrated in preceding pages. However, since Iolo had decided that the Bardd Glas was in fact 'cotemporary with Alfred, and is supposed to be the same person with Asserius Menevensis' (i.e. Asser, Alfred's ninth-century biographer),[41] he was obliged to remove Cato/Catwn from the title of this particular series altogether. In thus erasing the last faint link with the original 'Disticha' (of which, incidentally, he owned a copy), he also ensured that this body of 'traditional wisdom' became purely native, and Glamorgan-grown.[42]

But Iolo's greatest gift was for medieval poetry, which he attributed sometimes to known poets, sometimes to creations of his own, and often to characters known only as names in Welsh literary tradition: the Bardd Glas mentioned above is among the most notorious of these, having successfully infiltrated English medieval scholarship until very recently. Once he had given him the Christian name 'Geraint', Iolo was able to identify him with the harper 'Glascurion' (i.e. Glas-Keraint) mentioned in Chaucer's *House of Fame* (book III, line 1208), an association (including the connection with King Alfred) which was repeated in editions of Chaucer well into the late twentieth century.[43] Glamorgan's Norman period also produced some inspired works, notably in the poetry of the imaginary Rhys Goch ap Rhicert,

[40] *MAW*, III, pp. 100–16.

[41] The link is made through calquing the name 'Asser' as 'Azure'.

[42] Diana Luft, 'Encountering Iolo' (unpublished seminar paper: I am grateful to the author for allowing me to read her work). See also Williams: *IM*, pp. 228–9.

[43] See e.g. Larry D. Benson (ed.), *The Riverside Chaucer* (3rd edn., Oxford, 1988), p. 986. Iolo makes the connection to Chaucer explicit in NLW 13121B, p. 482, but there is no shortage of published channels for the spread of this idea. In his *English and Scottish Popular Ballads* (1882–98), Francis James Child accepted the connection between the ballad of the harper 'Glasgerion' (Child 67), first published in 1765 in Percy's *Reliques* (III, p. 43), Chaucer's Glascurion, and Iolo's Bardd Glas, whom he had discovered in an article in the *Cambrian Journal* (September 1858), 192–4; Thomas Price had reached the same conclusion in his *Literary Remains* (Jane Williams, *The Literary Remains of the Rev. Thomas Price*, I, pp. 151–2). G. J. Williams notes that the name Glaskirion appears among a list of ancient British bards in the second edition of John Bale's *Scriptorum Illustrium Maioris Brytanniae* (1557): like many other figures in Welsh literary tradition he is a name looking for an *oeuvre*. See Williams, 'Leland a Bale a'r Traddodiad Derwyddol', *LlC*, IV, no. 1 (1956), 15–25.

a precursor of Dafydd ap Gwilym, who left a joyous selection of troubadour-style pieces on love and nature,[44] and in the verses attributed to Robert Duke of Normandy, son of William the Conqueror. In a letter to the *Gentleman's Magazine* in 1794 Iolo claimed that Robert, having learned Welsh while a prisoner in Cardiff castle, 'became a bard' and was able to soliloquize in a passable sequence of *englynion* on the beauties of the oak tree he could see from his cell window. The poem, he claimed, is 'mysteriously allusive to the distressful incidents of the unfortunate and greatly injured Duke's stormy life'.[45] Over the years, Iolo wrote in the voices of a wide range of poets from many periods of Welsh literature: but with one poet above all he developed an intensity of relationship to match that of Chatterton with Rowley – Dafydd ap Gwilym.

[44] The poems were first published in Taliesin Williams (ed.), *Iolo Manuscripts* (Llandovery, 1848), pp. 228–51; see G. J. Williams, 'Rhys Goch ap Rhiccert', *Y Beirniad*, VIII (1919), 211–26, and Huw Meirion Edwards, 'A Multitude of Voices: The Free-Metre Poetry of Iolo Morganwg' in *Rattleskull Genius*, pp. 111–13. Iolo was much in favour of the Norman influence on south Wales, and praised this new style of poetry as being 'much more congenial to human nature in its civilized state' (NLW 13108B, p. 134).

[45] *Gentleman's Magazine*, LXIV (1794), 981–2. As G. J. Williams notes, the *englynion*, which begin 'Dar a dyfwys' ('Grows an oak') are obviously modelled on the brief sequence spoken by Gwydion in the Fourth Branch of the Mabinogi (Williams: *IM*, p. 322).

3

Poets and Patrons: Dafydd ap Gwilym and Ifor Hael

the dead have been wakened to put the living into a trance[1]

In 1789 the London-Welsh society known as the Gwyneddigion published *Barddoniaeth Dafydd ab Gwilym*, the first printed edition of the work of the celebrated fourteenth-century poet. By Iolo's time Dafydd ap Gwilym was an acknowledged star of the Welsh literary canon; his poems, and poems attributed to him, were extant in scores of manuscripts copied over many centuries. In the 1760s the Morris brothers of Anglesey had made a systematic attempt to gather the many texts together, and their collection was subsequently copied and added to by Owain Myfyr. Iolo, who had the opportunity to read and copy them during his period in London in the early 1770s, appears to have been overwhelmed by the poet's work, and began imitating him in his own poems, absorbing his techniques and his vocabulary. Dafydd's connections with Glamorgan entranced him; places and buildings took on a visionary quality. In 1784, deeply in debt after the failure of various business schemes, he had moved to Wentloog, an area just south of Newport where his wife had inherited land, to try his luck at farming. Visiting the ruined court of Dafydd ap Gwilym's patron Ifor Hael at nearby Basaleg, he wrote with some emotion to Owain Myfyr of the experience of walking in the footsteps of the dead:

> Yr wyf yn awr yn ysgrifennu attad o fann ag yr wyf yn ei ystyried yn fath o dir Cysegredig, hwnn yw'r tir a droediwyd lawer arno gan Ddafydd ab Gwilym, Morfydd, Ifor Hael a Nest wiwgoeth wenddoeth wynddaint, ar hyd lann afon Ebwy . . . Gwern y Cleppau yw un o'r Tai a breswyliai Ifor yn ei amser, y mae ynawr yn garnedd ambell darn o'r muriau yn lledsefyll ag eiddew yn eu mantellu, ag ynddo dyllau'r dyllüanod, a'r ystlymynod, ag ymmhlith y Carneddau isod y mieri'n tyfu a'r Llwynogod yn daeru . . . Y mae ynof ryw bruddder meddwl a chynnwrf Calon wrth edrych ar y Lleoedd hynn, darfu am Ifor, am Ddafydd &c eithr byw y Gân a brydawdd y naill ar clod a haeddodd y llall, a byw byddant tra phery'r Iaith Gymraeg.[2]

[1] Hardinge, *Rowley and Chatterton*, p. 10.
[2] BL Add. 15024, f. 199.

(I am writing to you now from what I consider a kind of Consecrated ground, the land trodden by Dafydd ap Gwilym, Morfydd, Ifor Hael and the fair, noble and wise Nest of the dazzling smile, along the banks of the river Ebwy . . . Gwern y Cleppa is one of the houses in which Ifor lived in his time, it is now a heap of stones with a few bits of wall barely standing, cloaked with ivy and full of the nests of owls and bats, and in the piles of rubble below the brambles grow and foxes lurk . . . – I am troubled in thought and roused in my heart when I look upon these places: Ifor is gone, and Dafydd &c – yet the song made by one and the praise earned by the other live on, and they will live as long as the Welsh Language survives.)

A school friend of Chatterton's evoked his similarly physical response to this type of 'consecrated ground':

He was always very fond of walking in the fields, and particularly in Redcliffe meadows; and of talking about these manuscripts and reading them there. *Come*, he would say, *you and I will take a walk in the meadow. I have got the cleverest thing for you, that ever was. It is worth half a crown merely to have a sight of it; and to hear me read it to you* . . . There was one spot in particular, full in view of the church, in which he always seemed to take a peculiar delight. He would frequently lay himself down, fix his eyes upon the church; and seem as if he were in a kind of extasy or trance. Then on a sudden and abruptly, he would tell me, that steeple was burnt down by lightning: that was the place where they formerly acted plays.[3]

In 1779, long before the collected volume was planned, Iolo had apparently sent four Dafydd ap Gwilym poems to Owain Myfyr (which may or may not have been forged). Then, in the mid–1780s, Iolo's letters to Myfyr and his co-editor William Owen (later known as William Owen Pughe) began dropping hints about a hitherto-unknown cache of Dafydd's poems, a collection made in Glamorgan.[4] After expressions of interest and indeed some persuasion on their part he sent them several pieces, most of which were too late for inclusion in the body of the edition, but which were published in the appendix. He also passed on new 'facts' about Dafydd's otherwise exiguous biography; like the forged poems, this information strengthened the poet's connection with south Wales, and particularly with Glamorgan. They include various versions of the romantic story of the poet's premature birth under a hedge on a cold and stormy night as the lovers Gwilym Gam and Ardudful were fleeing from

[3] Jacob Bryant, *Observations upon the Poems of Thomas Rowley*, p. 350; quoted in Taylor, *Thomas Chatterton's Art*, p. 44.

[4] 'I may possibly be able to send you something in the old way, particularly 5 or 6 pieces of Dafydd ab Gwilym', NLW 21286E, Letter no. 1103, Iolo Morganwg to Owain Myfyr, 1783; see also three letters to William Owen Pughe written in 1788: NLW 13221E, pp. 11–14, 25–32. Note that, save in the publications of William Owen, I use the form William Owen Pughe throughout for consistency.

their angry families to the safety of Ifor Hael's court. In one of them, a day after giving birth and marrying Gwilym, Ardudful dies and the child is baptized on his mother's coffin; in another, all survive to reach Basaleg, where they are welcomed and cared for until a reconciliation takes them back to Ceredigion. Both of these versions come from carefully named sources – one a book owned by a farmer, Efan Williams, from Llanblethian, and the other from a manuscript in which Mr Morgan Llywelyn from Neath had gathered information about the poet 'mewn rhan o'i gywyddau ef ei hunan, mewn rhan o ysgrifeniadau eraill ag hefyd mewn rhan o draddodiadau pen gwlad' (partly from his [DG's] own *cywyddau*, partly from other writings and also partly from local tradition).[5] These sources have proved, once again, to be rather elusive; but one can note, as in the story of the Twrch brothers, that same persuasive blend of different types of evidence which makes it very difficult to reject the whole account outright. In the event, the editors retained much of Iolo's contribution, keeping the dramatic storm scene and the connection with Ifor Hael, but resisting the implicit point of the story – that Dafydd was actually born in Glamorgan, somewhere near Llandaf – in favour of the stronger (and historically more likely) association with Brogynin, Ceredigion.[6]

The Dafydd ap Gwilym forgeries range from entirely new pieces to genuine poems 'doctored' with additional lines (often in praise of Glamorgan). In at least one instance, an entire poem is extrapolated from a surviving couplet quoted by another poet.[7] As G. J. Williams has shown, Iolo did not have a faultless grasp of the structures and grammar of fourteenth-century Welsh, and there are errors; but his imitations were clearly persuasive enough for the time. That the poems were not suspected for most of the nineteenth century, and not systematically analysed as forgeries until the twentieth, has been taken as an indicator of the low level of native scholarship and the comparatively recent development of literary criticism (both of which reflected the absence of Welsh-based institutions for higher education). But a major factor was the manuscript culture of Wales itself, the perfect terrain for forgery: texts had to be chosen and collated from hundreds of manuscripts scattered all over the country; some of them were in private hands, some in libraries, and many disappeared through neglect or accident. It was not difficult for Iolo to persuade the London Welsh that he had copied a text from a collection which had subsequently vanished. Moreover, solecisms could be explained as dialectal variations, and inconsistencies as scribal errors:

[5] NLW 13139A, pp. 77–85; the same information appears more or less verbatim in NLW 13221E, pp. 29–32, Iolo Morganwg to William Owen Pughe, 15 October 1788.

[6] For what is known of Dafydd's biography, see Rachel Bromwich (ed.), *Selected Poems of Dafydd ap Gwilym* (2nd edn., Harmondsworth, 1985), pp. xiii–xv. His connections with Glamorgan are explored in D. J. Bowen, 'Dafydd ap Gwilym a Morgannwg', *LlC*, V, no. 4 (1959), 164–73.

[7] For a forensic examination of the appendix poems, see *IMChY*.

> it seems to me by a close comparison of Mr O. Jones's collection of his works with some old MSS in this part of Wales, that the Northwalian transcribers of hi[s] Works have often changed the words of DG, substituting venedotian words for the original Silurian of the Author. I look upon the Glamorgan Copies of his works to be the best and most genuine extant.[8]

Iolo entrusted the preservation of these 'Glamorgan Copies' to a fifteenth-century copyist called Bedo Brwynllys, who, as he wrote some twenty years later, 'did Dafydd ap Gwilym . . . the same service that Pisistratus did Homer'.[9] Finding the poems 'numerously and very extensively fugitive in all parts of Wales', Bedo collected them together, and left a large volume 'in the Library of Raglan Castle';[10] the castle was subsequently burned to the ground by zealous Cromwellians, but other copies of his copy survived. The authenticating narrative, already oscillating between assertions of reliability (the dependable Bedo) and uncertainty (the destruction of the original), is further compounded by a nice twist, suggesting that Bedo was perhaps not so dependable after all: 'Bedo Brwynllys copied [i.e. imitated] after DGm with great success, and has left us about 150 pieces of poetry that possess a very superior degree of merit.'[11] The ambiguous 'copyist' who imitates as well as transcribes is a troubling figure: some of the poems published in the body of *Barddoniaeth Dafydd ab Gwilym*, notes Iolo darkly, are quite evidently not authentic. Two decades after the publication, and by now estranged from and bitterly resentful of Pughe and Myfyr (the latter, in an angry outburst, had gone so far as to accuse Iolo of forging some of the Appendix poems),[12] he used the figure of Bedo to cast doubt on their competence as scholars while keeping himself firmly out of the picture. That same cleverly distanced perspective appears in Rowley's 'translation' of and commentary on the poetry of the Saxon monk Turgot – a device which allowed Chatterton to express malicious scepticism about the authenticity of some of the texts he

[8] NLW 13221E, pp. 11–14, Iolo Morganwg to William Owen Pughe, 12 March 1788. 'Venedotian' and 'Silurian' were common terms for north and south at the time, and derive from the Roman names for the tribes associated with Gwynedd and south-east Wales.

[9] NLW 13158A, p. 333. There is a nice irony here: in his *Essay on the Original Genius and Writings of Homer: with a Comparative View of the Ancient and Present State of the Troade* (London, 1775), Robert Wood described Pisistratus as Homer's 'editor', whose task was to restore the 'scraps and detached pieces' to their 'correct form': he then, without irony, likened this relationship to that of Macpherson with Ossian. See Kristine Louise Haugen, 'Ossian and the Invention of Textual History', *Journal of the History of Ideas*, 59 (1998), 321.

[10] NLW 13158A, p. 333.

[11] Ibid., p. 335.

[12] Geraint Phillips, 'Forgery and Patronage: Iolo Morganwg and Owain Myfyr' in *Rattleskull Genius*, p. 421; G. J. Williams, 'Cywyddau'r Chwanegiad', *LlC*, IV, no. 3 (1957), 229–30.

had himself composed.[13] In another piece, the 'London Priest' John Ladgate, on receiving Rowley's 'Songs of Aella', thanks him with the lines:

> Nowe Rowlie ynne these mokie days
> Lendes owte hys sheenynge lyghtes,
> And Turgotus and Chaucer lyves
> Ynne ev'ry lyne he wrytes.[14]

By the 1780s a sophisticated reader, aware of the controversy, would not have been short of examples of the games with time and the dizzying levels of irony that writing like this displays. Was Iolo conscious of playing such games when, in a letter to William Owen Pughe just before the publication of Dafydd's poems, he expressed his gratification 'that DG will be brought once more into the land of the living through your efforts'?[15] Or when, in a letter to Owain Myfyr written in 1800, he expounded at some length on the sheer impossibility of a modern writer ever properly capturing the style and tone of an earlier age: 'Dafydd ap Gwilym is comparatively a modern, but who can copy after him? not a man living.'[16]

Perhaps because they were linguistically more accessible to a late eighteenth-century readership, the Appendix poems were often admired as examples of Dafydd ap Gwilym at his best. They are certainly among some of Iolo's most attractive pieces. Several of them dramatize moments in the Dafydd ap Gwilym 'story', from 'Cywydd i Forfudd ar ôl ei dwyn oddiar y Bwa Bach' ('Cywydd to Morfudd after stealing her from the Crooked One'), which refers to Dafydd's supposed abduction of his lover from her husband, to 'Y Cywydd Diweddaf a Gant y Bardd' ('The last Cywydd the Poet Sang'). But one of the best-known pieces, cited several times in the lengthy English introduction to the work and much loved throughout the nineteenth century, reinforces Dafydd's links with Glamorgan, and his patron Ifor Hael.[17] The celebratory 'Cywydd i Yrru yr Haf i Annerch Morgannwg' ('Poem Sending the Summer to Greet Glamorgan') reveals the joyous side of Iolo's passion for his native county which, as time went on, would be expressed more and more as bitter resentment against a perceived north Welsh literary hegemony.[18] As

[13] Cf. Taylor's comment: 'As the imaginary source of an imaginary poet, Turgot would weaken the demands for credibility and accuracy made on a fifteenth-century Rowley about the eleventh century' (*Complete Works*, II, p. 827).

[14] Ibid., I, p. 63.

[15] 'fod DG yn cael ei ddwyn unwaith etto i d[ir] y byw drwyddoch', NLW 13221E, p. 12, Iolo Morganwg to William Owen Pughe, 12 March 1788.

[16] BL 15030, ff. 12–13, Iolo Morganwg to Owain Myfyr, 17 June 1800.

[17] William Owen and Owen Jones (eds.), *Barddoniaeth Dafydd ab Gwilym* (London, 1789), pp. 522–5. The edition includes an English translation of the last few lines in its introduction, p. xxi.

[18] For the north–south rivalry in Iolo's work, see Cathryn Charnell-White, *Barbarism and Bardism: North Wales versus South Wales in the Bardic Vision of Iolo Morganwg* (Aberystwyth, 2004).

Welsh-language literature still tends to be very little encountered outside Wales, I reproduce the poem here in full, broken into sections with a literal translation. Even readers with no knowledge of the language should be able to see on the page something of the technical intricacies (*cynghanedd*) of the *cywydd* form – the system of rhyme (both internal and end rhyme) and alliteration on which Dafydd ap Gwilym wrought his deft and witty magic in the fourteenth century, and which Iolo here imitates with some skill:

I Yrru yr Haf i Annerch Morganwg

Tydi yr Haf, tad y rhwys,
A'th goedfrig berth gauadfrwys,
Tywysog gleiniog y glyn,
Tesog draw'n deffraw'r dyffryn!
Praff yw dy frisg i'n priffyrdd,
Prophwyd penial gwial gwyrdd;
Panelog, pwy un eiliw,
Pwyntiwr dedwydd y gwŷdd gwiw?
Peraist deganau purion,
10 Percwe brwys mewn parc a bron;
Pawr ar glawr y glaslawr glwys,
Per ydyw ail paradwys.
Rhoddaist flodau, a rhyddail,
Rhesau gwych ar deiau dail:
Cawn nodiau cywion adar
Can wanwyn ar dwyn a dar;
A'i gwrandaw'r gerdd fangaw falch
Ym mywyll, lle cân mwyalch;
Cawn genyd y byd o'i ben
20 A lluoedd bawb yn llawen!

(You, Summer, father of growth, with your hedge of richly covered treetops, sparkling prince of the glen, your warmth wakening the valley! Bold your path along our roads, prophet of the crowds of green twigs. Downy one, who is like you, blissful artist of the lovely trees? You have created pure playthings, a luxuriant web of perches in park and hill, and pasture on the lovely green earth, pure, a second paradise. You have produced flowers and plentiful leaves, rows of wonderful leafy houses. We hear the notes of the little birds as spring comes to hill and oak; we listen to the proud lovely song in the buds, where the blackbird sings. From you we have the world entire, and crowds rejoicing.)

Clyw fi Haf! o chaf i'm chwant,
Yn gennad ti'n d'ogoniant,
Hed drosof i dir Esyllt,
O berfedd gwlad Wynedd wyllt –

Gyr oni's b'och i'm goror,
Anwyla' man, yn ael mor.
F'annerchion, yn dirion dwg,
Ugein-waith i Forganwg
Fy mendith, a llith y lles
30 Dau-gan-waith, i'r wlad gynnes!
Dymgais a'm gwlad o'i hamgylch,
Damred a cherdded ei chylch;
Gwlad dan gaead yn gywair,
Lle nod gwych, llawn ŷd a gwair;
Llynoedd pysg, gwinllanoedd per,
A maendai, lle mae mwynder;
Arglwyddi yn rhoi gwleddoedd
Haelioni cun heilwin c'oedd.
Ei gwelir fyth, deg lawr fau,
40 Yn llwynaidd gan berllànau;
Llawn adar a gâr y gwŷdd;
A dail, a blodau dolydd;
Coed osglog, caeau disglair,
Wyth rhyw ŷd, a thri o wair;
Perlawr parlas, mewn glas glog,
Yn llànaidd, a meillionog!
Yno mae gwychion fonedd
A dâl im'aur mâl a medd;
Ac aml gôr y cerddorion,
50 A ganant a thant, a thôn:
Ymborth, amred i'r gwledydd
A dardd o honi bob dydd;
A'i blith, a'i gwenith ar g'oedd,
Yn doraeth i'r pell diroedd –
Morganwg ym mrig ynys
A byrth bob man, llan a llys!

(Hear me, Summer! O grant my boon: your own self as a messenger, in all your glory. Fly for me to Esyllt's land from the depths of wild Gwynedd; go until you reach the border, the beloved place, at the sea's edge. Take my fair greetings twenty times to Glamorgan; take my blessing, a beneficial tract, two hundred times to the warm land! Seek out my land and encircle it, travel its bounds: it is a country under a fair covering, a place of fine aims, full of corn and hay; there are lakes full of fish, beautiful orchards and stone houses where courtesy lives on as lords give feasts – the open generosity of a wine-giving lord. It will be seen for ever, my fair land, groved with orchards, full of birds that love the trees, full of leaves and meadow flowers. It has branchy woods and bright fields, growing eight types of corn, three of hay; a green patch of land in a fresh green cloak, open and clovered! There reside the excellent nobles who give me burnished gold and mead; and the many musical choirs with their harp and song. Nourishment to support the lands springs from her every day, her milk and wheat, rich and plentiful, sent to distant places: Glamorgan, the island's pinnacle, supplies everywhere, church and court!)

O'th gaf yr Haf i'th awr hardd,
A'th geindwf, a'th egindardd;
Dy hinon yn dirion dwg,
60 Aur-gennad, i Forganwg,
Tesog fore, gwna'r lle'n llon,
Ag annerch y tai gwynion:
Rho dwf, rho gynnhwf, gwanwyn,
A chynnull dy wull i dwyn;
Twynya'n falch ar galch gaer,
Yn luglawn, yn oleuglaer;
Dod yno'n y fro dy frisg,
Yn wyrain bawr, yn irwisg;
Ysgwyd lwyth o ber-ffrwythydd,
70 Yn rad gwrs, ar hyd ei gwŷdd;
Rho'th gnwd, fal ffrwd ar bob ffrith,
A'r gweunydd, a'r tir gwenith;
Gwisg berllan, gwinllan, a gardd
A'th lawnder, a'th ffrwythlondardd;
Gwasgar hyd ei daear deg,
Gu nodau dy gain adeg!

Ac y'nghyfnod dy flodau,
A'r miwail frig tewddail tau,
Casglaf y rhos o'r closydd,
80 Gwull dolau, a gèmau gwŷdd:
Hoyw feillion, dillynion llawr,
A glwysbert fflur y glasbawr,
I'w rhoi'n gof aur-enwog ior,
Ufudd wyf, ar fedd Ifor!

(If, Summer, I may have you in your finest hour and fairest growth, your time of springing forth, take your good weather, golden messenger, to Glamorgan. Bright morning, make the place content and greet the whitewashed houses: give growth, give the life-force with oak blossom to every hill: shine proudly on the whitewashed castle, brilliant, full of light. Lay your path through the country, in the lovely pasture, dressed in green; shake a load of sweet fruit, in bountiful course, across the trees; pour your crop like a torrent on every wood and heath and wheatfilled place. Clothe orchard, vineyard and garden with your fullness and your fruitfulness; scatter on her fair soil the sweet notes of your fair season! And in the time of your flowers and your fair thick-leaved treetops I shall gather the rose from the hedges, blossom from meadows, and the jewels of the trees, the bright clover, treasures of the ground, and the fair flowers of the green pasture, to place in memory of a gold-famed lord – for I obey him still – on the grave of Ifor!)

The poem takes its immediate inspiration from a *cywydd* believed in the eighteenth-century to be one of Dafydd's, but more probably attributable to his contemporary Gruffudd Llwyd, in which the poet sends the sun to Glamorgan, asking it to shine through the windows of various patrons.[19] The motif of sending a creature or an object as a *llatai* or messenger, usually on behalf of a lover, is characteristic of many Welsh poems of the Middle Ages, and Dafydd ap Gwilym was a supremely inventive exponent of the technique. Iolo's poem betrays its non-medieval origins mostly through its vocabulary – many words are either pure invention, or are only otherwise attested in later sixteenth or seventeenth century verse. Occasional slips, such as the mistaken medievalization of the verb *deffro* (to wake) as *deffraw*, and the presence of various 'favourite' Iolo words (*egindardd*, *rhwysg*) offer further proof of authorship, while phrases and whole lines are recycled from earlier Dafydd-style poems written in his own name.[20] The form, however, is handled with great confidence, and the couplets of the *cywydd* are packed with ornament and rhythmic variation, using the patterns of uneven stress produced by couplets rhymed alternately on an accented and unaccented final syllable (*llón* and *gw"nion*; *ffríth* and *gwénith*, or, for variation, with the monosyllable last, *góror/mor*). All of this combines to form a medieval texture, the effect of which is rather richer and deeper than that suggested by Susan Stewart's analogy of 'distressed forms' – that is, texts which have been 'antiqued' like furniture.[21] At their best, both Iolo and Chatterton are more actively engaged, more in love with their medieval languages than the image of a carefully applied patina of age implies. There is relatively little straight 'nature poetry' in the Rowleyan *oeuvre*, but one might compare the well-known opening description of summer in the 'Balade of Charitie', a text which, as we saw earlier, Iolo had received from Daniel Walters in 1782.[22]

[19] Rhiannon Ifans, *Gwaith Gruffudd Llwyd a'r Llygliwiaid Eraill* (Aberystwyth, 2000), no. 9; Lewis Morris was among those who attributed this poem to Dafydd ap Gwilym. For a full discussion of Iolo's poem, see *IMChY*, pp. 29–36, 178–9.

[20] *IMChY*, pp. 29–36. I am grateful to Barry J. Lewis for a medievalist's perspective on this poem.

[21] Susan Stewart, 'Notes on Distressed Genres', *Journal of American Folklore*, 104, no. 411 (1991), 5–31.

[22] Taylor (ed.), *Complete Works*, I, 644–5; the notes to the vocabulary are Chatterton's own. For discussions of Chatterton's use of landscape/pastoral/topographical modes, see Taylor, *Thomas Chatterton's Art*, pp. 262–312. On John Clare's reading of Chatterton for nature poetry 'against the grain', see John Goodridge, 'Identity, Authenticity, Class: John Clare and the Mask of Chatterton', *Angelaki*, 1, no. 2 (1994), 139.

In Virgynë the sweltrie sun gan sheene,
And hotte upon the mees* did caste his raie; *meads*
The apple rodded* from its palie greene, *reddened, ripened*
And the mole* peare did bend the leafy spraie; *soft*
The peede chelandri* sunge the livelong daie; *pied goldfinch*
'Twas nowe the pride, the manhode of the yeare.
And eke the grounde was dighte* in its moste defte* aumere.*
drest, arrayed; neat, ornamental; a loose robe or mantle

Chatterton's late-season lushness (Keats was a great admirer) is slower and less excitable than Iolo's energetic invocation to the summer's arrival; a closer seasonal parallel might be the shepherd's nostalgic lament in the 'First Eclogue' for his 'kinge-coppe-decked mees', 'tendre applynges' and 'spreedynge flockes of sheepe of lillie white'.[23] But both writers are involved in something more serious than pastiche: for Margaret Doody, Chatterton shows language 'being made before our eyes, coming at us with fresh unfamiliarity to challenge our powers of association and our knowledge of the way language works'. She sees in his 'two-tongued' style the logical conclusion of a tradition of double-voicedness inherent in Augustan poetry.[24] Reading Iolo's piece from a similarly dual perspective, as an 'eighteenth-century fourteenth-century poem', is an even more complex affair, since, beside the inherent double chronology, it exists both in an immediate Welsh context and a wider matrix of English-language literature – the two literary cultures to which Iolo had access and in both of which he wrote. One could of course argue that Iolo is here writing for a Welsh audience only – 'Poem sending the Summer to Greet Glamorgan' was not one of the pieces later translated in his English collection of *Poems, Lyric and Pastoral* (1794) – and yet the two main themes of the poem, landscape and patronage, are so thoroughly written into eighteenth-century literary tradition in English that a certain echo seems unavoidable.

Although the complex couplets of the *cywydd* provide a formal restraint, like a more supple, more subtle version of the Augustan couplet, the style of this poem is quite antithetical to most English landscape poetry of the period. Particularly striking is the absence of ordering prepositions: all is simultaneity, multiplicity and abundance.[25] There is little in the way of narrative to control it: the basic movement of the poem lies in the act of sending the sun from the

[23] Taylor (ed.), *Complete Works*, I, p. 307. This was the opening poem of Tyrwhitt's 1777 edition.

[24] Margaret Doody, *The Daring Muse* (Cambridge, 1985), pp. 225–31.

[25] The pioneering work on landscape perception for this period is John Barrell's *The Idea of Landscape and the Sense of Place* (Cambridge, 1972); see also Tim Fulford, *Landscape, Liberty and Authority* (Cambridge, 1996), Rachel Crawford, *Poetry, Enclosure and the Vernacular Landscape* (Cambridge, 2002) and the chapters on landscape, pastoral and Nature in David Fairer, *English Poetry of the Eighteenth Century 1700–1789* (London, 2003).

wilds of northern Gwynedd to the civilized south, and there are here no 'prospects' seen from an elevation, but rather an ecstatic view from above, a rushing over – more Gerard Manley Hopkins and Dylan Thomas than Thomson or Cowper or Dyer. The sun's eye view of the county does not preclude detail, such as the *percwe glas*, the web or lace formed by the greening twigs, or the song of a blackbird in a grove. But these things are not *placed* for us. The sense of abundance owes much to a medieval technique, of which Dafydd was a master, of piling up description, an overloading of the subject that, in a very un-eighteenth-century way, makes it hard to locate precisely in space and time. In fact, this type of poetry would seem to be quite resistant to the kind of visual ordering we expect from topographical and landscape poetry in English: it may not be inappropriate to compare the hypnotic rushing effect of the recurrent imagery of *Ossian*, whose images do, nonetheless, compose themselves into scenelets – a warrior by an oak by the stream – which could be, and often were, depicted visually. In other respects, however, Iolo's vision of Glamorgan conforms to what John Barrell sees as the pre-Picturesque equation of fertility with beauty: again the theme is a fairly constant one from classical sources onwards, and part of a general European inheritance which both Welsh and English poetry developed.[26] It is a celebration of plenitude, a *paysage riant*, albeit one, perhaps, on the verge of hysteria (Iolo, lacking Dafydd's amused veneer of self-mockery, could be accused in this poem of gushing).

In contrast to his many English poems in pastoral mode, there are very few people in this landscape – not a milkmaid or a shepherd in sight – but the good husbandry implied by the laden orchards and the wheat-filled fields, the whitewashed cottages and even brighter castles suggests a beneficent social order, which culminates in the evocation of the ideal civilized patron, Ifor Hael. Once again, it is tempting to read this for more than medievalism: the subject of patronage, after all, loomed as large in the Chatterton controversy as it did in Iolo's own life. Moreover, the very image of fruitful land under a benign ruler had an especial resonance for Iolo. As G. J. Williams perceptively noted, Iolo favoured praise poetry which turned its back on one important strand of native medieval Welsh poetic tradition, the celebration of martial prowess and the heroic ethics of the warrior prince, to focus instead on another aspect – also clearly present from the recorded beginnings of Welsh – the immediate bond of gratitude between the poet and the lord in the hall and the beneficial effects of the lord's generosity in a wider social sphere. It is in this context that Iolo, working on a hint from Leland, seems to have forged a number of *cywyddau* which he attributed to sixteenth-century poets, in praise of patrons who improved their land by planting orchards. These poems,

[26] Barrell, *The Idea of Landscape*, pp. 61–2.

georgic celebrations of agricultural improvement, paint an Edenic Glamorgan of vineyards, apricots, figs and cherries, in which Paradise is not some untouched pristine space but the result of good taste and, in both senses, cultivation.[27] Elsewhere he exclaims, with some vehemence:

> Celfyddydau yr hen Baradwys yw rhain a mwy er clod i'r genedl a ymarferai a hwynt nac y byddai fod pob un o'r gwyr yn ail i Arthur, neu yn hytrach yn ail i Ddiawl wedi lladd miloedd ar filoedd o'i gyd-ddynion . . . Gwych a fyddai cael hanes Celfyddydau Tangnef ymhlith y Cymry, a gwychach fyth a fyddai claddu yn anghof y pwll dyfnaf yn uffern, yr holl hanes y sydd am ryfel a Rhyfelwyr am *Frenhinoedd*.[28]
>
> (These are the arts of ancient Paradise and of more honour to the nation who practised them than if every man were to be a second Arthur, or rather a second Devil having killed thousands and thousands of his fellow men . . . It would be a wonderful thing to have a history of the Arts of Peace amongst the Welsh, and more wonderful still would be to bury in the oblivion of the deepest pool in Hell all history which deals with wars and Warriors and *Kings*.)

The Glamorgan of Iolo's past is a fertile and well-tended garden, a paragon of the arts of peace, a haven for the early Church and a cradle of learning and the arts; the generosity of patrons and of the fruitful land itself is a constant theme. But behind this contented stability lie, in David Fairer's words, 'all the things pastoral holds at bay – heroism, politics, money, war, time and death';[29] things which, as we shall see, will intrude increasingly in the English-language pastoral poems which Iolo published in 1794 against a background of war and revolutionary ferment.

In Dafydd ap Gwilym and Ifor Hael Iolo found the same inspiring and comforting model of patronage that Chatterton found in Rowley and Canynge, a model which, in Chatterton's case, has been read as a form of compensation for the lost father figure.[30] However one explains Iolo's motivation, he evidently shared Chatterton's desire for a physical connection to the past, and this, sometimes expressed in terms of raising the dead to life, found other productive metaphors of affiliation: in one wildly fantastic genealogy (correct only to his grandfather) he even, as Chatterton did with Rowley, wrote himself into the poet's blood-line as a descendant of 'one of the bastards of Dafydd ap Gwilym by Morfydd'.[31]

[27] See *IMChY*, p. 184.

[28] Cited in ibid.

[29] Fairer, *English Poetry of the Eighteenth Century*, p. 84.

[30] For a psychoanalytical approach to Chatterton's 'imposturous behaviour', see Louise J. Kaplan, *The Family Romance of the Imposter-Poet: Thomas Chatterton* (Berkeley and Los Angeles, 1987).

[31] Gwyneth Lewis, 'Eighteenth-Century Literary Forgeries', p. 150. On forgery and bastards (a surprisingly rich topic), see Groom, *The Forger's Shadow*, pp. 246–55.

The larger question remains unanswered: did Thomas Chatterton inspire Iolo the forger, as he clearly inspired the young William Ireland? Iolo's biographer G. J. Williams played very briefly with the idea in a footnote in 1956, and rejected it.[32] It is true that the hundreds of volumes of manuscripts which piled up in the cottage in Flemingston reveal no direct evidence for close reading or admiration of the poetry, and there is nothing (the lost letter to Daniel Walters excepted) to show that Iolo ever discussed Chatterton's creations in anything but dismissive and general terms. And yet, all the time that he was himself faking medieval poems and inventing druidic triads, two major authenticity debates were rumbling on, one of them on his doorstep in a city he knew extremely well. Iolo covered his own traces with exceptional skill (his own son, who piously edited reams of bardic material for the influential *Iolo Manuscripts*, published in 1848, had no idea that most of it was fiction), and he may simply have avoided Chatterton for reasons of self-preservation.

Part of the problem involved in positing direct influence lies in trying to ascertain how and when Iolo might have become aware of the complex nature of Chatterton's creations, and to map that against what we know of his own development. As a reader of literary journals and magazines in the 1770s he is very unlikely to have missed the controversy over the poems sparked by Tyrwhitt's edition of 1777, the preface of which states quite clearly that there is a question over authorship: although in the first edition Tyrwhitt declined to decide for or against the authenticity of the Rowley poems, subsequent editions included an Appendix arguing 'that they were written, not by any ancient author, but entirely by Thomas Chatterton'.[33] The second volume of Thomas Warton's *History of English Poetry*, which came out in 1778, also analysed the pieces and declared them spurious.[34] As we have seen, Iolo had his own theory about Chatterton as a forger (and some sense of his 'character') by 1782, when, thanks to Daniel Walters, he also read at least snippets of the poetry. During the rest of the 1780s, as he began imitating and then forging the Dafydd ap Gwilym poems and fleshing out a biography and a history of manuscript transmission which privileged Glamorgan, there is no further visible response to the poems or the controversy – unless, of course, the Dafydd poems in themselves constitute that response. He does, however, and most intriguingly, appear to have read William Barrett's 1789 *History and Antiquities of Bristol*, the most famous conduit for the 'thickening' material of Chatterton's historical imagination. Nine chapters of this work make extensive use of Rowley materials, including lengthy extracts from prose pieces such as Canynge's 'Cabinet of Antiquities', the heraldry and the genealogies, and

[32] Williams: *IM*, pp. 341–2 n. 164.

[33] This conclusion is advertised on the title-page of the third edition, published in 1778.

[34] Thomas Warton, *The History of English Poetry, from the close of the eleventh to the commencement of the eighteenth century* (4 vols., London, 1774–81), II, pp. 139–64.

Rowley letters and further poems.[35] In the introduction, Barrett also briefly acknowledges that this material remains controversial but declares (a favourite Iolo ploy) that publication is the only way of allowing readers to judge the matter for themselves. In December 1791, Iolo wrote a lengthy piece on Brandon Hill which closes with an oblique swipe at the Bristol historian:

> Stupid Bristol that never noticed the wonderful curiosities of nature that abound so much in every corner about it, almost if not entirely beyond what is to be met with in any part of Britain, and which crowdingly obtrude themselves so much on the half-opened eye, that one is astonished to think how the Demon of Idiotic Dullness could, with Barrett, pass by them daily without the least attention.[36]

It is not clear whether this is merely an ill-tempered way of disagreeing with Barrett's interpretation of the 'Roman Camps' either side of the Avon Gorge, or whether it suggests that he thought of Barrett as a fool (and a dupe?) because of his connection with the Chatterton material. If he were aware of Barrett's role in promulgating the forgeries, then the *History and Antiquities of Bristol* would have provided the perfect model of a historian more desperate for source material than truth; but then he was hardly in short supply of scholars of this type at home.

Whether the Bristol poet provided a direct model for Iolo in his forgeries is ultimately unknowable. Yet, in comparing the preoccupations and techniques and the curious proximity of both writers, it is impossible not to acknowledge what Gwyneth Lewis has called 'an intimate artistic connection between them'.[37] It sometimes feels as if Chatterton has just left the room. It does seem difficult to avoid the fact that, at exactly the right period, Chatterton's work offered Iolo a shining example of modern-medieval poetry supported by a cunningly wrought infrastructure of pseudo-historical documentation. Yet it is probably unwise to chase a single interpretation into the dangerous waters of motivation and intent; as others have shown, it is also possible to map the timing and development of his forgeries in relation to the highs and lows of his own connections with the London Welsh.[38] Besides, Iolo's response to reading Dafydd ap Gwilym's poetry in the 1770s seems too visceral, too creative and too personally involving to be merely the perverse product of a desire to emulate (and outdo) a notorious literary figure.

As with Chatterton, Iolo's fantasy of a sustaining relationship between a talented poet and a civilized patron was all the more poignant for never being

[35] For Barrett's role in the controversy, see Barry, 'The History and Antiquities'.

[36] NLW 13089E, p. 176. The piece is published in its entirety in Mary-Ann Constantine, *'Combustible Matter': Iolo Morganwg and the Bristol Volcano* (Aberystwyth, 2003), pp. 2–4.

[37] 'Eighteenth-Century Literary Forgeries', p. 90.

[38] See Phillips, 'Forgery and Patronage'.

realized in his own life. The contrast between the generous medieval lord rewarding poetic genius and the realities of making a living as a writer in late eighteenth-century Britain would come most sharply into focus in the years immediately after the appearance of the Dafydd ap Gwilym poems, when Iolo decided to publish the English poems he had been writing over the previous twenty years. His struggles to negotiate the financial and emotional pitfalls of patronage and publication raised new and deeply problematic issues of authenticity. And Thomas Chatterton would return to haunt him.

4

'What I really and truly am': Identity, Duplicity, Autobiography

> Sir,
> I send you some of my principal Subscribers which I have procured lately: the first of which is a Baronet!!! who speaks very highly of my 'Sonnet' in the prospectus – Good God, how great are my Expectations! what hopes do I cherish! As great as the unfortunate Chattertons were on his first entrance to London, which is now pictured in my Mind – & undoubtedly like him I may be building 'Castles in the Air' but Time will prove it.[1]

The Northamptonshire poet John Clare rose to fame in the 1820s, variously helped and hindered by a network of mentors, patrons, supporters and publishers, who offered advice and money, and took his verses in hand. His first collection, *Poems Descriptive of Rural Life and Scenery*, came out in 1820. When he went up to London, which he did on four occasions for various lengths of time, he became part of a literary circle centred around the *London Magazine* which included Charles Lamb, Thomas De Quincey and John Keats. A deliberate oddity in a bright-green jacket, Clare was billed from the beginning as 'the peasant poet' (as John Goodridge notes he tended, subconsciously or otherwise, to misspell it 'pheasant poet')[2] and was treated with a mixture of genuine admiration, affection and amusement. He was a success, but not a lasting one: he could not make a living as an author, and returned to village life irreparably dislocated by his experience of fame. He was declared insane at the age of forty-eight, and spent the rest of his life, over twenty years, in lunatic asylums, visited by the curious and the concerned, writing poetry in his own voice and under a variety of pseudonyms – most notably that of Lord Byron – to the end.[3]

The disintegration of John Clare is one of the most heartbreaking stories in English literature, and belongs very much to a particular time and place. Yet in outline, and even, unnervingly, in many details, it is a story that does very well for the middle period in Iolo's life, when, a generation before Clare, he also tried to make a name and a living as a poet in London. Like Clare, Iolo experienced

[1] From John Clare's first extant letter, to J. B. Henson (1818): Mark Storey (ed.), *The Letters of John Clare* (Oxford, 1985), p. 3.

[2] John Goodridge, 'Identity, Authenticity, Class', 142.

[3] Jonathan Bate, *John Clare: A Biography* (London, 2003); for an account focused on the London period, see Roger Sales, *John Clare: A Literary Life* (Basingstoke, 2002). Clare's Byronic persona is discussed by Russett, *Fictions and Fakes*, pp. 137–54.

the same bewildering trajectory from a regional and labouring-class background to the urban world of the literati ('Dear Peggy,' he wrote in 1791, 'I write now to inform you of my good success, I have within these few days been favoured with many names of the first rank, many of the most celebrated writers of the age, have recommendations to persons of great eminence at London.').[4] Reliant on influential friends and patrons at both regional and metropolitan level, Iolo made the same decision – or came under the same obligation – to market his work as a certain type of literary phenomenon, the production of a self-taught poet. He even has that same, slightly self-mocking, desperation for fame – 'Castles in the Air', the title of one of his poems, was originally intended as the title of his collection.[5] The financial and emotional cost of all this to himself and his family resulted in a mental breakdown and an eventual return to the beloved territory of childhood, where, although not clinically insane, he too would write through other men's voices. Most uncannily of all, the ghost of the young suicide Thomas Chatterton, appearing so ominously at Clare's moment of 'Greatest Expectation', was also waiting for Iolo in London.

The story is, of course (without the return home) also Chatterton's own; once again the sense of proximity between the two men is fascinating. But where the connections between their work as literary forgers of the medieval past can only be inferred or suggested, it is abundantly clear that, as in so many other instances, Clare's included, the story of Chatterton's life, his miraculous childhood, his struggles to find a patron, his journey to London and his iconic death, did directly affect Iolo. It can be detected, for example, in the way Iolo framed his own life for public consumption. In the brief autobiographical sketch which prefaced his collection of *Poems, Lyric and Pastoral* in 1794, he describes himself in his early years as introverted and misunderstood:

> I had worked at my father's trade since I was nine years of age; but I never, from a child, associated with those of my age, never learned their diversions. I returned every night to my mother's fire-side, where I talked or read with her; if ever I walked out, it was by myself in unfrequented places, woods, the sea-shore, &c. for I was very pensive, melancholy, and very *stupid*, as all but my mother thought.[6]

'What was supposed to be dullness in Chatterton was genius,' as John Davis would put it succinctly in 1806.[7] Like Chatterton, famously reluctant to read until he learned the alphabet 'from an old Folio music book', Iolo claimed that he learned to read:

[4] NLW 21285E, Letter no. 797, Iolo Morganwg to Margaret Williams, 19 February 1791.
[5] See NLW 21328A, a fair manuscript copy of the volume from the late 1780s.
[6] Williams: *PLP*, I, p. xvi. As G. J. Williams notes, the account of his childhood is demonstrably romanticized (Williams: *IM*, pp. 108–9).
[7] John Davis, *Life of Chatterton* (London, 1806), p. 9.

> In a volume of *Songs*, intituled *The Vocal Miscellany*; for, I could not be prevailed upon to be taught from any other book. My mother sang agreeably, and I understood that she learned her songs from this book, which made me so very desirous of learning it. This I did in a short time, and hence, I doubt not, my original turn for poetry.[8]

But the 'haunting' really began in 1792, by which time Iolo had moved to London after a period in Bath and Bristol collecting subscriptions for his intended publication. He spent the first part of the year with the lexicographer William Owen Pughe and his family in Pentonville, but by the summer he had moved out to cheap accommodation in – of all places – '12 Beauchamp Street, Brook's Market, Holborn', hardly a stone's throw from the room where Chatterton had died, apparently by his own hand, some twenty years earlier.[9] Here, frustrated by ill health, financial difficulties and guilt at having left his family with very little means of support, he seems to have suffered some kind of breakdown. A letter to his wife Peggy begins abruptly:

> Let me know immediately the first line of your letter whether my dear little children are all or any of them living. It has been for many months so fixed in my imagination that some if not all of them are dead that I have not been able to do any thing, but what trifles could be done in a very few days that I have been able to get the better of such thoughts. I have this three weeks had a sheet to correct, but am not able to look at it. I rise in the Morning early, for I never sleep, and walk about I know not where, often to the fields where I lie down under a hedge. I then come home, and pass the night in a manner so distressing that it will soon bring me to the grave.[10]

A month later he was still in turmoil, the obsession with his children's health still paramount. There are darker hints, too, in the invocation of Chatterton's name:

> tell me sincerely whether the little ones are alive. I cannot possibly put it for two minutes together out of my thoughts but that they are dead . . . I should not have been in this world now but from the hopes of still being of some help to them. It was from this street, and within a door or two, that poor Chatterton was obliged to force his way out of this good-for-nothing world.[11]

[8] Williams: *PLP*, I, p. xv. The *Vocal Miscellany*, much reprinted throughout the century, first appeared in 1733.

[9] NLW 21285E, Letter no. 810, Iolo Morganwg to Margaret Williams, 20 July 1792. Chatterton's 'suicide', so central to the Romantic myth of his life, may well have been an accidental overdose: see Richard Holmes, 'Thomas Chatterton: The Case Re-opened', *Cornhill Magazine*, 178 (1970), 203–51; Nick Groom, 'The Death of Chatterton', in Heys (ed.), *From Gothic to Romantic*, pp. 116–25.

[10] NLW 21285E, Letter no. 810, Iolo Morganwg to Margaret Williams, 20 July 1792.

[11] Ibid., Letter no. 811, Iolo Morganwg to Margaret Williams, 9 August 1792.

In October he was still wretched and Chatterton still on his mind:

> I have no means left in the World whereby I shall be able to extricate myself out of the difficulties which have over whelmed me. I have some things to do which, was I able to finish, would be of some profit to me, but a disorder in my head which alarms me very much, has for some time prevented me from doing any thing. I have five or six times since I have been here been afflicted with it. It is a perpetual pain and heat in my head. I feel it inwardly most. I sleep not a moment and have not slept for more than a month. I am frequently so delirious that I quite forget myself in every thing, especially at night. I am under the necessity of refraining from writing, for it hurts me very much, besides my thoughts are generally so confused that I can do nothing on that account. Laudanum gives me no relief but rather increases the internal heat in my head. You can not imagine how effectually this disables me from doing any thing. If I could remove to a better part of the Town, I mean a healthier place, I should perhaps be better. I am able to walk about however and am better in the air, but I can not walk about all day, and I perish with cold in my room. My Landlady keeps a shop in a distant part of the Town, she gets up about seven and breakfasts about eight, at which time I make my little tea, at night they come home. About nine o clock I have a little more tea if I have any, which is frequently not the case. And this is all the fire that I ever see. I have but one hope left now, which is that I shall soon die, for it is impossible for me to be relieved any other way. Send me one letter more, and let me see in it the names of my dear little ones. I shall never see their faces again. Poor Chatterton who lived and died almost the next door to where I am, found means, like myself, to keep his distresses unknown. There are some in this street that knew him well, he could not complain, and I can not, if I could, I have some reasons to think that things would have been otherwise than they are with me now. One letter more to inform me how you are, and how the little ones.[12]

Iolo invariably exaggerates his miseries when writing to Peggy, but this cannot be entirely dismissed as a defence-mechanism against guilt. It is certainly, as Geraint Phillips has shown, testimony to the effect of laudanum on his naturally lively paranoia; a justified fear of harassment by 'church-and-king' mobs and government spies cannot have helped him either.[13] But the influence of Chatterton himself is equally potent: self-identification is evident at every turn, in the description of the lodging, the poverty and mental anguish and, highly untypically, the hints at suicide.[14] Chatterton here is much more than

[12] Ibid., Letter no. 812, Iolo Morganwg to Margaret Williams, 27 October 1792.

[13] See Phillips, 'Math o Wallgofrwydd'.

[14] John Goodridge refers to 'horrific' statistics for suicide (and alcoholism and insanity) among the self-taught poets of the eighteenth and nineteenth centuries in 'Identity, Authenticity, Class', 133, 147 n. 9. There is an exceptionally stilted passage in Iolo's papers (NLW 21433E, no. 5) which laboriously sets out the reasons against suicide (the welfare of one's children being the most prominent): I agree with Geraint Phillips ('Math o Wallgofrwydd', 402) that it could well date from the summer of 1792.

a figure of speech – he has even talked to the neighbours about him. This is a real haunting, akin to the 'Ghosts of Otway & Chatterton, & the phantasms of a Wife broken-hearted, & a hunger-bitten Baby!' that pursued the hysterical and newly wed Coleridge in 1796.[15]

Because Iolo did not die or go mad, his London years have not usually been perceived as tragic: he has appeared far less of a victim than Clare, more active and manipulative, deviously constructing selves for his different audiences. Prys Morgan depicts him 'playing the noble savage' for the benefit of the English literati, while Gwyn A. Williams points out that during the latter half of 1792, the period of his greatest suffering in the letters to Peggy, he was 'up to his eyes in the fervour of *Jacobinism* and millenarianism' and spreading his ideas about bardism; the second Gorsedd ceremony was held on Primrose Hill at the autumn solstice that year.[16] He was also much taken up with 'Madoc fever' – the recently-revived hunt for a lost tribe of Welsh-speaking American Indians, the supposed descendants of a group of exiles who had left Wales in the twelfth-century with Madoc, prince of Gwynedd. Iolo and William Owen Pughe played pivotal parts in the collection and dissemination (and, in Iolo's case, invention) of information relevant to the search for these 'Madogwys'. Indeed, in 1791 and early into 1792, Iolo fully intended making the expedition himself, preparing for the rigours of the wilderness by sleeping rough, eating nuts and berries, and copying out lists of useful vocabulary.[17] The breakdown of the summer seems to have halted his plans. Both Gwyneth Lewis and Damian Walford Davies have since darkened this somewhat theatrical picture with thoughtful accounts of the pressures on Iolo as a political radical under the government of William Pitt; the heavy financial risk and the logistical complications involved in publishing by subscription, coupled with his liberal use of laudanum, cannot have helped matters either.[18]

This chapter offers a further version of Iolo Morganwg during this fascinating period of his life, an interpretation rooted in the facts of his social and economic condition, but dealing above all with issues of identity and authorial

[15] E. L. Griggs (ed.), *Collected Letters of Samuel Taylor Coleridge* (6 vols., Oxford, 1956–71), I, p. 275.

[16] Prys Morgan, *Iolo Morganwg*, p. 12; Gwyn A. Williams, *Madoc: The Making of a Myth* (London, 1979), p. 142.

[17] For Iolo's role in the Madoc fever of the 1790s, see Williams, *Madoc*, pp. 105, 128–40. NLW 21431E, no. 58 is a list in Iolo's hand of useful words in the Chipeway language, probably taken from Jonathan Carver's *Travels through the Interior Parts of North America, in the Years 1766, 1767 and 1768* (London, 1778).

[18] Note Lewis's comment that '[G. J.] Williams's suggestion that his work can be considered as the involuntary output of a compulsive liar does a disservice to the real social and political pressures which drove Iolo underground' ('Eighteenth-Century Literary Forgeries', p. 140); for the radical Iolo, see also Davies, *Presences that Disturb*, pp. 136–52 and Geraint H. Jenkins, *'Perish Kings and Emperors, But Let the Bard of Liberty Live'* (Aberystwyth, 2006). For publishing by subscription, see Mary-Ann Constantine, '"This Wildernessed Business of Publication": The Making of *Poems, Lyric and Pastoral* (1794)' in *Rattleskull Genius*, pp. 123–45, and for the effects of laudanum, see Phillips, 'Math o Wallgofrwydd'.

self-consciousness (both concepts thoroughly embroiled in the contemporary debates about authenticity). It explores the apparent paradox in Iolo's fierce defence of what he felt was his 'authentic' poetic voice in English, and his need to dissolve or mask himself by writing his Welsh poetry pseudonymously – a paradox which owes much to his conscious manipulation of the figure of the self-taught poet. The anxieties expressed so graphically as mental and physical distress in the letters to his wife also reveal themselves, in somewhat different form, in manuscript drafts of the short account of his life and work which appeared in 1794 as a preface to his *Poems, Lyric and Pastoral.*

Autobiography and the anxiety of reception

> The censure that will soon fall upon me does above all other things drive me mad.[19]

At precisely the point when Iolo was attempting to introduce himself to his reading public, autobiographical writing was becoming a feature of the literary landscape. Self-writing of various kinds had, of course, always existed, but as James Treadwell has shown, a rapid increase in explicitly autobiographical texts between the 1790s and 1830, combined with the critical reactions to them, mark the birth of what is effectively a 'new' genre.[20] By the end of Iolo's lifetime, memoirs and autobiographical writing in general were recognized as a distinct practice but, during its early stages, it was a mode of writing peculiarly fretted by anxiety. Such writing, Treadwell argues, far from revealing moments of intense communion with the private (and hence 'Romantic') self, in fact displays an acute awareness of the public sphere and an extreme self-consciousness about readership and the act of publication. The argument has especial force for works, like Iolo's, produced by subscription, since the immediate audience is known, personally or by name, to the writer – and indeed could be said to precede the work, both in being wholly instrumental in its physical production and in having their names quite literally listed at the front of the book. Iolo's audience, cajoled with specimens and fair copies, had been promised a result, but in 1792, for many reasons, the 'product' (confidently announced in various flyers of the previous year as imminent) was painfully slow in materializing: 'it would now be a heaven to me', he wrote to Peggy,

[19] NLW 21285E, Letter no. 812, Iolo Morganwg to Margaret Williams, 27 October 1792.

[20] James Treadwell, *Autobiographical Writing and British Literature 1783–1834* (Oxford, 2005). See also Felicity A. Nussbaum, *The Autobiographical Subject: Gender and Ideology in Eighteenth-Century England* (London, 1989) and, with a wider scope, Charles Taylor, *Sources of the Self: The Making of Modern Identity* (Cambridge, MA, 1989). For an interesting account of John Clare's self-writing, see Valerie Pedlar, '"Written By Himself" – Edited by Others: The Autobiographical Writings of John Clare' in Simon Kövesi and John Goodridge (eds.), *John Clare: New Approaches* (Helpston, 2000), pp. 17–31.

'if I could be sure of being able to send my books to my subscribers soon, and spend the remainder of my life, not only in a prison, but in the darkest dungeon – and spend eternity in Hell.'[21]

The numerous drafts of the preface and other unpublished writings (such as draft letters to potential subscribers which tail off in spluttering rage)[22] give some indication of the strain Iolo came under over the two or three years he spent getting the work through the press. The initial process of collecting subscriptions for his book had involved assiduous cultivation of the gentry in Bath and Bristol, and at this period he came into contact with writers and notables such as Hannah More, Harriet Bowdler, Hester Lynch Piozzi and Christopher Anstey. (He may or may not have met Ann Yearsley, who sent her name for the list in the summer of 1791, but he certainly claimed later to have discussed her 'frequently' with Hannah More).[23] Success with the *beau monde* was alternately exhilarating and intolerable. The same summer of 1791 saw him jeopardize the future of his work with an impulsive display of principle in the form of an open letter to several Bristol printers, withdrawing the subscription lists he had left in their shops lest they be contaminated by names from a blood-tainted city:

> for it is my fixed resolution not to disgrace my list with the names of any villainous abettors of the slave trade, who so exultingly rejoiced lately in your City, on the failure of the humane Mr Wilberforces Bill for the abolition of that inhuman traffic, for which Bristol is and always has been, so remarkably infamous.[24]

[21] NLW 21285E, Letter no. 811, Iolo Morganwg to Margaret Williams, 9 August 1792. Iolo's experience contradicts Paul Korshin's claim that the 'sense of obligation which pervades and often exacerbates the traditional patron-client relationship is usually diminished or wholly absent in the author-subscriber relationship', 'Types of Eighteenth-Century Literary Patronage', *Eighteenth-Century Studies*, 7 (1974), 464. For John Clare's discomfort with the subscription process, see Sales, *John Clare*, pp. 20–1.

[22] See e.g. NLW 21286E, Letter no. 1024 (a draft letter, probably to John Carthew, who acted as Pitt's private secretary) which begins 'I took the liberty of addressing a letter to you last week with proposals for publishing two small vols of poems, and I presumed to solicit the favour of your name sir without any money. I waited at your door in downing street this morning and was informed that I could not expect any answer.' It ends: '[there are] persons to be met with in the very lowest stations, who know more of human Nature than all the kings in the World, who will not allow that the blood which proudly boils in the dirty veins of Monarchs can possibly be as pure as that which streams thro the heart of the honest ploughMan, the harmeless Cobler, and the friendly and patriotic Chimney-sweeper in whom we find exibited more of the true dignity of human nature than than ever appeared in any King Emperor or any rascal whatever of that class.'

[23] See Mary-Ann Constantine, '"A Subject of Conversation": Iolo Morganwg, Hannah More and Ann Yearsley' in Davies and Pratt (eds.), *Wales and the Romantic Imagination* (forthcoming).

[24] NLW 21400C, no. 24a. The dispute is discussed in my *'Combustible Matter'*, pp. 14–19.

The results of this gesture do not seem to have harmed his prospects too badly, and the final list weighed in at over six hundred and fifty names, with 'Humanity's Wilberforce' proudly capitalized among them.

Poems, Lyric and Pastoral came out in January 1794, the fractious tone of its preface at odds with its soothing title. In the preface Iolo can be seen struggling to create a self-portrait which would appeal to a broad range of subscribers; because that range was so extraordinarily broad, the portrait is, like the volume, fraught with conflict. If the Hannah Mores and Elizabeth Montagus (and indeed, the dedicatee himself, the Prince of Wales) were intended to see and approve of the hard-working, plain-living, self-taught journeyman stonemason, and if the Romantically inclined were intended to see a Welsh Burns, a lyrical child of nature and a genius in the Chattertonian mould, there was still enough of the angry and resentful Jacobin (who, with 'an Ancient Briton's warm pride', rejected patronage in all its forms) for fellow radicals to take the book as a token of solidarity with anti-establishment causes.[25] Indeed, it is helpful to read the introductory preface as a sustained dialogue with potentially critical voices 'out there', an attempt to pre-empt and deflect a wide range of accusations from many different quarters ('the more explicitly a volume accounts for itself', notes Treadwell, 'the more obvious its dependence on the contested and uncontrollable literary public sphere').[26]

From the opening line, the reader is assaulted by a defiant tour de force of excuses for the delay in publication, from material and financial circumstances to the perfidy of the human race, politics, acts of God, and simple writer's block:

> My little publication appears after a pretty long delay. Some obstacles occurred from the nature of my situation in life: these were unavoidable, but mostly unforeseen; others were thrown in my way by the mean machinations of Envy, that appears to have been hurt at the success and valuable friendships that, for a little while, I met with at the opening of my subscription.[27]

There follows an angry refutation of rumours 'that I was going (some said I was gone) to America, with my subscribers' money in my pocket', and a string of further excuses for delay, including the disabling effects of ill health and the death of his beloved youngest daughter. Woven into these rather vociferous attempts to set the record straight (characterized by a 'querulous' tone noted disapprovingly by the *Critical Review*)[28] are moments of highly typical concern

[25] On Burns as a likely model, see below, pp. 70–1. Some radical responses to the volume are noted by Davies, *Presences that Disturb*, pp. 143–5.
[26] Treadwell, *Autobiographical Writing and British Literature*, p. 118.
[27] Williams: *PLP*, I, p. xi.
[28] *Critical Review*, 2nd series, 11 (1794), 168–75.

about the process of self-writing in itself: 'Some of my best friends have urged me to give some anecdotes of my life. I have little of any thing to say worth notice on this occasion.'[29] Several pages later the life-narrative is brought to a halt with a short paragraph that, in its combination of self-deprecation, apology and mild justification, reads like a template for the genre:

> This I imagine is more than enough of my history; it is of no importance to any one to know how many stones I hewed, or on how many grave-stones I have inscribed vile doggrel. Anecdotes of original impressions on the human mind may be of some philosophical use; and I have here honestly given my own. Unavoidable egotisms will be pardoned.[30]

Somewhere between this anxious politeness and the bouts of defensive aggression Iolo asserts his claim to the work in no uncertain terms:

> There were gentlemen of the first abilities that would have assisted me; but I could not think of accepting their very kind offers; for, I was from the beginning determined not to put the least imposition on the public, but to give them the real unsophisticated productions of the *self-tutored Journeyman Mason*.[31]

The assistance referred to here is literary rather than financial; and this is a declaration of authorial independence. As we shall see, Iolo knew exactly what he was doing in deploying the terms 'real' and 'unsophisticated': by 1794, the 'self-educated' poet was a well-established phenomenon, invariably introduced to the public as a product of 'natural genius', and representative, through a lack of formal education, of a poetry uncluttered with the borrowed sentiment of classical learning. The phrase 'the least imposition on the public', with its clear overtones of fraud, is especially telling (Iolo uses it of James Macpherson's *Ossian*; Owain Myfyr would eventually use it of Iolo himself), signalling as it does a reassurance to the public that they are receiving the genuine article. This neat declaration of honest good faith, however, took some time to achieve. The manuscript drafts reveal several versions of this section, with the argument varying slightly in each. One offers a fuller elaboration of the same idea, revealing that 'some poetical gentlemen' (he names only 'Mr Anstey of Bath') had offered to give his verses a 'polish they certainly want', but that he had resisted on moral grounds: 'I was fully, even resolutely determined that I would never like the Jack daw in the fable strut about in borrowed plumes.'[32]

[29] Williams: *PLP*, I, p. xiv.

[30] Ibid., p. xvii; note Treadwell's comments on the anxiety about 'egotism' expressed both by writers and critics: *Autobiographical Writing and British Literature*, pp. 63–4.

[31] Williams: *PLP*, I, pp. xii–xiii.

[32] NLW 21387E, no. 27.

Cautioning his readers that certain rumours had been spread to the contrary, he assures them that there is not 'in the whole world one person that can with truth print out a single line that he may call his own'. This is Iolo fiercely defensive of his authorial voice; the hint of some dark plot to discredit him is of a piece with the opening accusations, and entirely typical of the paranoia of this period. In another draft, his argument takes a scientific, not to say proto-anthropological, slant:

> nothing can be more reprehensible than those alterations by superior learning and abilities which are said to have taken place in most of the productions of uncultivated Genius that we hear of. Philosophers read these things, and they should not be deceived, for the sake of investigating the powers and properties of the human mind under all possible circumstance favourable and unfavourable, rather than for any intrinsic beauty or merit these crude scribblings possess.[33]

Here the poetry is pure data, a product interesting regardless of literary merit, because of who the author is and what he has done (there are clear echoes of Johnson's observation 'that there has rarely passed a life of which a judicious and faithful narrative would not be useful');[34] self-taught writers, he realizes, are especially vulnerable to accusations of 'alterations by superior learning'. But he also offers a more existential reason for holding one's authorial ground, evoking a powerful sense of self:

> I always submitted and that with gladness my verses to the Criticism of friends, but whatever faults they pointed out the Correction of them was always my own attempt . . . I never yet met with any person, who saw my subject so exactly in the same light as my self, or whose feelings, sentiments, experience etc perfectly corresponded with my own, and for that reason whatever ammendments they might propose their ideas never assimilated naturally with mine.[35]

Elsewhere that idea of individual uniqueness is expanded and given a class inflection:

> Let none be offended at an observation that I am now going to make. Some Gentlemen into whose hands I once put two or three of my pieces returned them with (what I could not call ammendments) altered, and additional lines and couplets, excellent in themselves but they never assimilated with my own ideas, those who have thro life walked the paths of opulence and science, view things from a point very different from there wherein the humble Pupil of uneducated simplicity and

[33] Ibid., no. 9.
[34] Samuel Johnson, *The Rambler* (6 vols., London, 1752), II, p. 209.
[35] NLW 21387E, no. 27.

wealthless rurality is placed; they rashly consider many things wrong because they never beheld them in the same light; I think that I do not appear very different in my *Castles in the Air* and *Stanzas written in London*, from what I really and naturally am. But in these pieces as they were once altered I was absolutely caricatured very oddly. I could not adopt a single line.[36]

Behind the short declaration of the published preface, then, lies a nexus of linked ideas to do with self-hood expressed variously as a strong distaste for any kind of false-seeming or mask-wearing, a fear of misrepresentation by others, a scientific concern for objectivity and a clear expression of individualism: that is, the impossibility of one person really knowing another, and in particular the impossibility of true sympathy or empathy across the barriers of class and circumstance. As it circles around and worries at the point from these many angles, Iolo's much-drafted preface amply demonstrates the 'self-consciousness' so typical of texts at the 'permeable border between public and private spheres'.[37]

The explicit self-writing of the preface is not the only place where such anxieties make themselves evident. The poems which, in Iolo's words, reveal him for 'what I really and naturally am' are also a site of endless worry and revision, a process visible right up to the moment of printing. I have shown elsewhere how the pressure of publication induced Iolo to rewrite an early poem so comprehensively that after innumerable drafts only six lines of the original remained untouched.[38] An even more instructive example can be found in a copy – in fact three pedantically careful copies – of a draft of 'Stanzas Written in London 1773' as corrected by the poet Christopher Anstey during Iolo's time in Bath in 1791. Anstey, the by-then elderly author of a successful satirical poem *The New Bath Review* (1766), had been helpful in setting Iolo up in his attempts to raise subscriptions for the book, advising him to print a specimen of his work in a proposal, and using his influence to procure names. Since, in these manuscripts, his suggestions and corrections to Iolo's poem are rather bitterly titled 'Anstey's interpolations', one may assume that the copies, all in Iolo's hand, were made after the initial euphoria of having a literary mentor had worn off.[39] The poem presents the sentiments of the young writer in 1773, on his first visit to London: he feels that he has been polluted by contact with the city and longs to return to the beauty and moral simplicity of his native Glamorgan. Iolo has used a different coloured pencil to mark the inter-

[36] Ibid., no. 9.

[37] Treadwell, *Autobiographical Writing*, p. 120.

[38] Constantine, '"This Wildernessed Business"' in *Rattleskull Genius*, pp. 139–43.

[39] NLW 21392F, nos. 52, 53, 54 (two of which are dated to 1791). The business clearly rankled for a long time: a lengthy draft letter to Mary Barker, written in 1796, refers again to his unhappiness with Anstey's corrections, and promises to include 'a copy [of] a piece as altered by Mr Anstey, with my observations upon it'. NLW 21285E, Letter no. 862, Iolo Morganwg to Mary Barker, 26 March 1796.

polations (here shown underlined), and, in one draft, added his own marginal comments:[40]

1.

When the sweet morn of Life appears
In retrospective view
How painful to trace back those years
When time unmarked by galling cares
On wings of pleasure flew.

2.

Then was I blest, e'er led astray
By Fame's alluring tale
When Reason's unambitious sway
Could ev'ry restless thought allay
And o'er my heart prevail.

3.

Why, Cambria, did I quit thy shore
Which erst I deem'd so fair
These realms of discord to explore
To dwell with strife and wild uproar
And breathe this tainted air.

a line of my own from another piece
Epistle to a friend in the County

4.

Dear Native Land, though thoughtless pride
Contemns thy humble plains
With Peace and Innocence supplied
The joys of nature still abide
Amongst thy cheerful swains.

5.

How pensive doth my mind survey
Those paths I traced alone
While yet in Childhood's morning gay
The Muse first lisped her infant lay
And made her efforts known.

See 4th stanza of Davona's Vale
and the [??] of Banks of the Daw

6.

Applauded by th' unletter'd swain
She felt her pinions grow
She pleased the Critics of the plain
Whilst Nature bade her simple strain
In artless numbers flow.

7.

On me in fair Glamorgan's Land
So sweet, methought, she smiled
Twas there I joined her tuneful Band
There every charm of Nature scan'd
And pour'd my woodnotes wild.

when first I join'd the tuneful Band
Epistle to a friend &c

8.

O blest Glamorgan sweet's thy scene
Thy wild romantic vales
Thy rivers deck'd with margins green
Thy tow'ring hills, thy sky serene
Thy health-inspiring gales.

Rivers deck'd with margins green in
A Translation from the Welsh

9.

May I to thee return again
With self-approving mind
To range once more my native plain
And free from every mental pain
To live with peace resign'd.

10.

Ah wretched me!Why did I long
While yet unknown to care
To join the city's madd'ning throng
To dwell her vicious sons among
And breathe her tainted air!

See 3rd Stanza

11.

Thou who art bless'd with innocence
Ne'er chuse thy dwelling here
Thy life, if blameless, gives offence,
Thy jeering friends will recompence
Thy virtues with a sneer.

12.

See fashion to the gaping crowd
Her gaudy plumes display
The vain, the wanton, and the proud,
Raise their tyranick shouts aloud,
And urge her sov'reign sway.

The vain, the wanton and the proud,
a string of Beads

13.

What myriads throng her giddy train
Blind to the charms of truth

Vice loudly chaunts her syren strain
And casts her wanton smiles to gain
The unexperienced youth.

14.

A while he shrinks, her dazzling throne
Still fearful to adore
But soon ashamed to stand alone
He claims some folly for his own
Some vice unknown before.

a very bold metonomy
Throne, for the person that sits thereon

It is however known at last, it seems

15.

Whilst Reason wakes, and virtue warms
Thy yet unconquer'd mind
O fly her vile polluted arms
Nor gaze upon her tinsel charms
Nor cast one look behind.

Reason wakes and virtue warms
Bead-stringing

16.

O fly! nor let thy gen'rous heart
Submit to her controul
She'll soon find out its weakest part
Will haunt thee with insidious art
And fascinate thy soul.

17.

Virtue, 'twas thy all-saving hand
Preserved me from the snare.
From schemes by fell Temptation plan'd
I heard thy call, thy dread command
And bless'd thy guardian care.

18.

Whilst toiling on life's boist'rous sea
'Gainst adverse passion's tide
Great pow'r I call, I bow to thee,
Thou, heav'nly monitor, shalt be
My pilot and my guide.

19.

Bid reason all her aid impart
To light my darksome way
To meek forgiveness move my heart
For those by whose insidious art
I've oft been led astray.*

See 5th stanza of Davona's Vale

20.
And thou from whom all virtue springs From a piece entitled Resolution
My soul with patience fill
Beneath the shadow of thy wings
Grant me to shun all hurtful things
And wait thy heav'nly will.

* *I've oft been led astray.* I here plead guilty, it seems – But I know not that I was ever led much astray at London, though I had to struggle with many temptations.

The blissful idealization of Glamorgan is one of the volume's core themes and, more than anything, links Iolo's English pastorals to his earlier Welsh poems and the imitations of Dafydd ap Gwilym. The latter, indeed, make a fleeting appearance in the published version of the poem, in an extraordinarily detailed footnote in praise of the county's whitewashed cottages (it extends over several pages and claims that the practice goes back to the ancient Britons); one of the 'sources' cited is Iolo's own 'Cywydd i Yrru yr Haf i Annerch Morganwg'.[41] Given his pedantic 'scrupulosity' in distinguishing every last 'and' interpolated by his mentor (see stanza two), it is perhaps surprising to find that Iolo's most frequent objection is that Anstey has recycled ideas and phrases which he (Iolo) has already used elsewhere; similarly, the 'bead-stringing' comments are in fact self-criticisms of his own lines. But there are more fundamental changes. What most disturbs him, it is clear, is the fact that Anstey has understood the poem to express the repentant thoughts of a young sinner longing to return home: the final footnote rather indignantly claims that – 'though I had to struggle with many temptations' – he is not guilty. (It is doubtless no coincidence that the imagery and the sentiment of the poem, particularly in the final stanzas, recall Cowper's hymn 'Temptation': 'O Lord, the pilot's part perform/ And guide and guard me through the storm').[42] Turning to the pre-Anstey drafts, and what would

[40] NLW 21392F, no. 52.
[41] Williams: *PLP*, I, pp. 17–18.
[42] John Newton, *Olney Hymns* (London, 1779), p. 231. Iolo greatly admired 'the (in my opinion) incomparable Cowper', and claimed to have walked out to the poet's house at Olney to deliver his copy of *Poems, Lyric and Pastoral* (to which Cowper had subscribed). He was not at home but, some months later, Iolo had a strange non-encounter with him during an evening in company at the house of one Mr Rose: the talk apparently turned on the 'origin of Poetical Genius', but 'during the whole time the Gentleman to whom I was not introduced never said [spoke] a word, for which reason I considered him as very deaf if not dumb also'. Rose explained some days later that this gentleman had been Cowper, who, suffering from a bout of depression, had been unwilling or unable to make himself known. NLW 21286E, Letter no. 983, Iolo Morganwg to Jonathan Rees, 28 March 1821.

become the final published version, however, the central idea of the poem is an even more subtle proposition, namely that the wickedness of the speaker's behaviour in London lies not in his actually succumbing to immorality, but in weak-mindedly pretending to be worse than he is:

16.
Thou must approach vile Folly's throne;
Reluctantly be vain;
Thy conscious innocence disown;
Affect, and boast, a vice unknown;
A guilt unpractised feign.[43]

In other words, the speaker's main crime is that of not being true to himself, of putting on an act – a distinction largely lost sight of in the Anstey version, which prefers the simpler pattern of the prodigal's return. This, then, apparently constitutes the 'absolute caricature' of Iolo's complaint, and it is interesting to see how both the poem and Iolo's rejection of Anstey's changes to it reveal that same concern with identity, of expressing 'what I really and truly am'. The expression of personal experience may seem to the modern reader somewhat muffled by the rather tame poetic diction and the very familiar topic (the rejection of city for country life was a much-worked theme in the eighteenth century and goes back at least to Virgil; Johnson's 'London' of 1738 was an admired model).[44] Yet there can be no doubt that Iolo felt he had invested this and other poems in the collection with his own, lived experience, and intended them to be read as such.

'Stanzas Written in London' is presented as a piece written twenty years prior to the date of publication and purportedly describes Iolo's first period in London. However, since, like many others in the collection, this poem was extensively revised, first by Iolo, then by Anstey, and then reclaimed by Iolo, more or less up to the last minute, it inevitably reflects his second period in London, when he again felt entrapped by the city's 'hell', and longed to return to Glamorgan. That double temporal perspective, although not acknowledged in the final version of the poem, is significant: it gives the lie, for one thing, to the title's claim 'written in 1773', since it is clearly not the poem it was then (and is thus, in a sense, a fake). Here another, highly perceptive, comment from the autobiographical drafts seems relevant:

[43] Williams: *PLP*, I, p. 21. The verse appears in more or less this form in all the earlier drafts: NLW 21328A, pp. 94–100 (stanza 20); 21329A, pp. 11–16 (stanza 14); 21330E, pp. 17–18 (stanza 14); 21331B, p. 13 (stanza 14); 21333B, p. 107 (stanza 14).

[44] In his own, annotated copy, of *Poems, Lyric and Pastoral* held at the National Library of Wales, Iolo has added the following lines from Johnson's poem, to be included in some future edition: 'Resolv'd at length from vice and London far,/ To breathe in distant fields a purer air/ And fix'd on Cambria's solitary shore/ Give to Saint David one true Briton more.'

> I find it very difficult even in my own emmendations, to avoid this consequence. For when I have pieces under correction written more than twenty years ago, tho I perfectly recollect my ideas and feelings, yet I find that time and reading has by insensible degrees made such a great change in my mind, judgment, language, so altered my sentiments, cooled some of my passions, and almost eradicated others, and even I think, awaked some that had heretofore been dormant, that I find it now, with all my efforts, impossible to express myself now at the age of forty six in the same manner I would have done at twenty. I feel that I am very often absolutely unable to resume ideas and feelings that were once my own, and that at the same time I perfectly remember, and that as well as a man become blind in advanced life may remember light and colours, but there is a wide difference between the memory, let it be ever so perfect, of what is past, and an actual experience of it.[45]

How any other person could hope to correct another is impossible to imagine, since even Iolo himself cannot become himself at twenty. This keen sense of the disassociated self is reminiscent of David Hume's description of the fragmented nature of individual identity as 'a bundle or collection of different perceptions . . . in a perpetual flux and movement', a kind of broken sequence of experiences held together by memory, or by the action of the imagination.[46] Like the poem, Iolo is not the entity he was in 1773. It is the same gap between the speaker and a former self or selves which Wordsworth, with more self-awareness but a similar anxiety, negotiates in 'Tintern Abbey': 'I cannot paint/ What then I was' (lines 75–6). Memory 'let it be ever so perfect' can only ever stand in for the actual experience, and so, as Margaret Russett observes, becomes in itself a kind of imposture.[47]

Iolo's autobiographical writings, both the poems and the preface drafts, offer an unusually nuanced account of what Hume called 'the fiction of a continu'd existence'.[48] Yet, even as they stress the irreducibility of private experience, they reveal an anxiety about remaining 'true' to an authentic identity and authorial voice – a voice which is modulated, revised, and occasionally tamed by the thought of its own reception in the wider, and politically complex, public sphere.

[45] NLW 21387E, no. 27.

[46] David Hume, *A Treatise of Human Nature* (3 vols., London, 1739–40), I, p. 439. For the wider eighteenth-century debate over the nature of self and personal identity, see Nussbaum, *The Autobiographical Subject*, pp. 30–57.

[47] Russett, *Fictions and Fakes*, pp. 41–3.

[48] Hume, *A Treatise of Human Nature*, I, p. 359.

5

Poems, Lyric and Pastoral *and the Self-taught Tradition*

Tri phrif anhepcor Awen;
Llygad yn gweled Anian;
Calon yn teimlo Anian;
a glewder a faidd cydfyned ag Anian.

The three primary requisites of poetic Genius:
An eye that can see Nature;
A heart that can feel Nature;
And a resolution that dares follow Nature.[1]

If autobiography is intrinsically 'nervous' about appearing in public, then the pressure to conform is doubled when, for reasons of gender or class, the writer is someone outside the normal boundaries of the literary sphere: in such cases acceptance depends on an ability to 'pass', to comport oneself correctly. The nervousness of self-writing is a marked feature of prefaces and introductions to the work of labouring-class poets. The shoemaker James Woodhouse is exemplary in this respect, beginning the revised edition of his poems with an 'Author's Apology' at his presumption in intruding upon a genteel readership for a second time, and reassuring them that he is not rising above his station.[2] Even patrons introducing their protegés take care to insist that decorum has not been breached: Hannah More's introduction of Ann Yearsley to her genteel public is at pains to reassure them that her fledgling poetic ambitions will in no way interfere with her duties as a wife and mother ('I have the satisfaction to tell you, dear Madam, that our Enthusiast is active and industrious to no small degree').[3] An inevitable strain between the desire to present the writer as some kind of prodigy (or 'natural genius') and the desire to be acceptable to a reading public is thus inherent in the genre, and we have already seen Iolo struggling to negotiate this in the drafts to his preface. Although in the preface to *Poems, Lyric and Pastoral* Iolo plays down the technical aspects of his craft ('it

[1] Williams: *PLP*, II, pp. 254–5.

[2] James Woodhouse, *Poems on Several Occasions: the second edition, corrected, with several additional pieces* (London, 1766); for Woodhouse and his patrons, see William J. Christmas, *The Lab'ring Muses: Work, Writing, and the Social Order in English Plebeian Poetry, 1730–1830* (London, 2001), pp. 183–210. The preface to Robert Burns's *Poems, Chiefly in the Scottish Dialect* (Kilmarnock, 1786) is probably the most influential example of the genre.

[3] From More's prefatory letter to Mrs Montagu; see Ann Yearsley, *Poems, on Several Occasions* (4th edn., London, 1786), p. xiv.

is of no importance to any one to know how many stones I hewed, or on how many grave-stones I have inscribed vile doggrel'), he does, as we have seen, emphasize his status as a labourer – much as he had done in the famous 'trailer' which appeared in the *Gentleman's Magazine* in 1789, which sets out his credentials as a hard-working, honest mason-poet ('sober, never seen in liquor').[4] But his determination to exploit this role alongside other, more provocative, voices, strains that picture of good behaviour to the very limits: indeed, it could be argued that the constraints imposed by the persona of the rural labouring-class poet are fundamental to the conflicted nature of the volume as a whole. Not least of the tensions is the fact that, within a Welsh context, the notion of a craftsman-poet does not have quite the same resonance: with far fewer official educational channels open to the majority of the population in the first place, it was hardly unusual for scholars and poets of the period to come from rural backgrounds, or even to practise a manual craft. Owain Myfyr was a self-made man. Nor, inversely, was it at all unusual for a craftsman to compose poetry: among Iolo's Glamorgan predecessors are the weaver Rhys Morgan and the carpenter Lewis Hopkin.[5] Iolo was perhaps distinctive within his circle of literary correspondents in never being able to break free of the financial need to work with his hands, but it is probably true to say that, in the eyes of his Welsh contemporaries, his craft was not the significant marker of his identity that it appears to be in many of his writings aimed at an English audience.

As Damian Walford Davies has put it, *Poems, Lyric and Pastoral* is 'strikingly politicized from the outset'; the book's fierce rhetoric, clad in the robes of Iolo's bardism, is directed against the religious, governmental and monarchical abuse of power.[6] The two volumes contain anti-slavery poems, anti-war poems and, most characteristically, an army of irritable footnotes attacking everyone from kings and priests to Grub Street hacks. And yet, oddly, that is not the main impression the collection makes on the reader. There is anger, and some anguish, in the collection, but surprisingly little of it is in the poems. A great many of these, like well-behaved sheep, gather on the gentler side of the fence, where life is indeed lyric and pastoral, and the landscape is green and pleasant (and, at times, not terribly interesting). In its meek adherence to the more conventional aspects of eighteenth-century pastoral, much of the work seems directly to contradict the various prescriptions for 'True Poetry' painted in the lively footnotes and asides. It is, with one eye shut, quite possible to read a deeply conservative message in the work: that the life of the peasant is a happy and healthy one, and that poverty and rurality guarantee a moral and spiritual superiority over wealth and city living. Open both eyes, and the focus goes awry, for this message

[4] *Gentleman's Magazine*, LIX, part 2 (1789), 976–7.

[5] *TLlM*, pp. 230–2.

[6] Davies, *Presences that Disturb*, p. 153.

is now interspersed with wolfish 'kingflogging notes' and passionate tirades against injustice. Or, as the reviewer in the *Gentleman's Magazine* put it bluntly (leaving little doubt of a preference for 'quiet and humble scenes' over the 'discontent of Faction or the wild enthusiasm of Reform'): 'There cannot possibly be a more heterogeneous and unnatural mixture than poetry and politicks.'[7]

It is possible to explain the contradictions in the work as the result of its twenty-year genesis: many of the tamer pastoral pieces are, in theory at least, the product of the 1770s, when Iolo was in his twenties. These are often, though not exclusively, gathered in the first volume; the political and bardic preoccupations of the 1790s come to the fore in the second. It is even possible to reconcile these opposites under the accommodatingly broad label of pastoral, by tracing a development from the conventional character of the contented shepherd to that more idiosyncratic lover of nature, the ancient British bard. But Iolo's deliberate decision to revise his earlier poems and present them as a generically and chronologically mixed bag ('all jumbled together')[8] works against this approach: the different types of poem were clearly meant to be read together. To treat the more docile aspects of the book, less palatable to modern readers, as a disguise, a kind of pastoral fancy dress intended to help a wolfish Welsh bard smuggle his esoteric brand of radicalism into the drawing rooms of Bath, Bristol and London, is to ignore the strength of Iolo's commitment to his more conventional English models. The notion of deliberate authorial manoeuvring, however, does have an especial force here, and it is worth looking more closely at how Iolo's poetry negotiates the main role he gives himself in the preface, that of the self-taught rural labourer.

Iolo was perfectly aware of what we might call a self-taught tradition, a kind of counter-version of English literary history which grouped the more famous labouring-class poets (with Shakespeare) in the category of 'natural genius'.[9] The idea of the untutored poet, who spoke or wrote directly from the promptings of nature, developed throughout the eighteenth century: Shakespeare, with his 'small Latin, and less Greek',[10] or 'warbl[ing] his native

7 *Gentleman's Magazine*, LXIV, part 2 (1794), 1113–14.

8 NLW 21387E, no. 39.

9 See Jonathan Bate, 'Shakespeare and Original Genius' in Penelope Murray (ed.), *Genius: The History of an Idea* (Oxford, 1989), pp. 76–97. Critical literature on the self-taught tradition in British poetry is a rapidly expanding field; key studies include Christmas, *The Lab'ring Muses*; Donna Landry, *The Muses of Resistance: Laboring-Class Women's Poetry in Britain 1739–1796* (Cambridge, 1990); John Goodridge, *Rural Life in Eighteenth-Century English Poetry* (Cambridge, 1995); idem (ed.), *The Independent Spirit: John Clare and the Self-Taught Tradition* (Helpston, 1994); Anne Janowitz, *Lyric and Labour in the Romantic Tradition* (Cambridge, 1998). Iolo has recently been included in Tim Burke (ed.), *Eighteenth-Century English Labouring-Class Poets: Volume III, 1780–1800* (London, 2003).

10 Ben Jonson, 'To the Memory of My Beloved, the Author Mr William Shakespeare: And What He Hath Left Us' in Geoff Parfitt (ed.), *The Complete Poems of Ben Jonson* (Harmondsworth, 1975), pp. 263–5, line 31.

wood-notes wild'[11] was often taken as the prime example. Thus Hannah More promised, in the letter to Elizabeth Montagu which prefaced Ann Yearsley's first collection, to 'send you some of her wild wood-notes'.[12] Christopher Anstey makes exactly the same connection by 'interpolating' the phrase 'woodnotes wild' into the seventh verse of Iolo's 'Stanzas Written in London'. The natural/ learned dichotomy which characterized much of the discussion of the period appears frequently in Iolo's own writings: in 'The Learned Ignorants' he attacks the 'book-poring pedants, by learning made fools/ Whose skulls are well-stuff'd with the rubbish of schools',[13] while his most famous bardic triad (cited above, p. 61) locates poetic genius in the eye and heart that can truly perceive nature, and a resolution that dares to follow her precepts. Iolo was familiar both with earlier writers in this tradition, such as the thresher Stephen Duck and the cobbler James Woodhouse (copies of whose work he owned in 1794),[14] and with contemporaries like the 'Bristol Milkwoman', Ann Yearsley, whom he may well have met. He read Burns avidly (and later, apparently somewhat less avidly, Robert Bloomfield).[15] His admiration for them can be found scattered throughout his manuscripts and in the letters:

> In the very best of our learned Poets we find a prodigious number of their best thoughts pilfer'd from Virgil, Horace, and many others. Let these Geniuses no longer strut about like the Jack daw in borrowed plumes. Let them restore to every bird his feather. and then we shall see them kick the beam when weigh'd against the Bristol Milkwoman or even poor Stephen duck. Shakespear and the Scotch Plowman will come terrible Giants to this field of battle.[16]

From the letters it is clear that Iolo was highly conscious of these writers, if not exactly as rivals (although professional jealousy may lie behind his brief and ungracious notes on Bloomfield), then as relevant points of comparison. He explained to Mary Barker in 1796 that his determination to resist all outside

[11] John Milton, 'L'Allegro' in John Carey (ed.), *John Milton: Complete Shorter Poems* (Harlow, 1968), p. 138, line 134.

[12] Ann Yearsley, *Poems, on Several Occasions*, p. x. Henry Mackenzie also used the phrase 'wood-notes wild' of Robert Burns (Pittock, 'Robert Burns and British Poetry', p. 197).

[13] Williams: *PLP*, I, p. 85. The poem is discussed in Davies, *Presences that Disturb*, pp. 177–83.

[14] A 'Catalogue of Books at London, May 20th 1794', NLW 13136A, pp. 137–57, notes 'Woodhouses Poems', p. 142 and 'Stephen Duck', p. 149.

[15] Iolo took detailed notes from James Currie's *Life of Robert Burns* (1800): NLW 13146A, pp. 3–7; extracts from Bloomfield's *The Farmer's Boy* (5th edn., 1801) appear to have been written out as examples of false or 'monotonous' rhyme or grammatical infelicity (NLW 13136A, pp. 237–40). It cannot have helped matters that Bloomfield's literary success, only five years after Iolo's *Poems, Lyric and Pastoral*, owed much to what John Lucas calls a 'backward-glancing' portrayal of 'rural virtues' that is not unlike Iolo's own: John Lucas, 'Bloomfield and Clare' in Goodridge (ed.), *The Independent Spirit*, p. 59.

[16] NLW 21419E, no. 24. The piece goes on to suggest that women poets, too, might have suffered a similar occlusion.

interference with his poetry stemmed 'from what was then very frequently said of Mrs Yearsley's Poems that had been published about four or five years before; . . . I had also, tho' upon no sufficient [a]uthority, heard anecdotes something similar of Robert Burns the Scots [P]loughman.'[17] A defensive letter written after the publication of *Poems* points up his own very different experience of publishing and marketing his work: 'I never had the good fortune of Mrs Yearsly whose business of procuring subscribers and collecting the money was done all by others, and by those whose influence precluded disappointment, Creech the Bookseller of Edinburgh and others in Scotland did the same for Burns.'[18] Like his declarations in the preface, his overtures to subscribers deliberately played the 'self-taught' card, as the response he elicited from Anna Seward makes clear: 'I do see genius pervading the mists of obscure birth, & incultivate education in the sweet & polished numbers of your Welch translation'.[19]

And yet, despite his admiration for and implicit claim of kinship with other self-taught writers, Iolo cannot be said to have modelled his own work on any of their varied approaches. One of the most striking aspects of the poetry of certain earlier 'peasant poets' of the 1730s, such as Stephen Duck and the housemaid Mary Collier, is their use of realism to explore the experience of rural labour. Their vivid descriptions of the hard work that lies behind such set-piece pastoral vignettes as haymaking or harvest produce, especially in Duck, a kind of anti-pastoral. The stifling threshing barn directly challenges the kind of idealized pastoral space that was already a cliché by the first half of the eighteenth century: 'No fountains murmur here; No Lambkins play/ No Linets warble and no Fields look gay.'[20] Sixty years later, Iolo's depictions of rural labour merely act as if none of this had happened:

> How happy the life of an innocent swain,
> That dwells with his herds and his flocks on the plain;
> Who labours abroad on his farm all the day,
> Now turning his fallows, now tedding his hay;
> Here cattle in fields of rich clover we view;
> Here lambkins in meads of a beautiful hue.[21]

[17] NLW 21285E, Letter no. 862, Iolo Morganwg to Mary Barker, 26 March 1796.

[18] NLW 21286E, Letter no. 1025, Iolo Morganwg to a female subscriber (very possibly Hannah More). This is a draft letter.

[19] NLW 21282E, Letter no. 459, Anna Seward to Iolo Morganwg, 12 July 1792. She also expressed her concern 'that nature made you the fatal present of a spirit & an imagination so raised above the sphere in which you were destined to move'.

[20] Stephen Duck, *Poems on Several Occasions* (London, 1736), p. 13.

[21] Williams: *PLP*, I, p. 60.

And this from a man who, in 1774, had written to his brother Thomas, also a mason, newly returned to Wales after giving up a job in London:

> I think it savours somthing of Indiscreation that [is] near a kin to madness for you to entertain such romantic notions of the pleasures of the Country, when you had (one should think) more experience than, the poets and Novel writers that very often turn your Brains the countrey it is true has pleasures and realy Superior to those of the Town, but the hardships that a working man must necessarily bear, there are far more than an equiavalent to them.[22]

In the preface, as we have seen, Iolo explicitly rejects giving any detailed account of his trade, and there is little in *Poems* which describes the world of work with any immediacy – and virtually nothing about stone-cutting. The fourth poem in the collection, 'Castles in the Air', plays metaphorically with the notion of his craft, but the idea of being a mason is more important than the work itself. Labour, indeed, is generally presented as a blessing:

> Toil's healthful hand with ease acquir'd
> Whate'er my bridled wish desir'd;
> All Nature's wants were well supplied,
> Nature, with little satisfied.[23]

Even the 'Song, written in 1785, *for the Use of a little select Society of Journey-men Masons, that met weekly to spend a chearful Hour at the moderate, and restricted, expence of fourpence*' is remarkably unspecific, and it is hard to feel the bite of metal on slate in lines like the following:

> Possessing Content, in the deep shades of Life,
> We leave to the Proud vain ambition and strife:
>
> . . .
>
> Nor envy the Rich – *we* no charms can behold
> In, what fears ev'ry conscience, vile silver and gold.[24]

The introduction to this poem, a thoroughly disarming blend of social criticism and piety, was 'an attempt', as Iolo explains, 'to write a rational drinking-song. Recommendation of duty is likewise one of its leading sentiments'. That prim declaration sounds a main theme of the collection: the necessity for restraint, the triumph of reason over passion, and a simple and unambitious life over fame and fortune.

[22] NLW 21285E, Letter no. 772, Iolo Morganwg to Thomas Williams, 26 August 1774.
[23] Williams: *PLP*, I, p. 25.
[24] Ibid., II, p. 82.

Iolo spent much of his life reading and writing about agricultural improvement; in the 1780s he was an innovative if rather unreliable farmer, and in the late 1790s he was sub-contracted to survey for the Board of Agriculture.[25] But although his manuscripts abound in descriptions of climate and soil, in lists of native and imported plants, in lovingly catalogued varieties of apple and in detailed diagrams for the perfect kitchen-garden, his English 'rural rhymes' are free of allusions to contemporary farming practice. It is to be regretted that he never tried his hand at a georgic poem in the style of John Philips's *Cyder* (1708), or of John Dyer, whose blank verse epic *The Fleece* (1754) offered a genially prescriptive survey of Britain's woollen industry.[26] This is a mode one could imagine Iolo adopting readily: an excuse to berate current practice and hand out advice on the use of lime and the correct breeds of animals, all combined in a hymn to his beloved county – the genre's engagement with ideas of Britishness would have offered particularly interesting scope. The idea gains even more force if one considers that Iolo's *bro* (locality) is quite literally ancient Siluria and, as John Goodridge has shown, the notion of a distinctive Silurian landscape, focused on the fertile lands of the borders, can be traced as a definite presence throughout eighteenth-century pastoral.[27] Yet even the poems 'inscribed to the Glamorgan Agricultural Society' simply state, rather than demonstrate, the idyllic life of the happy farmer:

> From sound, healthy sleep I rise up ev'ry morn,
> To toil in my fields with my cattle and corn,
> And prefer, whilst of rural employments I sing,
> The life of a *Farmer* to that of a *King*.[28]

Iolo was not alone in rejecting what William Christmas calls 'labour realism'. From the middle of the century, and particularly towards its end, many labouring-class poets turned away from the 'visceral workaday detail' of Duck and Collier to consider writing itself, and the implications of being a labouring poet rather than a poetic labourer.[29] Thus Ann Yearsley does not make much of her milk delivery, but her meditative and introspective pieces do explore her 'situation in life' in a distinctly personal mode. We find Iolo prescribing just this kind of approach in a draft which adds Virgil and Homer (again,

[25] See David Ceri Jones, 'Iolo Morganwg and the Welsh Rural Landscape' in *Rattleskull Genius*, pp. 227–50.

[26] For Philips, see John Goodridge and J. C. Pellicer (eds.), *Cyder: A Poem in Two Books* (Cheltenham, 2001), and Crawford, *Poetry, Enclosure and the Vernacular Landscape*, pp. 114–37; for Dyer, see Goodridge, *Rural Life in Eighteenth-Century English Poetry*.

[27] Goodridge, *Rural Life in Eighteenth-Century English Poetry*, pp. 181–2.

[28] Williams: *PLP*, I, p. 169.

[29] Christmas, *The Lab'ring Muses*, p. 161.

'natural poets') to the list of those who have lived and suffered without the insulating buffers of wealth:

> Incidents that harrow up the soul make good Poets, whence it is that our noble versifyers as Granville etc having from the very nature of affluence never experienced what Homer, Shakespear, Virgil and even Burns & Yearsley [experienced] are so very uninteresting in general.[30]

Once again, much of Iolo's own verse seems to shy away from this in actual practice, maintaining a kind of stylized decorum and deploying conventional character types and imagery that make even supposedly autobiographical poems like 'Castles in the Air' or 'Stanzas Written in London' appear didactic and generalized. He is much sharper and more immediate in prose.

There are further paradoxes. In *Poems*, and in numerous draft essays over a long period, Iolo makes a stirring case for a 'native British tradition', a vision of a literary inheritance which claims the primacy of Welsh over English in terms of belonging to the native landscape:

> It has always struck me forcibly that the knowledge of Nature and of its appearances in the Island and climature of Britain is strongly and prominently impressed on the Welsh Language . . . but nothing of this appears in the character of the English language, a language that was never properly educated in the School of Nature, a language that is, comparatively speaking, but of yesterday, nurtured up and formed in schools of art, and those none of the best or of the most illuminated ages.[31]

Where English is artificial, derivative and recent, a slave to the classics, Welsh boasts the 'Poetry of Nature in the Climate of Britain': a poetry that is both original and true to a lived 'British' experience. It is hard at this point to ignore the presence of James Macpherson, whose Ossianic writings really did introduce a breath of fresh, if rather damp, air into English poetry, and whose landscapes and language pushed at and broke the conventional poetic boundaries. As Hugh Blair noted in his *Critical Dissertation*, '[Ossian's] imagery is, without exception, copied from that face of nature, which he saw before his eyes; and by consequence may be expected to be lively. We meet with no Grecian or Italian scenery; but with the mists, and clouds, and storms of a northern mountainous region.'[32] Although *Ossian* may owe much of its stylistic character to a mid-century perception of primitive poetry derived from the Bible and

[30] NLW 21387E, no. 11. The phrase 'harrow up the soul' is used by the Ghost in *Hamlet* (Act 1, Scene V: 'I could a tale unfold whose lightest word/ Would harrow up thy soul'), and is cited in the discussion of Ossianic ghosts in Hugh Blair's *Critical Dissertation* (1763; 2nd edn., 1765): *PO*, p. 366.

[31] NLW 13103B, p. 47.

[32] *PO*, p. 384.

the work of Robert Lowth, it is also, as Derick Thomson has shown, inflected by the rhythms and cadences of Gaelic.[33] It cannot be said that Iolo's English poetry carries with it quite the same stamp of its linguistic and geographical origins, and one is inclined to agree with Gwyneth Lewis that the attempt to introduce 'a Welsh element into English poetry . . . is, artistically, not entirely successful'.[34] Lewis does argue, however, that the attempt should be taken seriously, and sees a genuine originality in Iolo's experiments with metre. In several poems in the collection this experimentation is made explicit: 'The Joys of Rural Life', claimed as one of his earliest compositions in English, introduces one aspect of the complex internal rhyme found in the Welsh poetry with a defiant comment to the effect that its cadences might well 'displease an English ear', but were pleasing to a Welsh one. Aesthetic appreciation, in other words, is not innate but culturally conditioned, something to be learned ('the fundamental charm, perhaps, in the poetry of all languages, is no more than a certain *something* which, by general custom and frequent usage, has been familiarized *to*, and is, consequently, expected or sought after *by*, the ear').[35] The introduction of a distinctively Welsh aesthetic into English seems to have been an early selling point for the volume: the poem accompanying the famous description of Iolo in the *Gentleman's Magazine* loosely versified a sequence of stanzas from the sixth-century 'Gododdin', while his printed 'specimen', left for subscribers in Bath and Bristol, was a sedate enough version of Dafydd ap Gwilym's 'The Fair Pilgrim'.[36] Several other pieces in the collection claim to be translations, or to be written in the Welsh manner. But the most obviously translated elements are the bardic triads at the end of the second volume, substituted belatedly at the request of certain friends 'in the room of the poems that were originally intended'.[37] These, rendered in a rather portentous prose, show the extent to which the antiquarian element in Iolo's work came to the fore late in 1793 when, encouraged by the publisher Joseph Johnson and others, he realized that Welsh bardism was potentially more marketable in the literary world than poetry. As Jon Mee has noted, his 'History of the Ancient British Bards and Druids' was advertised at the back of *Poems, Lyric and Pastoral*, with Johnson heading the subscription list.[38] In poetic terms, however, Iolo's boldest attempts to capture the feel of early Welsh verse (and a distinctive Welsh landscape) in English were never published. A piece like 'Hill of Snows', for

[33] D. S. Thomson, *The Gaelic Sources of Macpherson's 'Ossian'* (Edinburgh, 1952).

[34] Lewis, 'Eighteenth-Century Literary Forgeries', p. 173.

[35] Williams: *PLP*, II, p. 155; Gwyneth Lewis hears in this piece a 'haunting off-key harmony' (p. 174).

[36] Both were subsequently published in Williams: *PLP* ('Ode, imitated from the Gododdin', II, pp. 11–19; 'The Fair Pilgrim', I, pp. 74–84).

[37] *PLP*, I, p. xx.

[38] Jon Mee, '"Images of Truth New Born": Iolo, William Blake and the Literary Radicalism of the 1790s' in *Rattleskull Genius*, p. 176.

example, offers versions of early Welsh *englynion* which push English versification in more interesting directions than any of the translations, real or supposed, in *Poems* itself:

> Hill of snows – The swallow flies
> Near the ground and dreads the skies
> Seek out the sheltring nook for soon the storms arise.
>
> Hill of snows – The raven wakes
> Winds deeply murmur through the brakes
> Still snores the son of sloth nor care nor caution takes.
>
> Hill of snows – The billow swells
> Wisdom haunts the humble dells
> Calm happiness abides where peaceful nature dwells.
>
> Hill of snows – The mountain steep
> Pleasure dies her votries weep
> Th'unending paths of truth with dauntless ardor keep.[39]

The Welsh 'Eiry Mynydd' stanzas had been previously published by Lewis Morris in *Tlysau yr Hen Oesoedd* (1735) where, following Edward Lhuyd, they were introduced as druidic remnants. Iolo's cavalier but stylistically rather adept versions in English preserve a distinctive feature of the genre, the juxtaposition, or holding in balance, of observations from nature with sententious or moral maxims, while also taking the opportunity to introduce some of his own bardic precepts. In general, however, the Welshness of his sources is tamed by the process of translation.

If it is too much to expect Iolo to have produced a Welsh *Ossian,* one might consider that other Scottish model, Robert Burns. As we have seen, Burns clearly inspired Iolo to try his luck as a published poet in the late 1780s, and his example lay behind a later interest in collecting traditional song.[40] The manuscripts contain several extracts and notes taken from Currie's influential *Life of Burns* (1800), the longest of which describes the rootedness of the Scottish tradition in lived experience and real places. Its relevance to Iolo's own concerns as a bard of nature is obvious :

> The Lover associates his emotions with the charms of external nature, giving by this means a variety and liveliness not to be found in the poetry of Greece and Rome, or perhaps of any other nation – Scots lovesongs describe scenes of Rural courtship –

[39] NLW 21392F, no. 33 (extract).

[40] Daniel Huws, *Caneuon Llafar Gwlad ac Iolo a'i Fath* (Aberystwyth, 1993), and idem, 'Iolo Morganwg and Traditional Music' in *Rattleskull Genius*, pp. 333–56.

> are invocations of Lovers and their mistresses – the spot particularized, Ettrick Banks – Tweedside – Bush aboon Traquair &c the time also – as morning glooming &c – particularization more affecting than abstraction – generalization is the vice of poets whose learning overpowers their Genius.[41]

A good deal of this can already be found in *Poems, Lyric and Pastoral*, but what is most obviously lacking is the language. Another of Iolo's notes, on the word 'Holm – Scottish – The level low grounds on the banks of a river or stream', remarks that the 'Scots dialect is singularly copious and exact in the denomination of natural objects'.[42] Iolo had no access to a regional literary language to match Scots, one distinct from English but recognizable to an English readership, and one from which dialect words and idioms might be borrowed. For an English audience, Welsh had the opacity of Gaelic, and there was nothing – apart from anti-Taffy Fluellen-style comedy – in between.[43] Burns played with the full range of available registers, from the broadest Scots to the literary standard, and comparing even the relatively light Scots modulations of a poem like 'Now westlin winds and slaught'ring guns' with Iolo's not dissimilar 'Winter Incidents', one realizes how restricted the Welsh writer was by the narrow poetic register in which he worked: that the restriction was to some degree self-imposed is demonstrated by the development of the latter poem through several versions, in which various distinctive words and phrases (notably the 'clanking' of the wild geese) are gradually and relentlessly smoothed out.[44]

Iolo does occasionally hint at the possibility of some kind of cultural cross-over, a reawakened sense of natural landscape in English literature that had never been lost in Welsh. But here again his declarations rarely seem to match his actual practice:

> We never had pure british sceneries and sentiments in English Verse till Thomson lead the way and forced English poetry into the schools of Nature, wherein at length the English Muses has become matriculated, and has made a wonderful progress under the tuition of Cowper and many other of the present day, but of no preceding day, unless we may allow that of Shakspear, who certainly flung widely open the gates of Nature's School, but they were soon closed up and doubly barred, by Jonson, Donne, Cowley &c even the Great Milton himself was never able fully to

41 NLW 13146A, p. 3. Cf. James Currie (ed.), *The Works of Robert Burns: With an Account of his Life, Criticism on his Writings, &c.* (new edn., 4 vols., London, 1819), I, pp. 310–13.

42 NLW 13146A, p. 5.

43 Representations of Welshness and the Welsh language in the English press tended to be cumbersomely satirical. See Peter Lord, *Words with Pictures: Welsh Images and Images of Wales in the Popular Press, 1640–1860* (Aberystwyth, 1995); Pittock, *Celtic Identity*, p. 29 (and on the language as a marker of identity, pp. 116–19).

44 James Kinsley (ed.), *Burns's Poems and Songs* (Oxford, 1971), pp. 2–3; Burns's range of registers is explored in Pittock, 'Robert Burns and British Poetry'; for Iolo's 'Winter Incidents', see Constantine, '"This Wildernessed Business"' in *Rattleskull Genius*, pp. 139–43.

> enter into this school, that was closely guarded and all entrance into it forbidden by the scholastic Demon of Absurdity, whose reign we may now reasonably hope is now terminated.[45]

Thomson and Cowper are for Iolo the shining examples of the new turn for the better in English, but, certainly as far as 'nature poetry' is concerned, his own efforts in English also seem curiously devoid of their influence. He nowhere attempts to imitate their characteristic blank verse (often perceived, after Milton, as an expression of radical liberty from the 'bondage of rhyming'),[46] or to follow up a more meditative blend of introspection and natural description. It is hard to escape the feeling that the basic model for his 'sceneries' is William Shenstone, right down to the 'jessamine cot'; in both form and diction it is docile and relatively conservative. But perhaps this is not surprising. Iolo's Glamorgan landscape is after all, very unlike the Scottish Highlands, or even the image of Wales most obviously available to the British reading public in the latter half of the century: Iolo has little time for the essentially north Walian sublime introduced by Thomas Gray's poem *The Bard* (1757) and evoked in innumberable subsequent paintings and etchings.[47] Ancient British bard though he was, his backdrop was never one of craggy mountains and extremes of weather, but rather of safe havens, white cottages, orchards and gardens.

Two things should be stressed at this point. The first is that, by and large, adherence to conventional models of verse and expressions of conventional sentiment are rather the rule than otherwise among self-taught writers of this period. Any expectation that a labouring-class writer should directly challenge social and literary norms is doubtless informed by our perception of exceptional (and more readily accessible) voices, like those of Clare and Duck, rather than by the evidence of the mass of writers as a whole. Most of these writers aimed to emulate their literary models, not to subvert them: the radicalism, if any, of their work lies in their mastery of an idiom denied them by birth and circumstance, and in their ability to participate in a literary culture at all.[48] The second point to stress is that, in spite of its commitment to convention, *Poems, Lyric and Pastoral* is in fact a deeply idiosyncratic, and far from decorous, book. This becomes increasingly clear in the course of the second volume, as Iolo – at a very late stage in the work's development – begins to explore new aspects of pastoral, fulfilling an earlier declaration that its range should be stretched:

[45] NLW 13103B, p. 48.

[46] From the note on 'The Verse' added to *Paradise Lost*: Alastair Fowler (ed.), *John Milton: Paradise Lost* (Harlow, 1971), p. 39. Cf. J. C. Pellicer in Goodridge and Pellicer (eds.), *Cyder*, p. i.

[47] See Sam Smiles, *The Image of Antiquity: Ancient Britain and the Romantic Imagination* (London, 1994), pp. 47–53; Prys Morgan, *The Eighteenth-Century Renaissance* (Llandybïe, 1981), pp. 120–1.

[48] The point is made by Bridget Keegan, 'Rural Poetry and the Self-Taught Tradition' in Christine Gerrard (ed.), *A Companion to Eighteenth-Century Poetry* (Oxford, 2006), pp. 563–76; I am very grateful for the opportunity to see an advanced draft of this article.

The Author thinks Pastoral a species of Poetry that admits of as great a variety of subjects as any other whatever; and that it is not necessary, in the manner of modern Poets, to confine it solely to Love, and make his *whining swains* ring perpetual changes on the names of

Hard-hearted Phillis,
And cold Amarillis, &c. &c.

A Poet in the character of a Shepherd, an occupation the most proper of all others to represent primeval simplicity and virtue, describes objects as they naturally present themselves to the senses, and affect the mind; or utters sentiments that spring from the simple notions and inborn feelings of those that are unacquainted with the abstractions of philosophy, and the complex ideas derived from art. The shepherd, who is the representative and pupil of Nature, has, for his rural song, at least as great a diversity of themes as the more philosophic rhimer can boast of; who, if he pleases, may take to himself all the fine things of art, provided he leave the sylvan Bard in full possession of Nature.[49]

The most striking example, a poem titled 'The Horrors of War: A Pastoral', is a dialogue between a shepherd and a soldier in which the former calmly punctures all brash talk of glory and fame with his reminders of the bitter actualities of loss and destruction; a lengthy footnote condemns the barbarity of rulers who perpetrate wars regardless of the opinions of their own more civilized citizens.[50] In Iolo's version of radical-pastoral, trite rural swains and shepherds become pacifists ('The GAUL and the SPANIARD I deem/ Friends, innocent neighbours, and brothers to me'),[51] swords are emphatically turned into pruning hooks and Truth reigns triumphant :

Dark ERROR's code no more enthrals,
Its vile infatuations end;
Aloud the trump of Reason calls;
The nations hear! the worlds attend!
Detesting now the craft of Kings,
Man from his hand the weapon flings;
Hides it in whelming deeps afar,
And learns no more the skill of war;
But lives with NATURE on th'uncity'd plain:
Long has this *earth* a captive mourn'd,

[49] Williams: *PLP*, I, pp. 173–4.

[50] 'War and conquest are, generally speaking, the *aim* and *ambition* of monarchs in all ages; to them the slaughtering of 40 or 50,000 subjects, whose families are thereby reduced to misery and ruin, is a thing of no moment.' Williams: *PLP*, II, p. 143. Potential models for this poem are Thomas Warton's *Five Pastoral Eclogues, The Scenes of which are supposed to lie among Shepherds, oppress'd by the War in Germany* (London, 1745), and Chatterton's 'Eclogue The First', Taylor (ed.), *Complete Works*, I, pp. 305–8.

[51] Williams: *PLP*, II, p. 141.

But *days of old* are now return'd;
We PRIDE's rude arm no longer feel;
No longer bleed beneath Oppression's heel;
For TRUTH to LOVE and PEACE restores the world again.[52]

This, in 1794, with the kind of genteel sponsors he had, was both brave and foolhardy, as Iolo well knew. In another radical twist to a typically pastoral trope, Iolo's own brand of the Golden Age, a pre-Saxon, bardically administered Ancient Britain, is used to offer the possibility of something better, a model of 'primeval simplicity and virtue' from the past that must be reinstated in the present:

I'll sing the golden days of yore,
And bid my friendly cot restore
The virtues of primeval times:
The friend of *Age*, the Guide of *Youth*
I'll teach the laws of PEACE and TRUTH
In all my rural rhymes.[53]

The connections and parallels between Iolo's bardism and the bardic utopianism of William Blake (who was, it now seems likely, aware of Iolo's ideas during the period 1793–5) have recently been explored by Jon Mee.[54] For both men, political renewal in the present was a matter of recalling and releasing a spirit of liberty from the ancient British past. Moreover, as Mee has noted, both poets figure themselves as 'manifestations of "native genius", that is, bards who retained the authenticity associated with "uneducated poets"'.[55] That potentially contradictory combination of ancient wisdom and 'uneducated' native genius will be further examined below, but for now it is sufficient to note that the bardic and radical aspects of Iolo's poetry, coming as they do to the fore so strikingly in the last stages of the book's composition, are a major factor in unsettling the collection as a whole, and bear out Gavin Edwards's

[52] 'Ode, on Converting a Sword into a Pruning Hook': ibid., pp. 166–7.

[53] From 'Ode, to a Shepherd': ibid., p. 192. For the reclamation of pastoral by 1790s radicalism (in, for example, the work of Tom Paine), see Fairer, *English Poetry of the Eighteenth Century*, p. 99.

[54] The one certain link between Blake and Iolo is the fact that around 1806 William Owen Pughe commissioned Blake's now lost painting 'The Ancient Britons', based on a Welsh triad (see below, p. 128); Arthur Johnston, 'William Blake and "The Ancient Britons"', *NLWJ*, XXII, no. 3 (1982), 304–20; G. E. Bentley Jr., '"The Triumph of Owen"', ibid., XXXIV, no. 2 (1985), 248–61. Jon Mee has since persuasively argued that Blake may have seen Iolo's bardic triads circulating in manuscript late in 1793, '"Images of Truth"', pp. 174–5.

[55] Ibid., p. 177.

thesis that certain texts of the 1790s reflect the period's own uncertainties over possible directions and endings.[56]

Duplicity and double-voicing: 'the necessity of a lie'

The many contradictory forces at work in *Poems, Lyric and Pastoral* make it an instructive example of what Bridget Keegan has described as the 'double-voiced' nature of the self-taught tradition, one which strains to reconcile the conflicting demands of maintaining a demotic 'authenticity' – usually figured as a truthfulness to nature – with the acceptable language of high literature.[57] The virtual impossibility of achieving this in practice meant that the lives and works of writers like Ann Yearsley and John Clare were riven with anxieties about identity and ownership of their poetic voices – and in many ways remain so – as the many controversies, from the split between Hannah More and Ann Yearsley to the never-ending debate about editorial control of Clare's manuscripts bear out.[58]

Current criticism has tended to approach the question of poetic authenticity by asking how far labouring-class writers can be said to speak for their class, or for themselves, through the conventions of a literary language (and attendant ideologies) not their own. The issue, as we have seen, is complicated by the fact of patronage, through which an educated sponsor markets the verse of his (or often her) protegé(e) either by literally correcting and vetting their work, or by effectively doing so, in that the grateful poet sings what the patron wants to hear: again, the shoemaker-poet James Woodhouse is a particularly striking example of double-voicedness, his early poems to patrons contrasting painfully with the anger and resentment unleashed in his later epic (and autobiographical) poem *Crispinus Scriblerus*.[59] And there is a further catch: the supposedly untutored, unaffected, natural poet was expected to express himself or herself in an acceptably cultivated language, but if such poets were too persuasively literary they could often, as Iolo was acutely aware, be accused of plagiarism. As Clare would put it of the Village Minstrel:

[56] Gavin Edwards, *Narrative Order 1789–1819* (Basingstoke, 2005).

[57] Bridget Keegan, 'Nostalgic Chatterton: Fictions of Poetic Identity and the Forging of the Self-Taught Tradition', in Groom (ed.), *Thomas Chatterton and Romantic Culture*, pp. 210–27; see also Goodridge, 'Identity, Authenticity, Class'.

[58] The Yearsley controversy is discussed in Christmas, *The Labr'ing Muses*, pp. 235–66; Anne Stott, *Hannah More: The First Victorian* (Oxford, 2003), pp. 70–8; for the recent debate over Clare's copyright, see items in John Goodridge's 'Clare Criticism, 1970–2000' in Kövesi and Goodridge (eds.), *John Clare: New Approaches*, pp. 246–50.

[59] See Christmas, *The Labr'ing Muses*, pp. 183–210. *Crispinus Scriblerus*, much of which was written in the 1790s, was not published until 1896.

> malice mocks him wi a rude disdain
> proving pretensions to the muse as vain
> They deem her talents far beyond his skill
> and hiss his efforts as some forged strain.[60]

With authorial identity such a crucial aspect of their work, it is not hard to see why Thomas Chatterton might hold a particular fascination for such poets, and become a model peculiarly adapted to writers struggling against the inequalities of birth and fortune. The Romantics' Chatterton was after all both a poor charity-school boy and a natural genius, reliant on patronage, who, desperate for support and rebuffed by the suave society novelist Horace Walpole, was driven to destroy himself. And his poetic voice – which, in his lifetime, was already protean, supple and at the service of whoever would pay him best – was an endlessly contested area. Much of the debate that followed his death revolved around whether or not someone of his age and social class could produce the work he did. For many, it was easier to believe that the 'fifteenth-century' poems of the monk Thomas Rowley were what they claimed to be (or, as we have seen, that they were the work of some third person) than to believe that a poorly educated teenager could have composed them. With Chatterton, the connection between double-voicing and duplicity returns us to the question of literary forgery.

Like the labouring-class poet, the literary forger works in two voices, and in each case, the product, the poem, is invested with meaning twice over. First, it can be read for its content in its ostensible context: as a contemporary poem about nature or friendship, or a medieval hymn to charity. Secondly, when once the reader has knowledge of who the 'real' author is, it can also be read as an extraordinary feat, a tour de force, enhanced by the sense that certain boundaries, either social or chronological, have been transgressed. In both instances, too, the work itself is invariably swamped with authenticating devices, albeit deployed for diametrically opposed reasons: collections of labouring-class poetry usually begin with detailed life narratives proving that the author is who they claim to be;[61] literary forgeries bristle with antiquarian footnotes and manuscript references proving that the author is someone else. One of the most tantalizing aspects of *Poems, Lyric and Pastoral* is that it combines and confuses both categories at once.

Iolo was exceptionally sensitive to correction or criticism, in Welsh as well as English. For all the confident virulence of his criticism of others, he often

[60] Clare, *The Village Minstrel*, II, lines 1294–7; cited in Bridget Keegan, 'Boys, Marvellous Boys: John Clare's "Natural Genius"' in Kövesi and Goodridge (eds.), *John Clare: New Approaches*, pp. 65–76.

[61] Nicholas Roe, 'Authenticating Robert Burns', *Essays in Criticism*, 46 (1996), 195–218. Reprinted in Carol McGuirk (ed.), *Critical Essays on Robert Burns* (New York, 1998), pp. 208–24.

appears nervous about submitting his own work for judgement – witness the many drafts of an early letter to his mentor John Walters Sr., all of which open with a tortuous expression of deference;[62] or his lifelong habit of revising his work up to the very last minute, or of never finishing it at all. Geraint Phillips, noting his 'curious mixture of egotism and uncertainty', has argued that forgery offered Iolo a way of presenting his creations to others without taking responsibility for them, since infelicities and mistakes could be attributed either to the pseudo-author or blamed on the transmission history of the piece.[63] Once again it is tempting to compare Iolo's case with that of Clare: he initially kept his writing activities entirely secret, hiding his poems in a hole in the wall. When his mother came across them she assumed that he was improving his handwriting, and he watched her use them for lighting fires, unable to bring himself to claim ownership. Later, he adopted the strategy of pretending to his parents that he had indeed copied them from someone else:

> the love of rhyming which I was loath to quit, growing fonder of it every day, drove me to the necessity of a lie to try the value of their critisisms and by this way I got their remarks unadulterated with prejudice – in this case their expressions would be 'Aye, boy, if you coud write so, you would do'.[64]

The deception bought Clare the freedom to experiment until he felt sure enough of his poems to try them on the outside world.

But Phillips also locates the development of Iolo's forgeries in the specific circumstances of his relationship with Owain Myfyr. Myfyr did not 'own' Iolo in the way that Hannah More (at least briefly) owned Ann Yearsley, or Elizabeth Montagu James Woodhouse, but he was for many years an encouraging patron of Iolo's writings in Welsh, an occasional source of income and, through William Owen Pughe, Iolo's principal channel to publication in Welsh. For Phillips, the forgeries – particularly the Dafydd ap Gwilym poems and the huge selection of wisdom literature included in *The Myvyrian Archaiology* – were planted by Iolo as deliberate revenge for perceived slights against himself or (given the north Wales bias of the Gwyneddigion society) his beloved Glamorgan. They gave him a sense of superiority to the wealth and the combined learning of the London Welsh; they were a way of not being owned. One could take this further, and argue that literary forgery subverts the power relationship between poet and patron, as the patron becomes the one manipulated: here, the best parallel may be Chatterton's relationship with his small group of besotted Bristol antiquarians, to whom he effectively sold what they wanted to hear. The balance of supply and demand is subtly reversed. Until the deception is revealed,

[62] See below, pp. 87–8.
[63] Phillips, 'Forgery and Patronage', p. 408.
[64] Eric Robinson and David Powell (eds.), *John Clare by Himself* (Ashington, 1996).

however, the 'triumph' of the literary forger, beyond any immediate pecuniary advantage, remains private. Unlike certain forgers of art works, who paint signatures or messages on the blank canvass destined to become a Renoir or a Matisse – or, more pertinently, unlike William Henry Ireland, the young forger of the 'Shakspear' documents – Iolo, in his vast archive of manuscripts, gives us no confession, no moment of truth. The secret laughter imagined by Gwyneth Lewis in her poem 'Iolo Morganwg' is, with one curious exception, conspicuously absent.[65]

'Poor Williams' and 'old Iolo'

Iolo's idiosyncratic combination of humble stonemason and ancient British bard made its mark on literary London, as the reviews of *Poems, Lyric and Pastoral* bear out: 'a genuine Welsh bard, an original genius', wrote the *Critical Review*, 'who derives his poetical descent from Taliessin, and his inspiration from nature, for his situation in life is no higher than that of a working stonemason.'[66] Noting the bardic ceremonies held on Primrose Hill and praising the odes recited there for their 'sublimity of conception and loftiness of sentiment', the review quotes in its entirety the 'Ode, On Converting a Sword into a Pruning Hook' and expresses a lively interest in the doctrine of metempsychosis. The reviewer does, however, admonish Iolo for the 'strokes of petulant sarcasm' that blemish the collection as a whole, and suggests that he has overreached himself in his criticism of his betters: 'Neither', it warns, 'does it well become a writer, on his first appearance before the public, to speak contemptuously of men, or classes of men, who have long been in possession of its admiration or reverence.' The poet's claim to ancient wisdom is not permitted to override his 'situation in life'. Joseph Johnson's *Analytical Review*, also noting that the author is 'of humble birth, and by occupation a mason', gives the bardic side more prominence, repeating many of Iolo's claims about the ancient Welsh more or less verbatim,[67] while the *Monthly Review* begins by recalling a comment of Dr Johnson's to the effect that the work of 'an uneducated writer . . . compared with excellence . . . is nothing, but is very well for the person who wrote it', before assuring its readers that the productions of this Welsh mason 'deserve a more favourable sentence'.[68] No reviewer seems too troubled by the concept of a rural labourer who is also profoundly knowledgeable, not to say learned, in antiquarian lore. By the turn of the century, it seems, the stark opposition of untutored 'genius' and 'learning' has

[65] For Lewis's poem, see p. xvii; the curious exception is discussed below, pp. 208–10.
[66] *Critical Review*, XI (June, 1794), 168–75.
[67] *Analytical Review* (February, 1794), 196–200.
[68] *Monthly Review* (April, 1794), 405–14.

broken down sufficiently for the two concepts to come comfortably enough together in the figure of the bard.[69]

Some years later the combination was invoked again, when a writer in the *Critical Review* concluded his review of Robert Bloomfield's *Rural Tales* with the following plea:

> Neglected genius has too long been the reproach of England. To enumerate the dead would be useless; but it is not yet too late to mention the living, whose merits have in vain appealed to the public. We allude to a self-taught man, as humble in his situation as 'the Farmer's Boy', whose genius has been admitted, and whose profound learning in the antiquities of his own Country will be acknowledged and regretted when it is too late – Edward Williams, the Welsh bard.[70]

The author was almost certainly Robert Southey, whom Iolo had met some time before 1797, possibly through their shared interest in the 'Welsh Indian' Madoc story.[71] Southey was in Bristol and working on an early version of his epic poem *Madoc* (copies were circulating in manuscript) in 1795, at exactly the time that Iolo, now a published poet (although still an impoverished one) and with a declared interest in the legend, returned to the south-west. He may even have attended Coleridge's famous 'Lecture on the Slave Trade' at the Assembly Rooms before crossing to Glamorgan.[72] Damian Walford Davies has recently uncovered an oddly disconcerting picture of the 'Welsh Bard' through the eyes of the English Romantic poets. Coleridge, for example, alludes to an incident involving William Godwin, from which Iolo emerges as a highly sensitive and 'very meek' man, with an almost religious devotion to the memory of his mother.[73] Southey's account of him, written just after Iolo's death, is not dissimilar:

[69] For an enlightening exploration of this tension in the work of Thomas Gray, see R. J. Ellis, 'Plodding Plowmen: Issues of Labour and Literacy in Gray's "Elegy"' in Goodridge (ed.), *The Independent Spirit*, pp. 27–43.

[70] *Critical Review*, XXXV (May, 1802), 75. Iolo copied the paragraph out in NLW 21431E, no. 25.

[71] In a letter to his brother, Robert Bloomfield indicates his expectation that Southey will review *Rural Tales* as he had done *The Farmer's Boy* (BL Add. 28268, ff. 92–3, Robert Bloomfield to George Bloomfield, 3 May 1802). I am grateful to Tim Fulford for this reference and to Lynda Pratt for confirming the identification.

[72] Mary-Ann Constantine, 'Iolo Morganwg, Coleridge, and the Bristol Lectures 1795', *Notes and Queries*, 52, no. 1 (2005), 42–4.

[73] For Coleridge, Iolo and Godwin, see Davies, *Presences that Disturb*, pp. 167–76 and 'At Defiance'; the encounter with Godwin seems to have upset Iolo at the time, but for once he did not harbour a grudge, and (with a sly dig at Godwin's atheism), sent rather nostalgic greetings from Wales in 1811: 'I have a great regard for him, and hope that he is well, and as happy as a man of no future prospects can be.' NLW 21285E, Letter no. 888, Iolo Morganwg to George Dyer, 15 February 1811. Iolo's influence can also be seen at work in a brief note from Godwin to William Owen Pughe, written in 1805, asking if he has 'any further materials to afford me for my examination of the ancient Britons? . . . [T]he research I have already done increases my respect for the attainments of the Druids': NLW 13223C, p. 161, William Godwin to William Owen Pughe, 19 April 1805.

> Poor fellow! with a wild heart and a warm head, he had the simplicity of a child and the tenderness of a woman, and more knowledge of the traditions and antiquities of his own country than it is to be feared will ever be possessed by anyone after him.[74]

Though not unlike the benign old man evoked in the memoirs of Elijah Waring, this is not how Iolo Morganwg was seen by his Welsh contemporaries. Indeed, it is as hard to reconcile the feminized and 'child-like' Iolo of the Romantics with the often bitter character who emerges from the letters and writings, as it was for Meyerstein to square eighteenth- and nineteenth-century judgements of Chatterton. 'Poor Williams – a very meek man' is not so far from the lyricism of the 'poor unshelter'd Head' of Coleridge's 1794 version of 'A Monody on the Death of Chatterton' (or, indeed, Iolo's own references to 'poor Burns' and 'poor Stephen Duck').[75] Unlike Chatterton, of course, Iolo actively colluded in the process of his own sentimentalization. But, given that later self-educated poets like Clare were still struggling with the critical infantilization of natural genius (itself a legacy of the Chatterton myth),[76] perhaps the most striking feature of Southey's assessment is its easy combination of the 'simplicity of a child' with reputed 'knowledge of the traditions and antiquities of his country'.

Of all the English poets, Southey, with his explicitly Welsh project, was Iolo's keenest admirer. He worked a great deal of Iolo's bardic esoterica (much of it obtained through William Owen Pughe) into his epic, and provided 'old Iolo' himself with a cameo role as healer to the wounded Aztec leader (*Madoc*, Book 8, lines 3–7). In 1802 he was tempted enough by Iolo's Edenic version of south Wales to consider renting a house in the Vale of Neath, but not long after this, as his politics changed, he fell out of favour with his Welsh acquaintances. In 1805 William Owen Pughe noted disparagingly, 'Mr Southey's Madoc I understand will be published in a few days in a splendid 4to volume which none but the rich can get', and in 1813, unimpressed by his acceptance of the laureateship, Iolo remarked to his son that Southey was 'gone to the Devil' (as Caroline Franklin notes wryly, he was 'not speaking metaphorically').[77] But Southey, aptly enough, provides the final datable link between Iolo and Chatterton, with a comment which appeared in the preface to his and Joseph Cottle's 1803 edition of *The Works of Thomas Chatterton*:

[74] Robert Southey to Henry Taylor, 24 January 1827. C. C. Southey (ed.), *Life and Correspondence of Robert Southey* (6 vols., London, 1849–50), V, p. 285.

[75] On the 'lyrical' version of Chatterton, see Fairer, 'Chatterton's Poetic Afterlife', pp. 236–8, 245–8. 'Poor Burns' appears in NLW 21285E, Letter no. 886, Iolo Morganwg to David Williams, 8 January 1811; for Duck, see above, p. 61.

[76] Keegan, 'Boys, Marvellous Boys', pp. 67–9.

[77] NLW 21282E, Letter no. 363, Iolo Morganwg to William Owen Pughe, 20 February 1805; NLW 21285E, Letter no. 898, Iolo Morganwg to Taliesin Williams, 12 October 1813; and Caroline Franklin, 'The Welsh American Dream', p. 84.

> The Catch, by Chatterton's father, was received from Edward Williams, the Welch Bard; a man who, for his genius and learning and worth, is here mentioned with respect and regard.[78]

This 'mention' is out of all proportion with the importance of the contribution (which, not even part of the poet's own *oeuvre*, demonstrates once again how much the Chatterton myth entailed the talismanic accumulation of biographical scraps). It is far from obvious why, or indeed when, he may have sent it to Southey.[79] But that verdict of 'genius and learning and worth' shows how effectively, in the process of publishing his poems, Iolo had shifted the emphasis from the humble journeyman-mason to the 'Welch Bard', the scholarly purveyor of ancient truths. For all his deployment of the persona of the 'self-taught' poet, Southey did not include him in his collection of *The Lives and Works of the Uneducated Poets* (1831). As his engagement with the *Ossian* debate shows, it was increasingly in the scholarly-antiquarian arena that Iolo's battles over authenticity would be fought. But perhaps because the concept of genius was in itself so elastic, he never had entirely to relinquish the former for the latter (as David Fairer puts it, 'the genuine voice and the genuine text could sometimes gloriously coincide').[80] In a fascinating letter to the philosopher David Williams, written in 1811, Iolo set out his ideas about the nature of poetic genius most fully, arguing at length against the notion of poetic possession or frenzy ('If I well remember, you consider all poets (poor devils) as an incurable description of madmen. I cannot help it, but in return I have often been sorely tempted to consider most philosophers in a similar light.').[81] Poetry, he maintains, is not innate, nor in the gift of some external power, but 'as much a work of studious selection, of cool deliberation' as philosophy itself:

> The poet no less deliberately and coolly than the philosopher sends his mental powers in search of the beauties of nature, compares one thing with another, selects what appears to him most beautiful, affecting, and otherwise interesting, and to his purpose these, if he would be justly poetical, he must arrange and dispose of with judgement, use them on proper occassions, apply them with discretion, in due proportions so as to produce the desired effect. He must also study the powers and properties of the human intellect, acquaint himself with the human passions, their various modifications and operations. Hence he selects his most useful materials, and

[78] Joseph Cottle and Robert Southey (eds.), *The Works of Thomas Chatterton* (3 vols., London, 1803), III, p. 495.

[79] The 'Catch' appeared in the *European Magazine* in March 1792; no contributor is mentioned. There are at least three copies of the piece in the Iolo manuscripts: NLW 13089E, pp. 253–4; the other two copies are uncatalogued. I am grateful to Geraint Phillips for drawing them to my attention, and to Bethan Jenkins for details of the version in the *European Magazine*.

[80] Fairer, *English Poetry*, p. 167.

[81] NLW 21285E, Letter no. 886, Iolo Morganwg to David Williams, 8 January 1811 (draft).

> this, if he would with Homer, Shakespear, Cowper &c, be correct, he must do coolly, considerately and with philosophical deliberation, or his poetical productions will be very worthless things. Even his fictions must be to produce interesting effects analogous to the truths and other characteristics of philosophical history. Such must be the course and operations of poetical studies and exertions. Such was the process in the minds of Homer, Virgil, Horace, Shakespear, Milton, Akenside, Sargeant, Darwin &c.

Quite what is intended by the tantalizing thought that poetic fictions should produce 'interesting effects analogous to the truths . . . of philosophical history' is hard to say. The emphasis on 'coolness' (the word appears in various forms no fewer than seven times), may simply be a bid to persuade David Williams of his suitability to be a recipient of further help from the Literary Fund (the nub to which his letter finally gets round), but in Iolo's strikingly unfrenzied account of the workings of the poetic mind we find once more a notion of essential restraint which is fundamental to his bardic vision. The final (and, strictly speaking, far from genuine) bardic triad of *Poems, Lyric and Pastoral* triumphantly confirms that 'natural genius' and a solid education (if not necessarily a conventional one) were not, in themselves, incompatible:

> Three things thoroughly should all poetry be: thoroughly erudite; thoroughly animated; and thoroughly natural.[82]

[82] Williams: *PLP*, II, p. 256.

Part II: OSSIAN

6

'A multiplicity of copies': The Testimony of the Texts

He is a ghostly enough presence at times, but there is no getting away from Ossian. From the 1770s to the 1820s, across the entire span of Iolo's intellectual career, James Macpherson's creation and the controversy it provoked gave him a framework, a set of assumptions, and a vocabulary to work with – and against. He was not obsessed by *Ossian*, and never felt the need, as Edward 'Celtic' Davies did in the 1820s, to sit down and write a three-hundred page analysis of the poetic and antiquarian merits of the entire Ossianic *oeuvre*.[1] But, as for the generation of Welsh scholars who preceded him, the whole controversy was an irritant, with serious implications for the study of Welsh; no thorough analysis of Welsh poetry could avoid it. One of the many drafts of Iolo's great unpublished (and unfinished) work 'The History of the Bards' is a selection of notes on the development of poetry and the origins of alphabets, organized into a booklet with lined margins and headers. Two pages are titled (in a determined bold cursive) ***Ossian***: both are expressively blank.[2]

Wales seems on the whole to have resisted the melancholy seduction of the Highland bard. Ossian had his admirers (Edward Davies, who was under no illusions as to the historical veracity of the poems, thought them sublime and 'replete with generous sentiment'), but most of the Welsh intelligentsia reacted with hostility to the work and to its author.[3] The palpable *ad hominem* dislike of Macpherson amongst members of the Morris circle in the 1760s (where he is everything from 'a cheat' to 'chwiwgi lleidr defaid' ['a sheep-stealing rogue'])[4] stems partly from an alleged incident in which he claimed that 'he could soon make himself master of the Welsh Tongue, so as to translate any pieces *if there be anything worth translating* out of it' – a claim the indignant Lewis Morris

[1] Edward Davies, *The Claims of Ossian examined and appreciated: An Essay on the Scottish and Irish Poems published under that name* (Swansea, 1825).

[2] NLW 13108B, pp. 150–1.

[3] Davies, *The Claims of Ossian*, p. 327. For the Welsh reaction to *Ossian*, see Mary-Ann Constantine, 'Ossian in Wales and Brittany' in Gaskill (ed.), *The Reception of Ossian in Europe*, pp. 68–83.

[4] John H. Davies (ed.), *The Letters of Lewis, Richard, William and John Morris, of Anglesey (Morrisiaid Môn) 1728–1765* (2 vols., Aberystwyth, 1907–9), II, p. 544.

understandably found 'a little flashy & Romantic'.[5] But it is clear that a wider anti-Scottish sentiment is also in play, and that many of the Welsh intelligentsia shared a widespread English anxiety about the increasing influence of Scots figures in public life (Macpherson dedicated *Fingal*, tacitly, and *Temora* and the 1765 *Works*, openly, to the prime minister, Lord Bute);[6] this was further complicated by feelings of insecurity about Wales's own relationship with the English establishment. There is at times a palpable sense of rivalry, a fear of losing out, combined with a sense that Macpherson has been fighting in an underhand way (for William Morris, Macpherson had 'swynganu'r bobl allan o'i synhwyrhau' ('charmed the people out of their senses')).[7] Others were more confident that Wales would hold her own in any straight fight: 'I make no doubt', wrote Rice Williams to Thomas Percy in 1761, 'but the Welsh poetic genius, if properly ushered on stage, would make a much better appearance than any of the pigmy race of the Caledonian muses.'[8]

Under those circumstances it was unpatriotic merely to admire the poetic qualities of the work: Lewis and William Morris quickly closed ranks against their brother Richard in London for expressing even lukewarm praise: 'Clywed Bute a wnaeth y Myglwyt, mae'n debyg, yn canmol Ossian, ac ynta a ganodd ar ei ol' ('Grey-mane doubtless heard Bute praising Ossian, and started singing the same tune').[9] Unguarded expressions of literary appreciation were usually bitten back immediately. Evan Evans, whose *Some Specimens of the Poetry of the Antient Welsh Bards* (1764) was widely favoured among the Welsh, and by an interested number of English writers, as the Cambrian response to *Ossian*, wrote to Percy in 1762:

> I am now in my lucid intervals reading Fingal, and must own I am very much pleased with Ossian's poems: but that pleasure is much abated, when I find by the best Irish historians, that some of the heroes of his poems died some centuries before he wrote.[10]

[5] Lewis Morris to Samuel Pegge, 11 February 1761, in Hugh Owen (ed.), *Additional Letters of the Morrises of Anglesey (1735–1786)* (2 vols., London, 1947–9), II, p. 513. The circumstances of this boast are still unclear: see Constantine, 'Ossian in Wales and Brittany', p. 69.

[6] On anti-Scottish feeling in England, see Richard B. Sher, 'Percy, Shaw and the Ferguson "Cheat": National Prejudice in the Ossian Wars' in Gaskill (ed.), *Ossian Revisited*, pp. 207–45, and Dafydd Moore, 'The Reception of *The Poems of Ossian* in England and Scotland' in Gaskill (ed.), *The Reception of Ossian*, p. 24.

[7] Owen (ed.), *Additional Letters*, II, p. 594.

[8] Aneirin Lewis (ed.), *The Correspondence of Thomas Percy and Evan Evans* (Louisiana, 1957), p. 149. For Percy's involvement with Welsh matters at this time, see also idem, 'Ieuan Fardd a'r Llenorion Saesneg', *LlC*, VII, nos. 3–4 (1963), 172–92; D. Emrys Williams, 'Rice Williams: The Contact between Thomas Percy and Evan Evans', *NLWJ*, XVII, no. 3 (1972), 287–98.

[9] Davies (ed.), *Morris Letters*, II, p. 598.

[10] Evan Evans to Thomas Percy, in Lewis (ed.), *The Correspondence of Thomas Percy and Evan Evans*, p. 35.

As it turned out, Evans's cautious and scholarly work was no match for Macpherson, and although there are occasional signs of interest in the discovery of a potential Welsh 'epic', Welsh medieval literature remained a relatively specialized and poorly known area, and, except through Gray's Bard, failed to capture the public imagination.[11]

The *Ossian* controversy, periodically reignited, was still very much alive in the Britain of the 1790s and would continue, long after Macpherson's death in 1796, well into the nineteenth century. The next generation of Welsh poets and scholars inherited and continued the debate, albeit in a rather different political climate. In 1800, as he drafted and redrafted his defence of Welsh literary tradition for *The Myvyrian Archaiology*, Iolo was, to a quite remarkable extent, reading and responding to writers and critics involved in the debate of thirty and forty years earlier: Hugh Blair, Thomas Percy, the Morrises, Paul-Henri Mallet, Samuel Johnson and Macpherson himself. His immersion in the antiquarian concerns of a previous generation bears a striking resemblance to Katie Trumpener's account of the practice of the novelists who 'redeploy[ed] literary tropes thirty or forty years old with scarcely any consciousness of the passage of time'.[12] As was the case with these writers, Iolo's brand of cultural nationalism (expressed, like many others, under the sign of the bard) was itself formed in the crucible of the 1790s, with Jacobinism as an important and enduring element; yet in many ways it is also deeply reactionary, and his response to *Ossian* is inextricably both. In Iolo's case, of course, there is an extra twist, in that the impassioned claims for authenticity and the angry accusations against the kind of patriotic bias which blindly misreads sources and dares to falsify the historical record all come from a man simultaneously constructing his own fictions of the past.

The earliest datable reference to *Ossian*, or rather to James Macpherson, in Iolo's writings appears in a letter written in 1774, when he was working as a stonecutter in Kent. During this time, exiled from the newly discovered literary circles in London and from the vibrant poetic tradition at home, he wrote several letters and poems to friends and mentors. A letter to John Walters,

[11] See, e.g., Richard's comments to Lewis Morris, February 1763, on the Cambridge professor of Greek, Michael Lort, who 'says that Macpherson with his Galic poetry has set all the English antiquarians agog after the Welsh, in hopes to find something equal to it – ond ni welant fyth y fath beth ysywaeth (but alas they will see nothing of the sort)': Davies (ed.), *Letters*, II, p. 537.

[12] Trumpener, *Bardic Nationalism*, p. 12.

drafted at least six times, offers 'the following few Etymologies' for the lexicographer's approval.[13]

The two earliest drafts of this letter take explicit issue with James Macpherson's *Introduction to the History of Great Britain* of 1771, a work which, although it studiously refrains from using any Ossianic material as direct evidence, pulls together many of the points raised in the introductory essays to *Fingal* and *Temora.*[14] Macpherson claimed that the Highland Gaels were not, as most historians were agreed by then, an import from Ireland, but the aboriginal inhabitants of Britain: untouched by Roman civilization, they alone had preserved the model of the primitive Celtic society described by classical writers. Although, as Macpherson remarks sagely, 'etymology is a science frequently full of deception, and always unentertaining and dry',[15] much weight is given to the derivations of names of tribes and places, with most of the argument hinging on Macpherson's identification of the Gaels with Caesar's Gauls, peaceful populators of an otherwise empty Britain. Iolo's response was an indignant torrent of examples from Welsh poetry, contemporary philology, and Latin, proving instead that 'gallia (Celtic Gâl) is (I think) derived of the British Gâl which signifies the same as Iâl, pleasant, delectable, white &c':

> if this Etymology of Gallia be allowed, then Mr Macpherson's Chimerical notions will be greatly weaken'd by it, and consequently his history of the ancient Britons almost quite overthrown, for it Depends almost entirely on the Etymology he gives of Gallia, which he writes Gael, from the Eorse Gaethel, or the Irish, Giodhel, which is evidently a coruption of the British Gwyddel . . . Gwyddel (an Irishman) is the [same] as the Latin Sylvanus, or Sylvaticus, (q whether Sylva be from the Celtic yshelfa, from hely) the Bony scots & Irish may be displeased with such a name, but it certainly is the real truth. and perhaps the scots were called so from yscoetieit woodmen, or livers in woods, Synonymous to Gwyddelod, Mr Macpherson, following the vulgar corupt pronunciation of the Highlanders and some of ye Irish (for I have been told 'tis not so in all parts of Ireland) in Gael from Gaethel Erse or Goiddel Irish) asserts it to be the same with ye Latin Gallia, from whence, he concludes that the Highlanders as descendants of the Gauls, we[re] the real and only aborigines of

[13] NLW 21285E, Letter no. 777, Iolo Morganwg to John Walters, 18 September 1774. The other drafts, in approximately chronological order, are nos. 778 (the only other version to mention Macpherson), 780, 779, 776, with 774 as the final version sent to Walters in February 1775. Letter no. 785, an unfinished letter on the same subject to an unnamed addressee, declares 'the Etymologies of Mr James Macpherson & other Scotch writers could never give me the least satisfaction, as they are greatly forced and far-fetched, besides he often imposes on the world very ungenerously indeed . . . it is evident that Mr Macpherson has but very little if any knowledge of any of those dialects exept the Erse and that not as great as he would have the world believe'.

[14] James Macpherson, *An Introduction to the History of Great Britain and Ireland* (London and Dublin, 1771). Iolo is evidently responding to the section on the 'Ancient Names of Britain'.

[15] Ibid., p. 38.

this Island, pretending that they still retain their ancient appellation, *the muckle horned Deel gang away wi me! this will nae do mon.*[16]

A similarly excitable tirade disposes of any inherent primacy in the names Alban and Albion, dismissed as a classic tourist error made by the Phoenicians, who, having sailed up the west coast of Ireland, happened to come across Scotland before the rest of Britain, and mistook its name Al-ban ('high ground') for:

the name of the whole Island, and after their corrupt pronunciation called Britain Albion – tho the very Modest Mr Macpherson, denies our having the least knowledge of the Names Britain, Alban, Gallia, &c and that those words are not found in our Language, *Bravo O! Bravo O! well said Mon! the Deel tack me Mon thou art a muckle bony Loon.*[17]

Iolo's vehemence here is all the more striking given that this argument for the aboriginal status of the Scots Gaels championed by James Macpherson was not a remotely orthodox thesis for the time, and the book itself (largely because of its treatment of Irish sources) was very badly received.[18] But then Macpherson's treatment of the Welsh is itself less than flattering. The Cimbri, he claims in the *Introduction*, were a rough tribe who arrived some time after the settlement of the Gauls/Gaels, but before the civilized corn-growing Belgae: they represent the middle and least attractive state within a scheme of the development of societies which shares basic features with Adam Ferguson's *Essay on the History of Civil Society* (1767).[19] The Cimbri are not a primitive, clan-based, pastoral (and therefore innocent) group like the Gaels depicted in the *Poems of Ossian*, but represent instead the next stage of human development. They are property-owning, belligerent thugs, as yet unsophisticated by the third-stage restraints and graces of civilization. They had:

remained in the same rude barbarity which their ancestors brought with them . . . Recent injuries joined issue with their love of depredation. They made frequent incursions into the Belgic dominions; and it was from that circumstance that the Cimbri beyond the Humber derived their name of Brigantes, which signifies a race of freebooters and plunderers.[20]

[16] NLW 21285E, Letter no. 777, Iolo Morganwg to John Walters, 18 September 1774.

[17] Ibid. The response is obviously to Macpherson's off-hand comment, 'the Welsh use no appellation', *Introduction*, p. 39.

[18] William Ferguson, *The Identity of the Scottish Nation: An Historic Quest* (Edinburgh, 1998), pp. 233–4.

[19] See M. M. Rubel, *Savage and Barbarian: Historical Attitudes in the Criticism of Homer and Ossian in Britain, 1760–1800* (Oxford, 1978). The subject is further discussed below in chapter 7.

[20] Macpherson, *Introduction*, pp. 33–4.

Macpherson's 'freebooters' neatly correspond to Iolo's 'savage dwellers in the woods', as both writers summon etymology to defend their claims to primacy. Although Iolo's philology happens, in this instance, to be more or less accurate by modern standards (the word *Gwyddel* = Goidel = 'Irish' does indeed derive from a word which would come to play a significant part in his later creations: *gwŷdd*, meaning 'savage' or 'wild', or 'wooded'),[21] the ungraciousness on both sides is a reminder of how little love was lost between the Celtic-speaking countries for most of this period, and underlines the dangers of referring to a 'Celtic' response to the questions posed by the formation of a 'British' identity. Although an increasing number of scholars knew, from the work of Edward Lhuyd, of the linguistic affiliations linking the different Celtic-speaking countries, the concept of a shared Celtic culture, and of a kinship based on ethnicity, was still a long way off. The *Ossian* debate opened up rifts between Irish and Scottish Gaelic culture; religion and politics did much to keep Brythonic and Goidelic sides from exploring any shared sense of identity through the paradigm of linguistic cousinship. A lack of respect for (and ignorance of) Scots Gaelic culture would remain a feature of Iolo's later writings, but the essentially Scottish Enlightenment notion of the development of civilizations was, as we shall see, something he came to internalize thoroughly.

This version of Iolo's letter to Walters is only a draft; yet it is worth noting that it was at the very least a second draft, written out neatly and addressed, and one he may well have been intending to send. An earlier version, less coherent in its etymological explanations, is even more brutal in its comments on 'the modest, candid and impartial Sawney, Macpherson'.[22] Subsequent drafts of the letter, which was finally sent in February the following year, restrict themselves to a relatively sober list of etymological suggestions, suppressing all mention of Macpherson and the original impulse behind them; since something very similar happens in Iolo's later treatment of Macpherson, discussed below (pp. 99–100), this suppression would appear to be deliberate. The style of those first drafts, however, is not merely the exuberance of a youthful etymologist scenting his first kill: although published texts do make some attempt to rein them in, *ad hominem* attacks and sudden expletives are a distinctive feature of Iolo's writings to the end; Macpherson himself would be called worse than 'Loon'. A postscript to the letter to Walters cannot resist one last snap at his heels:

> Mr Macpherson in his Homer raised the Ghoste of the old Bard who soundly boxt his Ears, in his Introduction to the history of Britain. I think when it will be fairly

[21] See *GPC*, s.v. *Gwyddel.*

[22] NLW 21285E, Letter no. 778, Iolo Morganwg to John Walters, undated. For the abusive name 'Sawney', see Pittock, *Celtic Identity*, p. 31.

brought to the test he will find he has raised the Devil and that he can not be easily layed.[23]

Iolo, who enjoyed playing the devil, would indeed return, many years later, to plague Macpherson, or at least his reputation, in draft after angry draft during a period of intensive engagement with the issues of historical authenticity raised by the *Ossian* controversy. But by then, the authentic historical documents he defended were increasingly combined with those of his invention, and he had raised quite a few ghosts of his own.

'Many hundreds of manuscripts'

The Myvyrian Archaiology of Wales, published in three volumes between 1801 and 1807, was a landmark publication. It was the first serious attempt in Wales at gathering more than the 'specimens' presented so carefully and, alas, woodenly, by Evan Evans in his volume of 1764, and marks a shift from an earlier tradition of anthologizing the 'jewels' or 'beauties' of Welsh literature to a more solid attempt at chronological literary history.[24] The publication of the first volume at the turn of the century can be seen as significant, benefiting as it does from the general movement towards historicization and canon-formation in British literary scholarship of the mid-to-late eighteenth century,[25] while at the same time mirroring (and to some extent anticipating, since this is largely a nineteenth-century phenomenon) the efforts of those working in other European vernaculars, particularly the smaller and more neglected ones, to establish a national or cultural past through the concept of an unbroken literary tradition.[26] The motivation, in other words, is a dual one, and not without its tensions: as we shall see, the desire to be recognized as equal to,

[23] NLW 21285E, Letter no. 777, Iolo Morganwg to John Walters, 18 September 1774. 'Homer' boxing Macpherson's ears refers to the poor reviews of *The Iliad of Homer, translated by James Macpherson Esq.* (London, 1773).

[24] For anthologies preceding *The Myvyrian Archaiology*, see Catherine McKenna, 'Aspects of Tradition Formation in Eighteenth-Century Wales' in *Memory and the Modern in the Celtic Literatures*, CSANA Yearbook, 5 (Spring, 2006), pp. 37–60. I am grateful to Professor McKenna for allowing me a preview of this article.

[25] The critical debate over the development of English literary history is well summarized in David Fairer, 'Historical Criticism and the English Canon: A Spenserian Dispute in the 1750s', *Eighteenth-Century Life*, 24 (Spring, 2000), 43–64; see also Trevor Ross, *The Making of the English Literary Canon: From the Middle Ages to the Late Eighteenth Century* (Montreal, 1998); Jonathan Brody Kramnick, *Making the English Canon: Print-Capitalism and the Cultural Past, 1700–1770* (Cambridge, 1998); and Richard Terry, *Poetry and the Making of the English Literary Past, 1660–1781* (Oxford, 2001).

[26] See Joep Leerssen, 'Ossian and the Rise of Literary Historicism' in Gaskill (ed.), *The Reception of Ossian*, pp. 109–25; Anne-Marie Thiesse, *La création des identités nationales*.

and yet understood as different from, the English literary tradition, required some complicated intellectual footwork.

While stressing in their prefatory discussions the importance of the very earliest surviving Welsh poetry, earlier anthologies by Lewis Morris and Evan Evans had managed to avoid giving much of it either in the original or in English translation; neither, moreover, felt it necessary to present their material in chronological order.[27] And yet both writers express a very clear sense of working within a recognized literary tradition: as McKenna remarks of *Diddanwch Teuluaidd*, 'the earliest Welsh poetry is present to the anthology despite its absence from it'.[28] The first volume of the *Myvyrian* gives that tradition a material presence, beginning emphatically with poems attributed to the sixth-century figures Aneirin and Taliesin and working its way up to the Poets of the Princes, Dafydd ap Gwilym and the poets of the nobility of the fourteenth century. The subsequent volumes, which came out together in 1807, present a selection of historical, legal and religious prose texts, and an increasing quantity of wisdom literature, in the form of triads, proverbs and sayings, often attributed to certain characters. It is indicative of the different generic priorities of the period that the prose tales and romances, including the key texts known today as the Four Branches of the Mabinogi, are not included; they are promised for a putative fourth volume which, for various reasons, never materialized. All three volumes give the Welsh-language texts only, with no English commentary and no translations, but the dates, authors and titles of the poems are given in English in an opening list of contents. The texts themselves are footnoted, offering variant readings from a selection of manuscripts, and careful attention is paid, apparently at least, to the citation of sources. With its reputation irrevocably damaged by the exposure of Iolo's forgeries, most prevalent in the third volume, the *Myvyrian*'s valiant attempt to bring generic and chronological order to Welsh literary history, and indeed its profound influence on nineteenth-century Wales and beyond, has never been properly explored. And yet it was, and in many ways remains, a serious piece of scholarship.

The Myvyrian Archaiology was a collaborative work. The funding and much of the initial motivation for the project came from Owen Jones, by then a wealthy businessman in London and a leading light among the Gwyneddigion: his bardic name (Owain Myfyr) gave the book its title. The editorial work was the responsibility of William Owen Pughe, likewise settled in London, and by now thoroughly in thrall to Iolo's brand of bardism. Iolo's task was to

[27] Lewis Morris includes one poem ascribed to the 'ancient druids' and one to Taliesin in his sixteen-page *Tlysau yr Hen Oesoedd* (Caergybi, 1735); his later anthology, *Diddanwch Teuluaidd* (Llundain, 1763), is a collection of contemporary writers. Evans discusses Aneirin and Taliesin in the Latin dissertation which forms the centre of his tripartite *Specimens*, but most of his texts are eleventh- and twelfth-century.

[28] McKenna, 'Aspects of Tradition Formation', p. 52.

track down manuscripts. This involved travelling the length and breadth of Wales, much as Evan Evans had done before him, gaining access to libraries, chasing the trail of manuscripts in private hands, which had been lent and borrowed and occasionally stolen.[29] He went, as always, on foot, his correspondence with Pughe and Myfyr mapping the vagaries of his journey: anxious that he might run out of money, or that he had offended a potential donor, their letters chased him around the country, filled with advice, admonitions and the occasional cash-bill. He could be alarmingly silent for long periods at a time. It was during this period of manuscript-hunting that Iolo visited and worked in the famous library built by Thomas Johnes at Hafod, an archival treasure-house which burnt to the ground in 1807, a loss which would later prove a usefully unverifiable source for some of his forgeries.[30] A frustrating episode in 1800 saw Iolo, Pughe and Owain Myfyr's nephew Hugh Maurice turn up simultaneously at Dolgellau in a doomed attempt to gain entry to the famous, and by then famously inaccessible, library at Hengwrt. The previous summer, after a walk of nearly forty miles from Llanrwst to Llanelltud, Iolo fell asleep next to a limekiln and was overpowered by its fumes: had he not been saved by the kilner's wife, who sensed his trouble in a dream, he would never have woken again.[31]

Throughout the eighteenth century, even with a massive increase in printed books and a sharp decline in native patronage, Wales possessed a flourishing manuscript culture. It is important, as Catherine McKenna has warned, to realize that this was something quite different from the manuscript culture of literary coteries in eighteenth-century England: as in Ireland, and in Gaelic Scotland, transmission through copying had not been replaced by print.[32] Although pursued vigorously in the latter half of the eighteenth century by gentlemen, like the Morris brothers, who had a specifically antiquarian agenda, the copying of manuscripts was hardly the preserve of the privileged or especially well-educated. Nick Groom's depiction of Percy's circle as an exclusive scholarly elite whose dealings with manuscript culture 'emphasized a deliberate obscurity of sources' does not hold for Wales in this period.[33] The tradition of copying and swapping verses, both contemporary and ancient, did not therefore operate within a context of expected or even potential publication, and to speak of a work as being 'unpublished' in such a context is in some senses anachronistic,

[29] Glenda Carr, 'An Uneasy Partnership: Iolo Morganwg and William Owen Pughe' in *Rattleskull Genius*, pp. 451–4.

[30] On Johnes's social and agricultural experimentation at Hafod, see Elisabeth Inglis-Jones, *Peacocks in Paradise* (London, 1950). Shortly after the fire, Johnes wrote to Iolo for help in locating 'any blocks of marble fit for columns or for paving' to begin the rebuilding work (NLW 21281E, Letter no. 217, Thomas Johnes to Iolo Morganwg, 13 November 1807).

[31] For Iolo's account of this odd, quasi-mythical episode, see Mary-Ann Constantine, '"Seeing daylight all the way"', *Planet*, 172 (2005), 55–61.

[32] McKenna, 'Aspects of Tradition Formation' pp. 40–1.

[33] Groom, *The Making of Percy's 'Reliques'*, p. 38.

or at least inappropriate: poetic reputations did not rely on print. To recognize this is to go some way towards understanding the shift in outlook needed for Welsh scholars even to contemplate an undertaking like the *Myvyrian.* The editors' urgent concern that Welsh literature, by remaining unpublished, would effectively be consigned to oblivion, signals a fundamentally different perception of literary tradition.

In August 1800, with the collected materials nearing editorial completion, Pughe and Myfyr asked Iolo to prepare a short English introduction to the work; he worried at it on and off from about October, at one point taking it with him during a period of masonry work away from home, before finally sending a draft to Pughe in mid-December. 'A Short Review of the Present State of Welsh Manuscripts' forced Iolo to think a good deal about the concept of authenticity, and the piece is, first and foremost, a spirited defence of the reliability of the Welsh literary tradition. Because of the volumes' subsequently tarnished reputation it has never received much critical attention but, given the importance of the *Myvyrian* as a reference work throughout the nineteenth century in Wales, it can be seen as a key text in the development of a Welsh national consciousness. It is sharp in its condemnation of English attitudes to Wales:

> About the time when Wales was incorporated with England, government seems to have entertained an idea that it was not safe or politic to suffer the Welsh language to live; the use of it was discouraged, and all that could decently, and with saving appearances, be done, was attempted, to suppress and annihilate it. . . . Why Welsh Bibles were taken out of churches, as we have it recorded, and burnt; and English ones ordered to be used in the room of them, cannot now be well known: we trust that, however hostile the politics of this country were once towards our language, they have so far ceased to be so, as to become absolutely indifferent about the matter.[34]

Although Pughe and Myfyr succeeded in persuading Iolo to tone down some of his comments, the piece is equally harsh in its treatment of 'some of the first families in Wales', whose lack of *Amor Patriae* ('without a degree of which', one of the drafts notes grimly, 'persons of wealth and power are only so many rapacious Wolves or Tygers')[35] has condemned Welsh manuscripts to a shocking oblivion: 'patriotism and nationality . . . have almost disappeared in Wales'.[36] Above all, however, the piece returns again and again to the authenticity of the Welsh manuscripts, forming itself like a swarm of wasps around a fundamental challenge or accusation that is itself only dimly discernible ('hints, and even assertions, have of late been thrown out that we have none or none that

[34] *MAW*, I, pp. ix–x.
[35] NLW 13112B, p. 12 (the phrase has been crossed out).
[36] *MAW*, I, p. ix.

are authentic').[37] The open and public nature of the sources is elaborately demonstrated, with the principal owners of manuscripts named, and the main collectors and scholars of Welsh literature – heroic individuals battling against the increasing philistinism of the times – listed from the late sixteenth century onwards. The tone is defensive, and although Macpherson is never once mentioned directly much of the piece is clearly a response to the *Ossian* controversy and its aftermath. It seems written, at times, with clenched fists:

> The ancient Welsh literature has been viewed in very false lights. The Welsh nation and language, as we have just observed, had passed through half a thousand years of Roman learning and civilization, before the period wherein the oldest extant of our bards lived; they had also become Christian for so long a time before; of course a literary people. After having possessed the advantages of so long and luminous a period of knowledge, how unjustly are our ancient manuscripts viewed through the same medium with the fictions of modern times? We pretend to give nothing from oral tradition; we produce many hundreds of manuscripts of undoubted antiquity, marked with all the genuine characteristics of authenticity.[38]

'Fictions of modern times' and the scathing reference to 'oral tradition' would have alerted many readers to the Ossianic subtext here, as would a later reference to 'that *stubborn audacity*, which either withholds or gives false evidence'. But, as with the letter to Walters, it is only in the earlier drafts of this piece that the pressure of the *Ossian* debate is revealed. There are at least three long drafts,[39] most of them much fuller and angrier than the published version, and all laying great stress on the tangible nature of the proof on offer:

> The curious and learned are refered to those Libraries and MSS, which it is presumed they will carefully inspect, examine and even study, previously acquainting themselves with the language wherein they are written before they have the Audacity to call in question the authenticity of these poems or the genuiness of their antiquity. They are not given from pretended oral tradition of which no reciters can be produced, not from any MSS which are boldly asserted to exist but which are insultingly withheld from the eye of honest enquiry and rational sceptism.[40]

'Pretended oral tradition' and elusive manuscripts 'insultingly withheld' refer directly to incidents much earlier in the *Ossian* debate, as played out in the very public row between Macpherson and Dr Johnson in 1775. Johnson had

[37] Ibid.
[38] Ibid., p. xvi.
[39] In probable order of composition, these are NLW 13089E, pp. 262–73; NLW 13104B, pp. 119–30 and (very close to the published version) NLW 13112B, pp. 11–35.
[40] NLW 13089E, p. 270.

directly attacked the authenticity of the *Ossian* poems (and the honour of their author-editor) in comments which appeared in his *Journey to the Western Isles of Scotland*:

> I suppose my opinion of the poems of Ossian is already discovered. I believe they never existed in any other form than that which we have seen. The editor, or author, never could shew the orginal; nor can it be shewn by any other; to revenge reasonable incredulity, by refusing evidence, is a degree of insolence, with which the world is not yet acquainted; and stubborn audacity is the last refuge of guilt.[41]

Macpherson, via Johnson's publisher, called for a public apology and the removal of the offending lines from subsequent editions: when these failed to materialize (the second edition appearing in print almost simultaneously with the first), he seems to have written an angry letter, apparently threatening physical violence, to which Johnson famously replied: 'I will not desist from detecting what I think a cheat, from any fear of the menaces of a Ruffian.'[42] The day after the *Journey* appeared, Macpherson's publisher, Thomas Becket, wrote to the press to refute Johnson's challenge with the claim that Macpherson had actually left 'the originals of FINGAL and other poems of Ossian' in his shop 'for many months in the year 1762, for the inspection of the curious',[43] and this incident too appears in the *Myvyrian* drafts:

> It has been advanced as a proof of the authenticity of Ossian that Macpherson left a ms for SIX WEEKS in the hands of Mr Becket for the inspection and satisfaction of the curious. Admit the truth of this, tho we were not informed of it till ten or twelve years at least after, what can it prove? nothing but that one mss copy of Ossian existed at that time, which might have been a forgery of some not very ancient period. And till other, and considerably various, copies are produced, we must consider such a copy, if such ever existed, as being under a most violent presumption that it is a forgery.[44]

The argument between Johnson and Macpherson has been much discussed from both sides, with Johnson's requirement of written, tangible proof, his insistence that Macpherson 'shew the original', set against the Ossianic claims for the longevity of oral tradition.[45] There is no question, in the 'Short

[41] Samuel Johnson, *A Journey to the Western Isles of Scotland* (London, 1775), pp. 273–4.
[42] See Fiona Stafford, 'Dr Johnson and the Ruffian: New Evidence in the Dispute between Samuel Johnson and James Macpherson', *Notes and Queries*, new series, 36 (1989), 70–7.
[43] Cited in Howard Gaskill, 'What did James Macpherson Really Leave on Display at his Publisher's Shop in 1762?', *Scottish Gaelic Studies*, 16 (1990), 67.
[44] NLW 13112B, p. 19.
[45] See, e.g. Trumpener, *Bardic Nationalism*, pp. 67–97; Groom, *The Forger's Shadow*, pp. 107–14; Baines, *The House of Forgery*, pp. 103–20; Fulford, *Landscape, Liberty and Authority*, pp. 103–15. For more on Ossianic orality, see below, pp. 117–20.

review' and its drafts, as to which side of the debate Iolo is on: he is here at his most Johnsonian, scathing, sceptical, and professing scant regard for what he calls national vanity (a sin, he claims, from which Wales and the Welsh are happily free).[46] Besides the many direct citations and verbal echoes of Johnson, the whole tenor of Iolo's argument shows how far he has internalized the Englishman's assumptions in the authenticity debate. He is, for example, obsessively concerned with the materiality of the Welsh sources, and assures his readers of the physical, tangible nature of the available proof, as well as its abundance:

> When a time arrives, wherein we find a great multiplicity of such copies, we may be well assured that their original is a very ancient; for such a multiplicity of copies, of variations in readings, of apparent but very various antiquities, evinced by the effects of time in various degrees upon them, can never be produced but by a long series of ages. These things are, as we may term them, the grey hairs and wrinkles of old age, which never deceive those who behold them. The many copies extant of the ancient Welsh bards have been thus acted upon by time and by accident, of course they are authentic; or there must have existed a very great number of forgers somewhere, and at some time, as remote at least as the appearances of the greatly decayed manuscripts indicate, who combined thus to impose on the world; and in every age there must have been a succession of forgers who possess'd of a secret, very similar to that of Free Masons continued the fraud, and all to no purpose.[47]

To this momentarily dizzying vision of a secret brotherhood of forgers the draft version adds:

> Had even the hundredth part of such multifarious copies been produced of the Poems of Rowley, of what we find in Wales we should never have suspected their authenticity. Such copies of Ossian even of a thousand years subsequent to the time when they are said to have been produced, would have been deemed sufficient evidences of their authenticity.[48]

In June 1804 Iolo wrote a lengthy letter to the Scottish antiquarian Robert Macfarlan, who had been in touch with William Owen Pughe with a list of questions about Welsh literature.[49] Inevitably – Macfarlan had published a

[46] NLW 13089E, pp. 266–7; cf. NLW 13088B, p. 88: 'modern conjectures founded on nothing much better than National Vanity'.

[47] *MAW*, I, p. xvii.

[48] NLW 13112B, p. 21.

[49] Macfarlan, writing to William Owen Pughe in May 1804 (NLW 13224B, pp. 501–2), seems to have been responding to a review of Sharon Turner's *History of the Anglo-Saxons* (1801) in the *Edinburgh Review*, VI (January, 1804) which expressed scepticism as to the value of his Welsh sources (Macfarlan mistakes the issue, referring to the 'Vth Number'). I am grateful to Howard Gaskill for checking this.

Latin translation of *Temora* in 1769 and was busily engaged in translating more 'from the original Gaelic' – the arguments Iolo puts forward to defend the Welsh tradition are framed in terms of the Ossian debate. For the poems to be genuine, Iolo argues, copies of potentially early Ossianic manuscripts should have sprouted exponentially over the centuries, as they did in Wales ('of manuscripts of later centuries in the 13th, 14th, 15th & 16, we can at any time when called upon produce a hundred copies at least in London').[50] In order really to prove its point, however, this early poetry should itself exist in a wider manuscript context, encompassing the different branches of knowledge: 'history, laws, theology, ethics, astronomy, geography, agriculture, grammar, literary criticism, fables, romances, legends of saints, genealogies and even mathematics'.[51] In short (and the advice is, as ever, perceptive), 'to forge with any hopes of success in the Erse it would not do to fabricate an Ossian, or any thing else alone, you must forge in all the unavoidably concomitant branches of literary knowlege, at least in a great many of them'.[52] This of course is precisely what Iolo himself was doing, weaving a wide range of poetic, legal and annalistic material into the existing manuscript culture.

Another typically Johnsonian position, one which verges on caricature, is Iolo's own stubborn denial of the existence of any relevant Gaelic manuscripts, indeed of any early written culture in the Highlands at all. The letter to Macfarlan is quite explicit on this count. Correctly chastising his too-general use of the word 'Celt' (one of the side-effects of the *Ossian* scandal had been further to blur poorly grasped distinctions and encourage generalizations about 'Celtic', which was often used for Scots Gaelic at the time), Iolo writes:

> You ask Sir why are the Celts denied MSS. This is not the direct question. The appellation Celts is not proper here, for the Welsh, Irish, Bretons are Celts. They produce MSS. Welsh and Irish MSS are very numerous, but the Highlanders produce none.[53]

Again he summons up the fuss over the Ossian 'manuscripts', quoting a patchwork of Johnsonian phrases from the *Journey*; this time he also claims (although he does not specify when) that he had taken the trouble to inspect for himself the Gaelic manuscripts placed in the keeping of the London-based Highland Society, and found them 'chiefly meagre Genealogies, and Irish not Erse, and besides they are not of any considerable antiquity'.[54] ('What conviction', he adds, 'would have been effected by a few Irish silly Genealogies, even

[50] NLW 21285E, Letter no. 872, Iolo Morganwg to Robert Mcfarlan, 6 June 1804.
[51] Ibid.
[52] Ibid.
[53] Ibid.
[54] Ibid.

had they been Erse what purpose could they have answered towards Authenticating the Poems of Ossian?')[55] The *Myvyrian* drafts refer deprecatingly (and rather cattily) to the absence of early written proof:

> The capital but bungling fraud of printing the Erse translation from the original English of Ossian will never establish its Authenticity; this was not done till almost 40 years had elapsed from the Time it first came into existence in the English language . . . We hope that the Erse, that poor, and hitherto uneducated Sister of the Welsh, will be greatly benefited by a work that however fictitious, must be very interesting to the Caledonians, but we cannot help lamenting that a charge of fraud must for ever attach to the superior genius of Mr Macpherson.[56]

Authenticity is made wholly dependent on literacy and – in these writings, although, not, as we shall see, elsewhere – oral tradition is only mentioned with scorn. It is one of the glaring ironies of Iolo's work that his defence of Welsh integrity seems, at crucial moments, to be little more than a ventriloquism of the opinions of the great Englishman, some quarter of a century after their first publication.

Perhaps the most tantalizing aspect of the published version of the 'Short Review', however, is the systematic removal of all direct references to *Ossian*. In the closest draft, NLW 13112B, whole paragraphs, whole pages, match the published form more or less verbatim; but in every instance where the argument leads him to a comparison with Macpherson, that reference has been excised. Were it not for the same thing happening to the much-drafted letter to John Walters some twenty-five years earlier, one might assume that the cuts were the result of pressure from Pughe or Myfyr. Pughe was certainly responsible for suggesting that Iolo should drop another section directly attacking the main perpetrator of the malignant 'hints, and even assertions' against the Welsh tradition: John Pinkerton, who in various publications since the 1780s had developed a theory of Gothic origins which poured scorn on Celtic pretentions to antiquity and made specific allegations against the Welsh. Pinkerton's comments riled Iolo beyond endurance; a collection of furious snippets insulting him and his work has been carefully preserved in the

[55] Ibid. The London-based Highland Society was formed in 1784 along similar lines to the Gwyneddigion and Cymmrodorion societies, with the aim of preserving the language, poetry and music of the Highlands.

[56] NLW 13112B, pp. 21–2; cf. NLW 13104B, p. 125. References to a 'recently published' Gaelic *Ossian* are puzzling, however, since Macfarlan's three-volume Gaelic version did not appear until 1807. Iolo may have been referring to one of the various fragments published from 1778 onwards: see J. L. Robertson, 'Ossianic Heroic Poetry' (a translation of L. C. Stern, 'Die ossianischen Heldenlieder' (1895)), *Transactions of the Gaelic Society of Inverness*, XXII (1897–8), 264–7. Alternatively, he may simply have heard that the publication was imminent. I should like to thank Howard Gaskill for his help on this question.

archives.[57] But Pughe, tactful as ever, advised caution: 'Perhaps it would be better management for the text to be general against such foes, and throw his name into a sly note.'[58] There is no specific comment, however, on the many attacks against Macpherson. The effect of his absence on the final version is very strange. Although the prose is undoubtedly much stronger without the rather inelegant assaults, the gaps in the argument, and its unmistakable debts to the language of the controversy, conspire to summon him up: an unspoken presence jostling into the text.

[57] See the numerous pieces in NLW 21419E. Under the name 'Philistor', Pinkerton's 'Letters to the People of Great Britain, on the Cultivation of their National History' had accused Welsh scholars of dealing in fantasy: *Gentleman's Magazine*, LVIII, part 1 (1788), 499–501 (Iolo copied out the relevant section in NLW 21419E, no. 4). His *Dissertation on the Origin and Progress of the Scythians or Goths* (London, 1787) was 'predicated upon a belief in the congenital inferiority of the Celtic people' (*ODNB*); Iolo's copy of this work, held at the National Library of Wales, has various sarcastic comments in the margins.

[58] NLW 21282E, Letter no. 345, William Owen Pughe to Iolo Morganwg, 3 January 1801.

7

'Indelible impressions': Romans, Britons and the Legacy of Letters

The invisible presence of Macpherson is especially palpable around two-thirds of the way into the published 'Short Review', where, after a detailed (and well-informed) account of the nature of manuscript transmission, a new paragraph begins abruptly: 'Our bards were not barbarians. They were men of letters.' In the draft, this comment comes naturally out of a discussion of Gaelic illiteracy, which begins by co-opting the somewhat unlikely pairing of Hugh Blair and Samuel Johnson to prove its point:

> It is on all hands admitted that the Highland Scots knew nothing of Letters, even so late as the 15th Century (see Dr Blairs Dissertation on Ossian's Poems, p 219, 8vo Edit.) Dr Johnson justly observes that the Highland Bard was 'a Barbarian amongst Barbarians' the idle tale of these Poems having been, thro the long period of fourteen hundred years, retained by oral tradition, is only laughed at.[1]

Discussion of the progress of peoples towards civilization and, in particular, distinctions between savagery and barbarism, became central preoccupations of much eighteenth-century antiquarian and historical writing, and one of the main charms of *Ossian* for many readers was its depiction of a primitive 'first' stage of innocence and spontaneous human decency.[2] Welsh poetry had, in this precise context, already fared rather badly in an earlier head-to-head encounter with the Scottish bard, when the French reviewer of Evan Evans's *Specimens* concluded, 'Quand on compare ce ton avec celui des Welches, on verra la différence d'un peuple sauvage avec un peuple barbare' ('If one compares [Ossian's] tone with that of the Welsh poems, one will see the difference

[1] NLW 13112B, p. 29. Hugh Blair's remarks in the *Critical Dissertation* (1763; 2nd edn., 1765) were intended to prove that *Ossian* was more likely to be a genuine representation of third-century Caledonia than a fifteenth-century 'fake': *PO*, p. 355.

[2] See Rubel, *Savage and Barbarian*; Howard Weinbrot, *Britannia's Issue: The Rise of British Literature from Dryden to Ossian* (Cambridge, 1993), pp. 526–7, 541–8.

between a savage people and a barbarous people').[3] In his more thoughtful moments, Iolo seems to have subscribed to a notion of progressive stages in human development very like that proposed by Macpherson and Adam Ferguson: in a letter to William Owen Pughe, written in 1800, he complained that 'modern writers use the term Barbarian (as Dr Johnson did, *ut supra*) in a sense not sufficiently discriminate. The Caledonians, as represented in Macpherson's Ossian, without Agriculture without Arts, were savages and had not arrived at the State of Barbarism.'[4] But it cannot be denied that he himself is not always sufficiently discriminate, and in the drafts to the *Myvyrian* he uses the same quotation from Johnson in terms that are merely damning. For Iolo, as partly for Johnson, the 'barbarism' of the Scots Gaels is primarily revealed through their supposed illiteracy, but there are broader cultural considerations at work here as well. Like Macpherson, but for quite opposite reasons, he is keen to show that Wales and southern Britain were thoroughly romanized, and far from isolated:

> they had been for four hundred years at least a province of the Roman Empire in the most flourishing time of its learning, had been for so long a time Converts to Christianity, had at that time amongst them the most celebrated if not the only seminaries of learning in Britain; were beyond a doubt sufficiently acquainted with all the European Learning of that age.[5]

It is difficult to exaggerate the importance of the notion of *romanitas* in Iolo's vision of the British past. This is not an idiosyncracy: although, as Rosemary Sweet has argued, earlier Welsh antiquaries may not have been overly interested in excavating the material remains of their Roman past,[6] pride in the literary legacy of the Welsh Roman inheritance goes deep into Welsh conceptions of cultural identity. It is clearly marked in the thought of the Morris brothers and of many scholars before them, and can be found, transformed into legend, both in the long-enduring Brutus-myth (which ascribed the origins of 'Britain' to the arrival of Brutus after the fall of Troy) and in the medieval tale of 'Maxen Wledig'; it became, as Brynley F. Roberts has put it, 'one of the central

[3] Louis I. Bredvold, *The Contributions of John Wilkes to the 'Gazette Littéraire de l'Europe'* (Ann Arbor, Mich., 1950), p. 32. The piece, published in November 1764, was an extended version of an equally unfavourable draft review by Charles Wilkes; it was probably written by Jean-Baptiste-Antoine Suard, editor of the newly established *Gazette*, with some input from David Hume. See David Raynor, 'Ossian and Hume' in Gaskill (ed.), *Ossian Revisited*, pp. 156–7.

[4] NLW 13221E, pp. 75–8, Iolo Morganwg to William Owen Pughe, 19 December 1800. Rubel, a more recent commentator, also deplores the 'incredible vagueness of Dr Johnson's definitions of these concepts', *Savage and Barbarian*, p. 19.

[5] NLW 13089E, p. 270.

[6] Sweet argues that the 'Welsh prided themselves on having successfully resisted the Roman invasions and on having preserved their traditions distinct' (*Antiquaries*, p. 141), but does not take the literary legacy into account.

themes of medieval Welsh historiography'.[7] For Iolo, far from being the source of corruption implied by Macpherson ('[t]he debility which tyranny and luxury carried from Rome through all its dominions'),[8] the Roman presence was a deeply civilizing influence. The daylight metaphor used so often in the cause of bardism is here put to especially striking effect:

> The illuminated periods of the Greek and Roman Empires may be compared to one of the longest and brightest days of our summer, the evening twilight of which does not disappear before the Dawn or morning twilight of a succeeding day returns. All the nations who had for any length of time enjoyed the first day by having been within the Period and Pale of the Roman Empire, retained this summer twilight, never entirely lost the light of the preceding day. Such were the Welsh, Troubadours, Bretons, Italians &c, but the Gothic nations awoke to the second day as from a long winters night within which they had been born, all their knowledge consisted in a recollection of the dreams of that night.[9]

This confontation of Romano-Celtic enlightenment with Gothic ignorance and barbarity, inevitably heightened by association with the works of Pinkerton, not only neatly overturned the opposition set up by scholars like Thomas Percy (whose 'rampantly literate' Goths faced down the challenge posed by the oral Celts) but could also, as Cathryn Charnell-White has shown, be comfortably extended to include enemies closer to home.[10] In Iolo's planned 'History of the Bards', for example, the same binary opposition fits neatly over the north/south divide in Wales itself, with a civilized Roman south preserving an integrity, and a genuine poetic tradition, long since lost by the Scandinavian-influenced north.

In an interesting essay on the ruins of the Roman fort at Caerhun in Gwynedd, Iolo muses both on the visible and the less tangible aspects of the Roman legacy: 'indubitable vestiges of Roman Arts, Roman Mechanical Principles, Roman manners, usages, modes of expression etc. such as are not to be found in any other part of this Island.'[11] His comments on its effect on the Welsh language are worth quoting at some length:

> The Welsh are, probably, the only nation of all those nations that once composed the mighty and vast Roman Empire, who still, from that very luminous period, retain their ancient language not materially altered. Technology is always derived from the Arts

[7] 'Native Welsh historians sought a continuity of history from Roman Britain to dark-age Wales with all that that implied in terms of civilized origins and long-standing *Romanitas*': Brynley F. Roberts (ed.), *Breudwyt Maxen Wledic* (Dublin, 2005), p. xlvii.

[8] James Macpherson, *An Introduction to the History of Great Britain and Ireland* (London, 1771), p. 263.

[9] NLW 13138A, p. 279.

[10] Groom, *The Making of Percy's 'Reliques'*, p. 87; Charnell-White, *Barbarism and Bardism.*

[11] NLW 13103B, p. 45.

> and Sciences of the Periods wher[e]in it was formed. The Technology of the Welsh literary and mechanical arts and sciences was obvious[ly] form[ed] in the Roman ages of knowledge in Britain; it clearly utters the voice of such periods, and has brought down in the Ideas it expresses, in the peculiar acceptations of many of its words, some degree of the knowledge of those Arts and Sciences that gave it birth. It bears on its face indelible impressions of the Roman learning and knowledge, literary and mechanical; of these we observe obvious traces even in its oral dialects, and more particularly so in the Silurian Dialect, and this doubtless from the circumstance of one of the three great Roman Colonies (Isca Silurum) having been established in the very heart of the Country of the Silures. When the Saxon language became a dead language, much of that knowledge of which it was the Vehicle and Depository, died with it. It will, probably, be found to be a very General case that in very ancient living languages, something, perhaps much, of the knowledge of that period wherein they first became civilized and acquainted with letters, will be retained in them. Much of the manners, of the vulgar mythologies and opinions of such remote ages will be found alive in them.[12]

This is a powerful statement of one of Iolo's most fundamental beliefs: that a living language contains its own past, and can reveal a whole culture's history. 'Language' here is conceived of as spoken (it 'utters the voice of such periods', has 'oral dialects'), but some of the phrasing is revealingly visual: Welsh 'bears on its face indelible impressions', and displays 'obvious traces'. However its longevity is figured, the flow through time must be unbroken: it is precisely the discontinuities of English literary and linguistic history (Thomas Warton's *History of English Poetry* (1774–1781), begins of course not with Saxon poetry but with Chaucer) which prevent it from properly 'remembering' that period of early enlightenment.[13] Drawing a favourite (and, as we have seen, Ossianic) contrast between the tendency of English poetry to borrow its scenes of nature from the classics, while Welsh poetry has always drawn on the living landscape and 'climature' of Britain, Iolo remarks:

> A similar observation may be made respecting the impression made on the Welsh language by the Roman learning and civilization, the Welsh has felt these, the English has only heard of them, in these the Welsh has evidently had a practical experience, and knowledge. The English and its literature only a Theoretical or hearsay knowledge of it. Whence the catachrestical and otherwise unnatural acceptations of a prodigious number of its technical and other words and expressions.[14]

The clumsy last line enacts its own premise. And this is an audacious double twist: eighteenth-century English literature, dripping with Latinity, is nevertheless

[12] Ibid., p. 46.

[13] David Fairer (ed.), *Thomas Warton's History of English Poetry* (4 vols., London, 1998).

[14] NLW 13103B, p. 49. Cf. Blair's comments cited in chapter 2 (*PO*, p. 384).

disqualified from any meaningful relationship with Rome. Against the intimacy and length of Wales's involvement with *romanitas* Iolo sets the meretricious nature of English classicism, now revealed as the inevitable product of the Saxons' late arrival and their subsequent broken legacy of cultural blackouts.

A significant, if confusing, extension of the idea occurs in a previously cited letter to William Owen Pughe, in which Iolo compares Wales's early relationship with Rome to its current relationship with England. While denying that English as a language has had any positive influence on Welsh, he appears to suggest that on other levels it has been an improving force: 'our literature has been greatly affected by our connection with the English, and it is solely because this effect has not been extended into Caledonia, that its Inhabitants are still but one remove from the state of Savagism.'[15] In that deliberate alignment with Augustan England against Scotland there is no sense of the loss of innocence that for Macpherson comes with being part of the empire, English or Roman. But the disadvantages of this line of thinking for the development of a distinctively Welsh national consciousness are obvious, and indeed run counter to Iolo's own frequent tirades against English barbarism. His solution to that problem – as for many other historians and antiquarians fighting their corners for their own ethnic group – was simply to push everything further back, to claim a prior existence, and to prove that Welsh civilization, though enhanced by the benefits of occupation, was not simply the result of Roman interference. This pre-Roman refinement was expressed, once again, in terms of literacy.

'Lines of honesty': a bardic alphabet

In *De Bello Gallico* Caesar famously reports of the Druids of Gaul and Britain that they did not believe in committing their doctrine to letters, preferring to train their disciples, sometimes over twenty years, to remember 'a great number of verses'.[16] For all other things, however, they used 'Greek letters' (*Graecis litteris*), a phrase which has had a long history of interpretation.[17] Iolo was much preoccupied by this clue to pre-Roman literacy in Britain, and various manuscript notes show him wrestling with other authors on its possible significance. He was particularly inspired, it seems, by the suggestive semantic richness of the word *gwŷdd* (one of the primary meanings of which, as we saw above, is 'wild' or 'woody'). At some point early in the 1790s the manuscript pages

[15] NLW 13221E, Letter no. 14, pp. 75–8, Iolo Morganwg to William Owen Pughe, 19 December 1800. For the Roman Empire's place in the imagination of English writers at this period, see Suvir Kaul, *Poems of Nation, Anthems of Empire: English Verse in the Long Eighteenth Century* (London, 2000).

[16] Caesar, *The Gallic War*, trans. H. J. Edwards (London, 1917), Book VI, chapter 14.

[17] A. S. Owen, *The Famous Druids: A Survey of Three Centuries of English Literature on Druids* (Oxford, 1962), pp. 119–20.

start to fill up with speculations sparked by the happy discovery that 'wood' was also used metaphorically to mean 'verse, poetry' (the Welsh verse-form, the *cywydd*, is apparently related).[18] Taking the metaphors literally, Iolo scanned the early medieval poetry for references to what he believed was the practice of *naddu cerdd* ('to hew verse'), coining the term *gwyddawd* ('wood knowledge') as a calque on 'literature'.[19] Having thus satisfied himself that the ancient Welsh, like other ancient cultures, used to write on wood (he notes references to the practice in the Bible), and further encouraged by the fact that the word *gwyddor* means alphabet, it was not long before Iolo came up with a more authentically British version of the *Graecis litteris*, the bardic *coelbren*. This was a kind of primitive alphabet made up of notches on sticks, and initially comprising ten letters: it was derived, he claimed, from the three primary letters: /|\, which represent the ineffable name of the deity.[20] Iolo's interpretation of the name *coelbren* (a genuine word, to which he gave a new meaning) was, appropriately enough, 'stick of credibility'.[21] A draft letter written for the *Gentleman's Magazine* reveals that the alphabet was complete by 1792:

> Amongst other things retained by Tradition the Bards have a remarkable method of writing, inscribing, or engraving upon wood, – by cutting, notching, or scoring, letters or characters on slender billets. This is now only used as a probationary exercise imposed on a disciple, who produces, at his admission into the Order, the Alphabet with a stanza or two, cut in this manner on little square billets.[22]

To prove his point, Iolo set about carving his very own *peithynen*, a kind of abacus in which the wooden billets are combined to form sequences of bardic verses written in the *coelbren* script; this contraption may have been inspired by the so-called 'Staffordshire Clog', a wooden calendrical device also involving carved signs, an illustration of which he had carefully copied into one of his notebooks.[23] Iolo clearly relished his *coelbren* and made innumerable copies of tables comparing it with different scripts – medieval, Runic, 'Etruscan' – and noting with satisfaction that 'a whimsical Welsh Bard' had sent letters in the script 'over most of the continent of Europe as well into the tallons of Will Pitt: it occasioned dreadful alarms'.[24] In 1799, thanks as ever to the efforts of William Owen Pughe, the *coelbren* was included in Edmund Fry's *Pantographia,*

[18] See *GPC*, s.v. *gwŷdd* 1a and 1c. For detailed notes on the bardic alphabet and the development of letters and writing, especially writing on wood, see NLW 13097B, pp. 47–76, 191–5.

[19] NLW 13097B, p. 67.

[20] For an excellent account of Iolo's development of the *coelbren* and other alphabets, see Richard M. Crowe, 'Diddordebau Ieithyddol Iolo Morganwg' (unpublished University of Wales Ph.D. thesis, 1988), pp. 110–33.

[21] NLW 13097B, p. 62.

[22] NLW 13087E, pp. 22–4, dated 9 April 1792.

[23] Ibid., p. 13.

[24] NLW 13093E, p. 157.

an illustrated compendium of early alphabets from around the world; another version appeared in Pughe's *Grammar of the Welsh Language* in 1803. 'The Sanscrit Alphabet', he wrote delightedly to Iolo, 'agrees with Coelbren y Beirdd exactly in arrangement, number of vowels, consonants, and classes &c.'[25] The tempting field of Eastern scholarship, recently opened up to a European audience by scholars like Sir William Jones, offered further and yet stranger semantic possibilities for *gwŷdd,* as Iolo revealed in another bout of breathless etymologizing:

> Minerva the Goddess of knowlege and Wisdom was, by the ancient Greek and Romans, represented by an owl. The Bramins (says Mr Wilkins) represent their Goddess of learning and wisedom by a Goose, now *Gŵydd* in welsh is not only a Goose but seems to have signified 'knowlege, learning, Wisdom, &c' whence *Egwyddor, Arwydd, Cyfarwydd, Gwyddost,* thou knowest, *Danwyddyd* intelligence, (in Southwales,) *yn ei wydd* [is] obvious to him, *Gwyddfa* a conspicuous or obvious place, *Derwydd – Dy-er-Gwydd/* the prefixed particles *Dy* & *er* contracted into *der,* a man of learning of wisedom &c *Gwyddon* &c.[26]

In fact the rich variety of *gwŷdd* and its homonyns operated like a web of many strands: at the centre of it all, from Iolo's point of view, was *gwybod* (root *gwydd-*) the verb 'to know', a connection illegitimate in modern linguistics but understandably irresistible at the time. The *coelbren* and the mythology surrounding it represent, once again, the incarnation of a philological theory, the act of etymologizing made concrete: a literal metaphor. Much of Iolo's invention has this fundamentally poetic quality, although it rarely took quite such solid forms.

The inspired retrieval and restoration of a British native alphabet allowed Iolo to backdate a tradition of knowledge, science and education by at least 2,000 years. The reasoning behind this claim of longevity argued that the existence of a word in pure Welsh, patently not borrowed from anywhere else, must prove that the object or concept described has been in existence as long as the word itself. Since, according to Pezron, the Welsh/British language reached its mature, completed form some 4,000 years earlier, it can be easily proven that the Welsh (unlike the barbarous Saxons, obliged to borrow virtually all their theoretical and technological vocabulary), have been 'self-civilized' more or

[25] NLW 21282E, Letter no. 340, William Owen Pughe to Iolo Morganwg, 30 June 1800.

[26] NLW 13222C, p. 146, Iolo Morganwg to William Owen Pughe, 17 June 1800. 'Mr Wilkins' is Charles Wilkins, who had published a translation of the *Baghvad-Gita* (London, 1785). The profound influence of William Jones and others on Welsh scholars is discussed by Caryl Davies, *Adfeilion Babel: Agweddau ar Syniadaeth Ieithyddol y Ddeunawfed Ganrif* (Caerdydd, 2000), pp. 295–320. For more Eastern parallels, see, e.g., 'Phrases in common use in Glamorgan and also amongst the Persians and other Mahometans': NLW 13150A, pp. 249–50. *Gŵydd* (goose) and *gwŷdd* (wild, woody etc.), are not, alas, cognate.

less from the beginning.[27] The Romans merely added a further level of sophistication to an already complex society:

> almost every noun and verb in the Welsh language express with metaphisical precision all the object properties and agencies of Nature . . . refined and sublime ideas of Theology, philology. It has a multiplicity of terms definitive of all sorts of lines, circles, curves, angles simple and compound, figures of all the principal parts on very complicated machinery, as wheels of various kinds, screws, springs, etc. all the parts of a ship and its rigging, of all the parts of a house as rooms, chambers, pillars, every kind of aperture, (Goleuddor) & subdivision (cell, chor etc) every useful implement and process in Agriculture, in the smelting and refining of metals, in pharmacy etc. Its native terms in literature as Coelbren, peithynen, ebillwydd, Gwyddor, darllen, Cerdd, can etc. prove that they were not borrowed from any other nation.[28]

As Richard Crowe points out, and as Iolo's time with John Walters must have taught him, these were precisely the fields in which modern Welsh most needed words.[29] The lexicographers, in open daylight, were busy making them for the use of contemporary science and scholarship; Iolo was burying them in the past like fossils.

The *coelbren* expresses a wider contemporary preoccupation with the development of writing and an interest in comparing different scripts and alphabets. Indeed, it could almost be understood as a response to the challenge implicit in Thomas Astle's *The Origin and Progress of Writing* (1784):

> After the most diligent enquiry it doth not appear, that the Britons had the use of letters before their intercourse with the Romans. Although alphabets have been produced, which are said to have been used by the Ancient Britons, yet no one MS. ever appeared that was written in them – (I have several of these pretended alphabets in my collection; though they are only Roman letters deformed).[30]

But the need to find an orthography appropriate to the genius of the language goes back a long way, at least as far the 'Welsh runes' devised by the author of the ninth-century 'Nennius' manuscripts as a British counterpart to Saxon and Irish scripts.[31] Edward Lhuyd, in the early eighteenth century, had tinkered with the idea of spelling Welsh more effectively by using a combination of Greek and Roman letters, while Hugh Blair at one point had thought of

[27] For Pezron's influence in eighteenth-century Wales, see Davies, *Adfeilion Babel*, pp. 60–125.
[28] NLW 13089E, p. 303.
[29] Crowe, 'Diddordebau Ieithyddol', p. 188.
[30] (London, 1784), p. 96. Iolo refers to Astle in his letter to Robert Macfarlan.
[31] Ifor Williams, 'Notes on Nennius', *BBCS*, VII, part 4 (1935), 380–2.

producing a Gaelic *Ossian* entirely in Greek orthography.[32] The importance of spelling-systems in the development of Celtic and other minority languages is further considered in the final part of this book, but the need to represent the sounds of a language in as rational a way as possible was not only the province of philologists and antiquarians, and nor was it restricted to those at the Celtic margins looking for alternatives to the English (or Roman) norm. There were strong social and political dimensions to the linguistic work of English writers such as Joseph Priestley, John Horne Tooke and Thomas Spence, all of whom, in different ways and to varying degrees, wanted to produce a written language more accessible, more rational and closer to the spoken norm, a written language which would not exclude the common man.[33] Yet while a democratic, and indeed universalist, desire for phonetic transparency is certainly one aspect of Iolo's invention of the *coelbren*, it has an undeniably esoteric flavour, the aura of a 'secret code' known only to the cognoscenti.[34]

Indeed, given the subtlety of his manipulation of the Welsh manuscript tradition, Iolo's foray into the mechanics of early writing appears curiously naive, akin to the kind of messy, material forgery he scorns in Chatterton and William Henry Ireland.[35] His bardic alphabet brought him closer than any of his creations to being openly denounced as a forger, and should by rights have sparked off the 'Iolo controversy' which in fact took another century to materialize. The failed catalyst was another keen enthusiast for the *coelbren*, the Anglican priest and antiquarian Edward Davies, whose *Celtic Researches* (1804) explain that he had himself already postulated the existence of a druidic alphabet formed by leaves and twigs when, to his delight, 'Mr Owen presented me with a complete copy of it':[36]

[32] Kristine Haugen makes the interesting suggestion that Blair's proposed Greek spelling aimed to put Gaelic 'back', as it were, into Caesar's *Graecis litteris*: 'Ossian and the Invention of Textual History', 318.

[33] For Horne Tooke, see Olivia Smith, *The Politics of Language, 1791–1818* (Oxford, 1984), pp. 110–53; for Spence, see Anthea F. Shields, 'Thomas Spence and the English Language', *Transactions of the Philological Society* (1974), 33–64, and Joan C. Beal, 'Out in Left Field: Spelling Reformers of the Eighteenth Century', *Transactions of the Philological Society*, 100 (2002), 5–23. I am grateful to John Halliwell for this reference.

[34] See, e.g., NLW 13097B, pp. 54–5: 'it is certain that Ten letters used in that manner are sufficient for all the writing in any Language whatever, and of expressing, or articulating all the sounds of which the vocal organs of man are capable; but the manner of writing them can only be communicated to a Bard who previously to his admission into the order, or to the higher degrees of discipleship, has made a most tremendously solemn vow that he will never divulge it, or any of the Bardic Secrets to any one whatever who has not previously made such a vow: hence it is that I am not able to say anything more at present on the subject.'

[35] See his comments in NLW 13104B, p. 123 (cited above, p. 17).

[36] Edward Davies, *Celtic Researches, on the Origin, Traditions & Language, of the Ancient Britons* (London, 1804), p. 273. For a full account of this episode, see Moira Dearnley, '"Mad Ned" and the "Smatter-Dasher": Iolo Morganwg and Edward "Celtic" Davies' in *Rattleskull Genius*, pp. 425–42.

> Such are the *omen sticks*, *tokens*, *lots*, or *letters*, of the *Bards*. Let us only recollect the source, and the origin, of these characters, as before developed: that they were, in truth, only delineations of the *symbolical sprigs*, or *Druidical tokens*, the tops of certain *trees*, and *plants*; – I think, it will be acknowledged, that even their countenance carries the lines of honesty, and marks their genuine descent.[37]

Davies's enthusiasm drew attention to the *coelbren*. A letter from his friend Theophilus Jones shortly after the publication of *Celtic Researches* urged caution: 'I fear you have been imposed upon by Owen as to the Coelbren y Beirdd. I am very much mistaken if that Alphabet is not the manufacture of Ned Williams, & himself.' A later letter teased him with 'Woods & woody writing'.[38] Iolo's response to the publication took the form of a spectacularly ill-judged letter to Davies's principal supporter, George Hardinge, pointing out the many errors of fact and judgement in the work and lamenting that Davies had not sought his advice. He accuses him with particular vehemence of 'astonishing mistakes' in his translation of *Coelbren y Beirdd*, as 'Bardic Lots, Magic Lots, Lots of Druidism' – and indeed makes such an issue of this apparently minor point that it is hard not to see it as a furious response to trespass on private property, an unconscious declaration of ownership.[39] Hardinge, by then no great admirer of Iolo, passed the letter on to Davies, who gradually came to realize that he had been trusting unreliable sources. In 1809 he published *The Mythology and Rites of the British Druids*, which (while defending his own theory of the survival of Welsh druidism into the Middle Ages) made very specific claims against Iolo and Pughe, suggesting that their version of bardism was little more than a cover for revolutionary sentiment and revealed 'marks of gross misrepresentation, if not of absolute forgery'.[40] These claims, of course, complicated the by now de rigueur defence of Welsh sources with which the book opens, and although he had the weight of Sharon Turner's thoughtful (and English) *Vindication of the Genuineness of the Ancient British Poems of Aneurin, Taliesin, Llywarch Hen, and Merdhin* (London, 1803) behind him, Davies's efforts to separate the genuine from the spurious were inevitably compromised by his own hobby-horsical tendencies, not to mention his reliance on the apparently safe material in the

[37] Davies, *Celtic Researches*, p. 272.

[38] Cardiff 3.104, Letter nos. 92–3, Theophilus Jones to Edward Davies, 11 March 1804. (Cited by Dearnley, '"Mad Ned"', p. 434) and Cardiff 3.104, Letter nos. 112–13, Theophilus Jones to Edward Davies, 18 September 1806 (Cited by Dearnley, '"Mad Ned"', p. 436).

[39] Cardiff 3.104, Letter no. 41, Iolo Morganwg to George Hardinge, 29 May 1804.

[40] Edward Davies, *The Mythology and Rites of the British Druids* (London, 1809), p. 73.

three volumes of the *Myvyrian*. On the matter of the tree-alphabet which had so delighted him in *Celtic Researches* he says very little indeed.[41]

The eccentricity of Davies's work made him an inadequate adversary against Iolo in the cause of scholarly truth, and did little, in the end, to provoke a closer critical examination of bardism; it is possible, too, that the earlier, and more enthusiastic, *Celtic Researches* had the greater influence.[42] Yet he and his circle were not the only sceptical voices, and even Iolo's friends and admirers wavered. As early as 1793 Walter Davies (Gwallter Mechain) had written:

> In Anglesea, they suppose Coelbren y Beirdd to be wholly invented by you . . . I have the vanity to suppose myself something capable of distinguishing plausibilities from Inconsistencies. No do not think me conceited, or else you will do me injustice. Coelbren y Beirdd, if genuine, gives you applause and credit for the preservation; and if spurious, (as generally imagined,) it is not derogatory to your genius, for upon my word (which is a great thing) whoever invented it, he was no fool. The stream that carries me away most, is, its peculiarity of construction to express the Sounds of our Language. I can't but admire it for that. And I think it too compleat to be of an ancient Date. No ancient Alphabets have such exquisite Symmetry in their Formation. Therefore, take the glory of the Invention to yourself. But yet I stand in equilibrio, there is something to be said both pro. and con. Put your finger to the Ballance, and turn the Scale in your next Letter.[43]

Whatever that next letter contained, it was not the truth, and Iolo's bardic alphabet long outlived its maker, flourishing well into the nineteenth century. Sceptical voices were raised at frequent intervals, but the *coelbren* proved too important to lose, and became a symbol of bardic and national enthusiasm, appearing on gravestones and monuments such as the inscribed circles of stones left to commemorate eisteddfodau. It was used as a decorative visual shorthand for 'Welshness' on journals, and even seems to have had some success in the form of 'traditional' wooden *peithynau*, as nineteenth-century would-be bards strove to prove themselves worthy of the name by practising the ancient craft.[44] Iolo's son Taliesin Williams (somewhat unfairly, since he still had uniquely privileged access to the manuscripts of its only begetter) would win a prize at the Abergavenny eisteddfod of 1838 for an essay on 'Henafiaeth ac Awdurdodiad *Coelbren y Beirdd*' ('The Antiquity and Authority of *Coelbren y Beirdd*').

[41] The few brief references to *coelbrenni* in the work are on pp. 43, 453 and 490, each time in connection with his idea of bardic lots or sortilege. It may be that he felt he had sufficiently demonstrated his case in *Celtic Researches*, but at least one of his contemporaries thought the point needed further discussion, and was curious to know if Davies still credited 'the Authenticity of Mr Owens *Bardic Lots*' (Cardiff 3.82, Henry Payne to Edward Davies, 31 January 1810). I am very grateful to Moira Dearnley for this information.

[42] The work would later have an electrifying effect on the poet Robert Graves, who used the idea of the tree alphabet for his *The White Goddess* (1960).

[43] NLW 21280E, Letter no. 72, Walter Davies (Gwallter Mechain) to Iolo Morganwg, 16 May 1793.

[44] The National Library of Wales holds at least four *peithynau* from the Victorian period; the *coelbren* continues to resonate in the recent work of the artist Mary Lloyd Jones.

Conclusion

Iolo's main defence against the taint of 'Macphersonic imposture' is, then, largely aligned to what one might loosely term the 'English' side of debate; or rather, bearing in mind Dafydd Moore's comments on this point ('any idea of a firm dichotomy in response between Scottish and English figures is a myth'), the side which theoretically espoused rationality, scepticism and demands for material proof.[45] In the *Myvyrian* drafts, Iolo versus Macpherson sounds suspiciously like a replay of the fight with Johnson, or of the confrontation more recently staged by Nick Groom in which Thomas Percy and his English minstrels define a textual literary tradition against the misty orality of Ossian.[46] Implicit in his defence of the Welsh tradition are arguments taken for granted by them – that a literary tradition requires literature, and a script in which to write and transmit it, that culture cannot improve and develop in societies reliant on oral tradition alone. He shares many of their prejudices, is rude about the Scots as a people, and displays (for a man so keen on words) a surprising lack of knowledge and curiosity about Scots Gaelic itself.

In this at least he reflects one effect of the *Ossian* debate on the scholars of Wales: a strenuous desire to conform, to authenticate oneself in terms acceptable and familiar to those who may otherwise judge you beyond the pale. There are elements of this response in Evan Evans's excessively cautious handling of his texts: in cases where the language is deemed too obscure, the *Specimens* offers a dignified silence as a mark of editorial good faith, in deliberate contrast to the easy dazzle of Macpherson's translations.[47] A later, more broadly cultural, instance would be the trauma inflicted by the 'Blue Books' reports of 1847, where an investigation into the education and behaviour of the rural Welsh-speaking labouring classes 'uncovered' a society riddled, by English Victorian standards, with immorality. Although the resulting indignation did help to fuel nationalist fervour, a major result of the insecurity induced by the reports was a determined conformity, expressed, in M. Wynn Thomas's phrase, as an 'anxious Britophilia'.[48] Such cases express positions familiar to postcolonial

[45] Moore, 'The Reception of *The Poems of Ossian* in England and Scotland', p. 30.

[46] Groom, *The Making of Percy's 'Reliques'*, pp. 61–105.

[47] See, e.g., pp. 51–2 (discussing the poems of Taliesin). In the 'Short Review', Iolo criticizes Evans for his timidity: 'it is therefore to be regretted that the Reverend Evan Evans did not . . . investigate and point out the various things which embarrasssed him, instead of assigning all the difficulties to the language' (*MAW*, I, pp. xviii–xix). Cf., in a later context, Sarah Higley's claim that notions of narrative coherence and structure derived from English scholarship affected how Welsh scholars both read and edited the early verse. *Between Languages: the Uncooperative Text in Early Welsh and Old English Nature Poetry* (University Park, Pa., 1992).

[48] M. Wynn Thomas, *Corresponding Cultures: The Two Literatures of Wales* (Cardiff, 1999), p. 120. On the so-called 'Treachery of the Blue Books', see Prys Morgan, 'From a Death to a View: The Hunt for the Welsh Past in the Romantic Period' in Hobsbawm and Ranger (eds.), *The Invention of Tradition*, pp. 92–8.

criticism – in, for example, the ambivalence of Welsh attitudes to its dominant neighbour, or in the 'mimicry' of a perceived Englishness – and there is arguably still much work to be done on the precise nature of the double-voicing that can be read into texts of different periods.[49] Perhaps what distinguishes Romantic-period Wales from its later Victorian self (or selves) is a particular tone, which is neither craven nor apologetic. The *Myvyrian* introduction in its many forms, despite its debt to English models, is wired with a terrific confidence and a conviction of the strength and beauty of the Welsh tradition, 'now slowly returning, by an advancing reformation, to its ancient purity'.[50] Nor, as we have seen, does it shun explicit criticism of Anglo-centred British scholarship or government. Indeed, the work as a whole is a valuable testament to the complexity of Wales's relationship with England at this point: a canon-forming text designed for the use of Welsh-speaking scholars, but presented – for approval, but also as a challenge – to an English readership.

But Iolo's response to the problems posed by the *Ossian* debate and its aftermath does more than reflect a particular moment in Welsh–English relations. His defence of Welsh sources also sharpened his understanding of the workings of a manuscript culture through time. He realized, for example, that manuscript copies as individual items have little strength on their own, and that it is only through the complex interplay of versions that chronologies may be established and originals glimpsed – if indeed they can be captured at all. One of the most persuasive aspects of his account of the Welsh manuscript tradition is his understanding of its fluidity, its accommodation of variation and change, its 'grey hairs and wrinkles' and other marks of human fallibility. What clearer account of the problems associated with the concept of an 'original' text could there be than this?

> The copy of a negligent or unskilful transcriber gets into the hands of one who detects its errors, and in his own way corrects them; in the hands of another person, such errors are corrected in a different manner; a third supplies the defect, on ideas of his own, very different, sometimes, from either of the others; so does a fourth, a tenth, and possibly a hundredth. Thus will copies, in a long succession of years, differ greatly from each other; and perhaps, every one of them in some things from all the others; and when time has left the original at a very remote distance, it becomes imperceptible, where no copy by the author, or of or near his age, can with any probability be discovered.[51]

[49] See Aaron and Williams (eds.), *Postcolonial Wales*.
[50] *MAW*, I, p. xxi.
[51] Ibid., I, p. xvii.

His success as a forger, as we have seen in the case of the Dafydd ap Gwilym poems, owes much to his ability to evoke phantom lines of transmission that he himself had woven into the existing pattern. He is, in a sense, deploying the very same 'succession of forgers . . . possessed of a secret' that he holds up ironically a few lines later to mock incredulous critics. And his readiness to urge upon his reader the complexity of the evidence is completely disarming: 'to vouch for the truth or correctness of everything in ancient mss is not walking the legal, the honest, the open highway of truth'.[52] Letters do not mean fixity; the truth is not rigid. In a manuscript culture, mistakes and revisions are proof of a thriving organic existence, and individually imperfect copies together testify to the essence of a text, to its authentic self.

'I learned the alphabet before I can well remember, by seeing my father inscribe grave-stones.'[53] Iolo spent his whole life carving letters, and it is not hard to see the mark of his trade in his emphasis on tangible written proof – an abundance of manuscripts, a carved wooden billet. There is, however, a quite different side to his response to the *Ossian* debate, one which runs in a curious, and at times perverse, counterpoint to the development of his ideas about the written word. This is his own bardic version of oral tradition.

[52] Ibid., II, p. xi.
[53] Williams: *PLP*, I, p. xv.

8

'Singing with a voice as bright as ever': Last Bards

> Fond impious man, think'st thou yon sanguine cloud,
> Rais'd by thy breath, has quench'd the orb of day?
> To-morrow he repairs the golden flood,
> And warms the nations with redoubled ray.
> Enough for me; with joy I see
> The diff'rent doom our fates assign.
> Be thine Despair, and sceptred Care,
> To triumph, and to die are mine.'
> He spoke, and headlong from the mountain's height,
> Deep in the roaring tide he plunged to endless night.[1]

Iolo's passion for the processes of textual transmission and for the technology of writing can be placed under the sign of his father, the stonemason who taught him his letters 'before I can well remember'. But, as we have seen, in another version of his life-story he claims rather to have learned to read from his mother's 'volume of *Songs*, intituled *The Vocal Miscellany*'.[2] His father gave him a craft, but it is Ann Matthew's 'agreeable' voice that lies behind his true vocation: 'and hence, I doubt not, my original turn for poetry.'

Coming from a culture with its own tradition of public bardic poetry, and one in which oral tradition still played a significant part, Iolo might be expected to have some sympathy for the complex interaction of the written and the oral in Macpherson's work. Alternatively, given his obsession with textual authority, it would not be surprising to hear him echoing Johnson's opinion that an oral literature which 'merely floated in the breath of the people' is completely incapable of improvement and therefore of attaining the higher forms of expression.[3] In fact, neither is the case. Iolo is as scathing about *Ossian*'s claims to oral-traditionary longevity as he is about the 'non-existent' Gaelic manuscript tradition, but he defends his own version of orality with characteristic energy. Iolo's model of bardic orality has received little, if any, notice in recent discussions of the subject, and yet it deserves attention both as a contribution to a concept which, in the latter half of the eighteenth century, was still very much in the making, and as a further response to the *Ossian* debate.

[1] Thomas Gray, *The Bard* (Strawberry Hill, 1757), III, stanza 3.
[2] Williams: *PLP*, I, p. xv.
[3] Johnson, *Journey to the Western Isles*, p. 268.

As Roberta Frank has shown in her lively guided tour of eighteenth-century 'types' of bard, scholarly versions of the native oral poet sprang up like mushrooms during this period, from Homer himself to the assorted skalds, bards and scops of Britain's multicultural past: the stereotypes of oral behaviour developed for one culture (the skaldic verse-makers of the Vikings, for example) informed and to some extent even 'created' others (the elusive Anglo-Saxon scop).[4] Literary and historical models blended irrevocably, and by the end of the eighteenth century the bard was a familiar, if sometimes rather indistinct, figure in the intellectual landscape. In Britain and Ireland the debate focused on the specific historical problem of how to describe and explain early 'dark age' culture, both for the crucial period before historical records begin and for the later period of sparse native sources and tantalizing glimpses in the works of classical writers. At a time of defining and consolidating Britishness it was of more than academic interest to establish a claim to the earliest layers of Britain's past, and the Celtic 'fringes' were fierce in competing for what Joseph F. Nagy has called 'aesthetic, if not political, primacy' over Anglo-Saxon culture.[5]

The notion of oral tradition itself developed significantly during Iolo's lifetime as a result of intermeshed debates about the nature of the original source in a number of critical fields. As Nicholas Hudson has shown, the concept of an unwritten body of tradition running parallel with a written body of doctrine was familiar to the Roman Catholic church (the term 'oral tradition' is almost exclusively used in this theological context before the eighteenth century); the Puritan notion of an 'Ancient Constitution' provided a secular, legal parallel.[6] Neither, however, goes much beyond the idea of a loose package of beliefs handed down as an unwritten tradition of law or as part of a practising faith. But from biblical studies, and in particular the lectures of Robert Lowth, came the idea of a primitive poetic (although not, at first, specifically oral) language, one abounding in metaphor and aphorism.[7] These rhetorical characteristics would be reinforced by ethnographical writings from the New World, as travellers and missionaries like the Jesuit Joseph François Lafitau revealed something of the power of speech and ceremony in complex, and unlettered, societies. By the end of the 1760s classical scholarship brought its own revelations in the lucid writings of Robert Wood, whose gentle tact in introducing the idea that the

[4] Roberta Frank, 'The Search for the Anglo-Saxon Oral Poet' in Donald Scragg (ed.), *Textual and Material Culture in Anglo-Saxon England: Thomas Northcote Toller and the Toller Memorial Lectures* (Cambridge, 2003), pp. 137–60.

[5] Joseph Falaky Nagy, 'Observations on the Ossianesque in Medieval Irish Literature and Modern Irish Folklore', *Journal of American Folklore*, 114, no. 454 (2001), 439.

[6] Nicholas Hudson, 'Oral Tradition: The Evolution of an Eighteenth-Century Concept' in S. J. Alvaro Ribeira and James G. Basker (eds.), *Tradition in Transition: Women Writers, Marginal Texts, and the Eighteenth-Century Canon* (Oxford, 1996), pp. 161–76.

[7] Robert Lowth, *De Sacra Poesi Hebræorum Prælectiones Academicæ* (Oxford, 1753); translated by G. Gregory, *Lectures on the Sacred Poetry of the Hebrews* (2 vols., London, 1787).

father of genius, Homer himself, was illiterate indicates the strangeness of this new conceptual territory to a readership for whom art and civilization were unthinkable without letters: 'We are not far removed from the age, when great statesmen, and profound politicians, did not know their alphabet. I mention this undoubted fact to lessen the Reader's astonishment at any insinuation, that Homer could neither read nor write.'[8] Wood's work took a generation to have much impact, and even then it was not in Britain but in Germany that F. A. Wolf and G. A. Heyne took up his ideas in earnest. Indeed, much-debated as the subject was, there was considerable resistance to the notion of purely unwritten art, and even more to unwritten history. As Nick Groom shows, Thomas Percy's *Minstrelsy*, collection of old ballads though it was, remained defiantly textual in both conception and execution; and even Joseph Ritson, who was interested enough to 'prick down' songs not to be found in black-letter texts or printed garlands, saw the process of remembering and transmitting traditional songs as one of inevitable corruption: 'Tradition, in short, is a species of alchemy which converts gold to lead.'[9] Much of the resistance, like much of the enthusiasm, was a reaction to *Ossian,* which, more than any other text of the time, pushed the concept of orality into the foreground of antiquarian and literary discussion: indeed, as Kristine Louise Haugen observes, 'except for Vico, whose writings were not known in northern Europe, no one had presented a detailed or extensive account of oral poetry at the time of Macpherson's publications'.[10] The direct and indirect influence of many of these ideas can be traced in Iolo's bardism, but it is undoubtedly as a response to the challenges of *Ossian* and the subsequent controversy that his version of oral tradition takes its peculiar shape.

Recent work on *Ossian* has tended to portray it as extravagantly oral from the outset, and to see the publication of *Temora* in 1763, with the shift in emphasis to written proof, as the crucial point in the debate with Johnson at which Macpherson's credibility foundered: 'If he had not talked unskilfully of *manuscripts*', noted Johnson acidly, 'he might have fought with oral tradition much longer.'[11] While broadly true, this oversimplifies matters. As Haugen

[8] Robert Wood, *An Essay on the Original Genius and Writings of Homer: With a Comparative View of the Ancient and Present State of the Troade* (London, 1775), p. 248. The work was first printed privately (a few copies only) in 1769.

[9] Groom, *The Making of Percy's 'Reliques'*; Joseph Ritson, *Scotish Songs* (2 vols., London, 1794), I, p. lxxxi. During the 1790s Ritson persuaded Iolo to note down several pieces for him. See Mary-Ann Constantine, 'Chasing Fragments: Iolo, Ritson and Robin Hood' in Sally Harper and Wyn Thomas (eds.), *Bearers of Song: Essays in Honour of Meredydd Evans and Phyllis Kinney* (Cardiff, 2007), pp. 51–7.

[10] Haugen, 'Ossian and the Invention of Textual History', 315.

[11] James Boswell, *Life of Johnson*, ed. G. B. Hill, rev. L. F. Powell (6 vols., Oxford, 1934–64), III, p. 310. For Ossian's orality, see Groom, *The Making of Percy's 'Reliques'*, pp. 75–92 (but note that the name does *not* mean '"mouthy" (from the Latin *os*, mouth)' (p. 76)); Trumpener, *Bardic Nationalism*, p. 75.

has shown, the initial presentation of the *Fragments* was rather more tentative, its preface noting simply that the poems had been transmitted through the care of the bards, 'some in manuscript, but more by oral tradition'.[12] Although by 1762 Macpherson appears to have settled for an Ossian who did not know of writing at all, the Dissertation preceding *Fingal* nevertheless stresses that the later transmission of the poem was similarly mixed ('the translator collected from tradition, and some manuscripts, all the poems in the following collection').[13] With so little precedent to guide them, it is unsurprising that at various points in the development of the *oeuvre* Macpherson and Blair seem to hold different views, or at least to offer different emphases, in their comments on the subject. On one level, Ossianic orality seems surprisingly inadequate – full of breaks in transmission: 'The Celtic nations . . . once the masters of Europe . . . are very little mentioned in history. They trusted their fame to tradition and the songs of their bards, which, by the vicissitude of human affairs, are long since lost.'[14] Being 'destitute of the use of letters, they themselves had no means of transmitting their history to posterity' – indeed, as the later *Introduction to the History of Great Britain and Ireland* puts it, they 'were remarkable for their aversion to the study of letters'.[15] The poems themselves are predicated on loss and interruption; voices cut across each other, narratives shift and break. Ossian's act of singing is all that is keeping the deeds of Fingal and Oscar in living memory, and since he is singing to his widowed daughter-in-law, and is himself the last of his race, the prospects of survival do not look very inviting. The uncertainty of early tradition is encapsulated in a line quoted by Hugh Blair: 'His words came only by halves to our ears; they were dark as the tales of other times, before the light of song arose.'[16] Although it was often perceived and discussed, not least by Macpherson himself, as a would-be northern epic, even the later Ossianic poetry revels in this lyrical effect of brokenness and fragmentation: for Groom, Ossian exhibits the 'linguistic symptoms of senile dementia', his repetitions 'like the murmuring delirium of a mind dissolving into mist'.[17]

And yet, set against this is the poems' own insistence that the songs, and the voices of the dead, will be heard in 'future times':

[12] *PO*, p. 5; see Haugen, 'Ossian and the Invention of Textual History'.

[13] *PO*, p. 51.

[14] From the Dissertation preceding *Fingal* (1762): *PO*, p. 43.

[15] From the Dissertation preceding *Temora* (1763): *PO*, p. 205; *Introduction*, p. 1.

[16] Blair, 'Critical Dissertation' in *PO*, p. 352 (from 'The War of Caros', *PO*, pp. 112–13).

[17] On the distractions of the 'epic' label, see Dafydd Moore, *Enlightenment and Romance in James Macpherson's 'The Poems of Ossian': Myth, Genre and Cultural Change* (Aldershot, 2003), pp. 21–41; on Ossianic dementia, Groom, *The Forger's Shadow*, pp. 132–9; and on fragmentation in the work and its dissemination, Mary-Ann Constantine and Gerald Porter, *Fragments and Meaning in Traditional Song* (Oxford, 2003), pp. 21–49.

> But lead me, O Malvina, to the sound of my woods, and the roar of my mountain streams. Let the chace be heard on Cona, that I may think on the days of other years. – And bring me the harp, o maid, that I may touch it when the light of my soul shall arise. – Be thou near, to learn the song; and future times shall hear of Ossian.
>
> The sons of the feeble hereafter will lift the voice on Cona, and looking up to the rocks, say 'Here Ossian dwelt'. They shall admire the chiefs of old, and the race that are no more: while we ride on our clouds, Malvina, on the wings of the roaring winds. Our voices shall be heard, at times, in the desart; and we shall sing on the winds of the rock.[18]

And of course Macpherson did collect songs, which did tell of heroes known from medieval Gaelic and Irish literature. Although educated in the classics-centred world of the Scottish Enlightenment, he was born and brought up in a culture that was still largely oral, and was well aware of the social mechanisms that had produced and preserved Gaelic poetry within the clan society. He was perfectly aware, too, of the systematic cultural destruction that followed in the wake of the 1745 Battle of Culloden (in which members of his family were involved); by the time he began collecting in 1759 the old clan society had been irrevocably fragmented.[19] His version of oral tradition is thus both lived experience and nostalgic reconstruction:

> There can be no doubt that these poems are to be ascribed to the Bards; a race of men well known to have continued throughout many ages in Ireland and the north of Scotland. Every chief or great man had in his family a Bard or poet, whose office it was to record in verse, the illustrious actions of that family . . . And tradition, in a country so free of intermixture with foreigners, and among a people so strongly attached to the memory of their ancestors, has preserved many of them in great measure incorrupted to this day.[20]

Citing analogous traditions among peoples whose laws and histories date from before the advent of written sources, such as the Greeks, the Incas of Peru and the ancient Germans ('The care they took to have the poems taught to their children, the uninterrupted custom of repeating them upon certain occasions, and the happy measure of the verse, served to preserve them for a long time uncorrupted'),[21] Macpherson stresses time and again that tradition can only be depended upon among a people 'free of intermixture with foreigners' – the

[18] From *Fingal* (1762): *PO*, p. 114.
[19] Stafford, *The Sublime Savage*, pp. 17–20.
[20] Preface to *Fragments* (probably ghostwritten by Blair): *PO*, p. 5.
[21] From *Fingal* (1762): *PO*, p. 50 (on the Germans).

last phrase crops up more than once.[22] Nor does he ignore the question of technique, arguing that the language itself is inherently suited to produce a concatenated (and hence easily memorable) form of chanted song: 'Each verse was so connected with those which preceded or followed it, that if one line had been remembered in a stanza, it was almost impossible to forget the rest.'[23]

In a manuscript draft, Iolo flatly denies that any of this amounts to a definite 'Tradition':

> Had we been told that the Bardic Arts of traditional memory (and those well specified) were still preserved in the Scots Highlands, we might have given ample credit to Mr Mackpherson, and a Welsh Bard to whom these arts are known would not have insisted on old MSS, well knowing Tradition once become public is able to retain its learning for many ages, and even less subject to perversion or interpolation than writings are, is more open to detection, but in Scotland we hear of no such thing.[24]

Though the claims for a third-century provenance were audacious, Ossian is not such an unusual figure in the late eighteenth-century bardic landscape, performing the expected duties of praise and memorial long known from classical sources; nor, clearly, does Macpherson neglect to give some account of the 'Bardic Arts of traditional memory'. To what, then, was Iolo objecting?

The Last Bard

Eighteenth-century Wales had a thriving oral culture. Literacy, it is true, was increasing rapidly, and printed materials – chapbooks, ballads, almanacs and sermons – were devoured at all levels of society.[25] Manuscripts, as we have seen, were copied assiduously, and not only by scholars, and by the end of the century Welsh-language journals were reaching out to new audiences. Iolo's stint running a bookshop in Cowbridge gave him some insight into the (often hilarious) literary tastes of his rural clientele. And yet, although Wales does not seem to have had a tradition of great narrative ballads like those from which Macpherson conjured his *Ossian*, songs, stories, proverbs and local traditions and dialects were still thoroughly part of everyday life, and as Iolo travelled the country on foot he noted many of them: 'I have rambled over all Wales with all my ears open to every local word, idiom, peculiarity of pronunciation,

[22] Preface to *Fragments* (1760): *PO*, p. 5; *Fingal* (1762): *PO*, p. 50; and *Temora* (1763): *PO*, p. 205.
[23] *PO*, p. 49.
[24] NLW 13089E, p. 431.
[25] See Geraint H. Jenkins, *Literature, Religion and Society in Wales, 1660–1730* (Cardiff, 1978), pp. 33–54.

of construction and have attended more than perhaps ever anyone did before to the language in every part of the principality.'[26] His thoughts on the dialects of Wales – sadly never published – were, as Richard Crowe has shown, ahead of his time, as was his interest in folk tradition, amply documented by G. J. Williams and others.[27] Indeed, given the extent to which the written collection of oral folklore is now seen by its very nature to be fraught with problems of authenticity, it is perhaps surprising to find that the scraps of song, observations on local customs and many of the traditional anecdotes that appear in Iolo's manuscripts are, as far as can be ascertained, relatively free of theorizing or romancing; some even show a perceptive awareness of performance and context.[28] His bardic orality, however, is altogether different.

The material on bardism published during Iolo's lifetime includes the lengthy introduction to William Owen's *Heroic Elegies and Other Pieces of Llywarç Hen* (London, 1792) and an important essay, plus various remarks in footnotes, in the second volume of *Poems, Lyric and Pastoral*. As we have seen, he was circulating bardic triads in manuscript amongst regular clients at Joseph Johnson's bookshop in the mid-1790s, many of which would subsequently appear in *The Myvyrian Archaiology of Wales*. His ideas can be further enriched by drafts, notes and comments from the letters and the unpublished manuscripts, many of them towards the never-completed 'History of the Bards'. Much more would appear after his death. From this material, itself complex and evolving, it is possible to pick out certain fairly consistent ideas about orality and its role in the perpetuation of bardic tradition.

Iolo is peculiar in that his native oral poet is neither a literary construct (whether traditional like the figure of Ossian, or contemporary like Gray's *The Bard*) nor a scholarly reconstruction like Percy's medieval minstrels or the Scandinavian skalds. He is in fact his own 'last bard', the almost sole inheritor of the line in Britain, a distinction he claimed to have obtained as a young man at a ceremony preserved by a handful of elderly poets in Glamorgan. The oral nature of this inheritance was made clear in the letter (signed 'J. D.' but almost certainly by Iolo himself) published in the *Gentleman's Magazine* in 1789:

[26] NLW 13222C, pp. 161–4, Iolo Morganwg to William Owen Pughe, 15 February 1803.

[27] For dialect, see Crowe, 'Diddordebau Ieithyddol', pp. 237–301, and idem, 'Iolo Morganwg and the Dialects of Welsh' in *Rattleskull Genius*, pp. 315–31. For Iolo and folklore, see G. J. Williams, *Edward Lhuyd ac Iolo Morganwg: Agweddau ar Hanes Astudiaethau Gwerin yng Nghymru* (Caerdydd, 1964) and Williams: *IM*, pp. 35–72.

[28] Huws, 'Iolo Morganwg and Traditional Music'; Mary-Ann Constantine, 'Songs and Stones: Iolo Morganwg (1747–1826), Mason and Bard', forthcoming in *The Eighteenth Century: Theory and Interpretation*, 47, nos. 2–3 (2006), 231–49. For folklore and authenticity and the transition from orality to literacy, see Regina Bendix, *In Search of Authenticity: The Formation of Folklore Studies* (London, 1997); Dave Harker, *Fakesong: The Manufacture of British 'Folksong', 1700 to the Present Day* (Milton Keynes, 1985); Susan Stewart, 'Scandals of the Ballad' in eadem, *Crimes of Writing: Problems in the Containment of Representation* (Oxford, 1991), pp. 102–31.

> About the age of twenty he was admitted a *Bard* in the ancient manner; a custom still retained in Glamorgan, but, I believe, in no other part of Wales. This is by being discipled to a regular Bard, and afterwards admitted into the order in a Congress of Bards assembled for that purpose, after undergoing proper examination; and being also initiated into their Mysteries, as they are pleased to call them. Besides Edward Williams, there is, I believe, now remaining only one regular Bard in Glamorgan, or in the world: this is the Rev. Mr *Edward Evans* [*sic*], of *Aberdare*, a Dissenting Minister. These two persons are the only legitimate descendants of the so long-celebrated *Ancient British Bards*; at least they will allow no others this honourable title. Not but that there are excellent poets in considerable numbers in many other parts of Wales, who write both in Welsh and in English; but they have never been qualified as above: and what knowledge they have of the ancient laws and rules of Welsh poetry they derive from books.[29]

As G. J. Williams remarks, this is a thoroughly romanticized account of his education amongst Glamorgan's local poets.[30] The formative reading, book-borrowing and manuscript-copying described in his autobiographical writings are here transmuted into 'Mysteries' and a deprecating reference to those whose knowledge of poetry is merely 'derive[d] from books'.

Iolo's 'lastness' confers authority (it would, after all, have been difficult for most readers of the *Gentleman's Magazine* to question Mr Edward Evan of Aberdare as to the legitimacy of these claims)[31] and was never intended to signal the death of a tradition. Indeed, it is hard not to be struck by the lack of morbid nostalgia in bardism, given the overwhelming prevalence of the mood elsewhere. Even the obligatory negotiation of the legend of Edward I's massacre of the Welsh bards, the subject of Gray's poem and an episode of profound concern to many eighteenth-century accounts of Welsh literary history, is belligerently undefeatist:

> *Edward the Bardicide*, surnamed *Longshanks*, had caused many of the *Bards* to be massacred, and all were *severely restricted in the exercise of their ancient functions*. They were *Sons of Truth and Liberty*, and of course offensive to that age of *tyranny* and *superstition*; but the *Welsh* would not suffer them to be exterminated.[32]

[29] *Gentleman's Magazine*, LIX, part 2 (1789), 976–7.

[30] Williams: *IM*, pp. 465–6.

[31] Edward Evan[s], one of the Glamorgan 'Grammarians', died in 1798; Iolo has an account of his life in NLW 13159A, pp. 142–4. See R. T. Jenkins, 'Bardd a'i Gefndir', *THSC* (1946–7), 97–149.

[32] Williams: *PLP*, II, p. 223. Evan Evans's 'Paraphrase of the 137th Psalm' first appeared in the 1862 version of his *Specimens*; see Sarah Prescott, '"Gray's Pale Spectre"', and Trumpener, *Bardic Nationalism*, pp. 3–10. Evans, whose own work was a source for Gray, also corresponded with Percy on the subject in 1761. See Lewis (ed.), *Correspondence*, pp. 5, 11.

In a thoughtful analysis of Evan Evans's earlier treatment of the legend, Sarah Prescott shows how English and Welsh representations of the massacre legend influenced each other: Gray's ode of 1757 (still often used by literary critics today as a shorthand for a 'Welsh' perspective) was indeed much admired in Wales, and even to some degree 'internalized',[33] but it naturally posed problems for those who saw themselves as writing within a tradition that had *not* committed cultural suicide in a last gasp of defiance in the Middle Ages. What Katie Trumpener has called 'bardic nationalism' – the use made of the bard as a figure of resistance in the construction of Irish, Scottish and Welsh identities – is at odds with the English, and, increasingly, Romantic, image of the bard as a lone individual, since it draws inevitably on the historically grounded (and indeed, still just about visible) role of the poet as 'the mouthpiece for a whole society, articulating its values, chronicling its history' – if not, necessarily, 'mourning the inconsolable tragedy of its collapse'.[34] As Prescott shows, Evans's posthumously published 'Paraphrase of the 137th Psalm, Alluding to the Captivity and Treatment of the Welsh Bards by King Edward I' enters into a subtle dialogue with Gray to resist the notion of cultural annihilation; Iolo's tone, in radical 1790s style, is more polemic, and clearly owes much to a reinvigorated sense of opposition to the 'tyranny' of his own times: 'bardic nationalism' here joins forces with British radical resistance.[35] This tone can hardly be attributed to any inherent optimism in native Welsh literature: the earliest surviving poetry, the 'Gododdin', is a litany of dead warriors defeated by the English Northumbrians; Llywarch Hen, crippled with age, mourns a dynasty of lost sons; some centuries later, Gruffudd ab yr Ynad Coch would lament for a country devastated by the death of Llywelyn ap Gruffudd, the Last Prince. Indeed, the keynotes of elegy and loss – the ruined halls and nettle-covered hearths of Rheged[36] – would, with little or no adaptation, have been so perfectly in resonance with the melancholy, extinction-obsessed productions of the 'age of degeneracy' described by Fiona Stafford that one can only marvel

[33] For the localization of Gray's poem as part of the north Wales 'tourist trail', see Morgan, *The Eighteenth-Century Renaissance*, pp. 120–1; a printed proclamation for the midsummer Gorsedd in 1798 announced a prize for the 'Best Translation, into Welsh, of Gray's Ode – The Bard' (NLW 21282E, no. 325a).

[34] Trumpener, *Bardic Nationalism*, p. 6; the 'tragedy of collapse' works better in the Ossianic context than for Wales.

[35] 'We (the bards of Glamorgan) have been as severly persecuted by church and kingists as our glorious predecessors were by Edward the Bardicide', NLW 13221E, pp. 53–4, Iolo Morganwg to William Owen Pughe, 12 May 1798. It appears that 'some of the wilder democrats in London-Welsh circles found it hard to resist the temptation to urinate on Edward I's grave at Westminster'. Geraint H. Jenkins, 'Historical Writing in the Eighteenth Century' in Branwen Jarvis (ed.), *A Guide to Welsh Literature, c.1700–1800* (Cardiff, 2000), pp. 34–5; cited in Prescott, '"Gray's Pale Spectre"'.

[36] 'Aelwyd Rheged' in Jenny Rowland (ed.), *Early Welsh Saga Poetry* (Cambridge, 1990), pp. 426–8; translated by Tony Conran, *Welsh Verse* (2nd edn., Bridgend, 1986), pp. 130–2.

again at the missed opportunities for translation at this period.[37] A generation on from Gray, Evans and Macpherson, Iolo's tradition is all continuity: a handed-down flame of truth which boldly refutes Gray's pessimistic 'dying leap into endless night'. The bards, though weakened, survive their persecution at the hands of Edward I (not to mention centuries of misguided Catholic 'fable and superstition')[38] to bring their vital knowledge unsullied into the present.

Iolo's personal investment in the tradition gives his bardism a markedly performative quality. The Gorsedd, with its laying out of stones in a circle and its ceremonial sheathing of the sword, is centred on public utterance, on proclamation: what Iolo calls the 'Voice Conventional' is at the heart of the system. The power of the spoken word in the Gorsedd is revealed in the elaborately bureaucratic description of 'Bardism' published in 1792, which explains the various times and places at which proceedings must be announced, reveals the mottoes of the different regional 'Chairs', and outlines the ceremony itself.[39] More forcefully than this, however, in a section pondering the legal niceties of perpetuating the system during periods of dwindling membership, the spoken word has the power to summon bardism itself back into existence, should events ever conspire to render it 'dormant'. A single surviving bard might under such circumstances act 'arbitrarily' (having none of the usual channels for proclamation available) to revive the entire process:

> The arbitrary acts of a Bard, such as admission of an Ovydd, or any thing else, were done in consequence of a supposed, or implied decision of the Bards at a Gorsedd, existing in a necessary fiction to sanction an arbitrary act not otherwise allowed. In this fiction they always exist; they may be visible,[40] but cannot be virtually extinct; for the utility, and principles of their institution exist in nature. That being the case, the officiating agents of those principles are rather dormant than extinct; and to be called into action by proclamation.[41]

This 'necessary fiction' makes genuine 'lastness' impossible, since the system itself is always putatively present in nature, waiting to be summoned back into existence.

Iolo's bardic oral tradition begins, not in the social compact of poet and patron, but in religion: 'Bard' and 'Druid' were for him (as for Pezron and others) one and the same, aspects of the same function. Macpherson, much to

[37] Fiona Stafford, *The Last of the Race: The Growth of a Myth from Milton to Darwin* (Oxford, 1994), pp. 83–108; for 'an age prone to degeneracy', see Adam Ferguson's *Essay on the History of Civil Society* (Edinburgh, 1767), p. 394.

[38] Williams: *PLP*, II, p. 223.

[39] 'Bardism' in Owen, *Heroic Elegies*, pp. xxi–lxxx.

[40] 'Visibly' would make more sense here.

[41] Owen, *Heroic Elegies*, p. xlv.

his annoyance, had explicitly broken all connection between Druids and bards, depicting the former as a power-greedy priesthood before wiping them out altogether. Ossian himself lives in a curious kind of interstitial period, after the paganism of the Druids (quashed by his father Fingal) but before the arrival of Christianity: spirituality is limited to the ghosts of ancestors riding on the clouds. Iolo berates Macpherson for his 'bungling' in separating the two ('none could be a Druid without being a Bard and being either of these was the other of course and that unavoidably'), before adding, somewhat ominously, 'he knew not that there existed real Bards of the ancient uninterrupted succession in Britain whose testimony would one day arise against him' and suggesting for good measure that he be pilloried as a 'perjuror of intentional deceit'.[42] The theology so conspicuously lacking in *Ossian* is central to the bardic vision, in which the Druids, inheritors à la Stukeley of the true patriarchal religion, become the natural channel for a faith based on worship of the One God.[43] As such they have no problem in accepting Christianity: indeed, Iolo's Druids inevitably become not merely Christian but distinctly Unitarian in outlook.[44] Their steadfast commitment to oral tradition, even after the advent of letters, brings the primitive patriarchal religion down through the misguided 'error' of the Middle Ages to a newly enlightened period of civilized modernity. The imaginative power of that link between the very distant past and the present is palpable in a notebook entry Iolo made during a visit to the Rollright stone circle in the Cotswolds in 1802. Here, amid measurements and observations on the quality of the stone, he experiences a powerful and obviously religious connection to the past, but also comments on the disjuncture necessarily suffered by a stone circle in England. Cut off from its supposedly 'original' linguistic community, it has lost its ability to signify in the present:

> I was impressed with ideas of seriousness and drew a comparison between the modern idolatry of three Gods and the pure primeval religion of only one God for whose worship this place was once a temple open to the surrounding immensity of space of which there is not a single point uninhabited by the great father of all, the proper object of worship. In a field adjoining to the north stands a single stone 9 feet high nearly 6 wide & 2 thick called the Kingstone & the old King. And in the field next to it on the south are 3 stones about 6 or 7 feet high laying as it were their heads together, called the three whispering knights. Many circles in Wales larger than this.

[42] NLW 13091E, p. 300; see also NLW 13144A, p. 416.

[43] See Ronald Hutton, 'William Stukeley's Religion', *Antiquaries Journal*, 85 (2005), 381–94. I am grateful to the author for this reference. Iolo and Stukeley have much in common, though many of the similarities in their thought would have been masked by the latter's conversion to Anglicanism and the revision of his earlier theories in favour of the Trinity. Iolo's comments on his work tend to be derogatory.

[44] On Iolo's Unitarianism and the centrality of religious belief to the Gorsedd, see D. Elwyn J. Davies, 'Astudiaeth o Feddwl a Chyfraniad Iolo Morganwg fel Rhesymolwr ac Undodwr' (unpublished University of Wales Ph.D. thesis, 1975).

> No tradition whatever remains of the occasion or use of this circle. Where ancient languages are lost the knowledge and traditions contained in them sink with them into oblivion.[45]

Language is the key to continuity. Just as Macpherson stressed that orality could only operate effectively in a society 'free of intermixture with foreigners', so Iolo's bardism depends on the tenacious purity of Welsh, fixed and perfected (according to Pezron) some 2,000 years previously, to carry its truths unchanged across the centuries. His writings on this subject are abundant. The language is figured as both precocious in its maturity and copiously self-fertile:

> Hence it is that when the modern or living languages of all the other countries in Europe were like the newly litter'd cubs of the bear in their unlicked deformity yet unable to engage in or attempt anything of literature, the Welsh manufacturing its own materials produced for itself a wealth of words and phrases, a power of expression unknown to any modern language in Europe.[46]

'Surely', as he put it more bluntly elsewhere, 'the language that has within itself the most ample stores and resources on all occasions is not so barbarous as that which begs borrows and steals from all others.'[47] Such comments are in a long scholarly tradition of extolling the purity and inherent potential of Welsh, a tradition characterized by 'an undeniable spirit of confidence, even swagger',[48] and celebrated in such uplifting titles as John Walters's 1771 *Dissertation on the Welsh Language, pointing out it's Antiquity, Copiousness, Grammatical Perfection* (Cowbridge).[49] From other writings in his manuscripts it is clear that Iolo understood perfectly well how words change their meanings over time, and that Welsh had borrowed from Latin and French and continued to borrow from 'barbarous' English: but the lexicographical emphasis of the time was on restoring purity and on the creation of new words derived from Welsh roots. As Richard Crowe put it nicely, for Iolo Welsh was an 'ystorfa o bosibiliadau ieithyddol' (storehouse of linguistic possibilities),[50] with all necessary words and concepts potentially present. Language was approached not as a collection of words currently or formerly used in speech and writing, but 'fel cyfanswm o

[45] NLW 13174A (notes made during a journey from London to Merthyr, May–June 1802), pp. 5–7. For Stukeley, too, 'the unbroken and repetitive figure of a circle was "the most expressive of the nature of the deity, without beginning or end"' (Hutton, 'William Stukeley's Religion', p. 385.)

[46] NLW 13120B, p. 182.

[47] NLW 13089E, p. 303.

[48] Morgan, *The Eighteenth-Century Renaissance*, p. 81.

[49] A work, in the words of Prys Morgan, 'smarting with inferiority complex, shrill with boastfulness' (ibid., p. 72); for further detailed discussion of native scholarly attitudes to Welsh, see Davies, *Adfeilion Babel*.

[50] Crowe, 'Diddordebau Ieithyddol', p. 303.

eiriau potensial y gellid eu llunio' (as the sum total of possible words that could ever be devised).[51] By a clever suspension of the historical process, this potential could be retrospectively applied. As we saw in the case of the Dafydd ap Gwilym poems, Iolo differed from his fellow word-makers in his attempts to legitimize his creations by attesting their presence in ancient sources; the parallels with the 'necessary fiction' of an immanent bardic system, potentially summonable into existence at any time, are obvious. The survival and revival of Welsh in Iolo's lifetime – the efforts of the literary societies, the industriousness of lexicographers – must go some way towards explaining why Iolo, as a 'last bard', is so untrue to type.

'In the literature of the last bard', notes Stafford, 'there is no real attempt to cross the boundary between the primitive and the civilized, and the bard must remain with his race, preserved at an earlier stage of society.'[52] Iolo's passionate belief in the continuity of the Welsh language dissolved that boundary, and many others. A breathtakingly lyrical note from the manuscripts, possibly written in old age, captures the contradiction at the heart of his vision of Welsh. In an unusually Blakean conflation of biblical and personal mythology he insists that the fertile and copious language, which has lived through improbably vast tracts of time, is also perfect, unchanging:

> Iaith Gymraeg, yn ei llawn dyfiant cyn amser Inachus, (yn ei chof yn ymgadwyno damweiniau'r Byd er awr y floedd ai dug i fodoleb) yn cofio llong Nefydd Naf Neifion, yn cofio'r Greadigaeth, yn cofio ei hun yn gwlad yr Haf Deffrobani, yn cofio ei hun yn y lle y mae Constantinoblis yn awr, yn cofio ei phlant yn Llychlyn amser Urb ab Erin – wedi gweld ymerodraethau Cynteifion a mwyaf er hynny hyd yr awr hon a fu yn y Byd. Brenhinaeth Nemrwth Gawr – y Groegiaid, Rhufeiniaid, Rhyfain Babaidd, Siarlymaen, y Sawdeniaid, Diwygiad – wedi cadw gafael cadarn ar y ffydd yng Nghrist a gafodd ag a garodd er amser Pawl, Ilid a Bran Fendigaid – yn cofio ei hen fryddoniaid Beirdd Derwyddon – Prydain, Dyfnwal. Tydain Alawn Gwron, Hennydd ap Hu Lawnwaith, a Hu gadarn gydag aradr a Chan a Choelbren i Ynys Prydain, gwelodd awr geni mawredd mwyaf a fu erioed, hyd yr awr gwelodd awr angau miloedd o y hi ei hunan er hynny yn fyw fyth, ac yn ei blodau, heb un crychyn henain ar ei thalcun, heb un blewyn gwynn ar ei phenn, yn ymiachau oi holl ddolurau, yn canu mor loyw ei llafar ag erioed. – Dinas Cedyrn tyrrau beilchion, muriau ar ymgais cyrchu uchelderau'r nef wedi malurio yn un allwch y llawr. Cestyll gorthrymder gydag ei perchenogion, dim ond rhyw ychydigion o'u hesgyrn bregis yn ymddangos Beirdd Morganwg yn cynnal cof am y cwbl. Bydd fyw i weled y Byd yn bwrw ymaith ei holl Lwrwd ai fudreddi, ag i dderchafu Can Gorfoledd, Amseroedd a pheth gwell yn rai ddidranc a hithau yn un o'r Anfarwolion!!!
>
> Poed felly bo.[53]

[51] Ibid., p. 30.
[52] Stafford, *The Last of the Race*, p. 93.
[53] NLW 13120B, p. 393.

> (The Welsh language, grown to her full strength before the time of Inachus, (holds locked in her memory the events of the World since the hour of the cry that brought her into existence) remembers the ship of Nefydd Naf Neifion, remembers the Creation, remembers being in the Summer Land of the Deffrobani, remembers herself where Constantinople lies now, remembers her children in Llychlyn at the time of Urb ab Erin – has seen the first and greatest empires to this day that have been in the world. The kingship of Nimrod the Giant: the Greeks, the Romans, Holy Roman Empire, Charlemagne, the Sultans, the Reformation – has kept the same firm grasp on the faith in Christ that she has had and loved since the time of Paul, Ilid and Blessed Bran – remembers her old British Druid Bards – Prydain, Dyfnwal, Tydain, Alawn, Gwron, Hennydd ap Hu Lawnwaith, and Hu Gadarn [who came] with Plough and Song and Alphabet to the Island of Britain, she saw the hour of the birth of the greatest greatness that ever was, saw the hour of the death of thousands; despite this, is still alive, and blossoming, without a single wrinkle of age on her brow, without a single white hair on her head, healed of all her hurts, singing with a voice as bright as ever – The towers of the Strong Fortress, walls that tried to reach the heights of heaven lie crumbled in a heap on the ground. Castles of oppression lie with their owners, only fragments of their brittle bones showing: the Bards of Glamorgan retain the memory of all this. She will live to see the World throw off all its filth and corruption, and to raise the Song of Contentment, of Time and the Undying ones and she herself one of the Immortals!!!
>
> Let it be thus.)

In 1809 William Blake exhibited his now lost picture of 'The Ancient Britons', a work which, in size and ambition, seems to have been 'something of a summation of his artistic and metaphysical beliefs'.[54] It was composed around a translation of a triad supplied, in the words of Robert Southey (whose vocabulary for describing his Welsh acquaintances seems decidedly restricted) 'by that good simple-hearted, Welsh-headed man, William Owen, whose memory is the great storehouse of all Cymric tradition and lore of every kind'.[55] In the detailed *Descriptive Catalogue* which accompanied the exhibition, Blake's Britons are 'naked civilized men, learned, studious, abstruse in thought and contemplation',[56] who lived in the fifth century in the mountains of Wales. But, as with Iolo's Welsh language, they are not confined to the past. Blake, after all, is the ultimate visionary-antiquarian, and dissolves boundaries like no one else:

> they are there now, Gray saw them in the person of his Bard on Snowdon; there they dwell in naked simplicity; happy is he who can see and converse with them above the shadows of generation and death.[57]

[54] Smiles, *The Image of Antiquity*, p. 73.
[55] Cited in ibid.
[56] William Blake, *A Descriptive Catalogue: 1809* (Oxford, 1990), p. 39.
[57] Ibid., p. 42; also cited in Smiles, *The Image of Antiquity*, p. 74.

9

The Voice Conventional

> In verse knowledge may be conveyed along an unlettered path (if I may use such expressions) from one person to another and to very great numbers, from one place to another however distant, from one age to another even to very remote futurity.[1]

Iolo's Druid-bards are not the secretive priesthood of earlier antiquarians like William Stukeley or Henry Rowlands, or even of his contemporary and hated rival, the 'Harper to the Prince', Edward Jones. Rather than 'keeping their mysterious knowledge from the contemplation of the vulgar',[2] they are an active, and even democratic, group of instructors-of-the-people: 'the literal meaning of the word is, *one that maketh conspicuous*; and the idea intended to be conveyed is, a *Teacher*, or *Philosopher*.'[3] Hence the need for these priests to be poets: poetry was the medium of their message. Their wisdom is pedagogic, designed for widespread use: 'all are capable of learning a song, even the most illiterate.'[4] Its evangelical quality is highlighted in a bold comparison:

> my suggestions are highly countenanced by the example and practice of him *who spake as never man did*, whose *Sermon on the Mount* is a set [of] Aphorisms very much like those of the *Bards of Britain*, and who *wrote no book*, but trusted all his divine maxims to the care of *Orality*.[5]

– an observation which, elsewhere, is extended to include the Old Testament ('I can not help thinking that the Scripture Patriarchs had such a Scientific Tradition to which we owe the accounts of the Creation, the Flood, the book of Job and many things beside').[6] Besides the biblical precedent there were, as Macpherson, Wood and others had found, further useful parallels to be gained from the New World. An extract from Iolo's manuscripts, probably made during his 'Madoc' period in the early 1790s, summarizes or copies from a typical traveller's account:

[1] NLW 13108B, p. 3.
[2] Edward Jones, *Musical and Poetical Relicks of the Welsh Bards* (London, 1784), p. 2.
[3] Owen, *Heroic Elegies*, p. xxv.
[4] NLW 13089E, pp. 450–1.
[5] Williams, *PLP*, II, p. 225.
[6] NLW 13103B, p. 108.

> young men and women are taught by those Matrons and Chiefs to recite them [their traditions]. On numerous enquiries he found that all who related or recited them always agreed very punctually in the numbers of the years of their several Aeras, from which they date generally the times or years since events happened, or distinguished persons lived, in several instances found that they amounted to more than a thousand . . . from these Traditions he believed that an interesting Ancient History of North America might be compiled, and which might be in a great degree be depended upon and fairly admitted to be in the main true.[7]

Although the last sentence betrays some anxiety in its phrasing, this is nothing less than contemporary external corroboration of a reliable oral history stretching far back in time. Reliability, for Iolo, was dependent on technique, the use of song and 'aphorisms of morality in very concise, strong and luminous language' which could be readily committed to memory.[8] The transmission of ideas is thus intimately connected to form, which becomes inseparable from meaning:

> Of all the Aphoristical forms, used by the *Bards*, the TRIAD is the most common; it is short and simple; it is constructed on fixed and unalterable principles; the relations, resemblances and connexions, of its parts to and with each other, and an object or idea wherein all are centred, render it the most useful of any.[9]

Although it goes much further, this is not unlike Macpherson's declaration that the intricate concatenations of Gaelic verse make it 'almost impossible to forget the rest'.

Iolo's introduction to the sequences of triads published at the end of his *Poems, Lyric and Pastoral* in 1794 begins with an indignant response to John Pinkerton, the 'Critical Reviewer' who, reviewing the *Llywarch Hen* volume, had used the words 'lax and weak' in a discussion of the triads.[10] Mistakenly assuming that 'Goth' Pinkerton was referring to the form itself (he was actually criticizing the scholarship), Iolo points out that the triad form is the very opposite of lax, since 'too great closeness, brevity and compression are its great defects': he then tests his famous (and invented) triad on the nature of poetic genius against one of Samuel Johnson's aphorisms on the same subject, and finds to his satisfaction that the former comes off best ('O JOHNSON,

[7] NLW 13123B, p. 57; cf. NLW 13107B, p. 37, an extract from Percy's *Reliques* (III, p. x): 'The first attempts at Composition among all barbarous nations are ever found to be in Poetry and Song. The praises of their Gods, and the achievements of their Heroes, are usually chanted at their festival meetings. These are the first rudiments of history. It is in this manner that the savages of North America preserve the memory of past events; and the same method is known to have prevailed among our Saxon ancestors, before they quitted their German forests.'

[8] NLW 13108B, p. 3.

[9] Williams: *PLP*, II, p. 225.

[10] *Critical Review*, IX (October, 1793), 169–70.

hide thy diminished head! and thou, *Critical Reviewer* (*aut Pinkerton, aut Diabolus*), in calling this a weak production, what a weak *vermicule* doest thou appear!').[11] Although the triads in *Poems, Lyric and Pastoral* are all his own work, the form was genuinely used within Welsh literary tradition from an early period, and collections of them in various manuscripts from the Middle Ages onwards operated as mnemonic systems for cataloguing information relating to legendary, historical, legal or poetic tradition. Heroes, incidents, animals would be grouped together in threes, so that their stories could be readily recalled, often for allusive use in poetry:

> Three Fortunate Princes of the Island of Britain: Owain son of Urien, Rhun son of Maelgwn, Rhufawn the Radiant son of Dewrarth Wledig.[12]

Since many of these triads had long since lost their narrative context, they provided tempting material (and had done so for many antiquarians before Iolo) with which to reconstruct the early Welsh past. Iolo's triads, which he manufactured by the score, range across the different types with practised ease, nudging tradition in the directions he wanted it to go. Those of the famous 'Third Series', published in the final volume of *The Myvyrian Archaiology*, are his reworkings of an earlier genuine manuscript collection largely concerned with the early history of Britain. It is here that many of the evocative characters of Iolo's 'personal mythology', transformed from obscure references into the founders and benefactors of the Welsh nation, assume the characteristics by which they were best known in the nineteenth century: Hu Gadarn, the 'culture hero' and ploughman-king who first taught the Welsh their system of vocal song; the wise ruler Prydain fab Aedd; the bards Plennydd, Alawn and Gwron.[13] The 'Moelmutian' triads use legal language to evoke an ideal early British society, a kind of Golden Age, under the legendary leader Dyfnwal Moelmud: an essay in the manuscripts, scattered with typical cautious comments on the possibility of later additions, extrapolates an entire world from these texts.[14] Thus, instead of simply providing his country with an epic, Iolo, often working on speculative hints from early scholars, exploited the narrative potential inherent in the allusive, condensed lists to weave what Bromwich calls 'an elaborate verbal spider's web' of pseudo-history around his sources; it was one

[11] Williams: *PLP*, II, p. 218.

[12] Rachel Bromwich (ed.), *Trioedd Ynys Prydein: The Triads of the Island of Britain* (3rd edn., Cardiff, 2006), p. 8.

[13] For a detailed account of Iolo's manipulation of the traditional triads, see Rachel Bromwich, '*Trioedd Ynys Prydain' in Welsh Literature and Scholarship* (Cardiff, 1969); see also A. C. Rejhon, 'Hu Gadarn: Folklore and Fabrication' in Patrick K. Ford (ed.), *Celtic Folklore and Christianity: Studies in Memory of William W. Heist* (Santa Barbara, Calif., 1983), pp. 201–12.

[14] NLW 13088B, pp. 63–78. Compare the similar legal orientation of the early nineteenth-century Czech 'Manuscript of Zelená Hora', which also aimed to show 'the wisdom and peaceableness of early Slavonic social organization' (Evans, '"The Manuscripts"', p. 58).

from which it took Wales a long time to pull itself free.[15] The triads published earlier in Owen's *Heroic Elegies* and in *Poems, Lyric and Pastoral*, less tied to any original source, tend to be more abstract. Among the most influential outside Wales were the triads devoted to matters of theology, nuggets of bardic wisdom which many later historians and antiquarians found irresistible:

> All animated Beings are subject to three Necessities: *a beginning* in the *Great Deep* (lowest point of existence), *Progression* in the *Circle of Inchöation*, and *Plenitude* in Heaven, or the *Circle of Felicity*; without these things nothing can possibly exist but GOD.[16]

The nineteenth-century Swiss linguist Adolphe Pictet, earnestly revisiting these pieces with Kant in one hand and Leibnitz in the other, would conclude that the ancient Celts had indeed evolved, and tenaciously preserved, a moral philosophy of undreamed-of sophistication.[17]

Support for Iolo's assertion that the British druidic religion was entirely compatible with (and indeed a precursor of) Christianity appears in *Trioedd Pawl*, or 'Triads of Paul', a selection of which appeared in *Poems, Lyric and Pastoral.*[18] In an unpublished essay Iolo debates at length the propriety or otherwise of attributing the verses to St Paul himself.[19] He begins by reviewing the various channels through which the words of Paul might have reached the Ancient Britons, the most radical of which being that St Paul himself was the first apostle to Britain (a theory not of Iolo's invention, but to which his forgeries added some useful 'native' evidence).[20] Astutely realizing that 'Christianity could be orally, speedily, and extensively taught by Bardic verse and aphorisms and much more so than could be done in writing',[21] Paul had availed himself

[15] Bromwich, *'Trioedd Ynys Prydain' in Welsh Literature and Scholarship*, p. 13.

[16] Williams: *PLP*, II, p. 241.

[17] Adophe Pictet, *Le Mystère des Bardes de l'Ile de Bretagne ou la Doctrine des Bardes Gallois du Moyen Age Sur Dieu, la vie Future et la transmigration des Ames* (Geneva, 1856).

[18] Williams: *PLP*, II, pp. 251–4. John Williams added more of 'Paul's Triads', all from Iolo's manuscripts, in the first volume of *Barddas* (Llandovery, 1862), pp. 290–344; he summarizes part of Iolo's unpublished essay on the triads in a footnote on pp. 290–1.

[19] NLW 13119B, pp. 263–74, 287–93. Some of the strategies deployed in the essay are discussed below, pp. 203–07.

[20] The theory, which supported Protestant claims to a Christianity independent of the influence of Rome, appears in earlier writers such as Parker, Camden, Speed and Henry Rowlands; it was used by Thomas Burgess, Bishop of St David's, in his pamphlet *Christ, and not Saint Peter, the Rock of the Christian Church; and St Paul, the Founder of the Church in Britain* (Carmarthen, 1812) to urge the Government against granting further privileges to Catholics. Burgess (who knew Iolo) does not cite *Trioedd Pawl*, though he does use another of Iolo's triads from *The Myvyrian Archaiology* (see n. 22 below). Later devotees of the theory have made more liberal use of Iolo's material: see, for example, R. W. Morgan, *St Paul in Britain, or, The Origin of British as opposed to Papal Christianity* (Oxford, 1861), pp. 202–3; Lionel Smithett Lewis, *St Joseph of Arimathea at Glastonbury* (Altrincham, 1955).

[21] NLW 13119B, p. 268.

of this useful indigenous mode of spreading the Word, and his verses had survived long enough to be written down in the Middle Ages. Another possibility, sparing the saint the necessity of a visit to Britain, is that a British bard, such as Caradoc ap Brân or his father Brân the Blessed, may have converted to Christianity in Rome and recast the tenets of their new-found creed in traditional form.[22] The bulk of the essay (discussed in the final part of this book) offers a fine example of the elaborate feints and double bluffs Iolo could deploy in presenting his own forgeries to the outside world, but there is much here too which is relevant to his concept of orality. The closing paragraphs, for example, move into a discussion of how 'unauthorized' native material could be perceived in relation to the canon of scriptural writings:

> It is not unreasonable to think that in the primeval ages of Christianity there were many Apostolical writings, tho' not in our present Canon, that were in the languages, adapted to the manners, and state of civilization of the several nations that in those ages were converted to Christianity. Why might not Paul's Triades in the Welsh language be accounted amongst these?[23]

In this version of events, Iolo claims a place for Welsh and other traditions that remained unknown and invisible 'because they were not in either the Greek or Latin Languages'. By establishing a presence for his own language, back in the 'primeval ages of Christianity', he sets up the possibility of differently transmitted, but equally valid, legacies of Christian belief. Although he may not have intended to sound anything other than scholarly and broad-minded, his subsequent suggestion gestures towards an alternative version of Christianity itself: 'I have often wished that the Apocryphal Christian Scriptures were collected into a volume and published; amongst them, Pauls Triades might, perhaps, merit a place.'[24] That modest 'perhaps' is surely a decoy: this body of texts would form, if not a counter-Bible (since he is constantly at pains to stress the perfect fit between bardism and 'pure' Christianity), then at least a parallel (and in his view, more faithful) version of the Scriptures, one capable of disturbing the orthodoxies of established religion. As a Unitarian he was in any case deeply critical of the Church, writing to Hannah More in 1792: 'I cannot help lamenting its depravity, for depraved it certainly is.'[25] What is most striking, though, is the parallel with his own body of work, which similarly feeds off and

[22] Various forged triads in *The Myvyrian Archaiology* support the theory that Brân was the founder of Christianity in Britain (e.g. the 'tri Menwedigion Teyrnedd', *MAW*, II, p. 63); for Iolo's interpretation of Welsh tradition on this point, see Bromwich (ed.), *Trioedd Ynys Prydein*, pp. 290–2.

[23] NLW 13119B, pp. 291–2.

[24] Ibid., pp. 292–3.

[25] NLW 21286E, Letter no. 1023, Iolo Morganwg to Hannah More, undated draft.

disturbs the authorized version of Welsh literary history: Iolo is himself a creator of Apocrypha, a rewriter of beginnings.

In a final twist, Iolo offers the suggestion that Paul's Triads might renew their 'original' didactic purpose in a further propagating act of translation:

> Perhaps in more elegant English than that into which I have been able to translate them, they might be, with advantage, introduced into schools as a childs book. They are more capable of being easily retained in memory than any thing in prose possibly, that has yet appeared. And their sentiments are not inferior to those of that most excellent school book, *The Oeconomy of Human Life*.[26]

The reference to Robert Dodsley's immensely popular *Oeconomy* (which, first published in 1750, had run to some two hundred editions by the end of the century) shows the extent to which the pedagogic element of Iolo's bardism grew out of, and was aimed at, a genuine taste for didactic, moral literature among the reading public.[27] But the allusion has a further force since the *Oeconomy's* anonymously published precepts of virtuous conduct (written in a prose style explicitly derived from those bedrock texts of early primitivist discourse, 'the book of Job, the Psalms, the works of Solomon, and the prophets'), claimed on the title page to be 'translated from an Indian Manuscript written by an Ancient Bramin' with 'an Account of the Manner in which the said Manuscript was discovered in a Letter from an English Gentleman now residing in China, to the Earl of ★★★★'.[28] Though this piece of exotic literary subterfuge was subsequently acknowledged as such, the parallels between Iolo-as-Paul and Dodsley-as-Bramin are striking: both offer their readers a moral guide for their times, in the guise of an earlier, pristine source of wisdom. The difference has something to do with lightness of touch. Whereas Dodsley's 'authenticating' narrative has two or three moments of self-referential archness (when he mentions the impossibility of checking the translated text against an original, or notes that 'many would suppose it to be the work of a European'), Iolo appears rather to be grappling earnestly with problems of authenticity which he himself has created.

Iolo also produced reams of proverbial triads conveying traditional folk wisdom, or rules for good conduct; as we saw earlier, these were often attributed to figures of wisdom like Catwn Ddoeth or Bardd Glas. They have the closest affiliation with the kinds of oral sayings he must have collected on his travels; although again, while some of them sound persuasively homespun, others

[26] NLW 13119B, p. 293.

[27] See Donald D. Eddy, 'Dodsley's *Oeconomy of Human Life*, 1750–1751', *Modern Philology*, 85, no. 4 (1988), 460–79. All citations in this paragraph are from the opening 'letter from China' in a 1779 edition of the *Oeconomy*, printed by H. Jennings, Holborn.

[28] Cited from a reproduction of the title-page of the first edition in Eddy, 'Dodsley's *Oeconomy of Human Life*', 472.

seem to be translations of or calques on material from John Ray's *A Compleat Collection of English Proverbs* (1670) or Benjamin Franklin's popular and long-running *Poor Richard's Almanac* (1732–57). His comments on these pieces show how subtle he could be in manipulating his contemporaries.[29] In a letter to Owain Myfyr written in 1805 he made a case for including 'indelicate' material in the forthcoming volume of the *Myvyrian*:

> in those ages of good sense tho destitute of modern refinement, strong and impressive Language, figures, similes &c were deemed the most proper things imaginable on many occasions, for example, no language can be more proper to chastise or castigate an ungrateful scoundrel than that of the following proverb
>
> Cos dîn Taeog ag ef a gâch yn dy ddwrn,
>
> In all our Collections of English proverbs we find another exactly like it.
>
> Scratch a Churls arse and he will shit in your fist.
>
> See Ray's proverbs &c.
> In collections of ancient things of this nature no man of sense ever thought of omitting such things. The indelicacies of Horace of Ovid, of The Provençal Troubadours, of Chaucer, of Lydgate, of Skelton, &c are all carefully retained.

Noting that 'Macpherson and Chatterton ruined their causes by their excess of refinement, of delicacy of sentiment', and concurring with those who feel that much modern refinement is in fact a sign of squeamishness and degeneracy, he adds:

> English Gentlemen will soon[er] or later appear critically acquainted with our Language, these will detect modern ideas and sentiments, and be thence induced to consid[er] a very great part, if not the whole of the Archaiology, a modern fabrication, that Wales as well as England has had its Chatterton[s] as well as Scotland its Macphersons.[30]

'Indelicacy' can thus be considered as another authenticating device, a kind of chronological local colour: Owain Myfyr was especially pleased with the proverbial triads, and the third volume of *The Myvyrian Archaiology*, for which this material was intended, is the richest in Iolo's forgeries.

Another marker of the authenticity of bardic tradition, according to Iolo, is its silent rejection of the ideas of the twelfth-century writer Geoffrey of Monmouth, whose *History of the Kings of Britain* (*c*.1139) had provided the Norman rulers with a glamorous account of the early history of their newly-conquered territories. It entered Welsh literature in an adaptation, which many Welsh scholars believed was the source for Geoffrey's own work, known

[29] See Phillips, 'Forgery and Patronage', pp. 418–19.
[30] BL 15029, ff. 124–5, Letter no. 1124, Iolo Morganwg to Owain Myfyr, 13 July 1805.

as *Brut y Brenhinedd* (literally the 'Brutus' of the Kings). The term refers to the legendary line of descent from Brutus, who was supposed to have washed up on these shores to found a new race of 'Britons' after leaving Troy; this origin story still had some currency in eighteenth-century Wales and was espoused, for example, by Lewis Morris a generation earlier. Although Welsh literature borrowed freely from Geoffrey's work (which had itself drawn on and adapted certain Welsh traditions in the first place), Iolo goes to great lengths to defend bardism from its pernicious influence:

> All the fabulous writings in the Welsh are in prose, the most noted of them all is that Romance of Brutus and his Trojans by Geoffrey of Monmouth. Some of our modern historians who, it seems, are such patriots as to love their own Country and nation better than Truth, have in their defence and vindications of Geoffrey endeavoured to press the old Bards into their service. But however the sence of a single line or couplet may be perverted, there is not one of our honest old '*song inditers*' that ever mention or allude to the story of Brute. Whatever our modern Brutes (for such I esteem all lovers of falshood) may say.[31]

Again, the echoes of Johnson (turned this time against his compatriots) are clearly audible: the argument extrapolated from this, however, is a much larger one, based on the premise that 'long narrations and declamations in prose were unmanageable things for Tradition'.[32] Poetry is the only appropriate channel for the earliest period, and therefore the only reliable source for knowledge of that period; prose, being later and easier to manipulate, is inherently suspect. Behind this assumption lies one of the fundamental tenets of eighteenth-century primitivist thought, namely that poetry (associated with the spoken word) is the 'original' language of natural expression, and that prose (a product of written culture) requires civilization and art. When working on his 'History of the Bards' Iolo took copious notes on this subject from Percy's *Reliques*, Blair's *Dissertation*, Mallet's *History of the Northern Antiquities*, Denina's *Revolutions of Literature*, Ritson's *Essay on National Song* and many others to prove the intimate connection between poetry, orality, originality and truth: 'Thus unanimous are the learned of all countries that Poetry was antecedent to Prose . . . felt it not only expedient, but necessary, to be ample in my authorities.'[33] The triads, inevitably, were the most perfect expression of this truth.

[31] NLW 13106B, p. 133.
[32] Williams: *PLP*, II, p. 223.
[33] See NLW 13107B, pp. 36–43 and 66–70 for the extracts; citation at p. 69.

'The most excellent Institution that ever appeared in the World'

Bardic tradition, we learn, was above all a *well-systematized science*, to be firmly distinguished from 'wildly confused popular stories of we know not what, old wives tales'.[34] The sheer regulation of the bardic system most assures the purity and reliability of its oral tradition. It is a world of extraordinary bureaucracy:

> The *Didactic Songs* and *Aphorisms* of the *Bards* were always laid before their *Grand Meetings*, *Conventions*, or *Curialities*, of the *Solstices* and *Equinoxes*; there they were discussed with the most scrutinizing severity, if admitted at the first they were re-considered at the second meeting; if then approved of, they were ratified or confirmed; otherwise they were referred to the *Triennial Supreme Convention* for ultimate consideration, where all that had been confirmed at the *Provincial Conventions* were also recited, and the disciples, that there attended from every Province, enjoined to learn them, that thereby they might be as widely diffused as possible; these were recited for ever afterwards, annually at least, at every *Curiality*, or *Convention*, in *Britain*: this being the practice, it was impossible for *perversion* and *interpolation* to take place, every thing of this kind would be soon detected and rejected; all the *Bardic Traditions* were thus to be for ever recited *annually* at one or other of the four *Grand Meetings* of the year: being thus guarded in *every Province*, it was impossible for them to deviate materially from *Truth*.[35]

This is a long way from the multi-version fluidity of the source as described in a manuscript context, when Iolo could write that 'Truth requires not a severe formality of language, and modes never to be deviated from.'[36] It is also, like much of the absurdly legalistic detailing of the ins and outs of bardism, difficult to read seriously (indeed, difficult to read at all). But there are productive ways of approaching it. As some of his contemporaries noticed, Iolo's bardic system reflected his radical politics: Edward Davies remarked caustically that his Ancient Britons appeared suspiciously familiar with doctrines of equality and fraternity unheard of before the French Revolution.[37] Iolo's bards are (at least in theory) anti-hierarchical and explicitly committed to the defence of Truth and Liberty, and there are obvious parallels to be drawn between the history of their persecution and the harrassment of radicals under the government of William Pitt: indeed, Gwyneth Lewis has argued that the whole edifice of bardism was a kind of double camouflage (buried in the past, and in a 'strange' language) for radical thought and activity after direct opposition became impossible. The equation between bardism and radicalism needs, however, to be carefully nuanced, and to be contextualised more minutely. The French

[34] Williams: *PLP*, II, p. 220.
[35] Ibid., pp. 220–1.
[36] *MAW*, II, p. ix.
[37] Davies, *The Mythology and Rites of the British Druids*, p. 60.

Revolution went through several crucial stages in the early 1790s, and British radicals were closely involved in drafting the legislation for what should have been a new world order: Tom Paine was an active member of the new Convention; Mary Wollstonecraft, in Paris early in 1793, helped to draft ideas about female education for the Girondist Committee of Public Instruction; the Welsh Dissenter, educationalist and internationally acclaimed political writer, David Williams, with whom Iolo would later correspond, was instrumental in the revision of the 1791 constitution.[38] This rigmarole of Druids and Triennial Supreme Conventions is saturated with the language of politics: the processes of 'convention', 'ratification' and 'consideration' are, in 1794, dangerously electric with meaning. But beyond the lexical resonances of Iolo's bardism is a more complex ideological positioning. After all, the notion of tradition, the influence of the past over the present, plays a vital role in two of the key British texts of the revolutionary period, and it is a complicated irony that Iolo's systematized and unalterable truths seem to owe more to the tradition of generational interconnection described in the *Reflections* of Burke (whom he loathed) than to the radical rejection of the bonds of the past that lies at the heart of Paine's *The Rights of Man*.[39] The paradox is not unique. Recent critics have noted similar manifestations of inflexibility and restraint at the heart of more orthodox British radicalism in the 1790s – the result, according to Saree Makdisi, of an ideological investment in the notion of individual rights.[40] Indeed, Iolo's fantasies of bardic legislation and 'fixed orality' can look like an extreme example of what Jon Mee has recently identified as a major preoccupation of the period: the containment of 'enthusiasm' through both self-regulation and external control. The 'Bardism' essay preceding the *Heroic Elegies* starkly emphasizes the former:

> To be admitted into this class, the first requisite was unimpeached morals; for it was indispensably necessary that the candidate should above all things be a good man. He was seldom intitiated into anything considerable until his understanding, affections, morals and principles in general had undergone severe trials. His passions and faculties were closely observed, and exercised, when he was least aware of it; at all times, in all places, and on every occasion possible, there was an eye, hid from his observation, continually fixt upon him; and from the knowledge thus obtained of his head and heart, and in short his very soul scrutinized, an estimate was made of his principles and mental abilities.[41]

[38] Janet Todd (ed.), *The Collected Letters of Mary Wollstonecraft* (London, 2003), p. 221; for David Williams, see Davies, *Presences that Disturb*, pp. 8–54.

[39] Cf. Gavin Edwards on Burke's vision of society as 'an endless and beginningless process of keeping a promise', *Narrative Order*, pp. 45–6.

[40] Saree Makdisi, *William Blake and the Impossible History of the 1790s* (Chicago, 2003).

[41] Owen, *Heroic Elegies*, p. xxxvi.

Mee, like Makdisi, finds the great exception to this self-regulating tendency in that other contemporary Ancient Bard, William Blake, whom he describes as constantly seeking 'an outside to the discourse of regulation, a perspective from Eternity'.[42] And in this context the contrast between Blake and Iolo could hardly be greater. Save for the occasional gem of a phrase, the language of the 'Voice Conventional' (particularly as it appears in the posthumous *Iolo Manuscripts*) stands in rigid, not to say uptight, opposition to Blake's energetic biblical-Ossianic mode:

> By voice conventional is meant – the recitations given in Gorsedd of the oral traditions retained by the bards of the Island of Britain, relative to circumstances and sciences that had been conventionally verified, and ultimately established in efficiency; for nothing can be admitted as substantiated in truth, but that which has been progressively submitted to the national Gorsedd of bards, until ratified thereby, and which has, consequently, been publicly inculcated by conventional promulgation, and by efficient vocal song.[43]

Even the would-be 'luminous' triads have very little poetry in them: those that are not simply lists of names tend to be rather earnest lists of abstractions with none of the disturbing contradictions and ironies of the Blakean *Proverbs*. It is odd to think of these two men with their different bardic manuscripts, passing in and out of Joseph Johnson's shop, eccentric, obsessive, radical and marginal, and with so much in common; yet if Iolo, like Blake, felt he had to 'create a system rather than be enslaved by another man's' the results – with occasional exceptions, such as the eulogy to the Welsh language cited above (p. 127) – were startlingly different.

Another instructive parallel to Iolo's bardic tradition occurs in the work of the Irish historian Geoffrey Keating, whose influential *History of Ireland* appeared in an English translation in 1723.[44] For Keating, as for Iolo, the main problem lay in persuading his readership of the reliability of his version of the past, and his account is full of assurances that the sources he is using to write his history have been 'preserved incorrupt, without Falshood or Interpolations'.[45] Here we learn how the poets and historians of Ireland 'met once every three Years at the Palace of *Tarah*, to Debate upon the most important Concerns of State':

> In this Assembly, the ancient Records and Chronicles of the Island were Perused and Examined; and if any Falshoods were detected, they were instantly Erased, that

[42] Jon Mee, *Romanticism, Enthusiam, and Regulation* (Oxford, 2003), p. 292.
[43] Williams (ed.), *Iolo Manuscripts*, p. 444.
[44] *The General History of Ireland . . . collected by the learned Jeoffrey Keating DD. Translated by Dermo'd O'Connor* (2 vols., London, 1723).
[45] Ibid., II, p. 10.

> Posterity might not be imposed upon by False History; and the Author, who had the Insolence to abuse the World by his Relation, either by perverting Matters of Fact, and representing them in improper Colours, or by Fancies and inventions of his own, was solemnly Degraded from the honour of sitting in that Assembly, and was dismissed with a Mark of Infamy upon him.[46]

Iolo's bardic tradition also has its Mark of Infamy: any hapless bard who transgressed 'was, for the most minute deviation from the truth, to be publickly degraded at a Congress by ordering a sword to be unsheathed and blood drawn from his forehead and breast, and he could never afterwards be readmitted'.[47] Keating's Assembly produces a body of evidence 'disposed into the archives of the island as a venerable and authentick Collection, whose Veracity was to be relied upon, and never was questioned by future Ages, who called this Body of Records the *Great Antiquity*'.[48] Tom Paine would not have approved, but this is very like Iolo's version of tradition, with the important difference that Keating's 'authentick' history (admirably entrusted to 'a select Committee of nine') is a written, manuscript one, the product, as Bernadette Cunningham has put it, of 'an understanding of the historical record that placed a premium on the written word and perceived laws as written documents'.[49] Iolo's fully-accountable orality, his oral paper trail, is thus a peculiar mirror image. Although it is clearly derived from book-bound notions of correction and authenticity, writing, in this world, has become 'scribblecraft', the instrument of untruth:

> If a manuscript has a little of the mould of age on it, we admit blindly more of what it says as *truth* than becomes a wise man. *Letters* can transmit lies to posterity through a long, dark, and unknown, as it were, subterraneous passage: *Bardic Tradition* walks in open day and beaten tracks, exposes itself to the *eye of light*, as its own language emphatically has it. *Macpherson*, *Chatterton*, *Pinkerton*, and others, could never have sported with *Bardic Tradition* as they have done with *Letters*.[50]

Quite how one should reconcile the war of contradictions between Iolo's fixed orality and his fluid literacy is a difficult question. Both are summoned as needed to defend the authenticity of Welsh tradition, and both can be seen as responses to specific problems raised by the *Ossian* debate. Although they appear fundamentally at odds, there are nonetheless moments in Iolo's work when the two sides come together in a very satisfying union. One is the

[46] Ibid., I, p. 67.
[47] NLW 13097B, p. 251.
[48] Keating, *The General History of Ireland*, II, pp. 8–9.
[49] Bernadette Cunningham, *The World of Geoffrey Keating: History, Myth and Religion in Seventeenth-Century Ireland* (Dublin, 2000), p. 64.
[50] Williams: *PLP*, II, pp. 221–2.

account, mentioned in chapter 2, of how, on the basis of a story he had heard from an aged inhabitant, Iolo had persuaded the churchwarden to dig up a grave in Llantwit Major graveyard in order to find an early inscribed stone known as the Samson cross: in this case, faith in oral tradition quite literally retrieves the carved-stone writings of the past. Another is an origin myth, presumably all his own, giving a 'mythological' account of the birth of the bardic letters – something which he carefully distinguishes from his 'historical' account of the development of literacy in Britain. It is a glorious act of summoning, akin to the calling into being of the complex world of the Gorsedd which Iolo, the Last Bard, retrospectively legitimized through his own 'necessary fiction':

> Of the Ten letters however I may additionally observe, we derive them from the three rays of light which appeared coinstantaneously with the Deity's utterance or audible pronunciation of his Name, when as coinstantaneously all the world, all the Creation leaped as it were, or started into existence with a loud shout of joy, so celestially melodious and musical that it conferred life and intellect, to all created existences . . . Einigan Gawr (Einigan the Great), son of Menw ap Teirgwaedd (Menw son of the Three Voices) was the person . . . who from the appearances of the three rays of light drew or engraved them on the ground as the symbol of the voice or word that was uttered coinstantaneously with their appearance. He afterwards engraved them on a stone which he found at the side of the River Llifonwy, this he carried about him as a memorial of the Creation and the manner of its coming into existence, and as the Symbol of the Wonderful Being who in the audible utterance of his Name gave it its existence.[51]

This is the spoken word made visible: an oral tradition inscribed in stone.

Iolo's bardism is among the many curious products of a period in which, however briefly, it became possible to rethink the structures of religion and society as never before. It is an attempt to frame new codes of conduct, based on notions of virtue and morality that were shared, at some level, by other radical thinkers of the 1790s. As early as 1792 Iolo was describing it as a 'severe inflexible morality', and that, in a sense, is what it became: by the middle of the nineteenth century, the unpredictable, angry and highly individualistic tone of the footnotes to *Poems, Lyric and Pastoral*, or the manuscript essays, was more or less obliterated by the solemn and disembodied voice of the published *Iolo Manuscripts*, something alarmingly like Keating's Great Antiquity: 'that never was questioned by future ages'. And yet, as we shall see, it is this very lack of individuality which ensured the continued success of his vision, his version, of

[51] NLW 13097B, p. 56.

the Welsh past: for most of the nineteenth century Iolo was at his most dangerously influential when he appeared to be least present.

Fig. 1. *Iolo Morganwg 1798* by William Owen Pughe.

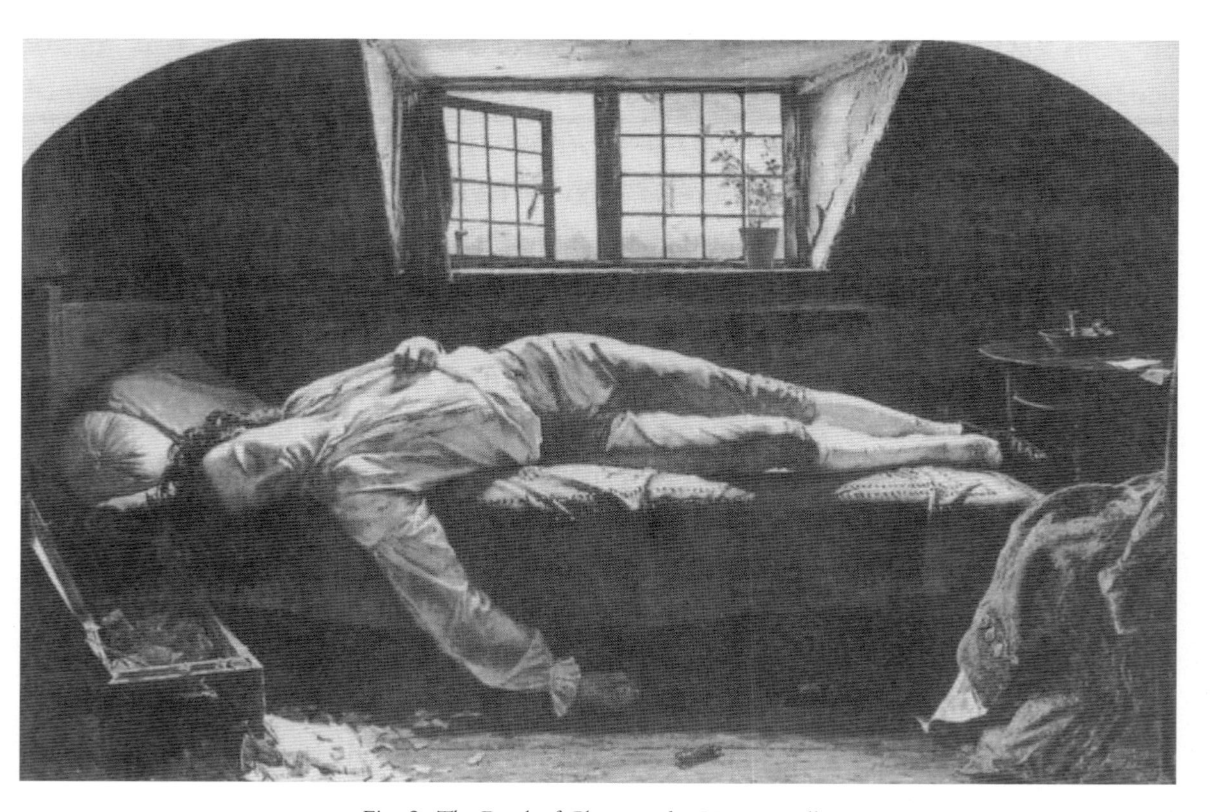

Fig. 2. *The Death of Chatterton* by Henry Wallis.

(*) 236

Rhof henw gyda rhwyf hinon
Athwydd teg i'r wlad hon,
Fra gair o wir gariad (Fr. a Ll. Hop.)
Iarlles Arglwyddes pob Gwlad,
Be bai ar gred bybyr gri
Na bai rydd i neb roddi,
Ni fedrai fwnai fynag
Neb o Forgannwg roi nag,
Bei caeth i Fardd bywiog can
Y Byd oll, a bod allan,
Ef a gai heb ofwy gwg
Ei gynnal yn Morgannwg.

Dafydd ab Gwilym ai Cant,
medd llawer Copi (fal L. Morys)
Gruff. Llwyd ab Dafydd ab
Einion medd eraill.

Gruff. Llwyd ab Dafydd ab Einion
Lygliw ai Cant medd pob Copi er a welais
i oddieithr un sef un Llyfr o eiddo Mr. Sion
Bradford yr hwn ai rhoddai i D. ab Gm.
eithr Llyfr arall, gwell ei awdurdod
yr ysgrifenllaw Llywelyn Sion o
Langewydd, gwr deallus a gofalus iawn
ai rhydd i'r Gruffudd uchod, — y mae'r
Cywydd hwn i'w weled agos ymhob Casgliad
o hen Gywyddau a welais i ym Morgannwg
a phob un yn gytun gydlais yn ei roddi
i'r unrhyw Brydydd. er hyn i gyd ni
allaf lai na meddwl yn gydfon a Mr.
Lewys Morys fod y Cywydd uchod yn
debygach herwydd dychymyg, Trefn, a
Barddoniaeth, i waith D. ab Gm. nag i eiddo
un Bardd arall er a welais i etto, oddieithr
gwaith y Bedo Brwynllys. Io. Gm.

C. i anfon yr Haf i Annerch Morgannwg,
(o Lyfr Mr. Sion Bradford.) [illegible]

Dydd i'r Haf tad y rhwysg,
A'th goedfrig berth gaeafrwysg,
Tywysog gleiniog y glynn,
Tesog braw'n deffrau dyffryn,
Praff yw dy frig i'n Prydydd,
Proffwyd pennial gwial gwydd,
Paneloo pwy un eilir,
Pwyntiwr dedwydd y gwydd gwin,
Peraist deganau purion,
Percwe brwys mewn parc a bron,
Pawr ar glawr y gladlawr glwys
Per ydyw ail Paradwys,
Rhoddaist flodau a rhyddail,
Rhesau gwych ar deiau dail,
Llawn nodiau cynion adar,
Can wanhwyn ar dwyn a dar
A'i gwrandaw'r gerdd fangaw falch
Ym mywyll lle can mwyalch,

Llawn gennyd y Byd o'i Ben
A llonedd bawb yn llawen,
Clyw fi'r haf, a chaf i'm chwant
Yn gennad ti'n d'ogoniant,
Aed drosof i Dir Esyllt
O Berfedd Gwlad Gwynedd wyllt,
Gyrr onid boch i'm gordd
Anwyla man yn ael môr,
F'annerchion yn dirion dwg
Ugeinwaith i Forgannwg,
Fy mendith a llith y lles
Dan gannwaith i'r wlad gynnes,
Dyngais am gwlad o'i hamgylch
Damred a cherdded ei chylch,
Gwlad dan gaead yn gywair,
Lle nod gwych llawn yd a gwair,
Llynnoedd pysg, gwinllanoedd per,
A maendai lle mae mwynder

Fig. 3. Iolo's poem attributed to Dafydd ap Gwilym ('Cywydd i Yrru yr Haf i Annerch Morgannwg').

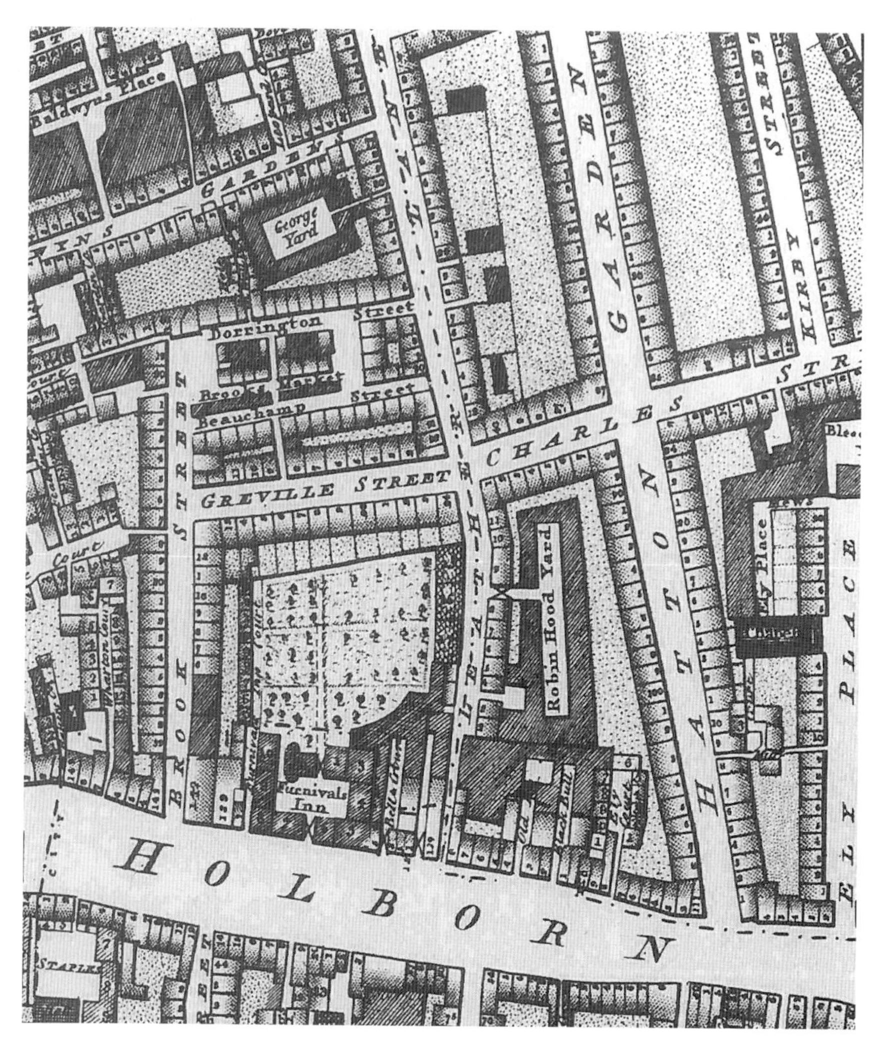

Fig. 4. 1790s Holborn, showing the proximity of Iolo's lodgings to Chatterton's 'garret'.

Fig. 5. James Macpherson, unknown artist after Sir Joshua Reynolds.

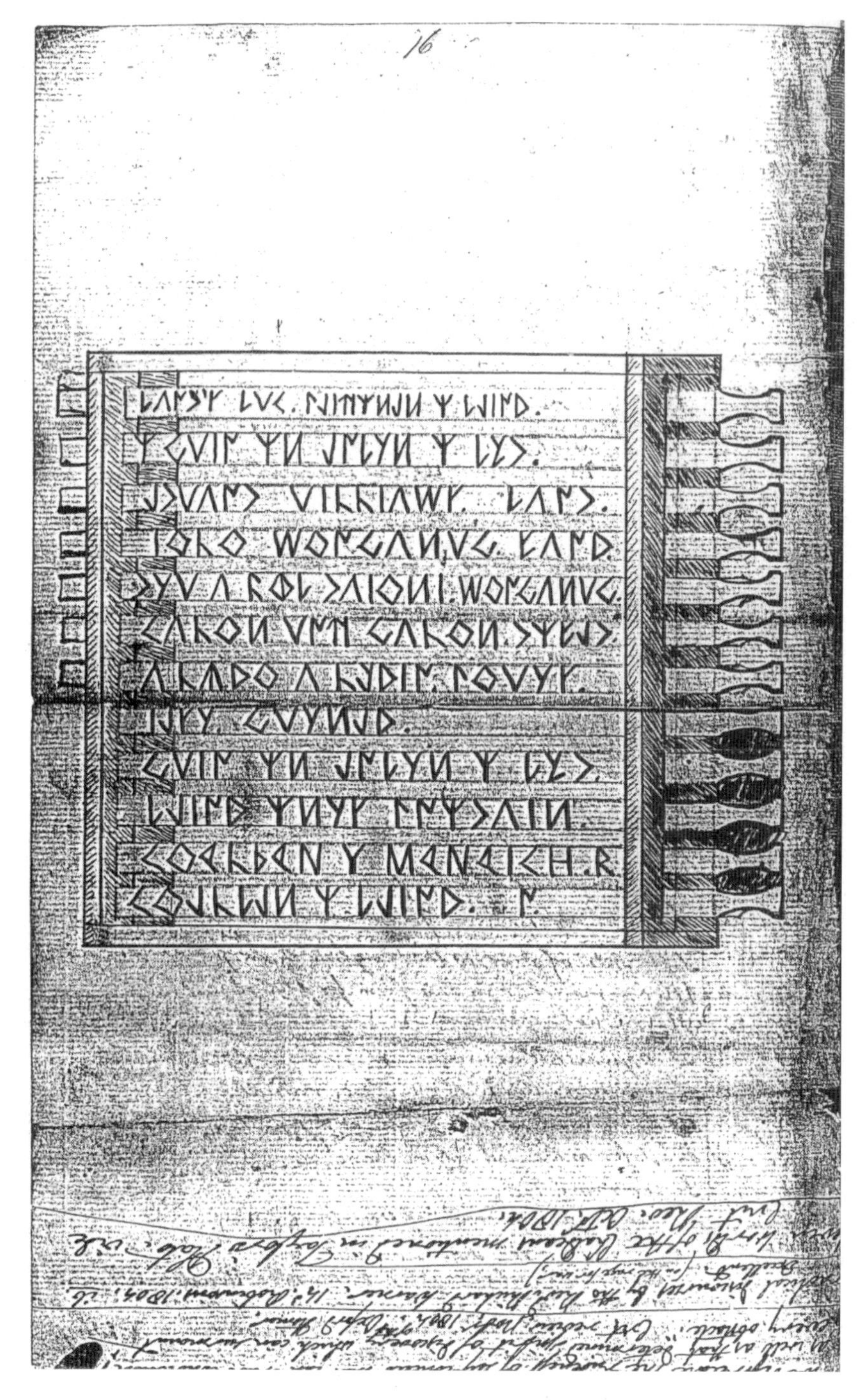

Fig. 6. Iolo's bardic alphabet, 'Coelbren y Beirdd'.

THE
B A R D.
A PINDARIC ODE.
I. 1.
'RUIN ſeize thee, ruthleſs King.
'Confuſion on thy banners wait;
'Tho' fann'd by Conqueſt's crimſon wing,
'They mock the air with idle ſtate!
'Helm, nor Hauberk's twiſted mail,
'Nor even thy virtues, Tyrant, ſhall avail
G3
'To

Fig. 7. One of William Blake's watercolour illustrations to Gray's *The Bard*.

La Bretagne
et la littérature orale
en Europe

Centre de Recherche Bretonne et Celtique
Centre de Recherche et de Documentation sur la Littérature Orale
Centre International de Rencontres des Cultures de Tradition Orale

Fig. 8. La Villemarqué by Alexandre Le Bihan.

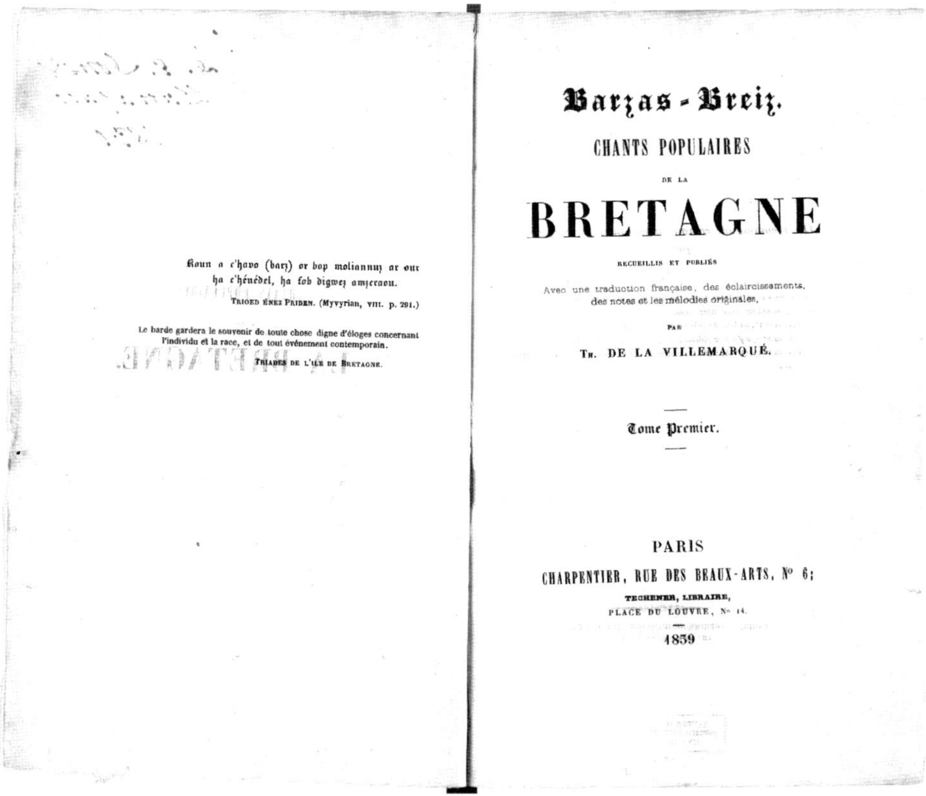

Koun a c'havo (barz) or bop moliannuz ar our ha c'hénédel, ha kob digwez amzeraou.

TRIOED ÉNEZ PRIDEN. (Myvyrian, VIII. p. 291.)

Le barde gardera le souvenir de toute chose digne d'éloges concernant l'individu et la race, et de tout événement contemporain.

TRIADES DE L'ILE DE BRETAGNE.

Barzas-Breiz.

CHANTS POPULAIRES

DE LA

BRETAGNE

RECUEILLIS ET PUBLIÉS

Avec une traduction française, des éclaircissements, des notes et les mélodies originales,

PAR

TH. DE LA VILLEMARQUÉ.

Tome Premier.

PARIS

CHARPENTIER, RUE DES BEAUX-ARTS, N° 6;

TECHENER, LIBRAIRE,

PLACE DU LOUVRE, N° 14.

1839

Fig. 9. Title page of the 1839 *Barzaz-Breiz*.

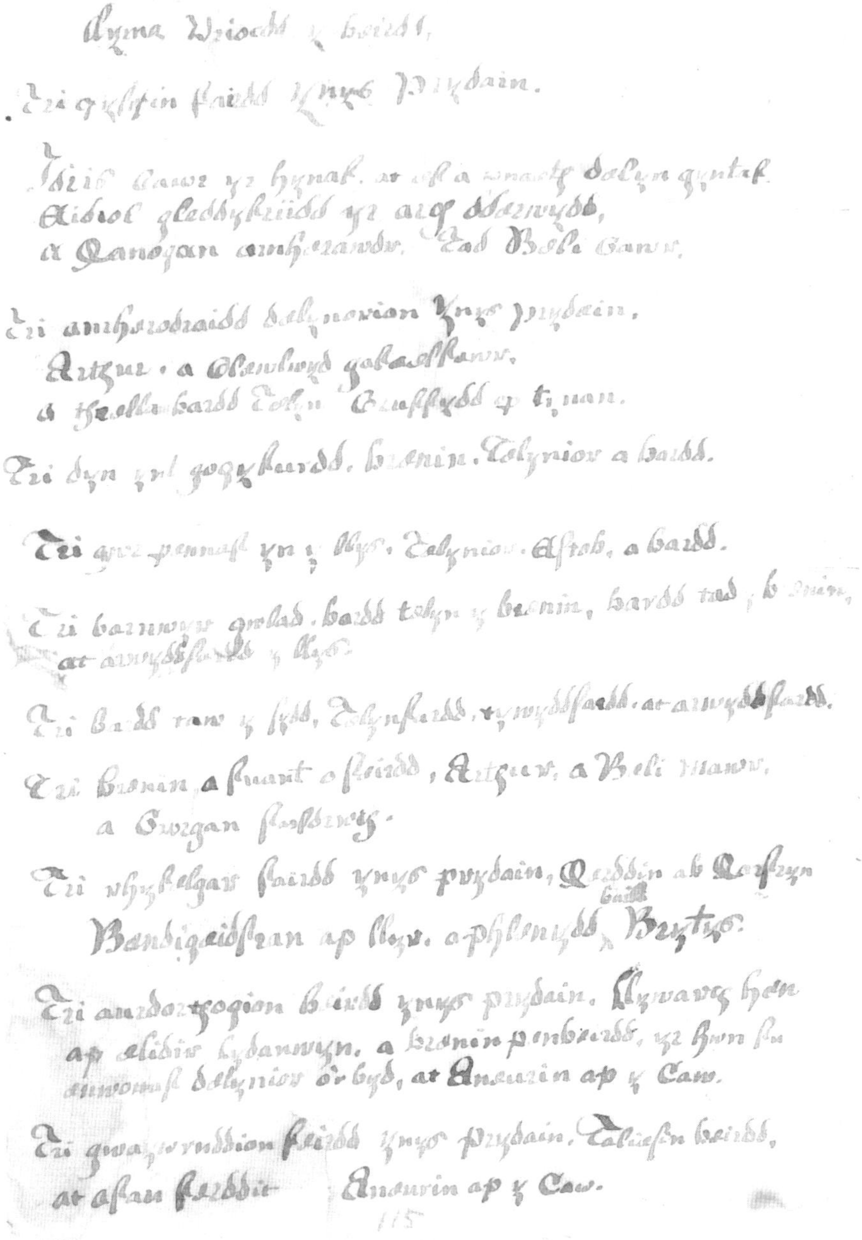

Llyma Drioedd y beirdd,

Tri [illegible] feirdd Ynys Prydain.

Teir [illegible] Cawr yr hynaf. ar [illegible] a [illegible] delyn gyntaf.
Eidiol gleddyfrudd yr [illegible] [illegible],
a Gwgan [illegible]. [illegible] Beli Gawr.

Tri amherodraidd delynorion Ynys Prydain,
Arthur, a Glewlwyd gafaelfawr,
a [illegible] bardd Telyn [illegible] y [illegible].

Tri dyn yn gogyfurdd. brenin. Telynior a bardd.

Tri [illegible] yn y llys. Telynior. [illegible], a bardd.

Tri [illegible] gwlad. bardd telyn y brenin, bardd teulu y brenin,
ar [illegible] y llys.

Tri bardd [illegible] y llys, Telynfardd, [illegible]. ar [illegible].

Tri brenin a fuant o feirdd, Arthur, a Beli Mawr,
a Gwgan [illegible].

Tri [illegible] feirdd Ynys Prydain, [illegible] ab [illegible] [illegible]
Bendigeidfran ap Llyr. a [illegible] Brytys.

Tri [illegible] beirdd Ynys Prydain. Llywarch hen
ap Elidir Lydanwyn, a Brenin penbeirdd, yr hwn fu
[illegible] delynior o'r byd, ar Aneurin ap y Caw.

Tri [illegible] feirdd Ynys Prydain. Taliesin beirdd,
ar [illegible] feirdd Aneurin ap y Caw.

115

Fig. 10. Iolo's 'bait': the forged triads sent to Edward Jones.

Part III: LA VILLEMARQUÉ

10

'Je suis barde!'

A letter from France

In February 1821 the attorney William Vaughan returned from Paris with a letter to be put into the hands of 'Mr Edward Williams, or any other member of the Society of Bards you deem most appropriate'. It was from the French historian and philologist Claude Charles Fauriel, best known now for his work on the folk-songs of Greece and the literature of Provence. The letter, forwarded to Iolo, shows that Fauriel's interest also extended to matters Celtic, and offers a detailed, if somewhat apologetic, insight into the state of Celtic studies in France at this time.[1]

As far as Fauriel was concerned, the study of Welsh language and literature had been badly neglected ('comme nulle') in France. The long wars between Britain and France had not only affected commerce but had also hampered the exchange of scholarship, and the Académie Celtique had done little to remedy matters: its interests had remained firmly on French soil, and were mostly directed towards Brittany. However, with no Breton-language manuscripts, few printed books of interest, and works of scholarship at best of a maverick tendency, there had been, until recently, very little to report.[2]

But things were improving. Le Gonidec's Breton grammar had already marked a new seriousness of intent: his Breton dictionary, to appear shortly,

[1] NLW 21283E, Letter no. 5705A, C. Fauriel to Iolo Morganwg, 6 January 1821. For Fauriel's role in the Celtic revival in Paris, see Francis Gourvil, *Théodore-Claude-Henri Hersart de la Villemarqué (1815–1895) et le 'Barzaz-Breiz' (1839–1845–1867)* (Rennes, 1960), pp. 63–5 (hereafter Gourvil, *La Villemarqué*); Jean-Yves Guiomar, 'Le *Barzaz-Breiz* de Théodore Hersart de la Villemarqué' in Pierre Nora (ed.), *Les lieux de mémoire III. Les France* (7 vols., Paris, 1992), II, pp. 526–65.

[2] For the dissolution of the Académie Celtique, founded under Napoleon in 1805, see Bernard Tanguy, *Aux origines du nationalisme breton: le renouveau des études bretonnes au XIXè siècle* (Paris, 1977), p. 275, and idem, 'L'Académie Celtique et le mouvement bretoniste devant la révolution française' in *La Révolution Française dans la conscience intellectuelle bretonne du XIXème siècle*, Cahiers de Bretagne Occidentale, 8 (Brest, 1988), pp. 127–44.

would also doubtless be of interest to Welsh scholars.[3] It would not be hard to persuade some of the members of the Société des Antiquaires de France (which replaced the Académie Celtique in 1814) to turn their attention to the language and literature of Wales. And, in the rising generation of younger scholars then in Paris, Fauriel knew of several 'jeunes gens d'un esprit élévé & sérieux' (intelligent and committed young people) already working in areas for which a knowledge of Welsh and of the early history of Wales was indispensable. Although he could not count himself among the latter group, his own academic interests had also led him, albeit haphazardly and with interruptions, to the study of things Welsh. Resolved now to continue these researches with more energy, he would be grateful for the opportunity to 'take occasional advice from one of the current heirs of the doctrines and traditions of the ancient Welsh Bards'. And he would be delighted if, through their mutual correspondence, he could help to make the work and the aims of the bardic society better known in France, and thus contribute 'to a fraternity of knowledge which would usefully commemorate the ancient national fraternity between the Kymri of Great Britain and those of Gaul'.

In the rest of the letter Fauriel gives a more specific account of his own reading, asking what books had appeared since the date of his last acquisition, the third volume of *The Myvyrian Archaiology of Wales* (1807), and enquiring expectantly after a putative fourth volume.[4] He then expounds with some enthusiasm on the 'philosophical and religious system of the ancient Welsh bards', known to him through the essay prefacing the poetry of *Llywarç Hen* (1792) and the notes and translations in *Poems, Lyric and Pastoral.* He has spoken of this system, he says, with some of the finest philosophical minds in France, and has been urged on more than one occasion to publish something on the subject. But he has been waiting for more information, more material, before embarking on this difficult and important task.

Fauriel's original letter went to Iolo, and Vaughan sent a copy to Thomas Burgess, bishop of St David's, who was by then vice-president of the Cambrian Society; he also had a translation made and sent to the editors of the *Cambrian* and *Seren Gomer.*[5] But a subsequent letter from Vaughan, written in May, shows that the French scholar's enthusiasm for the works of the 'talented and knowledgeable' Edward Williams had failed to provoke a response. Angry with Iolo for having neglected to provide the local branch of

[3] J.-F.-M.-M.-A. Le Gonidec, *Grammaire celto-bretonne* (Paris, 1807); idem, *Dictionnaire celto-breton ou breton-français* (Angoulême, 1821). See Louis Dujardin, *La Vie et les Oeuvres de Jean-François-Marie-Maurice-Agathe Le Gonidec, Grammairien et Lexicographe breton (1775–1838)* (Brest, 1949) (hereafter Dujardin, *Le Gonidec*).

[4] Fauriel had favourably reviewed the three volumes in 1818; see Guiomar, 'Le *Barzaz-Breiz*', p. 562, n. 16.

[5] NLW 21283E, Letter no. 506, Will[iam] Vaughan to Iolo Morganwg, 28 February 1821. The Welsh translation appeared in *Seren Gomer*, IV, no. 67 (1821), 112–14.

the Cambrian Society with a translation (into Welsh) of the bardic rules and regulations, Vaughan reproached him:

> I therefour beg you will return me the English Copy as soon as possible – I saw Mr Fauriel has not fared better, I have however Now done my Duty – And if the learned Sons of Cambria sleep and are regardless of those who seek to do her honour, it seems a Pity the whole community – should share the Blame.[6]

Why did he not reply? It is possible that he was daunted by Fauriel's approach; perhaps, and more likely, he simply never got round to it. Never a prompt or reliable correspondent, he was now seventy-five, plagued as ever by illness and increasingly feeling his age. And he was busy with various projects, chief among them the publication of his manuscript *Cyfrinach Beirdd Ynys Prydain* ('The Secrets of the Bards of the Island of Britain'). This work, over forty years in the making, set out to prove once and for all the priority and superiority of the Glamorgan poetic system, established, according to Iolo, before the fifteenth century and subsequently perverted by Dafydd ab Edmwnd and the poets of the north. It is a learned and devious compilation, cleverly layering its sources in a series of partial revelations going back through time: the extracts, supposedly taken from poets and scholars such as Lewys Morgannwg, Meurig Dafydd, Dafydd Benwyn and Dafydd Llwyd Mathew show that the true system of bardic metres had been kept alive as an alternative tradition in the south, until they were gathered together into a single book by Llywelyn Siôn to form a compendium of a bardic order that had long been 'dan encudd a choll yn eigion y Tywyllwch' ('hidden and lost in the depths of Darkness').[7] Thirty years on from *Poems, Lyric and Pastoral*, the business of publication was proving as troublesome as ever: a letter to the bishop of St David's, alarmingly reminiscent of the Preface to his poems, catalogues the 'many and unforeseen, and (as I should have once thought) inconceiveable obstacles' that had befallen the manuscript en route to the printers.[8] It would not appear, in fact, until three years after Iolo's death, published in all good faith by the dutiful Taliesin.

At this period, too, Iolo was instrumental in setting up various local 'Bardic' societies or Chairs, writing for example in June 1821 to the Revd David Lewis Jones in Carmarthen of his desire to 'Establish a Bardic Chair (Cadair wrth Gerdd Dafod) on the genuine ancient Principles or System of Yr Hen Gymry, in Dyfed'.[9] Many of the local societies devoted to the furthering of

[6] NLW 21283E, Letter no. 506, Will[iam] Vaughan to Iolo Morganwg, 28 February 1821.

[7] Taliesin Williams (ed.), *Cyfrinach Beirdd Ynys Prydain* (Abertawy, 1829), p. 2. For a discussion of this work, and the impressive scholarship on which it is based, see Williams: *IM*, pp. 375–8.

[8] NLW 21286E, Letter no. 985, Iolo Morganwg to Thomas Burgess, 10 November 1821.

[9] Ibid., Letter no. 984, Iolo Morganwg to David Lewis Jones, 5 June 1821. A letter from W. J. Rees later in the year talks of establishing another Cambrian Society in Gwent: NLW 21282E, Letter no. 419, W. J. Rees to Iolo Morganwg, 21 November 1821.

Welsh language, literature and history which sprang up all over Wales in the first half of the nineteenth century have a distinctively Iolo-inspired inflection. He was also involved in the arrangements for the provincial eisteddfod, held that year in Caernarfon, where, though he was not able to attend, 'it went off gloriously . . . No less than 11 harpers, 13 datgeiniaid [declaimers] and 26 bards were present'.[10] Only two years after his coup at Carmarthen, where he had succeeded in making the Gorsedd ceremony an integral part of the eisteddfod, the ancient rituals of his own invention, fraught with their complex ideological load, were fast becoming one of the highlights in the calendar of respectable Welsh society.[11] The final decade of Iolo's life saw a remarkable shift in the nature and context of his bardic vision, and indeed in his status within Wales. The concretization, if not the realization, of the vision brought its own complications. The shift in the ideology of bardism brought about by the change in social context will be discussed in more detail below, but from being one among many visions of a better world circulating among the radicals and poets of London in the 1790s, bardism was now part of the establishment in the newly industrialized, and newly embourgeoised, society of south Wales; it was also making its mark at a national level. Iolo himself was by now something of a Grand Old Man, the 'rough honest' character of Elijah Waring's *Recollections*. Perhaps the most telling marker of this transition appears in the flyleaf of a copy of Edward 'Celtic' Davies's *The Claims of Ossian Examined and Appreciated*, published in 1825. Here, the man who came closest to accusing Iolo publicly of playing foul with his sources during his lifetime expresses his deep esteem for him, just months before his death:

> To Mr Edwd Williams, Bard.
>
> The following Work is on account of his very laudable exertions, and important services in promoting the cause of Welsh Literature, very respectfully presented
>
> by the Author, April 29th 1826.[12]

There is no need whatever to see irony here, but with hindsight the appropriateness of the gesture, and of the gift itself, is pleasing.

The bardic evangelization of these last years of Iolo's life did not, however, extend to Paris or Brittany. Indeed it is hard, in any of his writings, to find

[10] NLW 21282E, Letter no. 418, W. J. Rees to Iolo Morganwg, 3 November 1821.

[11] Geraint H. Jenkins, 'The Unitarian Firebrand, the Cambrian Society and the Eisteddfod' in *Rattleskull Genius*, pp. 269–92.

[12] Uncatalogued copy of Edward Davies, *The Claims of Ossian*, held at the National Library of Wales; several pages have brief annotations in Iolo's handwriting. I am very grateful to Huw Walters for passing on his discovery. Iolo's son mentions receiving the 'gift' in June 1826 (NLW 21284E, Letter no. 705, Taliesin Williams to Iolo Morganwg, 14 June 1826): since Iolo died in December of that year he must have been thinking about *Ossian* until very close to the end.

much intellectual interest in fellow Celts across the seas. Items of Breton and Cornish vocabulary, derived from Lhuyd and Borlase, appear in his many word-lists, and he was interested in exploiting their potential for his own reconstructions of words in the Silurian dialect.[13] But although in one note the Bretons themselves appear, together with Troubadours and Italians, as one of the peoples who never quite lost the light of Roman civilization,[14] they are treated less courteously in the 'Institutional Triades' of 1794:

> *Tair cenedl a lygrasant, a fu ganthynt ar ddysg o Farddoniaeth Beirdd Ynys Prydain, drwy gymmysg oferbwyll, ac o hynny ai collasant; y* GWYDDELOD, CYMRY LLYDAW, *a'r* ELLMYN.[15]
>
> Three nations corrupted what was taught them of the British Bardism, blending with it heterogeneal principles, by which means they lost it; the *Scots* (Irish), the *Letavian Cimbri**, and the *Germans.*
>
> * The Bretons of France.

France itself, though never perceived as a particularly Celtic country, appears as an object of goodwill from an early period, and Iolo's treatment of the French as a people has none of the casual bigotry of his comments on the Irish and the Scots. In a society which, as Linda Colley has shown, was deeply marked by anti-French sentiment, this is worthy of note.[16] A poem possibly first drafted in the late 1770s pours scorn on the warmongers who 'with well-directed cannon balls / Knock down a thousand harmless Gauls'; reworked over many years, this sentiment would expand in a revolutionary context into a long treatment of the author's feelings of compassion and solidarity with 'brother[s] born in France'.[17] Although critical of Napoleon, Iolo never saw the French as the great enemy, and even the famous 'invasion' at Fishguard in 1797 merely provoked amusement: 'Breeches, peticoats, shirts, shifts, blankets, sheets (for some received the news in bed,) have been most wofully defiled in South wales lately on hearing that a thimble-full of French men landed on our coast.'[18] Above all, however, and particularly during the intensely productive and politicized years in London, France was the country minting a new world order, with its own institutions, laws and ceremonies: and although Iolo agreed that those institutions had been tarnished by the actions of those who

[13] See, for example, NLW 13142A, pp. 95–110, 115–17, 127–9, 131–42, 145–60, where Welsh words appear with Breton or Cornish cognates.

[14] NLW 13138A, p. 279.

[15] Williams: *PLP*, II, pp. 229, 232 (Iolo's translation).

[16] Colley, *Britons: Forging the Nation.*

[17] For a discussion of this poem, see Constantine, '"This wildernessed business"', pp. 139–43.

[18] For the Fishguard episode, see NLW 13222C, p. 132, Iolo Morganwg to William Owen Pughe, 7 March 1797.

ran them, he maintained that the founding principles were sound.[19] Indeed, even late in his life, he felt that French institutions offered the most suitable model for a culture wishing to attain genuine national status. There is more than a little irony in the fact that only a few days before Fauriel addressed his letter to the Welsh bard, Iolo had written to the Revd David Richards of his plans for a Welsh Academy on the lines of the Académie Française, famous for its draconian guardianship of the virtue of the French language (linguistic purity being a subject that exercised Iolo to the point of mania following his split with the 'Southcottian' William Owen Pughe):

> Would it not be possible Sir to institute A Welsh Academy for the cultivation of the Language and Literature of Wales; and above all for emancipating or rescuing the language out of the Tallons of those who of late years have been overwhelming it with corruption, barbarism, and by a most capricious (I had almost said Southcottian) orthography, and Hottentotic idiom and construction. so shamefully cacophonizing our most powerful and beautiful language, I have no room for all my ideas on the subject at present. – The Academy that I would humbly propose should proceed as much as possible on the Plan of the French Academies of Inscriptions, of Belles Lettres &c I mean as far as circumstances would admit, for it would be madness at present, and I fear for a long time to come, to think of such nobly supported and endorsed Colleges as those of the French Academies are, what I would humbly suggest in the incipient state of such an Institution, would be to establish a Welsh Corresponding Academy.

'I hope', he added tactfully, as ghosts from the radical past loomed briefly, 'that the Term Corresponding will not offend on this occasion.'[20]

But if Iolo was in no hurry to establish contact with Brittany or Gaul, his 'philosophic and religious system', bardism, had already crossed the English Channel. Its influence there, as in Wales and to some extent in England, would grow more noticeable as the century progressed. This chapter traces the posthumous effect of Iolo's ideas on one of the main exponents of Celtic Romanticism in France, a Breton aristocrat who began studying in Paris in 1833–4. Although too young at the time of Fauriel's letter to be one of the 'jeunes gens' of the rising scholarly generation, he was the beneficiary of that surge in interest in matters Celtic, and he came to know many of the new scholars personally. Like them he was encouraged in the early stages of his work by Fauriel – but he was positively inspired by Iolo.

[19] In an essay, possibly drafted during his time in London, Iolo states 'that an antichristian spirit prevails in it [the French Convention] at present I also firmly believe, but this does not consist in, but in a departure from, republican principles': NLW 13136A, p. 166. A similar qualified definition of 'Jacobinism' appears in a draft letter, probably written in 1804: NLW 21286E, Letter no. 1038, Iolo Morganwg to [George Hardinge?].

[20] NLW 1895Ei, Letter no. 1182, Iolo Morganwg to David Richards, 26 December 1820.

'Je suis barde!'

On 11 October 1838, at a particularly sumptuous eisteddfod held in Abergavenny under the auspices of the Society of the Cymreigyddion, Théodore-Claude-Henri Hersart de La Villemarqué was admitted as a Bard of the Island of Britain. He wrote to his family shortly afterwards, full of excitement:

> je suis barde maintenant, vraiment barde! 'barde titré', et j'ai été reçu selon les anciens rites des V et VI siècles, qui se sont transmis jusqu'à nous.[21]
>
> (I am now a bard, a true bard! a 'titled bard', and I was sworn in according to the ancient rites of the V and VI centuries, handed down to the present time.)

In his stockinged feet, he had sworn an oath of loyalty on the naked blade of a sword, and received the blue ribbon of initiation ('the true colour of the bards') before making a speech – apparently in Breton – to the assembled company.[22] As he emerged from 'the circle of mystic stones' where Taliesin and Merlin had stood before him, he had felt 'a sort of religious shiver' and had vowed to devote himself to the cause of bardism, to love God and his native land even unto death:

> Les ombres illustres des anciens Bardes semblent se lever devant mes yeux et me demander sévèrement: 'Qu'as-tu fait, toi, pour mériter l'investiture des couleurs sacrées?' Hélas, je n'ai rien fait jusqu'à présent! mais je nourris, dans mon âme, un projet qui réjouira les ombres des défunts, s'ils peuvent encore s'intéresser aux oeuvres des mortels. Je veux élever un temple, dont j'ai déjà jeté les fondations. J'ai commencé à rassembler en Armorique, les fragments épars de leurs chants oubliés, pour en composer un poëme en leur honneur, que je dédierai: à la Bretagne, à la Cambrie, à toute l'Europe et aux générations futures, for ever.[23]
>
> (The illustrious shades of the ancient Bards seem to rise before my eyes and ask me sternly: 'What have you done to merit the investiture of the sacred colours?' Alas, I have done nothing as yet! But I cherish, in my soul, a project which will delight the shades of the dead, if they are still interested in the works of mortals. I will raise a temple; I have already laid the foundations. I have begun to gather together, in Armorica, the scattered fragments of their forgotten songs, to make a poem in their honour, which I shall dedicate to Brittany, to Cambria, to the whole of Europe and to future generations, for ever.)

[21] Pierre de La Villemarqué, *La Villemarqué, sa vie, ses oeuvres* (Paris, 1926), p. 52.

[22] See C. de Jacquelot, 'L'Eisteddfod d'Abergavenny en 1838', *Le clocher breton* (Avril, 1913), 2587–91 and (Mai, 1913), 2600–5, for the claim that this speech was given in 'la langue bretonne ancienne'; Fañch Postic, 'Premiers échanges interceltiques: le voyage de La Villemarqué au Pays de Galles', *Armen*, 125 (2001), 39–40.

[23] Jacquelot, 'L'Eisteddfod', 2604.

That project was the *Barzaz-Breiz*, the 'songs of the Breton people', published some months later in 1839. This work, created *Ossian*-like from the 'scattered fragments' of Brittany's song tradition, would become mired for over a century in a bitter controversy about its origins and intentions: La Villemarqué, like Iolo, would be both credited with retrieving and accused of inventing a noble Celtic past for his people. His ordination as a bard (he would add his new title 'Barz-Nizon' at the book's second printing in 1840) is a significant moment in the development of a self-consciously 'Celtic' relationship between Wales and Brittany. It can be safely assumed that the illustrious shade it most delighted was the only begetter of the Gorsedd ceremony himself, dead by then a dozen years.

The Abergavenny episode can be seen as a node, or a knot: a place at which ideas, lives and ideologies tangle, and take on new directions. To claim that the Breton Celtic revival was wholly the result of La Villemarqué's response to ideas that originated with Iolo would be misleading, but it is possible to focus some of the wider issues of Celtic Romanticism through that moment of connection between these two creators and reclaimers of tradition. Their 'relationship' is admittedly a tenuous, not to say tenebrous, one, and not merely because of its posthumous nature. La Villemarqué's connection with Iolo has none of the drama of Iolo's own agonized relationship with the ghost of Chatterton in Holborn in the 1790s: for the young Breton, Edward Williams was a name among a group of respected Welsh scholars, a copier of ancient manuscripts and joint editor of *The Myvyrian Archaiology*. It was the literature and ceremony of bardism that inspired him; writing in the first half of the nineteenth century, he could not have known how much of it was in fact Iolo's creation.

La Villemarqué's first contacts with Wales were the indirect result of various earlier encounters between the Bretons and the Welsh. Welsh scholars had long been interested in Brittany: Edward Lhuyd had travelled there in 1701, while the pan-Bretonizing work of the Abbé Paul Pezron, the *Antiquité de la nation et de la langue des Celtes* (1703), was known in Wales well into the nineteenth century.[24] But more consciously 'inter-Celtic' relations begin with Thomas Price 'Carnhuanawc' (1787–1848), vicar of Llanfihangel Cwm Du, Breconshire, a talented and energetic man with a lifelong commitment to Welsh language and to literature.[25] Price belongs to the generation of Iolo's son

[24] Prys Morgan, 'L'Abbé Pezron and the Celts', *THSC* (1965), 286–95; Davies, *Adfeilion Babel*, pp. 60–125.

[25] For biographies of Price, see Jane Williams ('Ysgafell'), *The Literary Remains of the Rev. Thomas Price, Carnhuanawc* (2 vols., Llandovery and London, 1855); Stephen J. Williams, 'Carnhuanawc, 1787–1848, Eisteddfodwr ac Ysgolhaig', *THSC* (1955), 18–30; and Janet Davies, 'Carnhuanawc', *Planet*, 65 (1987), 40–7. Price's links with Brittany are discussed by Prys Morgan in 'Thomas Price "Carnhuanawc" (1747–1848) et les Bretons', *TRIADE: Galles, Ecosse, Irlande* (1995), 5–13, and by Jean-Yves Le Disez, *Étrange Bretagne: récits des voyageurs britanniques en Bretagne (1830–1900)* (Rennes, 2002), pp. 109–28.

Taliesin, the generation that did much to give Iolo's ideas about the civilizing and educative role of the bardic tradition a concrete form. He was at the heart of a dynamic group of men and women, all fervent supporters of Welsh music and language, who organized literary events and competitions, and generally encouraged the nobility and gentry of Wales to see themselves as patrons of a noble culture. Their efforts led to the establishment in 1833 of the society known as Cymreigyddion y Fenni (The Welsh Society of Abergavenny), famous for the splendour of its eisteddfodau and counting among its members the historians Jane Williams and Angharad Llwyd, the translator Charlotte Guest, Sir Charles Morgan of Tredegar and, a central figure, Augusta Hall, Lady Llanover, wife of the MP Sir Benjamin Hall, in whose library at Llanover Court Iolo's manuscripts would come to be housed.[26]

Price's devotion to Welsh and his many talents and interests (besides his philological and historical interests, he was a gifted artist and a craftsman) make him in some ways a natural, if more personable, successor to Iolo himself. They met at least once, in 1824, when Price visited Iolo in Flemingston. Some months later at the eisteddfod in Welshpool he urged his audience not to forget the 'literary and antiquarian services' of the old bard:

> And when you are enjoying the gratifications of the present season, and feasting upon the luxuries of intellectual enjoyment; and may they be enhanced to you a thousand fold! yet do not forget the services of this poor old man : and let it not hereafter be said that while the natives of the Principality were indulging in pleasure and gaiety, poor Iolo Morganwg was passing his last days in obscurity and indigence.[27]

'After this', notes Price's editor, 'a small subscription was made for him.' A letter from Taliesin several months later, urging Iolo to show some gratitude for the efforts Price had made on his behalf, suggests that even in old age it was hard for him to accept charity.[28]

At the same eisteddfod Price took a prize for an essay on 'the mutual relations between Wales and Armorica'.[29] His particular interest in Brittany went back to his time as a young man in Brecon, when he had encountered French prisoners of war of Breton origin; he taught himself some Breton and read widely. Convinced by a passage in John Hughes's *Horae Britannicae* (1819) that the Welsh owed a debt of gratitude to the Bretons since their St Garmon had rescued the Welsh from the Pelagian heresy, Price wrote to the British

[26] For the Cymreigyddion, see Mair Elvet Thomas, *Afiaith yng Ngwent: Hanes Cymdeithas Cymreigyddion y Fenni 1833–1854* (Caerdydd, 1978); eadem, *The Welsh Spirit of Gwent* (Cardiff, 1988).

[27] Williams, *Literary Remains*, II, p. 129.

[28] NLW 21284E, Letter no. 693, Taliesin Williams to Iolo Morganwg, 28 October 1824.

[29] Williams, *Literary Remains*, II, p. 118.

and Foreign Bible Society urging them to return the favour by commissioning a translation of the Bible into Breton.[30] The lexicographer Le Gonidec was chosen for the task, and in the summer of 1829 Price travelled through Brittany and down to Le Gonidec in Angoulême, bearing a precious copy of Dr John Davies's Latin–Welsh *Dictionarum Duplex* (1632). His well-informed *Tour through Brittany made in the year 1829*, published after his death, shows that he met various scholars and historians in Morlaix and Brest.[31] Discussions with them about the state of Welsh language and letters had given rise to thoughts of further meetings, perhaps involving a Welsh delegation to Rennes for 'a sort of eisteddfod', but nothing immediate came of it.[32] In the end it was Price's friendly correspondence with Le Gonidec which brought the two sides together.[33]

In February 1834 the Welsh–Breton connection was strengthened by the arrival in Gwent of the writer and art-historian Alexis-François Rio, who married Apollonia Jones of Llanarth Court and quickly became part of the Cymreigyddion circle. There were now firm plans to invite a Breton deputation over to Wales, headed by Le Gonidec. In 1837 an essay topic was set on the 'influence of Welsh on the literature of Europe', and Price wrote to Le Gonidec with the suggestion that he compete: declining the invitation because of the pressures of his new employment, Le Gonidec recommended two young students of his in Paris, Auguste Brizeux[34] and Hersart de La Villemarqué, and asked if Price would be willing to correspond with them as well.

Price's warm response earned him, a few weeks later, a rapturous letter from La Villemarqué stating his intention to try for the essay prize, and assuring him of his profound admiration and respect.[35] The letter came with a cutting from a newspaper describing a Parisian 'Breton Banquet' at which La Villemarqué had

[30] Ibid., II, p. 149.

[31] Ibid., I , pp. 1–111. The *Tour through Brittany* includes much of the material from the earlier eisteddfod essay, which was not printed.

[32] Williams, *Literary Remains*, II, p. 164. Like Price, the Methodist minister David Jones visited Brittany on behalf of the Bible Society in 1824, and helped to awaken Breton interest in Welsh affairs. See Fañch Postic, 'Propositions pour un enseignement bilingue en 1836: un mémoire inédit de Y.-M.-G. Laouénan', *BSAF*, CXXX (2001), 437–66 and Dujardin, *Le Gonidec*, pp. 77–81, 257–67.

[33] The letters are included in Williams, *Literary Remains*, II, pp. 165–79.

[34] For Brizeux's key role in French/Breton Romanticism, see Heather Williams, 'Writing to Paris: Poets, Nobles and Savages in Nineteenth-Century Brittany', *French Studies*, 57 (2003), 475–90.

[35] Williams, *Literary Remains*, II, pp. 223–4. The letter is reprinted and commented upon by Fañch Postic in 'La Villemarqué et le Pays de Galles (1837–1838): deux lettres inédites de Thomas Price', *TRIADE: Galles, Ecosse, Irlande* (1995), 17–19. A tantalizing comment by Jane Williams, editor of the *Literary Remains*, indicates that this was 'the first of many received by Mr Price from the Comte Théodore Hersart de La Villemarqué'. The rest of the correspondence is sadly not extant, apart from the two letters from Price preserved in the La Villemarqué archive at Keransquer and published by Postic. The essay 'on the influence of Welsh', submitted in French, seems to have been written, but did not win the prize.

reminded his listeners of the bonds connecting the two countries, and had toasted (not for the first time or the last) 'nos frères du Pays de Galles' (our brothers from Wales). He also included a review of his recent publication, the manuscript of the *Life of Sainte Nonne*, and described his current project, a collection and translation of 'the songs of the Armorican Bards' which would be the 'first work of its kind in France and Brittany'. Having thus established his patriotic and scholarly credentials, La Villemarqué could allow his enthusiasm full flight:

> Ce sera un bien beau jour pour moi, Monsieur, que celui où je pourrais vous voir dans cette sainte terre de Cambria. Oh! j'y ai rêvé bien souvent, je me figure y trouver les mêmes coutumes et les mêmes traditions que dans notre chère Bretagne. L'invasion anglaise se fait-elle sentir? Avez-vous, comme nous, conservé vos longs cheveux et les Magous [*sic*] des vieux Kymru? Etes-vous bien toujours les descendants de Hu Gadarn?[36]
>
> (It will be a fine day for me indeed, Monsieur, when at last I meet you in the sacred land of Cambria. Oh! I have dreamed of it often enough: I imagine I will find the same costumes and the same traditions as in our beloved Brittany. Is the English invasion very palpable? Have you, like us, kept your long hair and the Magous [*sic*] of the ancient Kymru? Are you still truly the descendants of Hu Gadarn?)

This vision of Wales, born of his studies in Paris and fed by *The Myvyrian Archaiology* and other works of Iolo and William Owen Pughe, provides a neat Romantic counterpoint to Price's own wryly recalled expectations of Brittany some years earlier, when, advised by a group of 'gay Parisians', he had mentally prepared himself for 'something egregiously outlandish and untamed, something between the Esquimaux and the Hottentot, which should concentrate all the distinguishing characteristics of the savage of both hemispheres'.[37] The differences between the two men are instructive. La Villemarqué's opportunity to discover Wales for himself came soon enough. Some months later he, Le Gonidec and Brizeux were made honorary members of Cymreigyddion y Fenni, and the following year, although neither of the other two could be of the party, La Villemarqué and five other Breton representatives sailed from St Malo to Southampton, and made their way to Abergavenny.[38]

[36] Postic, 'La Villemarqué et le Pays de Galles', p. 19 (he suggests that 'Magous' is probably for 'Bragou', the distinctive baggy trousers of Breton peasant costume).

[37] Williams, *Literary Remains*, I, p. 10.

[38] Le Gonidec was by this time seriously ill; he died on 11 October 1838, the day La Villemarqué was made a bard. The poet Alphonse de Lamartine had also been invited, but could not attend. There is some debate about the number of Breton delegates but, besides La Villemarqué and the Rios (returning from Brittany), they certainly included Auguste-Félix du Marc'hallac'h, Jules de Francheville, Louis de Jacquelot and Antoine Mauduit. For details of this journey, see Francis Gourvil, *Un centenaire: L'Eisteddfod d'Abergavenny (Septembre 1838) et les relations spirituelles Bretagne-Galles* (Morlaix, 1938).

The assembled worthies of Glamorgan were no doubt less hirsute than he had imagined, but La Villemarqué's experience in Wales did nothing to destroy his illusions: here indeed, if not in quite the sense he had imagined it, were the descendants of Hu Gadarn.[39] The 1838 eisteddfod was one of the most splendid of all those held by the Cymreigyddion and it is not difficult to imagine the impact of its three days of ceremony and celebration on the Breton guests.[40] The first day began with a great procession, over two and half miles long, with a line of costumed bards and druids – headed by Iddil Ifor and Iolo's son Taliesin – and a riot of banners and symbols (among them a giant six-foot leek) enthusiastically proclaiming simultaneous devotion to Wales and loyalty to the British crown. Besides the competitions and the accompanying speeches there were splendid dinners (every toast, every speech was recorded in newspapers in detail), and on the second evening a costumed ball, at which La Villemarqué wore the bright blue traditional costume of a peasant from Kerne/Cornouaille. Even before their arrival, members of the Breton delegation were the object of much attention in the Welsh and English press: their presence was taken as a flattering mark of international interest, and La Villemarqué in particular – widely believed to be a special envoy from King Louis-Philippe – was treated as a guest of honour.[41] On the second morning he was presented with a handwrought silver drinking horn, or *corn hirlas*, as a 'token of the union of the two races'.[42] The themes of union and reunion would be elaborated endlessly throughout the festivities, in toasts and speeches on both sides. At one of the dinners Louis de Jacquelot read out verses written for the occasion by the poet Lamartine, who had not been able to attend. 'Un toast aux Bretons et Gallois réunis, dans le pays de Galles, en commémoration de l'unité de race' (A toast to the Bretons and the Welsh

[39] La Villemarqué's impressions of his time in Britain are recorded in a series of letters, some of which were published by his son Pierre de La Villemarqué in *La Villemarqué, sa vie, ses oeuvres*; further details appear in Fañch Postic, 'Premiers échanges', but some material remains unpublished in the archive at Keransquer. La Villemarqué's report to the Ministry of Public Instruction was published as 'Un rapport de M. de la Villemarqué', *Le clocher breton* (Février, 1906), 1096–9 and (Mars, 1906), 1109–12.

[40] The event was covered in detail by local newspapers, both Welsh and English: the *Hereford Times* issued a double supplement, used extensively by C. de Jacquelot (the great nephew of one of the original delegation) in 'L'Eisteddfod' and by Gourvil, *Un centenaire*. For a detailed account in Welsh, see Mair Elfed Thomas, *Afiaith yng Ngwent*, pp. 127–37.

[41] See, e.g., the announcement in *Seren Gomer*: 'Mae y Gymdeithas hon wedi creu cymmaint cynhwrf yn y Byd Llëenyddawl, mal y mae sôn am dani trwy holl Ewrop, yn enwedig yn Ffrainc, lle y sylwir ar ei Thestunau gyda hyfrydwch hyderus. Oherwydd paham, mae Louis Philippe, Brenin y Ffrancod, wedi penderfynu danfon Cenadwr, ar draul y Llywodraeth, i Gylchwyl nesaf y Gymdeithas' ('This Society has caused such a stir in the Literary World, that there is talk of it throughout all Europe, especially in France, where its Topics are noted with ardent delight. For which reason, Louis Philippe, King of the French, has decided to send an Ambassador, at the Government's expense, to the next gathering of the Society'). *Seren Gomer*, XXI, no. 274 (1838), 220.

[42] Jacquelot, 'L'Eisteddfod', 2601.

reunited in Wales, in commemoration of racial unity) takes as its central image the idea of an ancient broken sword, whose fractured halves are joined together in a ritual of recognition whenever Bretons and Welsh meet. The imagined ceremony would itself become part of the Gorsedd ritual following the second wave of cross-Channel relations at the end of the nineteenth century.[43] After Lamartine's poem came another long speech, this time by Rio, also exalting the newly rediscovered relationship. His declamatory finish: 'No, no, King Arthur is not dead!' apparently earned him several minutes of applause.[44] But perhaps the most striking contribution was La Villemarqué's *Kan Aouen Eisteddvod* ('Inspiration-Song of the Eisteddfod'), which he sang during the dinner on the first evening with apparently extraordinary results:

> l'un des Bretons d'Armorique conviés à la fête de famille que leur donnaient leurs frères de Cambrie, venant à entonner un chant de bienvenue, dans l'idiome de son pays, se vit compris et salué des applaudissements d'une foule en délire, soulevée tout entière, comme par un effet électrique, aux accents d'une voix qu'ils reconnaissaient après treize cents ans![45]
>
> (one of the Armorican Bretons invited to the family celebration by their Cambrian brothers performed a song of welcome in the language of his own country, and found himself understood and greeted by the delirious applause of the crowd, brought to their feet as if by electricity at the sound of a voice recognized after thirteen hundred years!)

In his biography of La Villemarqué, Francis Gourvil was scathing about the curious hybrid language of the piece, claiming that its faux-antique Cambricized Breton would in fact have been 'equally unintelligible' to natural speakers of either language.[46] But that electric moment of recognition (induced no doubt as much by the 'warm, vibrant' voice of the performer and the familiar tune as by the revelation of a few obviously equivalent words and phrases) was irresistible.[47] La Villemarqué recounted his triumph to his parents, and wrote a third-person account of it into the last paragraphs of his report to the Ministry of Public Instruction: a printed version of the song, he claimed, had already run through two successive editions, and several thousand copies were now scattered across south Wales – 'où il se chante en ce moment' (where it

[43] Price apparently translated some of the stanzas into English on the spot. For the 'broken sword' ceremony, see below, p.193.

[44] Jacquelot, 'L'Eisteddfod', 2589. The same rallying cry concludes the Preface to the *Barzaz-Breiz*: '*Arthur n'est pas encore mort!*': *BB* (1839), I, p. lxxviii.

[45] 'Un rapport de M. de la Villemarqué', 1112; see also Jacquelot, 'L'Eisteddfod', 2591, who says that the crowd stood on the benches and threw their hats in the air.

[46] See Gourvil, *Un centenaire*; in 1938 Gourvil offered a prize for the best translation of the piece in the *Ouest-éclair*, with some amusing results.

[47] Jacquelot, 'L'Eisteddfod', 2591. Postic, 'Premiers échanges', 39, mentions the shared tune without identifying it.

is being sung at this moment).[48] The episode perfectly illustrates his profound belief in the mutual intelligibility of Breton and Welsh, a key concept in the *Barzaz-Breiz* and in many later works. Again, one can only wonder what Price (who had tactfully read out an English translation of the song before La Villemarqué sang it) made of this performance. His conscientious experiments carried out ten years earlier in Brittany had led him to conclude 'that, notwithstanding the many assertions which have been made respecting the natives of Wales and Brittany being mutually intelligible through the medium of their respective languages, I do not hesitate to say, that the thing is utterly *impossible*'.[49] But at the Abergavenny eisteddfod – and La Villemarqué was far from being alone in this – such scruples were overwhelmed by a powerful emotional reaction to the idea of a common language, a common culture and a common blood. Glowing reports of 'Barz Nizon' and John Jones (Tegid) holding animated conversations in some kind of mutual tongue appeared shortly afterwards in *Seren Gomer*, and, some months later, even inspired a series of *englynion*.[50]

La Villemarqué remained in Britain for some months after the eisteddfod to fulfil his literary mission for the Ministry of Public Instruction: he was to look for any surviving Breton manuscripts in the libraries of Wales, London and Oxford, and to study the most important manuscripts in medieval Welsh. For the first three months he remained the guest of the Llanover family, moving between Llanover Court and their residence at Aber-carn. There were numerous visits to other well-to-do families in the area, and several excursions and trips, including a tour of several days that took La Villemarqué, in the company of Sir Benjamin Hall and the Chevalier Bunsen, down to Bristol, and thence to Glastonbury and Stonehenge. Christmas and the New Year were passed, with Thomas Price, at Dowlais, home of Sir Josiah John and Lady Charlotte Guest. By this time Charlotte Guest, assisted by Thomas Price and John Jones (Tegid), was well advanced with her English translations of the medieval Welsh tales, whose publication as *The Mabinogion* would earn her a considerable reputation. She had, in fact, already made contact with La Villemarqué, having briefly employed him a year earlier to copy several extracts from Chrétien de Troyes' *Yvain ou le Chevalier au lion* as comparative material for the Welsh 'Iarlles y Ffynnon' ('The Lady of the Fountain').[51] There was some strain in the relationship between the two even at this stage, as their respective diaries reveal; by

[48] 'Un rapport de M. de la Villemarqué', 1112. The song was indeed printed, with Welsh and English translations, by Thomas Williams: *Can–aouen Eisteddfod, written in the Breton language, for the Abergavenny Cymreigyddion Anniversary October 10th 1838* (Crickhowell, 1838).

[49] *Literary Remains*, I, p. 35.

[50] Ieuan ab Gruffydd, 'Le Conte Hersart de La Villemarqué, (Bardd Nizon)', *Seren Gomer*, XXII, no. 281 (1839), 46; a series of *englynion* by 'P' appeared in ibid., XXII, no. 288 (1839), 275.

[51] Revel Guest and Angela V. John, *Lady Charlotte: A Biography of the Nineteenth Century* (London, 1989). La Villemarqué's visit is described on pp. 107–9.

January 1839, La Villemarqué had apparently tried to persuade Rees, the publisher of 'The Lady of the Fountain', to add his name to the title page of the publication. Relations would rapidly deteriorate as, back in Paris, he threatened to bring out a French translation of the Welsh romance 'Peredur' ahead of Lady Charlotte (in the end, her translation appeared first). But his time at the Guests also showed him another aspect of Wales, not the lovely hills and streams which reminded him of home, or the romantic vision of Chepstow castle bathed in 'le plus beau soleil du monde',[52] but the roaring and grinding forges of Guest's ironworks at Dowlais. The sooty face of industry did not dismay him; indeed it seems, from his letters home, to have enhanced an already theatrical experience. He watched the furnaces from his bedroom window at night, 'jouissant de ce spectacle extraordinaire' (exalted by this amazing spectacle).[53]

In February 1839 he finally spent a few days at Jesus College, Oxford. The relative brevity of his stay there has often been commented upon: the consultation of manuscripts was, after all, the official purpose of his visit, which was funded by a public grant of some 600 francs.[54] It is hard to know what he really made of texts like those found in the Red Book of Hergest or how much he relied on the support of scholars like Thomas Price and John Jones: the latter was with him in Oxford, and would later supply him with a copy of *Peredur*. The real extent and nature of La Villemarqué's knowledge of Welsh is a subject of some dispute, and will be examined more thoroughly below, but there is an undoubted gap between his actual grasp of the language, and his opinion (rooted in his conviction of the mutual intelligibility of Welsh and Breton) of his own linguistic ability.

It is worth noting here that, during La Villemarqué's time abroad, the Committee for the Ministry of Public Instruction, notwithstanding strong support from Fauriel, had in fact turned down his request to publish the *Barzaz-Breiz* for a third and final time: they were, according to the report, nervous of being duped by 'some new Macpherson'.[55] And yet, the *froideurs* of Lady Charlotte apart, nothing in his six-month visit to Britain seems to have sobered the enthusiasm of this young and ambitious scholar. The letters home, the official report to the ministry, and the accounts of him by others all radiate confidence, energy and self-esteem. Ordination as a bard, and the lavish attention bestowed upon him during his stay, must have seemed a glorious confirmation of his belief in himself and his work. Price's 'Tour through Brittany' is once again an instructive counterfoil: the Welsh clergyman travelled with

[52] Postic, 'Premiers échanges', 36.
[53] Ibid., 42.
[54] See comments by Gourvil, *La Villemarqué*, p. 71, Guiomar,'Le *Barzaz-Breiz*', p. 540, and Postic, 'Premiers échanges', 42.
[55] Guiomar, 'Le *Barzaz-Breiz*', p. 539.

what Le Disez has characterized as an Enlightenment mentality, an approach based on observation and cautious questioning which, if it did not always approve of what it found, was at least prepared to test, to consider, to be surprised.[56] La Villemarqué, on the other hand, brought a kind of dazzling conviction, which seems mainly to have reflected back at him. Indeed, the Wales which welcomed La Villemarqué with so much fanfare can look at times like a curious conspiracy to confirm an ideal: the Society of the Cymreigyddion of Abergavenny was, without doubt, of all the Welsh societies active at that time the one most likely to show him what he was looking for in 'la sainte terre de Cambrie' (Cambria's sacred ground).

La Villemarqué's stay in this charmed circle introduced him to what appeared to be a working contemporary model of a Celtic-speaking culture, in what appeared to be an ideally organized society. In the context of the eisteddfod, the Welsh language enjoyed both prestige and honour, with – what must have seemed extraordinary from a Breton perspective – the blessing and active encouragement of the local aristocracy and literati. This ideal of a deep-rooted and benevolent paternalism appears constantly, in one form or another, in the *Barzaz-Breiz*. In Wales, La Villemarqué felt that he had seen it at work, and his report to the Ministry of Public Instruction is eloquent on the social virtues of such occasions:

> Le lord s'y asseoit à côté du barde tailleur ou savetier, et la noble lady, vêtue du costume national, y prend place auprès de la femme ou de la fille du pauvre joueur de harpe, qui pleure de joie en l'entendant lui adresser familièrement la parole dans la chère et sainte langue de leurs communs aïeux. Le peuple du pays de Galles est en effet d'autant plus attaché à son aristocracie que cette aristocratie comprend mieux ses devoirs et a plus à coeur de lui prouver qu'elle veut partager avec lui des biens plus précieux que les fruits grossiers de la terre.[57]
>
> (The lord sits next to the bard, who may be a tailor or cobbler, and the noble lady, dressed in national costume, takes her place beside the wife or daughter of the poor harp player, who weeps with joy at hearing her speak to him in familiar tones in the dear and sacred language of their common ancestors. The Welsh people are especially attached to their aristocracy because this aristocracy understands its duties, and is keen to show that it wishes to share with them benefits far more precious than the gross fruits of the earth.)

Reality was a good deal more precarious. Both linguistically and politically south-east Wales was a complex area at a complex time. Not far beyond the orderly parades, the grand dinners and the *awdlau* written 'to congratulate Sir

[56] Le Disez, *Étrange Bretagne*, p. 110.
[57] 'Un rapport de M. de la Villemarqué', 1110–11.

John Guest on his baronetcy',[58] lay a world of serious unrest and a growing class antagonism born of rapid industrial expansion. Only months after La Villemarqué left the country, south Wales saw the first Rebecca riots and, in November 1839, one of the most dramatic events in the Chartist movement, when seven or eight thousand people from the mining valleys – some of them from Tredegar and Dowlais, from the very works whose 'spectacle' had so impressed him – marched on Newport in what has been called the most serious insurrection in nineteenth-century Britain. At least twenty people died, most of them marchers shot by troops.[59]

The language, too, was in a perilous state of flux, alternately boosted and depleted by the effects of migration, as workers from west Wales and England sought lucrative employment in the iron industry.[60] Although at the time of La Villemarqué's visit, Welsh in Monmouthshire was relatively healthy in terms of numbers of speakers, the social upheavals of industrialization (and the attitudes of the largely English factory owners) would soon effect a rapid fragmentation and decline. The first thing La Villemarqué saw on entering the town of Abergavenny was a banner bearing the slogan: 'Oes y Byd i'r Iaith Gymraeg' (translated by the Society as 'The Duration of the World to the Welsh Language'). But the world was shifting, and although it may not have been evident to a visitor from Brittany, most members of the various Cymreigyddion societies scattered across Wales were acutely conscious of the need for an effort to preserve and maintain the use of Welsh in public affairs.

The relative conservatism of the Abergavenny group was not, however, merely reactionary: as Sian Rhiannon Williams has noted, they were progressive in the challenges they made to the indiscriminate use of English in law courts, in their calls for more Welsh-speaking clergy and in their insistence on Welsh-medium education. Both Benjamin Hall and Josiah John Guest became Liberal MPs, and received radical backing when they stood against Tory opponents. On the other hand, the more overtly radical elements were discouraged: the harpist Llywelyn Williams, whose father, Zephaniah Williams, was one of the architects of the Newport rising, was not a welcome guest at Llanover Hall.[61] But other Cymreigyddion societies did not necessarily follow suit: the group at Sirhywi counted among its members one 'Horne Tooke' (D. J. Griffiths), a bardic name much disapproved of by Thomas Price, as

[58] This was one of the set topics for 1838: see. e.g. 'Awdl Gyfarchiadawl i Syr John Guest ar ddyrchafiad i radd Barwnig', Cyfansoddiadau a Beirniadaeth Cymreigyddion y Fenni, NLW 13960E, nos. 54 a–d.

[59] David J. V. Jones, *The Last Rising: The Newport Insurrection of 1839* (Oxford, 1985).

[60] Sian Rhiannon Williams, 'The Welsh Language in Industrial Monmouthshire *c.*1800–1901' in Geraint H. Jenkins (ed.), *Language and Community in the Nineteenth Century* (Cardiff, 1998), pp. 203–29; eadem, *Oes y Byd i'r Iaith Gymraeg* (Caerdydd, 1992).

[61] Guest and John, *Lady Charlotte*, p. 106; the authors note that he did, however, receive support from the Guests.

being 'Anghymreigaidd' ('Unwelsh') and 'yn sawrio gormod o ymbleidiad gwladwriaethol' ('smelling too much of political prejudice').[62] There were, then, inheritors of the radical strain in Iolo's bardism: the bookseller John Davies (Brychan) was one of them, a man for whom the struggle for the Welsh language was intricately bound up with the struggle for workers' rights, and who mocked the ceremonies and the politics of the Llanover set. But La Villemarqué, fêted and dined by the aristocracy more or less incessantly for the duration of his visit, did not see, or look for, the things which might have complicated his response.

It is a long way from the first Gorsedd on Primrose Hill to that of the eisteddfod in Abergavenny. What La Villemarqué took from his experience in Wales and gave to Brittany had already been translated and adapted by time and changing social context. This mediation undoubtedly diffused some of the differences between the Breton aristocrat and the Welsh stonemason, but the translation of bardism to Brittany was not without its own tensions. Many of the questions raised at the beginning of this book in the dialogue between Iolo and Macpherson resurface, though in new forms, when Iolo and La Villemarqué are brought together. The dearth of medieval manuscripts in Breton gives a new twist, for example, to the debate over oral and literary sources in the construction of a national past: like Iolo, La Villemarqué called on oral tradition to summon up his country's early history but, unlike Iolo, he had no parallel ancient manuscript tradition to support him. Like Iolo's Wales, the Breton version of a pure Celtic race had to negotiate the position of Brittonic in relation to other Celtic groupings, with the Continental Gauls taking the place of the Irish/Scottish Gaels. And running through it all, in a distinctive dark counterpoint to the enthusiasm of the trip to Wales, there is one major faultline: religion. From the *Barzaz-Breiz* onwards, La Villemarqué sought to reframe and reclaim the central tenets of bardism (and, for good measure, much of early Welsh literature) for the true Catholic faith. Among the many forces swirling around the stone circle of the 1838 Gorsedd, the collision of Protestantism and Catholicism would produce some of the most curious results.

The *Barzaz-Breiz*, like other works wrapped for years in the smog of an authenticity debate, has at last emerged into a more interesting critical light. For two decades now, since the publication of some of La Villemarqué's early collecting notebooks, the materials have been available to examine the relationship of the published poems with the raw oral tradition from which they derive.[63] The genesis of the work and the development of its three critical editions have been (as far as currently limited access to the archive will

[62] NLW 13183E1, no. 252 (undated note in Price's hand).
[63] Donatien Laurent, *Aux sources du Barzaz-Breiz: la mémoire d'un peuple* (Douarnenez, 1989).

permit) minutely situated in the historical moment, identifying it as a key text in the growth of a 'Bretonist' movement in Paris and Brittany in the 1830s and 1840s.[64] And it has most recently been studied as a work (albeit an idiosyncratic one) to be read within the general context of European, particularly German, Romanticism.[65] But, although Guiomar's study of 'Bretonisme' rightly acknowledges the importance of the idea of Wales to scholars and historians of the period, La Villemarqué prominent amongst them, there has so far been no close examination of the *Barzaz-Breiz* as a work drawing on a specifically Welsh Romanticism, a work much indebted to Welsh scholarship still deeply marked by the ideas of Iolo Morganwg.

[64] Tanguy, *Aux origines du nationalisme breton*; Jean-Yves Guiomar, *Le bretonisme: les historiens bretons au XIXe siècle* (Mayenne, 1987); also idem, 'Le *Barzaz-Breiz*', and idem, 'Quand les bretonistes répudièrent la Gaule (1840–1850)' in Paul Viallaneix and Jean Ehrard (eds.), *Nos ancêtres les Gaulois* (Clermont-Ferrand, 1982), pp. 195–201.

[65] Nelly Blanchard, 'Une fiction pour s'inventer: le *Barzaz-Breiz* (1839–1845–1867) dans le mouvement romantique' (unpublished Ph.D. thesis, Université de Bretagne Occidentale, Brest, 2004).

11

'La langue de Taliésin': Wales and Welsh in the Barzaz-Breiz

The forces that brought the *Barzaz-Breiz* into existence were negative: it was born of a vacuum, an absence. As La Villemarqué discovered early in his studies in Paris, Brittany appears in the works of various medieval French and Latin authors as a place renowned for its storytelling and poetry; the *lais bretons* and the Arthurian tales of Marie de France, Chrétien de Troyes and others invoked 'la Bretagne' as the source of their material and inspiration. In 1815 the abbé Gervais de La Rue published his *Recherches sur les ouvrages des Bardes de la Bretagne armoricaine dans le Moyen âge*, in which he listed many of these citations and suggested that those lost sources might yet be found. His suggestion that scholars from the province redouble their efforts in the search for the Breton language originals was, as Gourvil has noted, a major catalyst for La Villemarqué, giving purpose and direction to his research.[1] At the age of nineteen he wrote an admiring letter to the elderly La Rue, full of patriotic fervour: 'je suis Breton Monsieur, et tous les Bretons vous ont voué comme moi un culte tout particulier depuis que vous avez fait briller d'un si vif éclat la gloire littéraire de leur pays' ('I am Breton, Monsieur, and all Bretons, like myself, hold your name in particular reverence since you have made the literary glory of their country shine with such brilliance').[2] In it he announced that he was already working on a great project that would revive the literary fortunes of Brittany. He received a kind, but careful, reply from the abbé:

> J'ai fait vraiment, Monsieur, un tour de force extraordinaire en m'avisant d'écrire sur vos bardes armoricains et sur leurs ouvrages, quand je n'avais pas une seule ligne de leurs poésies dans leur langue.[3]
>
> (It was, Monsieur, an extraordinary tour de force on my part to write on your Armorican bards and their works when I had not a single line of their poetry in their own language.)

[1] Gourvil, *La Villemarqué*, pp. 10–18.
[2] Ibid., p. 14.
[3] Ibid., p. 17.

That 'tour de force' is worth noting, reading as it does like a gentle warning on the perils of presuming too much; another note of caution at the end of the letter suggests that La Villemarqué approach his material 'free from local partiality'. The material in question was the collection of folk-songs which would form the *Barzaz-Breiz*, a tour-de-force if ever there was one: La Villemarqué had already decided that the gap in the medieval written records could be filled by turning to oral tradition.

According to Donatien Laurent, he may have begun collecting songs and ballads as early as 1833.[4] At the family home of Plessix-Nizon, a manor house some ten miles west of Quimperlé in Cornouaille/Kerne, he began to note down songs from the servants and the itinerant beggars who came to the manor, and especially to his mother, for charity or medical help. Indeed, it was probably La Villemarqué's mother, Ursule de la Feydeau, la Dame de Nizon, who began making notes of these songs in an old recipe book, and she certainly helped him to organize his material. In the successive introductions to the three editions of the *Barzaz-Breiz* she comes to occupy a progressively significant part (perhaps because of filial piety, perhaps because La Villemarqué needed to distance himself) in the genesis of the collection. What the notebooks unquestionably reveal, however (and the point was still fiercely debated as late as the 1970s), is that La Villemarqué had a fluent grasp of Breton from childhood. It was not, of course, 'correct' from a scholarly point of view, since all his formal education was necessarily through French: uncertainty over correct forms and spellings would keep him revising the Breton texts of his songs through all three editions. But, however much he may have altered his sources, they were real enough: like James Macpherson, La Villemarqué was alert to, and an early recorder of, the oral traditions around him. The notebooks reveal a corpus of songs in many ways typical of later collections from the region, but with a handful of unique or rare texts which must have given him every reason to believe many of his own claims about the antiquity of the tradition.

As with Macpherson, and perhaps with Iolo too, it took distance to bring this familiar tradition into a new focus. La Villemarqué's studies in Paris and the company he kept there gave Brittany a glamour he may not have found at home. At the Pension Bailly, where he took up lodgings in 1834, and through his studies at the École des Chartes, he became part of a group of young, predominantly Catholic, Bretons: a kind of Paris version of the Cymmrodorion. Quite apart from the revelation of La Rue's *Recherches*, Brittany

[4] For a detailed analysis of the genesis of the *Barzaz-Breiz*, see Donatien Laurent, 'La Villemarqué, collecteur de chants populaires: étude des sources du premier *Barzaz-Breiz* à partir des originaux de collecte (1833–1840)' (unpublished Ph.D. thesis, University of Brest, 1974). The major findings of this investigation, and the notebooks themselves, were published as *Aux sources du Barzaz-Breiz*. For a general introduction to the tradition and its nineteenth-century collectors, see Mary-Ann Constantine, *Breton Ballads* (Aberystwyth, 1996).

was acquiring a new profile in literature and scholarship, as an incipient Romanticism slowly inverted the traditional stereotype of the province from backward to primitive, a place lost in (and to) time. Historians like Augustin Thierry and Aurelien de Courson were placing an increased emphasis on the early links with Wales; the Breton language was gaining some dignity through the works of Le Gonidec. At the soirées of the de Courcy brothers, La Villemarqué and others planned and discussed the future of Breton literature, the new histories and the role of religion. A new interest in the life of the peasantry was generated by Brizeux's poetic idealizations in *Marie* (1835), while Émile Souvestre produced a series of vivid articles on popular poetry published in *Revue des Deux Mondes* in 1834 in which the Breton people themselves are figured as the 'last of' their kind.[5]

La Villemarqué was not long before contributing to this growing surge in interest. His first publication was of a paper delivered at a congress, organized by the Institut historique in November 1835, on the influence of Celtic language and literature on the language and literature of France.[6] It is hardly a polished piece, and the Welsh sources, radically misspelt, have a throwaway exotic glamour – but it is interesting to note that even at this stage he refers to Edward Davies, the Triads, *The Myvyrian Archaiology of Wales*, the laws of Hywel Dda, and includes a lengthy citation of the famous elegy to Llywelyn ap Gruffudd by Gruffudd ab yr Ynad Coch (just recognizable as 'Griffon, fils' Inad le vieux'). Three years before the journey to Wales he was thus on at least a nodding acquaintance with names from several medieval Welsh sources. There is, however, no mention of the songs he had collected himself.

But they did begin to appear in his next publications, mostly produced for journals like the Catholic *L'Echo de la Jeune France*. Here, elaborate and evocative descriptions of his travels in the Breton countryside show how his reading had predisposed him to see the songs as fragments of the past. His discussion of the ballad of the 'Plague of Elliant' opens Breton folk-song out to a wider, and historically deeper, concept of oral tradition, which sounds very much like an echo of Iolo : 'le Bardisme ou la littérature celtique, n'est autre chose, comme celle de tous les peuples primitifs, que l'*histoire chantée*. La voix du barde donnait une âme à chaque événement'[7] ('Bardism or Celtic literature is, like that of other primitive peoples, nothing other than *sung history*. The voice of

[5] Detailed accounts of this period can be found in Guiomar, *Le bretonisme*; Tanguy, *Aux origines*. See also the essays by Bernard Tanguy, 'Des celtomanes aux bretonistes: les idées et les hommes' in Jean Balcou and Yves Le Gallo (eds.), *Histoire littéraire et culturelle de la Bretagne* (2 vols., Paris, 1987), II, pp. 293–334, and Donatien Laurent, 'Des antiquaires aux folkloristes: decouverte et promotion des littératures orales' in ibid., II, pp. 335–54. Souvestre's collected articles appeared as *Les derniers bretons* (Paris, 1836).

[6] Théodore Hersart de La Villemarqué, 'La langue et la littérature de la Celtique sont-elles entrées comme élément dans la formation de la langue et de la littérature de la France?', ed. J.-Y. Guiomar, *BSAF*, CXVII (1988), 61–93.

[7] 'Un débris du Bardisme', *L'Echo de la Jeune France* (15 March 1836), 264.

the bard gives each event a soul'). The ancient Celts are, we learn, still very much alive in Brittany, protected, like Macpherson's Gaels, from too much 'foreign intermixture': 'Dans nos montagnes, au contraire, et nos vallées profondes, à l'abri du contact des villes de toute influence francaise, *le passé revit dans le présent*' (In our hills, on the contrary, and in our deep valleys, safe from contact with the towns and all French influence, *the past lives again in the present*).[8] There is also, as various critics have noticed, a marked streak of anti-French sentiment. All these themes would form important strands in the *Barzaz-Breiz*.

The *Barzaz-Breiz* was La Villemarqué's most significant work, the one for which he became known: it gained him international standing, election to the Institut de France and, in 1846, the Légion d'Honneur. It had three incarnations, stretching across his career, from the 1839 edition, which had fifty-three songs in two volumes with facing-page translations (modelled directly on Fauriel's *Chants populaires de la Grèce moderne*, 1824–5), to the edition of 1845, augmented to eighty-six songs with a much-expanded introduction and notes. The third single-volume edition of 1867 added little in terms of content, but changed the format, reducing the Breton text in font size and consigning it to the bottom of the page.[9] The songs are arranged chronologically in order to span centuries of Breton history from pagan druidic times onwards: rather like Macpherson, La Villemarqué appears to have reworked traditional material in the light of his theories of the past, and his alterations to the pieces he collected range from minimal interference (but often zealous over-interpretation) to the wholesale recreation of texts. Critics have seen a fundamental ideological shift between the editions of 1839 and 1845, from the celebration of a Gaulish-Celtic inheritance, which Brittany, by virtue of its language, had best preserved, to a 'Bretonist' stance, more confrontational with France.[10]

Having failed to gain the support of a cautious Comité Historique, La Villemarqué, like Iolo, had to find the money to publish his work privately; unlike Iolo he did not have to resort to subscription, but persuaded his family to shoulder the costs. Given how close the first edition of the work was to completion by the time La Villemarqué visited Wales, it is hard not to be impressed by the breadth (and weight) of the young author's knowledge. The collection is richly referenced; sources in medieval Welsh literature are especially prominent, and Iolo's mark is heavy on many of these: indeed, the very name of the work is a neologism derived from Iolo's word *barddas*, while the title-

[8] Ibid., 268. The suspension of historical time in primitivist perception of the Celtic-speaking cultures is interestingly analyzed by Pittock, *Celtic Identity and the British Image*, pp. 36–9: 'Primitivism's commitment to the past was thus both profound and vacuous, for the past it praised was dehistoricized' (p. 37).

[9] For a detailed account of the growth and composition of the three editions, see Gourvil, *La Villemarqué*.

[10] See Guiomar, 'Le *Barzaz-Breiz*'.

page boasts a triad from *The Myvyrian Archaiology* on the duties of the bard. By 1839, La Villemarqué was thus familiar with (or at least aware of) a significant number of Welsh or Welsh-related texts, from medieval works like the *Vita Sancti Dubritii*, the *Historia Brittonum* and Geoffrey of Monmouth to John Davies's *Antiquae Linguae Britannicae* (1621) and more recent studies, including Evan Evans's *Specimens* (1764), Thomas Pennant's *Tour in Wales* (1778–83), Edward Jones's *Musical and Poetical Relicks of the Welsh Bards* (1784, 2nd edn., 1794) and its later revised incarnation *The Bardic Museum* (1802) and Sharon Turner's *Vindication of the Genuineness of the Ancient British Poems* (1803), as well as the journals *The Cambrian Quarterly* and *Y Greal* and the manuscripts of the Red Book of Hergest and Liber Landavensis. From the Iolo 'stable' come *The Myvyrian Archaiology of Wales*, Iolo's *Poems, Lyric and Pastoral*, William Owen Pughe's *Heroic Elegies*, *Barddoniaeth Dafydd ab Gwilym* and the *Welsh and English Dictionary* (1793–1803); on several occasions, La Villemarqué acknowledges the advice of friends and scholars in Wales. Of these references, which were further enriched in 1845, *The Myvyrian Archaiology* is by far the most cited, with forty references in 1839, fifty-two in 1845 and forty-four in 1867.[11] Gourvil, who finds La Villemarqué's extensive use of Welsh sources rebarbative, sees them as a form of youthful showing off; but his understanding and use of this material deserves to be looked at rather more closely.

The introduction opens with a citation from the historian J.-J. Ampère to the effect that if anywhere has kept its bards in possession of druidical traditions it must be Armorica, the only region which, despite union with France, 'est restée celtique et gauloise de physionomie, de costume et de langue, jusqu'à nos jours' ('has remained Celtic and Gaulish in its physiognomy, its costume and its language to this day').[12] This distinctiveness, says La Villemarqué, has long been interpreted as mere barbarousness: but such is the fate of all small countries (and, in a gesture of Celtic solidarity, he cites the Welsh, Irish and Highland Scots as examples) in the eyes of their larger neighbours, as the political and military tyranny of the latter soon turns to 'intellectual despotism'. In response to the implicit question in Ampère's statement (are modern Breton poets the true descendants of the ancient Celtic bards?), he begins by providing his readers with a brief sketch of the latter, culled from ancient authorities (Caesar, Tacitus, Strabo) and sealed with a quotation from Iolo's 'Laws of Moelmud', which details the duties of the bard as an inculcator of virtue and wisdom, one of the three 'pillars' of the society.[13] The advent of Christianity and the arrival of the insular Britons (among them, apparently,

[11] Blanchard, 'Une fiction pour s'inventer', p. 281.
[12] *BB* (1839), I, p. i.
[13] *MAW*, III, p. 291.

the poet Taliesin himself)[14] did not fundamentally alter the nature of bardism in Brittany: 'les poètes nouveaux ne brisèrent point la harpe des anciens bardes, ils y changèrent seulement quelques cordes' (the new poets did not break the harp of the ancient bards, they merely changed a few strings).[15] The 'earliest' songs of the *Barzaz-Breiz* itself are summoned as testimony to this period of transition. But while the change of religion is relatively smooth, La Villemarqué makes no attempt to claim for Brittany a continuous learned bardic tradition as Iolo had done for Wales. He acknowledges instead a sea-change, as 'poésie savante' in Brittany gave way to 'poésie populaire'.The popular poets, the poets of the peasantry, are thus the ragged inheritors of the druidic-bardic mantle: deferring again to *The Myvyrian Archaiology*, La Villemarqué notes that for this reason Brittany is counted among the nations which corrupted *barddas* by blending it with 'heterogenous principles'.[16]

Although from this point onwards he should, as he claims, be discussing popular poetry, the rest of the introduction and the notes to many of the songs return constantly to the ancient tradition, blurring the focus and implying linguistic and cultural survival and continuity. The impoverished poets of Breton-speaking Brittany are irresistibly cast as bards in the ancient style. Poets and musicians, they celebrate the actions and events worthy of memory; they dispense praise and blame; they play the *rebek* (a kind of triple-stringed harp). The blind ones among them, he notes, even use a version of the ancient bardic alphabet, carved on wood, to help them recall the themes of their songs: the reader is here directed to the account of *Coelbren y Beirz* (by 1845, transcribed as *Koelbren ë beirz*) in Edward Jones's *Musical and Poetical Relicks*.[17] A discussion of songs composed by young clerics or students explains that their compositions are never written down, and that this is in accordance with the Wisdom of the Bards of the Island of Britain, who maintain that oral memory is a more faithful and dependable medium than letters. Following Lhuyd, La Villemarqué also makes much of the tercet form, seeing a three-line single rhyme stanza as an indicator of the antiquity of Breton tradition: 'used by the druids to transmit their knowledge to their pupils', it appears in those songs which the editor feels certain date from the 'sixth to the tenth' centuries.[18] Although one of the main aims of the *Barzaz-Breiz* was to set out a chronological history of the province through song, the introduction manages to produce a vision of a contemporary Brittany whose closest parallel is the early

[14] On the tradition of Taliesin's sojourn in Brittany, see John T. Koch, *De Sancto Iudicaelo rege historia* and its implications for the Welsh Talieisin' in Joseph Falaky Nagy and Leslie Ellen Jones (eds.), *Heroic Poets and Poetic Heroes in Celtic Tradition: A Festschrift for Patrick K. Ford*, CSANA Yearbook, 3–4 (Dublin, 2005), pp. 247–62.

[15] *BB* (1839), I, p. xvii.

[16] Ibid., I, p. xviii.

[17] Ibid., I, p. xxxii; *BB* (1845), I, p. xxxiv.

[18] *BB* (1839), I, p. lx.

medieval Welsh past: a Brittany suspended in time. The high point of this game of temporal equivalence is the elaborate demonstration that early medieval Welsh poetry, though abstruse to modern Welsh scholars, could still be enjoyed by the average Breton peasant. A parallel text gives a few lines of a poem from *The Myvyrian Archaiology* in 'sixth-century Breton' (in fact a heavily Bretonicized version of the Welsh) and in 'modern Breton': not only, claims La Villemarqué, can all but four of the words of the fragment be found in any Breton dictionary, but they are in fact in daily use ('journellement employés') among the peasantry of the various regions of Brittany:

> dont le moins intelligent comprendrait les vers du barde du VIè siècle, et ces quatre mots eux-memes, qui manquent dans quelques vocabulaires, sont encore en usage parmi le peuple du Morbihan, où Taliésin a passé la moitié de sa vie.[19]
>
> (of whom the least intelligent would understand the lines of the sixth-century bard, and those four words, missing from several lexicons, are still in use amongst the people of the Morbihan, where Taliesin spent half his life.)

The scholarly smokescreen is much thicker here, but an interesting parallel can be drawn between this attempt to ratify the Breton oral tradition through the actual presence of Taliesin (there is the faintest implication here that Taliesin's very words have survived, almost physically, as breath in the mouths of the people) and Iolo's similar determination to have him (not to mention Aneirin, and Dafydd ap Gwilym and many others) born or at least based for a time on Glamorgan's soil. And in La Villemarqué's earlier report, that breath, that spoken language, is given a greater capacity for survival and endurance than the fragmented texts themselves:

> la langue de Taliésin est exactement celle que parle aujourd'hui les paysans de la Basse-Bretagne; nous leur avons lu des fragments de ses chants, et ils les ont compris, tandis que les savants gallois ne les entendait qu'avec peine.[20]
>
> (the language of Taliesin is exactly that spoken today by the peasants of Lower Brittany; we read them fragments of his poetry, and they understood them, where the Welsh scholars could only understand them with great difficulty.)

Although references to Wales crop up, sometimes in quite unlikely places, in the notes to the more lyric pieces, La Villemarqué's debts to Welsh scholarship are heaviest in the collection's 'earlier' bardic material. The very first piece in the 1839 edition was *Diougann Gwenc'hlan / La Prédiction de Gwenc'hlan* ('The Prophecy of Gwenc'hlan'), the dramatic first-person lament of a dark-age bard, blinded and imprisoned, predicting the destruction of his enemies. In the

[19] Ibid., I, p. lxiii.
[20] 'Un rapport de M. de La Villemarqué', 1098.

introduction, La Villemarqué had already explained that, until the eighteenth century, the Bretons had possessed a collection (*receuil*) of Gwenc'hlan's poems: although this collection was now lost, it was still possible to find fragments of his poems in oral tradition. The bard, identified with the 'Cian, qu'on appelle Gueinchguant [*sic*]' of the *Historia Brittonum*, is made an approximate contemporary of Taliesin and Aneirin.[21] La Villemarqué's interest in the character of Gwenc'hlan has a complex prehistory, which need not be repeated here, but the notion of a famous lost Breton manuscript attributed to a fifth-century bard was not his own. For present purposes La Villemarqué's motives and intentions during what became known as the 'affaire Gwenc'hlan' are of less importance than the poem which finally emerged in 1839, and the image of bardism it conveys.[22]

The piece, readily dismissed by Gourvil as a 'chanson factice' (an artificial song, i.e. a fake), does not obviously display many of the characteristics of popular Breton song (qualities which are clearly discernible in the idiomatic echoes elsewhere in the collection), but its lyrical first-person melancholy has a certain poetic power:[23]

Pa guz ann héol, pa goenv ar môr Mé war kana war treuz ma dôr	Quand le soleil se couche, quand la mer s'enfle, je chante sur le seuil de ma porte
Ma oann iaouank mé gané-fé ma zo deut koz kanann ivé	Quand j'étais jeune, je chantais; devenu vieux, je chante encore
Mé gan enn noz, mé gan enn dé Ha mé zo keûet koulskoude	Je chante la nuit, je chante le jour et je suis chagrin pourtant

(When the sun sets and the sea swells, I sing at the threshold of my door
When I was young I sang: grown old, I am still singing.
I sing the night, I sing the day, and I grieve nonetheless.)

Having catalogued his infirmities in some detail, the bard then has a vision of two symbolic animals, a boar and a sea horse, in mortal combat, and the poem finishes with his curse on the prince who has thrown him into the dungeon.

'Cette pièce', the notes claim, correctly enough, 'est tout à fait dans le goût des poésies des plus anciens bardes Gallois' ('This piece is quite in the style of

[21] *BB* (1839), I, p. xii. La Villemarqué is reacting to earlier attempts by Evan Evans and Sharon Turner to turn 'Cian, qui vocatur Gue[ni]ith Guaut' into an equally fictitious 'Gwyngwn'. A famous section of the ninth-century *Historia Brittonum* roughly synchronizes the activities of five poets (of whom only Taliesin and Aneirin are associated with a surviving corpus of poetry) with the reign of Maelgwn Gwynedd.

[22] Francis Gourvil, '"Voleur" sans le savoir: Prosper Mérimée et "Gwenc'hlan" en 1835', *Nouvelle revue de Bretagne* (March–August, 1949), 104–15, 211–22, 299–306.

[23] *BB* (1839), I, pp. 4–5.

the oldest Welsh bards').[24] Five points of obvious correspondence are explained. Like Taliesin, Gwenc'hlan believes in the 'three circles of existence and in the dogma of metempsychosis'; like the famous Llywarch Hen, he suffers physically and emotionally (a heartfelt translation gives the French reader a taste of the Welsh bard's complaint – 'je suis vieux, je suis seul, je suis décrepit' (I am old, I am alone, I am decrepit)); extensive use is made of animal epithets (his chief is a wild boar, Taliesin's a warhorse); like Aneirin, Gwenc'hlan sings in his chains, and there are exact correspondences to medieval Welsh verse in a line describing warriors with blood up to their knees and in a verse about an eagle, reminiscent of the 'Eryr Pengwern' stanzas of Llywarch Hen.[25] In 1845, he added final confirmation of their close affinity in the unmistakeable traces of alliteration and in the uncanny similarities of tone:

> Les chants des poètes gallois, contemporains de Gwenchlan, portent la meme empreinte profonde de mélancolie, de fatalisme et d'enthousiasme; ils respirent le meme esprit prophetique et national.[26]
>
> (The songs of the Welsh poets, contemporary with Gwenc'hlan, bear the same deep marks of melancholy, fatalism and enthusiasm; they breathe the same prophetic and national spirit.)

The critics liked it, the *Gazette de France* asking enthusiastically, 'Y a-t-il, par exemple, quelque chose de plus terrible que ce passage de la prédiction de Garenc'hlan [*sic*], l'un des débris les plus authentiques du bardisme primitif?' ('Can there be anything more sublime than this passage from the prophecy of Garenc'hlan [*sic*], one of the most authentic relics of primitive bardism?').[27] The absence of any obvious parallels in recorded Breton oral tradition (there are echoes in popular prophetic material, but nothing at all like it in the songs)[28] makes it easier to read this piece as a kind of poetic back-formation, generated by its own notes. It appears to be a textbook bardic poem precisely because it is.

This is not the case with the next piece, which, although it leans equally heavily on Welsh sources for its erudite notes, does at least have a healthy abundance of related texts in the song tradition with which it may be compared. In 1845, the Gwenc'hlan poem was ousted from its opening position in the collection by 'Ar Rannou/Les Séries' ('The Parts'), also

[24] Ibid., I, p. 10.

[25] The references in the notes direct the reader to 'Dr Owen's Pughe' [*sic*] *Dictionary* (2nd edn., 1832) and a selection of poems from the *The Myvyrian Archaiology of Wales*.

[26] *BB* (1845), I, p. xvii. The shared 'prophetic and national spirit' is also noted in BB (1839), I, p. vx.

[27] *Gazette de France*, 15 October 1839.

[28] For the Gwenc'hlan legend and its possible survival in oral tradition, see Mary-Ann Constantine, 'Prophecy and Pastiche in the Breton Ballads: *Groac'h Ahes* and *Gwenc'hlan*', *Cambrian Medieval Celtic Studies*, 30 (1995), 87–121.

known as 'The Druid and the Child'. When, in 1867, the storm finally broke over La Villemarqué and his editing of the *Barzaz-Breiz*, this song was one of the most controversial, and most discussed. La Villemarqué introduces the piece as 'one of the most peculiar and perhaps the most ancient in Breton poetry'.[29] It is, he claims, a pedagogical dialogue between a Druid and a child, containing a summary, in twelve questions and twelve answers, of druidical doctrine concerning fate, cosmogony, geography, chronology, astronomy, magic, medicine and metempsychosis. In a neat formulation of much nineteenth-century thinking on oral tradition, he adds:

> Chose extraordinaire, l'empire de la coutume est tel en Bretagne, parmi le peuple des campagnes, que les pères, sans le comprendre, continuent d'enseigner à leurs enfants, qui ne l'entendent pas davantage, le chant mystérieux et sacré qu'enseignaient les druides à leurs ancêtres.[30]
>
> (It is an extraordinary thing, but tradition is such a powerful force amongst the Breton peasantry that fathers, without understanding it, continue to teach their children, who do not understand it either, the mysterious and sacred song which the druids taught their ancestors.)

To complete the transformation, these obligingly empty vessels are changed in the 1867 edition from 'pères' to 'mères':[31] what was once male and hieratic is now in the mouths of mothers and nurses.

Because the song is recapitulative, building up a sequence of questions and answers from one to twelve like the English 'Green Grow the Rushes-O' (to which it is distantly related), all the elements assemble in the final set. In the traditional versions, those elements vary considerably from area to area, making it difficult to produce a standard 'type' against which to judge La Villemarqué's transformations. J.-J. Boidron's analysis of some forty versions (including La Villemarqué's) is a helpful point of reference for comparative purposes.[32]

> *The Druid*
> Fair one, bright son of the Druid, speak
> Fair one, what will you have?
> What shall I sing you?

[29] *BB* (1845), I, p. 1.
[30] Ibid.
[31] *BB* (1867), p. 1.
[32] J.-J. Boidron, *'Gousperoù Ar Raned' ha gourspered 'Ar Rannou': Les 'Vêpres des Grenouilles' ou 'Les Séries' des druides* (Rennes, 1993). Because the poems were very much aimed at a non-Breton-speaking readership, my translation of the *Barzaz-Breiz* piece is based on La Villemarqué's French, which itself does not always give an accurate rendering of the Breton.

The Child
Sing me the twelfth series
So I may learn it now

The Druid
Twelve months and twelve signs, the last but one is the Archer, shooting his barbed arrow. The twelve signs battle: the blessed Cow, the Black Cow with the white Star is coming from the Forest of Plunder. The barbed arrow in her breast, her blood flowing everywhere, lowing, her head raised up. The horn sounds: fire and thunder! Rain and wind, thunder and fire! Nothing remains, not a single Series . . .

Eleven armed priests, coming from Vannes: their swords are broken, their robes are bloodied and their crutches are of hazel. Of three hundred only eleven remain.

Ten ships seen coming from Nantes: Woe unto you! woe unto you, men of Vannes!

Nine little white hands on the table in the courtyard near the tower of Lozarmeur, and nine mothers groaning. Nine korrigan dancing with flowers in their hair and woollen cloaks, around the spring in the light of the moon. The sow and her nine piglets by the door to her sty, grunting and snuffling, snuffling and grunting. Little ones! Run to the apple tree, the old boar will teach you a lesson.

Eight winds whistling; eight fires with the Great Fire, in May, on the mountain of War. Eight heifers white as foam grazing on the Deep Island; eight white heifers of Our Lady.

Seven suns and seven moons: the chicken has seven planets; there are seven elements in the flour of the air (atoms).

Six little children made of wax brought alive by the power of the moon: if you don't know it, I do.

Five zones of the earth; five parts of eternity; five rocks upon our sister

Four stones for whetting, Merlin's whetstones, sharpening the swords of the brave.

Three parts in this world, three beginnings and three ends, for men and oak alike. Three kingdoms of Merlin, with golden fruit and bright flowers, little children laughing.

Two oxen harnessed to a shell: they heave, they strain. See, what a wonder!

No series but Necessity: Death, father of suffering. Nothing before, nothing after.

Such a rich confusion of images offers considerable scope for interpretation. Caesar, Strabo and William of Malmesbury are all summoned to help make sense of the song, but the majority of the references are Welsh – eight to *The Myvyrian Archaiology*, one to Edward Jones's *Bardic Museum* and one to Iolo's *Poems, Lyric and Pastoral*; William Owen Pughe's dictionary is also cited.

Before examining the 'druidic' doctrine, however, there is the question of the title. In French, it is unambiguously 'Les Séries, ou le Druide et L'Enfant' (The Series, or The Druid and the Child); in Breton, it is given simply as 'Ar Rannou'. *Rann*, like the Welsh *rhan*, means a part or a section; the plural *rannou* could therefore be taken to mean a series of parts. In Breton oral tradition, however, the common name for this song is 'Gousperou ar Ran*ed*', with *ran* here meaning 'frog or tadpole' – 'The Frog's Vespers'. An endless point of debate in the eventual controversy over the authenticity of the *Barzaz-Breiz* was whether La Villemarqué could legitimately translate *rann* in the song as *série* (in the sense of 'sequence'): traditional versions certainly use it ambiguously enough, enabling devouts and sceptics to split into two camps. Gourvil, La Villemarqué's antagonistic biographer, assembles a few traditional examples with which to pour scorn on the druidic version and stubbornly translates it as 'frog' wherever possible ('What shall I sing? The loveliest frog you know').[33]

A few examples from La Villemarqué's commentary on his own version show how he used his Welsh sources when interpreting the song.[34] The first Series –

Heb rann ar red heb-ken	Pas de série pour le nombre un: la
Ankou, tad ann anken	Nécessité unique; le Trépas, père de la douleur
Netra kent, netra ken.	rien avant, rien de plus.

(No series but Necessity
Death, father of suffering
Nothing before, nothing after.)

– is an obvious echo of the famous comment in Caesar's *De Bello Gallico*, that the Gauls worship Dis, the god of death, and La Villemarqué duly points this out. But there are also echoes (not acknowledged here) of Iolo's Welsh triads, such as this one from the sequence published in 1794:

Tri phrif anffawd Abred, Angen, Anghof, ag Angau.

The three great, or primary, infelicities of the *Circle of Inchöation*: *Necessity*, *loss of Memory*, and *Death*.[35]

33 Gourvil, *La Villemarqué*, p. 406.
34 All quotations from the song are from *BB* (1845), I, pp. 1–15.
35 Williams: *PLP*, II, pp. 235, 242 (Iolo's translation).

The second series links directly to Welsh mythology, with the oxen confidently identified as a reference to an early Celtic flood myth, in which Hu Gadarn, with his two oxen, Ychain Bannawg, pulls a 'crocodile' (as La Villemarqué translates *afanc*) from Lake Llion, thus rescuing the earth from the universal deluge. The flood myth, like Hu Gadarn himself, is once again Iolo's work.[36] So far, La Villemarqué appears to be citing his dubious sources in all good faith. Elsewhere, however, he is considerably more creative. Discussing the comparison between the life of a man and the life of an oak tree in the third series, he cites a phrase from Taliesin: '"Chêne est mon nom", dit-il' ('"Oak is my name", he says'), with a note adding the 'original' Welsh: 'Derou . . . henou i'm.' A glance at the relevant passage in *The Myvyrian Archaiology* reveals the significance of the omission marks. La Villemarqué's 'citation' is highlighted in bold:

Derw buanawr	(**Oak** swift his shout
Rhagddaw cryneu nef a llawr	heaven and earth trembled before him
gelyn glew dryffiawr	a strong warrior enemy
ei **enw ym** peullawr	his **name in** a writing tablet)[37]

In effect, the three words have been taken almost at random, and, with scant regard for grammar (and indeed, in the case of **ym**, meaning), turned into a gnomic statement; this is then used to elucidate a line of Breton verse, which is itself either the author's own creation, or conjured from an ambiguous (and now missing) original. The traditional versions of the song contain images quite as surreal as any in the *Barzaz-Breiz* version, but Boidron offers no parallel for this line.[38] Elsewhere in the notes appear references to relatively familiar Welsh legendary figures, such as Gwion Bach, the little boy set by the witch Ceridwen to watch the cauldron of inspiration in the story of Taliesin, and Merlin – although here it should be noted that, since La Villemarqué did

[36] See above, p. 131.

[37] *MAW*, I, p. 30. The extract is from the *Cad Goddeu* (The Battle of the Trees). Marged Haycock's emended text and translation for this section are as follows: 'Derw buanawr/ Racdaw crynei nef a llawr/ <Glesyn> glew drussyawr/ Y enw ym peullawr' ('Oak [was] swift his shout/ Heaven and earth trembled before him/?Bugle, a brave warrior/ His name [is kept] on a writing tablet'): 'The Significance of the 'Cad Goddeu' Tree-List in the Book of Taliesin' in M. J. Ball, J. Fife, E. Poppe, J. Rowland (eds.), *Celtic Linguistics: Reading in the Brythonic Languages. A Festschrift for T. Arwyn Watkins* (Amsterdam, 1990), p. 324.

[38] Boidron, *'Gousperoù Ar Raned'*, pp. 236–7. Traditional versions of the song might include any of the following: eleven hunting dogs returning from the chase; eleven piglets with a sow; ten ships loaded with wine; nine armed sons returning from Nantes with their shirts bloodied, their swords broken; seven suns and seven moons; six brothers and sisters; five black cows crossing the land of God; four ducks singing the *exaudi*; three fingers of gold; two wheels in a mill; a silver finger for Mary.

in fact discover a ballad about Merlin in Breton oral tradition, his appearance in the eclectic cast of this song is perhaps understandable.[39]

One further interpretation is of particular interest here. In his analysis of the twelfth series, La Villemarqué compares the words 'fire and thunder! Rain and wind, thunder and fire!' with a few lines from Gruffudd ab yr Ynad Coch's thirteenth-century elegy for Llywelyn ap Gruffudd. In this, one of the most famous poems in Welsh literature, the poet's grief at the prince's death is mirrored in an anguished landscape of wind and rain, with land and sea thrown into turmoil. La Villemarqué comments coolly:

> Cette concordance de doctrine est frappante. Évidémment l'auteur cambrien connaissait une partie des secrets dont l'Armoricain fait un si pompeux étalage, et il avait puisé au même courant traditionnel. Les bardes gallois du moyen âge, il ne faut pas l'oublier, étaient les descendants convertis des Druides, prêtres du dieu Bel, et les paysans du Gladmorgan, sans comprendre la portée du terme, donnent encore à ceux d'aujourd'hui le nom très-caractéristique d'*initiés de la vallée de Bélen.* (Ed. Williams, *Poems*, t. II, p. 161). Le barde armoricain le mériterait bien plus.
>
> (This concordance of doctrine is striking. Evidently the Welsh author partly knew some of the secrets that the Armorican poet here displays with such pomp, and he drew on the same traditional current. The Welsh bards of the Middle Ages, we must not forget, were the converted descendants of the Druids, priests of the god Bel, and the peasants of Gladmorgan [*sic*], ignorant of the meaning of the term, to this day give them the highly characteristic name of *initiates of the valley of Belen.* (Ed. Williams, *Poems*, vol. II, p. 161) The Armorican bard is far more deserving of this title.)

Having dismissed the Welsh poet for his somewhat inadequate grasp of the bardic mysteries (so much more satisfyingly displayed in the Breton song), La Villemarqué proceeds to weave in another Welsh source, this time to one of Iolo's own footnotes in *Poems, Lyric and Pastoral*:

> *Bardism* has also been for time immemorial under some degree of persecution; its regular professors are known in *Glamorgan* by the nick-name of *Gwŷr Cwm y felin*, and generally supposed to be *infidels, conjurors*, and we know not what.[40]

Iolo used the phrase 'Gwŷr Cwm y Felin' to describe the group of Dissenting scholars or grammarians who were responsible for the literary revival in Blaenau Morgannwg during the eighteenth century; and it is true, although it is not mentioned in the relevant footnote, that he saw in them a direct link to the

[39] Laurent, *Aux sources*, pp. 286–96; Mary-Ann Constantine, 'Neither flesh nor fowl: Merlin as bird-man in Breton folk tradition', *Arthurian Literature*, XXI (2004), 95–114.

[40] Williams: *PLP*, II, p. 161.

patriarchal religion of the Druids.[41] But the god Belen must be La Villemarqué's own interpolation: *Cwm y felin* is a simple place-name, meaning 'the valley of the mill'. Given that the Breton for 'mill' is 'melin', exactly the same as the Welsh, La Villemarqué's transformation of the word into 'the valley of the god Belen' requires something more than the eye of faith. Although it has recently been suggested that 'these references are truthful – that is to say, La Villemarqué did not deform or alter them to suit his thesis, which does not exclude his being inspired by them in the first place',[42] it is clear that his use of Welsh sources in this poem alone ranges from mistaken innocence, to profound ignorance, to pure deception; his actual knowledge of Welsh remains remarkably difficult to define. His use of the *Myvyrian* in particular is, even given the rich and strange mix contained within its pages, selective, eccentric and highly manipulative. As Gourvil suspected, the scholarly apparatus for this poem is as creative a compilation as the poem itself.

There are many other examples of La Villemarqué turning to Welsh sources throughout the *Barzaz-Breiz*. The ballad of the plague of Elliant gains chronological depth from being linked to the sixth-century plague that killed Maelgwn Gwynedd; the Merlin poems are elucidated with copious references to the ninth-century *Avalleneu* and to Geoffrey of Monmouth's *Vita Merlini*; the witch Eloisa boasts of her powers in the language of Taliesin. In some, Iolo's influence is especially marked: 'La Fiancée en Enfer' ('The Betrothed In Hell') gives rise to a long, bardically inspired explanation of the progression of souls through the various circles of being;[43] 'La Fête de Juin' ('The June Festival'), sees in the custom of the dance-leader wearing a bunch of blue, green, and white ribbons clear evidence of its 'origine druidique' in a solstice ritual.[44] Other references are most interesting for the glimpses they give of the young author's contacts with Wales. A song placed early in the chronology is 'Ar Vugel Laec'het' / 'L'enfant supposé' ('The Changeling'), in which a mother, by pretending to prepare a meal for ten people in an eggshell, tricks the changeling into exclaiming:

Vit dek, mamm kez, enn eur blusken!	Pour dix, chère mère, dans une coque!
Gwélez vi ken gweled iar wenn	J'ai vu l'oeuf avant de voir la poule blanche;
Gwélez mez ken gwéled wézen	j'ai vu le gland avant de voir l'arbre

[41] See NLW 13138A, pp. 104–6; NLW 13121B, pp. 335–8.

[42] Boidron, *'Gousperoù Ar Raned'*, pp. 214–15.

[43] *BB* (1839), I, p. 135. The progression of souls comes from William Owen Pughe, *A Dictionary of the Welsh Language, Explained in English* (2nd edn., London, 1832), II, p. 214, s. v. Hanfod.

[44] *BB* (1839), II, pp. 227–8 (with references to the 'Bardism' in William Owen, *The Heroic Elegies and Other Pieces of Llywarç Hen* (London, 1792), pp. 37, 39, 42). The 1845 edition expands this to include a 'recollection' from one of the participants to the effect that they remember priests wearing bardic colours and playing a kind of ivory harp: *BB* (1845), II, pp. 326–7.

Gwelez mez ha gwélez gwial	J'ai vu le gland et j'ai vu la gaule
Gwélez derwen é c'hoat Brézal	j'ai vu le chêne au bois de Brézal
Ha kent na wéliz kémend all	et n'ai jamais vu pareille chose[45]

(For ten, mother dear, in one shell! I have seen the egg before seeing the white hen; I have seen the acorn before seeing the tree; I have seen the acorn and the gall; I have seen the oak in the forest of Brézal; but I have never seen anything like that.)

The comparatively brief notes to this song cite 'une tradition galloise analogue, que nous ont racontée les paysans du Glamorgan' ('an analogous Welsh tradition, recited to us by the peasants of Glamorgan').[46] This turns out to be a similar story containing a 'Welsh triplet', disguised in heavily Bretonicized orthography, which corresponds 'almost exactly' to the Breton verses of the *Barzaz-Breiz*. The Welsh version is presented as the sole remaining debris of the ancient song, which must therefore date to the period before the separation of the two peoples; Geoffrey of Monmouth's *Vita Merlini* (in which Merlin makes a similar pronouncement about having seen an acorn grow into an oak) provides a further chronological anchor. As Donatien Laurent has pointed out, the correspondance between the two traditions is indeed striking, especially if one allows for the fact that La Villemarqué has very probably transformed a Breton story and rhyme, much like the Welsh one, into a full-blown ballad.[47] But the sources cited here are also interesting for other reasons. The triplet, La Villemarqué implies, is a find of his own, collected from the Welsh-speaking peasantry of Glamorgan: if this were really the case it would be a fine example of his ability to communicate in Welsh, and of the use he made of his time in Wales. But written sources are also given, and Thomas Crofton Croker's 'The Brewery of Egg-shells' reads very like a synopsis of the Breton ballad, even down to the tender moment of recognition of the sleeping returned child, while a contribution to the *Cambrian Quarterly* makes it clear that La Villemarqué's Welsh 'triplet' was in fact a four-line *pennill*.[48] Jane Williams of Aberpergwm, who seems to have provided Croker with much of the Welsh material included in the third volume of his *Fairy Legends*, was an

[45] *BB* (1839), I, pp. 28–9.

[46] Ibid., p. 32.

[47] Donatien Laurent, 'Tradition and Innovation in Breton Oral Literature' in Glanmor Williams and Robert Owen Jones (eds.), *The Celts and the Renaissance: Tradition and Innovation* (Cardiff, 1990), pp. 91–9.

[48] See Thomas Crofton Croker, *Fairy Legends and Traditions of the South of Ireland* (3 vols., London, 1825–8), I, 65–76; and *Cambrian Quarterly*, II (1830), 86–7. The story is there introduced as 'translated almost literally from the Welsh, as told by the peasantry', and the *pennill* runs: 'Gwelais vesen cyn gweled Derwen,/ Gwelais wy cyn gweled iâr/ Erioed ni welais verwi bwyd i vedel/ Mewn plisgyn wy Iâr!' (I have seen the acorn before the oak/ I have seen the egg before the hen/ But I have never seen food for the harvest supper / Cooked in the shell of an egg!)

active member of the Llanover circle, and it seems quite possible that La Villemarqué's contact with 'les paysans de Glamorgan' was entirely mediated through her.[49]

Other folk contacts, some mentioned in passing, also help to confirm the shared Welsh–Breton heritage. In 'Les Fleurs de Mai' ('The Flowers of May', added in 1845) a reference to the traditional practice apparently recorded in Wales and Brittany of dressing with flowers the graves of girls who die in May, concludes with the elegant and eerily pre-Arnoldian assertion that all the best parts of Shakespeare are Welsh (or is it Breton?):

> Shakspeare [*sic*], auquel les traditions et les coutumes bretonnes fournirent plus d'un vers charmant, a enchâssé ce dernier trait, comme un joyau de prix, dans son poëme sur le Gallois *Kymbeline*.[50]
>
> (Shakespeare, who found in [British/Breton] traditions and customs the inspiration for more than one delightful line, has worked this detail, like a rare jewel, into his poem on the Welshman *Cymbeline*.)

As this curiously misleading sentence shows, the characteristic feature of La Villemarqué's style is a parenthetic ability to imply connections and influences which, on closer inspection, cannot quite bear the suggested load. Even today, proving him 'wrong' is a surprisingly fatiguing business, since his secret lies in the accumulation of half-truths which need careful sifting (and some of which, it must be said, have occasionally resolved themselves into unexpected new truths).[51] In this context it is easy to sympathize with Nelly Blanchard's decision to read the whole of the *Barzaz-Breiz* as a creative work, to treat La Villemarqué's erudition as a form of fictional discourse, a rhetorical strategy designed to impress and persuade his readers. Hers is an appealing and liberating approach which can ignore the smaller specific questions of authenticity, the untangling of which can so easily become a pedantic game of reappraising sources and giving him marks out of ten for accuracy.[52] But it is perhaps dangerous to cut quite so free. Those sources do, after all, matter; they exert a force. To treat the book as a sealed container ignores the tradition onto which the *Barzaz-Breiz* was a window, albeit an elaborate stained-glass one. It does make a difference if a song existed in popular tradition before being rewritten, because it is precisely in the gap between the traditional and the rewritten versions that ideology, taste and motivation can be properly analysed. These

[49] See Croker, *Fairy Legends*, III, p. 159.

[50] *BB* (1845), II, p. 266.

[51] Some of Donatien Laurent's most successful work on the Breton tradition has started from a hint from La Villemarqué, overturning the general assumption that his 'Celtic' connections are a priori suspect. See especially the studies of Merlin (*Aux sources*, pp. 286–96) and Skolan/Ysgolan, 'La *gwerz* de Skolan et la légende de Merlin', *Éthnologie française*, 1, 3–4 (1971), 19–54.

[52] Blanchard, 'Une fiction pour s'inventer'.

questions apply equally to the deployment of references: La Villemarqué's use and abuse of his academic sources really needs to be treated as more than camouflage or rhetoric. As Anthony Grafton's entertaining and instructive work on the history of the footnote suggests, the prime authenticating mechanism of scholarship, its copious citings of sources and authorities, remained a site of extraordinary manipulative potential well into the nineteenth-century's era of apparently solid objectivity.[53] Indeed, faced with La Villemarqué's relentlessly subtle meshing of erudition and wilful misrepresentation, one longs for the noisier and more idiosyncratic commentaries of the previous century.

La Villemarqué's debt to Wales can also be measured negatively: he was inspired by Welsh material, but reacted against it too. Although in 1837, with the prospect of his visit to Abergavenny before him, he had written to Thomas Price of his dream of visiting 'cette sainte terre de Cambria', and although he was genuinely overwhelmed by the event itself, his attitude to Wales is far from one of straightforward adulation. Many of the references to Wales in his work are not acts of homage to the country that is the source of bardism, but something more aggressive. Like Iolo, La Villemarqué singlemindedly subsumed sources to his own needs: the needs of his *patrie*, his *bro* (locality), and the needs of his religion.

[53] Anthony Grafton, *The Footnote* (London, 1997).

12

Translating Wales

On 11 November 1840, Lady Charlotte Guest noted acidly in her diary that La Villemarqué had entered an essay for the October eisteddfod at Abergavenny on the influence of Welsh traditions on the literature of Europe. She was not impressed:

> His essay was really very amusing to me. He made great use of my Mabinogion and scarcely made any acknowledgement. On the contrary he delicately insinuated that I did not write the book myself, a degree of moral turpitude which he dare not openly accuse me of. The secret of all this is his anger at being unable to forestall me in the publication of Peredur March 1839.[1]

Guest's translation of 'Peredur', one of the Welsh romances, was done at white-heat between March and July 1839 after hearing that La Villemarqué had persuaded Tegid to send him a copy of the Welsh text, and was planning to forestall her with his own translation into French. She worked furiously, barely stopping to give birth to her fifth child (she would have ten children in all), and was triumphant to discover that she had won the race. In fact, it seems that Tegid had not provided La Villemarqué with an English crib for his copy of the Welsh text, and that the task was simply beyond him.

In 1842, La Villemarqué further antagonized Lady Charlotte by publishing French translations of three Welsh Arthurian romances under the decidedly ambiguous title *Contes populaires des anciens bretons*.[2] The tales themselves (generally known by the names of their heroes as *Owain*, *Geraint* and *Peredur*) were of obvious interest to a French audience, being versions of three romances by

[1] *The Diaries of Lady Charlotte Guest: Extracts from her Journals 1833–1852, edited by her Grandson the Earl of Bessborough* (London, 1950), p. 117. See also Guest and John, *Lady Charlotte*, pp. 107–9.

[2] Th. Hersart de la Villemarqué, *Contes popularaires des anciens bretons* (2 vols., Paris, 1842). In a copy held at the National Library of Wales a nineteenth-century reader has written, in French, several caustic comments, and replaced the ambiguous 'bretons' in the title with the word GALLOIS ('Welsh'). (Copy from the library of David Nutt, acquired in 1914.)

Chrétien de Troyes, *Yvain*, *Éric et Énide* and *Perceval*.[3] They also happened to be the only three Welsh tales published with English translations by Charlotte Guest between 1838 and 1840.[4] Guest's role in the work is mentioned briefly in the preface to the *Contes populaires*, which revisits (with yet another account of the rapturous reception he received upon declaiming his poem) the young author's visit to Wales in 1838, and outlines the original object of his research into the Welsh manuscripts. This was 'de les rechercher, de les traduire, et de constater quels rapports ils pouvaient avoir avec l'ancienne littérature francaise' (to search them out, to translate them, and to see what links they might have with early French literature). He then pays ambiguous homage to the work of 'une jeune Galloise . . . lady Charlotte Guest', who

> se réserva la première partie de cette tâche, et voulut bien m'y associer: elle fit imprimer plusieurs textes originaux, et poursuit leur mise en lumière avec une intélligence et un courage au-dessus de tout éloge; j'entreprends seul la seconde en ce moment.[5]
>
> (reserved for herself the first part of this task, and was kind enough to involve me in it: she published several original texts and pursued [or, is pursuing] their elucidation with an intelligence and courage beyond all praise; I alone am currently undertaking the second [or, just possibly, 'I am currently undertaking only the second'].)

It is, as ever, hard to say if La Villemarqué is being deliberately vague here, or simply careless, but the phrasing certainly leaves it very unclear exactly which 'tasks' are being undertaken (or have been completed) by whom. The implication in any event is of a partnership of equals, with La Villemarqué involved from the beginning, and this is confirmed in the preface's closing image:

> Telle voudrait paraître la publication de ces contes, fruits poétiques mûris autrefois sous un double rayon du soleil d'Armorique et de Cambrie, aujourd'hui cueillis pour l'Europe, par une Galloise et un Breton.[6]
>
> (Such is the desired aim of the publication of these tales, poetic fruits ripened long ago under a double ray of sun in Armorica and Cambria, gathered today on behalf of Europe by a Welshwoman and a Breton.)

[3] Ceridwen Lloyd-Morgan describes the three Welsh tales as 're-tellings of the French narratives, and often very free re-tellings at that': 'French Texts, Welsh Translations' in Roger Ellis (ed.), *The Medieval Translator*, II (London, 1991), p. 49; the direction of influence/adaptation would not, of course, have been generally agreed in La Villemarqué's day.

[4] Gourvil, *La Villemarqué*, pp. 96–7; for Lady Charlotte's translations, see Rachel Bromwich, 'The Mabinogion and Lady Charlotte Guest', *THSC* (1986), 127–41, and Sioned Davies, 'Cyfieithu'r Mabinogion' in J. E. Caerwyn Williams (ed.), *Ysgrifau Beirniadol XIII* (Dinbych, 1997), pp. 16–30.

[5] *Contes populaires*, I, p. xv.

[6] Ibid.

In reality, the 'partnership' was far from sunny. On receiving a copy of the book from La Villemarqué himself in May, Guest wrote in her diary that he had relied almost totally on her own translations of the three romances: 'he has followed me servilely throughout and taken all my notes, without acknowledgement except in one unimportant instance'.[7] An enthusiastic review of the book (together with the *Barzaz-Breiz*) in the English *Athenaeum* in July prompted Guest and her friend George Clark to write an angry response, sent by her publisher William Rees, which openly accused La Villemarqué of 'piracy' and gave a detailed account of his procedure:

> To the English edition were appended certain notes, some of which were derived from sources strictly local, and the whole collected together from very various authorities. These notes are also appropriated in the French translation, – sometimes absolutely unchanged, sometimes a little altered, or taken to pieces and rearranged, and often transposed from one story to another. Throughout the whole work there is not any acknowledgement of the appropriation, and except in a passage in the notes, the only mention of Lady Charlotte Guest is in an extremely flippant paragraph in the introduction.[8]

If his translations lacked imagination, La Villemarqué's plagiarism is at least inventive; Guest could not accuse him of servility in his use of her notes. Most of the references cited are to 'original' medieval sources such as *The Myvyrian Archaiology* or Gerald of Wales, sources which we know he used in the *Barzaz-Breiz* before his visit to Wales. He introduces much of his own material from Brittany; in some places he expands on her observations, and there is at least one more fantasy-translation entirely of his own creation, again apparently working directly from *The Myvyrian Archaiology*, which purports to be a hymn of praise to the great god Hu, sung by a victim about to be sacrificed in a stone circle.[9] On the other hand there are plenty of correspondences in matters of detail: it is at least suspicious that La Villemarqué should, like Guest, have felt the need to provide a separate elucidatory note to the phrase 'trees of equal height'.

But helping himself too liberally to Lady Charlotte's translation and notes was only one of the acts of piracy in the *Contes populaires*, which performs a kind of double appropriation, one actual, one retrospective. La Villemarqué argued that Brittany was the ultimate source for the three French romances, and the birthplace of the Arthurian cycle as a whole. The premise required that he produce 'originals', and these, naturally enough, came from the *Barzaz-Breiz*,

[7] *The Diaries of Lady Charlotte Guest*, p. 133.

[8] *Athenaeum*, 772 (1842), 734.

[9] *Contes populaires*, II, p. 292: 'Le serpent du karn'. *MAW*, I, pp. 72–3 reveals that he had spliced together the last six lines of 'Marwnad Uthyr Pendragon' ('Elegy for Uthyr Pendragon') and the first seventeen of a poem simply entitled 'Armes' ('Prophecy'). The 'translation' (which he modestly admits may not be entirely accurate) looks like very bad sight-reading.

which between 1839 and 1845 underwent considerable augmentation, particularly of its earlier historical and mythological section. The 'Perceval/ Peredur' material is discussed in the 1845 edition in notes to a sequence of 'fragments épiques' relating to a 'national hero' whom La Villemarqué called 'Lez Breiz' ('Defender of Brittany') and incorrectly identified with a ninth-century chief called Morvan.[10] The sequence begins with an episode strongly reminiscent of the opening of the Peredur/Perceval story: a naive young boy marvels at the arms and armour of a passing knight before running off to join the court, leaving his mother unconscious with grief. The notes discuss the affinities between the different international versions to arrive at the foregone conclusion of the primacy and purity of the Breton.

La Villemarqué is especially interesting on the nature of the transformations this 'primary source' has undergone. The song, he claims, crossed from Brittany to Wales in the ninth century, where it was initially sung in the Breton manner but later reworked as prose:

> mais toute poésie, toute naïveté, tous les détails charmants de l'original, la forme même, si dramatique et si piquante, ont complètement disparu dans son récit terne et sans vie, qui n'est qu'un résumé, du reste.[11]
>
> (but all the poetry, all the innocence, all the delightful details of the original, even the form, so dramatic and piquante, have entirely disappeared in his dull and lifeless rendition, which is, for that matter, little more than a resumé.)

This degeneration, he argues, has less to do with the passage of time than with the passage from one culture to another. The Breton oral tradition is thriving after nine centuries because 'elle a de profondes racines dans les souvenirs nationaux' (it has deep roots in national memory). The absence of such roots in Wales has obliged the Welsh to graft the story onto one of their own. Chrétien de Troyes and Wolfram von Eschenbach are also accused of lacking in naturalness, with, if possible, the German even heavier, more dragging and more montonous than the Welsh. All are charged with 'plagiarism' from the Breton source:

[10] *BB* (1845), I, 127–84. This proto-epic seems in fact to be based on several traditional ballads relating to a sixteenth-century aristocrat, Jean de Lannion, known as 'Les Aubrays' or 'Lezobré' (see Gourvil, *La Villemarqué*, pp. 421–6). The procedure recalls Macpherson's use of the Gaelic ballads, but the impulse to create 'national' narrative from traditional songs is widespread and apparently irresistible by the mid-nineteenth century: see Constantine and Porter, *Fragments and Meaning*, pp. 39–45.

[11] *BB* (1845), I, p. 178.

> Ce n'est pas, au reste, la seule fois que les étrangers ont gâté, en y portant la main, les traditions de la Bretagne; nous en verrons d'autres exemples. On dirait qu'il en est des souvenirs nationaux commes des plantes délicates qui ne peuvent vivre et fleurir qu'au lieux où elles ont vu le jour.[12]

> (This is not, for that matter, the only occasion on which foreigners have ruined Breton traditions with their improvements; we shall see other examples. It could be argued that national memories are like delicate plants which can only live and flower in the places where they first saw the light.)

It takes a sheer effort of will to remember that this 'delicate' (but surprisingly tenacious) plant is pure mirage, generated by the very sources accused of ruining it: La Villemarqué here demonstrates to perfection the position of the 'scholar-pickpocket' which, as Anthony Grafton points out, had been wittily described by Jacob Thomasius as early as 1673.[13] His subtle appropriations complicate J.-Y. Guiomar's argument that the 1845 *Barzaz-Breiz*, shifting as it does to a more 'Bretonist' position, enlisted Wales as a main source of support in defining Breton culture against France: 'ce qui signifiait pour le Pays de Galles signifiait aussi et de même pour la Bretagne' (what signified for Wales did so also, and in the same way, for Brittany).[14] This, while true in general, overlooks the fact that the Welsh support brought its own problems. The discourse of brotherhood, of shared origins and language and history, of mutual understanding, has its moments of breakdown, of violent reaction. This is one of them: here the Welsh are firmly, along with the French and the Germans, *étrangers* (foreigners).

Nowhere is this conflicted attitude to Wales better displayed than in the question of orthography. The standardization of any language – the establishment of notions of correct usage in grammar and spelling – is fraught with ideological complications. Even for a spectacularly 'successful' language like English, definitions of linguistic correctness can flush out a whole range of anxieties and preconceptions. In a minority language with very little written tradition to rely on, efforts to standardize often reveal deep insecurity. Cultural if not national pride requires a 'native' orthography in order to avoid being spelled, as nineteenth-century Breton often was, through the language of one's

[12] Ibid., p. 183. Something similar happens in the ballad 'Ar Breur-Lez / Le Frère de lait' ('The Foster Brother') when La Villemarqué accuses Gottfried Bürger's famous poem *Lenore* (from which it is at least partially derived) of being a degenerate form of his Breton 'original'. See Mary-Ann Constantine, 'Ballads Crossing Borders: La Villemarqué and the Breton *Lenore*', *Translation & Literature*, 8, no. 2 (1999), 197–216.

[13] 'More than one scholar has plagiarized material from another while simultaneously accusing the victim, in the relevant footnote, of having done the same. Few readers will have the tenacity to check the story for its accuracy, and most will assume that the elegant pickpocket, and not the dishevelled victim, has told the truth': Grafton, *The Footnote*, p. 14.

[14] Guiomar, *Le bretonisme*, p. 541.

oppressive neighbour. Debates over the spelling of Breton (which continue to this day) thus tend to be tied up with a double determination to be taken seriously and to distinguish the language from French.[15]

As a disciple of Le Gonidec, La Villemarqué was involved in language reform from very early in his career. His later comment on that period is a vivid reminder of the initial transition from spoken to written Breton:

> Il voulait bien prendre la peine de me donner des leçons d'une langue que je parlais alors sans règles, et s'intéressait vivement au textes populaires dont j'allais commencer l'impression; ce qu'il y avait d'incorrect dans l'orthographe, les mots ou les phrases, il le redressait et expliquait les expressions, et m'aida plus d'une fois à retrouver le fil à travers le dédale des versions souvent embrouillées.[16]
>
> (He took the trouble to give me lessons in a language which I spoke at that time without rules, and he took a keen interest in the popular texts which I was preparing to publish; where there were faults of orthography, vocabulary or phrasing he corrected and explained them, and more than once he helped me find the thread through a labyrinth of tangled versions.)

As Iolo imbibed the lexicographical ideals of John Walters, so La Villemarqué came to see Le Gonidec's aims of purifying the vocabulary of Breton and rationalizing its orthography in terms of a 'restoration' which necessarily involved linguistic expansion – in both cases the process of creating new words runs parallel with the creation of the 'old' texts in which they are legitimized. When Le Gonidec died, he undertook to publish the *Dictionnaire français–breton* (1847), adding many words of his own, often derived from Welsh, and a lengthy essay on the history of the Breton language.[17] In an earlier essay on *L'avenir de la langue bretonne* ('The Future of the Breton Language'), published in 1842, La Villemarqué had written of the need to persuade Bretons, and the clergy in particular, to adopt a logical and 'national' orthography, no longer calqued on that of French: he devoted much energy to trying to convert the Breton clergy to his system, making enemies in the process, since many found the new system daunted their congregations, long used to hymns and other religious texts in a literary language that took much of its vocabulary from French. La Villemarqué, equating the purity of language with moral purity,

[15] See James Milroy and Lesley Milroy, *Authority in Language: Investigating Language Prescription and Standardization* (3rd edn., London, 1999). Standardization is still highly politicized in Brittany, a fact which (irrationally but powerfully) has much to do with way the nationalist movement developed during the Second World War: see Gwenno Sven Myer, 'Y Cylchgrawn Llydaweg *Gwalarn* (1925–1944): Ei Amcanion, ei Iaith, ei Gyfraniad i Lenyddiaeth' (unpublished University of Wales MA thesis, 1998); Fañch Broudic, *La pratique du breton de l'Ancien Régime à nos jours* (Rennes, 1995).

[16] Gourvil, *La Villemarqué*, p. 34.

[17] Tanguy, *Aux origines*, I, pp. 200–33; the essay is republished in ibid., II, pp. 9–108.

was zealous to the point of accusing one priest of 'heresy' in his adherence to this 'jargon mixte'.[18]

La Villemarqué's belief that the modern spoken Breton of the peasantry maintained a purity lost from the written record added an extra twist to all this: since the contemporary songs were records of the past, they could be transcribed into Le Gonidec's orthography and treated as de facto medieval documents. From there, it was a relatively small step to using the same technique on real medieval texts in Welsh: like the ambiguous adjective 'breton', La Villemarqué uses Le Gonidec's orthography to emphasize a kinship with early Welsh written sources which sidelines later Welsh developments altogether. Indeed, it can appear like an act of aggression: the title-page quotation for example, from *The Myvyrian Archaiology*, has been drastically Bretonicized, to the extent that a Welsh reader would have to look hard to make sense of it. The Welsh, which has been taken slightly out of context from the middle of a longer sentence, is:

> a chov a chadw ar bob moliannus ar wr a chenydl; a phob dichwain amserau
>
> (and memory and retaining everything praiseworthy of man and nation/tribe; and every occurrence of the times)

On the flyleaf to the 1839 edition of *Barzaz-Breiz* this is 'cited' as follows:

> Koun a c'havo (barz) or bop moliannuz ar our ha c'henedl, ha fob digwez amzeraou.
> Trioed Énez Priden. (Myvyrian, t. III, p. 291)
>
> Le barde gardera le souvenir de toute chose digne d'éloges concernant l'individu et la race, et de tout événement contemporain.
>
> Triades de l'Ile de Bretagne

The sense of the line is only very slightly altered, and the translation is accurate enough; but the whole character of the language has changed, as if put into heavy disguise. Where a close cognate exists, La Villemarqué has simply substituted Breton words for Welsh (*koun* for *cof*, *enez* for *ynys*, *ha* for *a*, and, more radically, *digwez* for *dichwain*); Breton plural endings are provided (*-ou* not *-au*), and the whole line is further dressed up with the characteristic *k*, *z*, *c'h* of Breton orthography. It is not a translation into Breton, but something more curiously half-way.

La Villemarqué's creeping colonization of Welsh texts did not go unnoticed or unchallenged, especially after he made his practice more explicit. In 1850, he published an anthology of Welsh poets, *Poèmes des bardes bretons du VIè siècle*, which blurs the boundaries between the two languages still further by

[18] Ibid., I, p. 156.

presenting a selection of texts attributed to Taliesin, Aneirin and Llywarch Hen in the rational and 'historical' spelling established by Le Gonidec ('le Jhonson [*sic*] de la péninsule', as he nicely puts it).[19] His claims to have taken his texts, not from *The Myvyrian Archaiology*, but from a careful collation of original manuscripts, are met with cynicism by Gourvil, who notes various anomalies, and points out how little time he would have had for such minutely detailed work during his brief visit to Oxford in 1838.[20] Contemporary critics also voiced doubts: Ernest Renan, in his influential essay on 'La poésie des races celtiques' (first published in *Revue des deux mondes* in 1854) felt that the texts had been rendered effectively unusable on both sides of the English Channel since, to the majority of Breton speakers, Le Gonidec's system was as opaque as the original Welsh.[21] The preface to a new edition of the work in 1860 responded in decidedly injured tones to the negative criticisms the book received. The aim, he explained again, was to 'rétablir scientifiquement les textes sous leur forme première' ('to return the texts by scientific methods to their original form'). The Welsh spelling of these texts, the spelling of *The Myvyrian Archaiology*, was a 'travesty' which left texts 'unrecognizable to the eye': it was 'un système arbitraire de l'invention des Gallois' ('an arbitrary system invented by the Welsh') which had disfigured the old orthography and masked the primitive style.[22]

La Villemarqué's antagonism towards Wales has two main sources. The most paradoxical is his *bretonisme* which, although inspired and largely fuelled by the idea of a renewal of the early relationship with insular Britain, is based on a theory of the primacy or purity of Armorican/Breton sources, which obliges him to appropriate or reject crucial aspects of Welsh literary history. The other, more straightforward, reason is his religion. Notions of moral and religious truth are so powerfully woven into his vision of the language and the people who spoke it that some collision with Nonconformist Wales would appear unavoidable.

La Villemarqué's Catholicism, particularly in the earlier stages of his career, was not without its radical aspects. As J.-Y. Guiomar has noted, the Pension Bailly, where La Villemarqué stayed on his arrival at Paris, was far from narrow-minded, and there were various outlets for the discussion of literary and philosophical ideas.[23] Many of the young Bretons who stayed there were, like La Villemarqué, from families whose traditional grounds for legitimacy – they

[19] Th. Hersart de la Villemarqué, *Poèmes des bardes bretons du VIé siècle* (Paris and Vannes, 1850), p. x.

[20] Gourvil, *La Villemarqué*, p. 119.

[21] The passage was omitted in the better-known version of Renan's essay published in 1860 (see Gourvil, *La Villemarqué*, pp. 119–120).

[22] The *nouvelle édition* was published under a slightly rearranged title: *Les bardes bretons: poèmes du VIè siècle* (Paris, 1860). The citations are from pp. 4–5.

[23] Guiomar, *Le bretonisme*, pp. 62–78.

were aristocratic, regional and Catholic – had been turned upside down by the Revolution and its aftermath (La Villemarqué's mother had lost many members of her family). The Pension Bailly provided a safe place in which the relationship between monarchy, religion and state could be reconsidered. In the decades between 1820 and 1850 the situation was relatively fluid and relatively progressive: many of the students had a social and spiritual agenda which went beyond merely being apologists for the *ancien régime*.

There is, however, an undeniably reactionary flavour to La Villemarqué's vision of Brittany, and his investment in this ideal world could be decidedly confrontational. A striking outburst occurs in the introduction to the *Barzaz-Breiz*, in a passage describing how, in pre-Reformation Wales as in modern Brittany, the most important religious festivals were held at the solstices, just as the druidical assemblies had been. On these great public occasions people danced, sang, played games and held races and wrestling competitions; but that link had been broken by Protestant reform:

> Innocentes et pures joies sanctifiées par la religion, qui vous a enlevées au peuple de Cambrie? Quels plaisirs vous ont remplacées? Qu'êtes vous devenues? Les sectes protestantes qui déchirent et dépoétisent ce malheureux pays, ont ôté à ces fêtes tout caractère religieux: il n'en reste que de débris sauvés à grande peine par les bardes, ces gardiens de la nationalité galloise, qui désormais ne s'appuie plus que sur les moeurs, la langue, et les traditions. En Bretagne, elles ont conservé leur génie primitif, et la religion a continué d'être l'âme de ces solennités qui promettent encore a nos vieux usages, à nos croyances vénérables, à notre langue, et à notre littérature rustique, de longues années d'existence.[24]
>
> (O innocent and pure joys blessed by religion, who has taken you from the people of Cambria? What new pleasures have replaced you? The Protestant sects which tear apart and depoeticize this unhappy country have erased all religious character from these festivals: all that remains is the debris rescued with great difficulty by the bards, those guardians of Welsh nationality, now reduced to a reliance on mere custom, language and traditions. In Brittany, these events have kept their original character, and religion has remained at the heart of these solemnities which promise many long years yet of existence to our language and to our rustic literature.)

'Mere custom, language and traditions' – the written manuscript tradition, a main support of Iolo's argument for the continuity of Welsh, is here bypassed as a kind of monumental debris, so many dead letters. La Villemarqué's source is living and endlessly replenished: time passes in Wales, but not in Brittany. Again, the ironies are piquant, given how much of Iolo's own inspiration stems from a similar conviction, and how much importance he, too, placed on a continuity which survived long periods of religious 'untruth'.

[24] *BB* (1839), I, p. lxxiii.

This passage attacking the 'sectes protestantes' would, somewhat belatedly, provoke an angry response from a Welsh Protestant clergyman based in Quimper.[25] The Revd J. Williams, himself equally horrified by the public displays of Catholic religion – the *fêtes* and the *pardons* – by which La Villemarqué set so much store, found ample material in his own experience of Breton life to refute and return all charges of moral misconduct.[26] Accusing La Villemarqué of abusing his position as an 'expert' on Welsh matters, he expressed his concern that his prejudice would in fact 'damage the renewal of contact between these two branches of Celtic'.[27] La Villemarqué chose not to alter the offending paragraph in the third edition of the work, which came out seven years later.

In the light of such events, the failure of societies such as the archaeological *Association bretonne* to develop real links with their Welsh counterparts seems the less surprising. In fact, the heady beginnings in Abergavenny bred little further enthusiasm for cross-Channel relations for most of the nineteenth century. In 1857, La Villemarqué set up the *Breuriez Breiz* (the Brotherhood of Brittany), a literary society which used bardic names as noms de plume, but (bar a few details such as the wearing of green, blue and white scarves) did not have the overtly religious-druidic connotations of the Gorsedd. He appointed himself *Penn-Sturier* (Chief-Pilot) and developed a penchant for handing out diplomas to poets who were willing to publish in the new orthography.[28] The society met infrequently, and soon ran into difficulties.

Despite two further, briefer, visits to Britain made in 1855 (to Oxford and Cambridge, where he looked at early manuscripts), La Villemarqué's intellectual relationship with Wales did not develop in any interesting ways. Most of his Celtic scholarship seems to derive from the early, extraordinarily energetic period of his student days. Indeed, for all his religious frisson in Abergavenny it was not La Villemarqué who introduced the Gorsedd to Brittany, and it took another half a century for institutionalized bardism to take root there. He may possibly even have retarded it, since the druidic pretensions of the *Barzaz-Breiz* became one of the chief targets of his adversaries in the subsequent controversy. In 1867, during a supposedly 'International' Celtic Congress which had attracted disappointingly little interest from Wales, R. F. Le Men issued

[25] J. Williams (Pasteur Gallois à Quimper), *La Basse Bretagne et le pays de Galles: quelques paroles simples et véridiques adressées a M. le Comte Hersart de la Villemarqué* (Paris, 1860). See Jean-Yves Carluer, 'Missionnaires gallois et protestants bretons, les réalités et les ambiguïtés d'une solidarité interceltique, 1832–1940', *TRIADE: Galles, Ecosse, Irlande* (1995), 47–67.

[26] For other examples of the Protestant response to Catholic Brittany, see Le Disez, *Étrange Bretagne*.

[27] 'Il est même à craindre que les détails erronés que vous donnez sur les Gallois ne portent atteinte au rétablissement des rapports entre les deux branches celtiques' (Williams, *La Basse Bretagne*, p. 7).

[28] Gourvil, *La Villemarqué*, pp. 143–5.

a direct challenge to La Villemarqué's authority: 'Jouez au barde, à l'archibarde, ou même au druide, mais n'essayez pas de faussez l'histoire avec vos inventions' ('Play at being bard, arch-bard, or druid, but do not attempt to falsify history with your inventions').[29] La Villemarqué's speech to this conference, attended by only four Welsh delegates, two of them already resident in Brittany, revisited the theme of a racial brotherhood between the Breton/Britons on either side of the English Channel, and dwelt nostalgically, once again, on his own successes at the 1838 eisteddfod.[30]

The development of links with Wales fell to the next generation of revivalists, who founded the Union Régionaliste de Bretagne in 1898 and attended the pan-Celtic eisteddfod at Cardiff the following year. Having introduced the ceremony of repairing the 'broken sword', derived entirely from Lamartine's poem written sixty years earlier, the 'grand druide' Jean Le Fustec returned with the Gorsedd regulations and translated them: the first Breton Gorsedd was celebrated in Carnac in 1904. Gorsedd members also saw to it that the Welsh national anthem 'Hen Wlad fy Nhadau' was translated into Breton, thus simultaneously reaffirming and creating the 'shared cultural heritage' that is common currency in Wales and Brittany today. Philippe Le Stum's excellent study of this very literal act of translation shows how the Breton Gorsedd was implicated in various aspects of the cultural revival (the *emsav*) during the first half of the twentieth century, some more savoury than others.[31]

The appropriation and reinterpretation of 'bardism' a hundred years after Iolo's time is another story. But in its early stages at least, it is clear that pan-Celticism did not come easily, even within the closer linguistic groups. In the work of La Villemarqué, Brittany's relationship with Wales is fraught with its own neuroses: the motherland, *la sainte terre de Cambria*, was both adored as an ideal, and rejected as a reality.

One of the most unnerving aspects of La Villemarqué's involvement with Welsh Romantic scholarship is the almost total invisibility of Iolo himself. The abundant notes and clever citations of the *Barzaz-Breiz* and other works bear marked traces of Iolo's ideas: there are bardic footprints everywhere. But the trace is almost always mediated through the various works published by William Owen Pughe or through *The Myvyrian Archaiology*, and it is clear that La Villemarqué had no sense at all of Iolo as a character, or even as an author.

[29] The offending comment (made in the Preface to Le Men's new edition of the *Catholicon*) was subsequently pasted out. See Tanguy, 'Des celtomanes aux bretonistes', p. 331.

[30] Th. Hersart de la Villemarqué, 'Les Bretons d'Angleterre [*sic*] et les Bretons de France', *Revue de Bretagne et de Vendée* (1867), 337–56.

[31] Philippe Le Stum, *Le néo-druidisme en Bretagne: origine, naissance, et développement, 1890–1914* (Rennes, 1998), pp. 28–34; see also Michel Nicolas, *Le séparatisme en Bretagne* (Brasparts, 1986), pp. 97–9, for 'Blut und Boden' inspired readings of the triads in extremist circles during the Second World War.

Questions of influence and exchange are, for this reason, harder to analyse: because Iolo has little presence as a character in La Villemarqué's work, this is no flyting, as with Macpherson, nor a haunting, as with Chatterton, but something more insidious. Where Iolo himself responded to particular and highly controversial works – *Ossian*, the Rowley poems and the storm of writings that surrounded them – La Villemarqué is dealing with successful forgeries: texts, ideas, rituals inextricably woven into the genuine materials on which he based his own idiosyncratic research.

He seems, instead, to have poured all his historical imagination into the character of Owain Myfyr, whom he credits, in an extraordinary fairy-tale first outlined in the *Contes populaires des anciens bretons* and lavishly expanded in the introduction to *Poèmes des bardes bretons*, with singlehandedly taking up the cause of Welsh literature against the indifference of the English and the indolence of the Welsh. In an opening passage strongly reminiscent of the 'Short Account of Welsh MSS' (written, of course, by Iolo), La Villemarqué rhetorically asks his readers whether they would not have expected the revival of Welsh letters to have begun under the auspices of the British royal family, or to have been motivated by some noble descendant of the Welsh princes, eager to preserve his family's glorious deeds; or, failing that, at least by some educated clergyman, or generous *bourgeois de Galles*? But no:

> L'auteur de la publication littéraire qui fait le plus d'honneur au pays de Galles et qui est incontestablement l'une des plus importantes des temps modernes, n'était ni roi, ni prêtre, ni noble, ni bourgeois, c'était un paysan. Il s'appelait Owen Jones, et naquit en 1741, au comté de Denbigh, dans la vallée de Myvyr, dont il prit le nom plus tard, suivant une coutume des bardes gallois.[32]
>
> (The author of the literary publication which does most honour to Wales and which is without doubt one of the most important in modern times was neither king nor priest, neither aristocrat nor bourgeois: he was a peasant. He was called Owen Jones, and was born in 1741, in the county of Denbigh, in the valley of Myvyr, from which, according to a custom of the Welsh bards, he later took his name.)

There follows a sentimental account of Myfyr's youth, describing how, as a young man tending sheep on the hills, he would often turn his eyes to the splendour of Snowdon, that mystical mountain which, surely, he must have climbed to sleep the sleep of poetic inspiration, an inspiration which would nourish his dream of reviving the former glories of his native land. Realizing that the only way to achieve his goal, and to break down the barriers of class snobbery, was by becoming rich, he made his way to London, where, shilling by shilling, he built up his fortune with his one dream always in mind . . . And

[32] La Villemarqué, *Poèmes des bardes bretons* (1850), p. ii.

so on, to the final scene in a London graveyard, where a stone blackened by time, wind and fog stands upright, facing (somewhat inconveniently, but La Villemarqué's solution is ingenious) east:

> C'est la tombe de Owen Jones; l'attitude de son grant funèbre, dans le cimitière d'Allhallows, fut la sienne durant toute sa vie. Inébranlable en ses desseins, alors même qu'il était pauvre et que le vent de l'adversité l'assaillait le plus violemment, il eut toujours les yeux tournés vers l'oeuvre de lumières et de progrès que l'amour sacré du pays faisait briller pour lui, à l'horison, comme le lever d'une nouvelle aurore.[33]
>
> (It is the gravestone of Owen Jones; and his funeral monument, in the Allhallows cemetery, stands as he stood all his life. Unshakeable in his intentions, although he was poor and the winds of adversity assailed him fiercely, he always had his eyes turned towards the work of light and progress which the sacred love of his country caused to shine for him, on the horizon, like the rising of a new dawn.)

La Villemarqué's account effectively subsumes the collective efforts of the Gwyneddigion, and the joint efforts of the three editors of *The Myvyrian Archaiology*, into the work of a single man: Owain Myfyr becomes not only the prime economic mover of the Welsh cultural revival, as he undoubtedly was, but also its superlative scholar, tireless copyist, scrupulous editor and visionary. The same introduction ends with a list of the author's debts of gratitude to various people (with Lady Guest, thanked fulsomely for her scholarship, at the top): among them, La Villemarqué salutes the memory of 'Taliésin Williams, fils d'un des éditeurs du Myvyrian' ('son of one of the editors of the Myvyrian'). Iolo's anonymity could not be more assured.

Forgery and Translation

The tangle of texts involved in La Villemarqué's complex relationship with Wales, Paris and Brittany is instructive. One way of looking at some of the issues surrounding forgery is to think of them as symptoms of translation, of the movement between states. The passage of a text from one language to another is an exceptionally vulnerable moment, a moment at which identities are simultaneously lost and remade. The difficulties imposed in the representation of any text in a new language mean that discussions of translation have (and have had for long time) an emotional palette remarkably similar to those

[33] Ibid., p. xv.

involving forgery, with words like deception, travesty and appropriation all implying some fundamental act of betrayal of the source.[34]

Many other literary forgeries, *Ossian* most famously, have involved literal linguistic translation, and Macpherson's treatment of his Gaelic sources formed – for those prepared to believe that there were Gaelic sources in the first place – a central part of the debate. The Committee of the Highland Society's *Report . . . into the Nature and Authenticity of the Poems of Ossian*, drawn up by Henry Mackenzie in 1805, made the question of translation central: as Susan Manning has argued, Mackenzie felt that Macpherson's main fault lay in a verbose and too explicit rendering of the more compact and fragmented originals, their specificity 'frequently lost in words, of which the sound pleases the ear, but which are of a general, indeterminate sort'.[35] (Macpherson himself was more gung-ho about the process, having, by 1773, moved from initial protestations of literalness to the claim that 'A translator, who cannot equal his original, is incapable of expressing its beauties.')[36] A similar but more positive notion of the expansion of the source is implied in Iolo's closing comments to his 1794 essay on the triads:

> After what I have said of the origin and occasion of the *Triades*, the candid reader will rather attend to the nature of the sentiment than to the cramped mode of expressing it, and judge of their author's abilities, by what, with such ideas, he would have performed in the modern modes of literature, rather than what he was necessitated to do we know not how many centuries ago, when written dissertations were not known, and could be of no use.[37]

Here the reader is being asked to turn the oral into the written, the primitive into the modern, through a process of expansion which aims above all to explain, to make explicit. Iolo's confidence in this process represents the obverse side of the 'untranslatability' topos that frequently attached itself to the Celtic languages, expressed sometimes as a reluctance or refusal to be 'done into English', sometimes as the possession of an ineffable sensual rhetorical experience: 'There is, in the original Gaelic . . . an effect produced, to which no combination of words in the English language, which the Committee could either command or procure, can at all do justice.'[38] Here, the inability to cross from one

[34] For a useful overview of changing (and unchanging) perceptions of translation, see the selected extracts in Douglas Robinson, *Western Translation Theory: From Herodotus to Nietzsche* (Manchester, 1997).

[35] Susan Manning, 'Henry Mackenzie and Ossian, or, the Emotional Value of Asterisks' in Stafford and Gaskill (eds.), *From Gaelic to Romantic*, pp. 136–52.

[36] *PO*, p. 412.

[37] Williams: *PLP*, II, p. 227.

[38] Manning, 'Henry Mackenzie and *Ossian*', p. 146.

language to another can be read as a kind of awed respect for the original. But forgery has no such respect, and no truck with such silences.

The exegetical use of footnotes, beloved of all the writers discussed here, is a typical feature of the translation-as-expansion process, from Chatterton's quaint vocabularies to La Villemarqué's stifling reams of erudition. Since the past is necessarily fragmentary or obscure, the possibilities for its interpretation, its translation into the present, are open wide. Imagination, passion, perversion, take possession of the empty spaces. Because this filling-in process is so much like the workings both of 'real' scholarship and of what we now think of as fiction, it is very hard to explain literary forgery's distinctiveness, and tempting to explain it as an extreme or aberrant version of one side or the other (Ruthven's attempt to break down the dichotomy between them, and to claim forgery for literature, does, as Patrick Herron points out, generate its own internal paradox).[39] But it is surely its status as both-and-neither that makes literary forgery something else again: a kind of zombie, an 'unliterature' (and its famed ability to bring the dead to life is relevant here). A similar 'in-betweenness' is the current favoured territory of translation studies, as postcolonial thinking about the relationships between cultures and languages moves away from models of aggression and betrayal to a more dialogic stance.[40]

The translation paradigm in its various forms can be applied readily enough to the many other transitions explored in this book, from the wrench of the oral into the written to the transformation of manuscript into print; few crossings appear more vulnerable than that of the autobiographical act, translating the self from a private to a public sphere. In each case the preservation of an authentic original is at stake, with the 'translator' open to accusations of falsification or betrayal: this, I suspect, is what Iolo is reaching to express in his 'Stanzas Written in London', and this is why the enactments of Welsh or Breton identity in London and Paris have such an inevitably theatrical flavour.

Forgery has been called 'a translation without an original',[41] but this is not quite accurate: it usually grows out of something, a hint, or a seed; it is a growth that feeds off the original, covering it and distracting from it, like ivy or mistletoe. A folk-song becomes a druidic document, a name on a tomb is given a life, an *oeuvre*. And the transformation can be a slow and subtle process, as Edward Davies noted of Macpherson's imperceptible shift from editor to author: 'A great change was effected; but it was effected by degrees. – The old *woollen* stockings, by repeated mendings, were gradually converted into *silk*.' A stray and decontextualized comment in Iolo's manuscripts, possibly a quotation, offers

[39] Patrick Herron, 'Ruthven's *Faking Literature*, Forging Literature and Faking Forged Literature', *Jacket*, 17 (2002) (http://jacketmagazine.com/17/herron.html, accessed 18 July 2006).

[40] Susan Bassnett, *Translation Studies* (3rd edn., London, 2002), pp. 5–6; see also Susan Bassnett and Harish Trivedi (eds.), *Post-Colonial Translation: Theory and Practice* (London, 1999).

[41] See Gauti Kristmannsson, *The Role of Translation in the Construction of National Literatures in Britain and Germany 1750–1830: Translation without an Original* (Frankfurt am Main, 2005).

a similar image: 'mend it as the Highlander mended his gun. He gave it a new stock, a new lock, and a new barrel.'[42] To which, on a less homely note, one might add Gwyneth Lewis's brilliant insight that 'the godhead described in [Iolo's] Theological triads is a progressive entity, committed to the improvement of his creation by emendation'. In seeking therefore 'to restore what had been lost, or become deteriorated, or to cast it off, and substitute a better in its stead', Iolo himself is performing the necessary role of his bardic priests, 'duty-bound to emulate their God's constant revision of the works of his creation'.[43]

[42] Davies, *The Claims of Ossian*, p. 84; NLW 13130A, p. 175.
[43] Lewis, 'Eighteenth-Century Literary Forgeries', p. 232.

Epilogue

13

Epilogue: 'I have fairly caught the gudgeon'

> I had known and must all persons of any reading know numerous instances of respectable Talents having wandered astray led along by false lights, but I never could have believed that they had knowingly and willfully so deviated from the paths of Truth . . . I had always believed that a concatenation of unconscious mistakes that often fall to the lot of the fairest intentions had unfortunately been the undiscerned seducers of such writers; I never believed that a man of literature could possess such a depravity of heart as would have induced him to write and publish, wilful and premeditated falsehoods.[1]

'[M]ae'r twyllwr wedi ei ddal' ('the imposter has been caught'). Thus Sir John Morris-Jones in an exultant preface to G. J. Williams's analysis of the Dafydd ap Gwilym poems in 1926.[2] At last, he says, 'the myth of honest Iolo' is exploded: he is now revealed for what he was, a 'hateful man driven by hate', who corrupted literary and historical sources and set Welsh scholarship back by decades: 'And there is reason to fear that it will be another age or so before our literature and history are clean of the traces of his contaminated hands.'[3]

It is hard to resist the lure of character and personality. From a critical distance, Iolo's creations fit clearly enough into the Europe-wide phenomenon of Romantic nationalism; they are social and historical manifestations of a wider pattern. Yet most writing on Iolo cannot help but succumb to more personal questions of his motives and intentions, and the answers vary in emphasis with each critical agenda. For some the main factor is his obsession with Glamorgan and hatred of north Wales; for others it is his addiction to laudanum, or simply some crucial defect of his personality (G. J. Williams, Iolo's most thorough and most patient biographer, refers frequently and somewhat helplessly to 'that thing' in his mental make-up, brought on, perhaps, by

[1] NLW 21319A, p. 60. Iolo is fulminating here against Edward 'Celtic' Davies.

[2] *IMChY*, p. v.

[3] 'Ac y mae lle i ofni y bydd ein llên a'n hanes am oes neu ddwy eto cyn byddant lân o ôl ei ddwylo halog ef': *IMChY*, p. xvi.

an unhealthy attachment to his mother).[4] For John Morris-Jones, who had been closely involved in the establishment of the new University of Wales at the turn of the century, and was zealous in his efforts to set Welsh scholarship on a new and rigorous track, Iolo and his work had to be not so much rejected as exorcised. Recent criticism is less inclined to deplore his wickedness, and readier to forgive or at least reinterpret his forgeries as creative works driven by nascent nationalism, or by a combination of political and religious zeal.

In *The Forger's Shadow* Nick Groom shows how rapidly the 'myths' of various literary forgers and the controversies that surrounded them suffocated interest in their actual creations: the poems of Rowley and Ossian, much read and admired by the rising generation of Romantics, dropped out of critical sight almost within that generation, and have remained marginal to the canon ever since. For Groom, the focus on biography with its endless speculation about motive is a distraction, albeit a potent one, from the works themselves. Although the 'Iolo controversy' was delayed until over a century after his death, its effects in Wales have been similar: John Morris-Jones's criminalization of 'Iolo the imposter' and the subsequent heated exchanges for and against him kept the debate, until late in the twentieth century, revolving around his intentions and personality. As a result (and very like Chatterton), it is as a character, rather than an author, that Iolo is known in Wales today.[5] His minimal presence on the syllabus in departments of Welsh literature and history is an inevitable result.

Groom is right therefore to say that 'it is not enough to accuse forgeries of being deceitful and morally wrong'.[6] But intention, motives, compulsions are still forces to be reckoned with. As Jack Lynch argued recently in an analysis of the autobiographical 'Confession' of William Henry Ireland, the effect of any piece of writing depends on the reader's understanding of the writer's aims.[7] The various recensions of Ireland's account of his notorious 'Shakespere' forgeries reveal an unnerving compulsion to lie about everything from birth dates to death-bed scenes, and to revise endlessly versions of the same events: the 'true confession' of forgery is itself a fake. One difficulty raised in reading this kind of material (and the many drafts of Iolo's autobiographical preface to *Poems, Lyric and Pastoral* pose similar problems) is the danger of an overly literary response, and here the question of authorial intention seems entirely legitimate. It is something like the effect created by the novelistic device of the 'unreliable narrator', which positions the reader, in a kind of pact with the author, knowingly outside the distorted perspective of the story-teller. To read Iolo in the twenty-first century on the morality or immorality of forging literary and historical

[4] Williams: *IM*, p. xxxviii ('y rhywbeth hwnnw a oedd yn ei yrru ddydd a nos' (that thing which drove him day and night); p. 94 (on his mother), and *passim*.

[5] Marion Löffler's forthcoming book in this series explores the nineteenth-century 'myth' of Iolo.

[6] Groom, *The Forger's Shadow*, p. 15.

[7] 'Ireland's Chatterton', Plenary lecture at a conference on 'Romanticism and Forgery', University of Bristol, 29 November 2003.

sources is necessarily to read him within an ironic frame. But it is disconcertingly hard to know whether, like an author, Iolo is knowingly manipulating his readership – winking at us across two hundred years – or whether in fact we are reading someone pathologically trapped inside his own version of events (whichever version it happens to be at the time). One's grasp of the writing changes accordingly.

The mass of manuscripts collected from Iolo's cottage in Flemingston hold surprisingly few clues to suggest an ironic, self-aware level to his forgeries. His own son Taliesin, who selected the texts published after his death as the *Iolo Manuscripts* (1848), had no qualms about their authenticity. It is possible that the mass and confusion of papers in themselves worked in his favour, although G. J. Williams suggests that he must have been careful to remove the more obvious traces of his activities. Given his unremittingly scathing stance towards the controversies of his own day, it is particularly interesting to come across instances where he seems to give the notion of forgery itself more room for manoeuvre. Such instances, perhaps inevitably, perhaps subconsciously, occur most frequently when he is introducing his own creations.

A good example is an unpublished essay written to accompany 'Trioedd Pawl' ('The Triads of Paul') discussed earlier. In it, Iolo can be seen working carefully, and at times laboriously, through arguments for and against the authenticity of the triads, with the issue of precisely identifying authorship exercising him over several pages:[8]

> Pauls Triades may be by some supposed to have been produced by a Pia fraus of some ancient Christian Bard. I confess that it might possibly enough be so, but if this gave weight and authority to Doctrines the most important that ever blessed Mankind I shall be greatly at a loss to know how and in what I am to censure, to discover wherein the turpitide lies, and its magnitude, it is hard to say that the author did not mean well or that he was not a good man and Christian, and we can not discover that this fraud has produced hitherto any bad effect.[9]

The concept of 'Pia fraus', or 'Pious fraud' is introduced with disarming ingenuity: the results of such activity, he argues, are so clearly beneficial to humankind that the author can hardly be accused of failing to be 'a good man and Christian'. 'Pia fraus', forgery which furthered the aims of the Church, was widely practised (though not officially condoned) at all levels in medieval ecclesiastical culture, and often took the form of forging title deeds – a rewriting of origins – to prove the claims of religious establishments to their land; it was especially common in Britain in the century after the arrival of the Normans.[10]

[8] NLW 13119B, pp. 267–74, 287–93. The essay is continuous, but several blank pages have been inserted (pp. 275–86).

[9] NLW 13119B, pp. 273–4.

[10] See M. T. Clanchy, *From Memory to Written Record* (2nd edn., Oxford, 1993), pp. 148–9, 318–27.

Eighteenth-century historians were familiar with the concept, and Thomas Warton uses the phrase 'pious fraud' in the discussion of post-Conquest Britain which opens the first volume of his *History of English Poetry* (1774).[11] If one were looking for a riposte to John Morris-Jones, a benign explanation for Iolo's own forgeries, the notion of pious fraud provides a useful paradigm: Iolo's bardism was above all an explicitly religious affair, aimed at moral and spiritual regeneration. Gwyneth Lewis argues this point most persuasively, viewing 'literary forgery as the religious and artistic cornerstone of the gorsedd's philosophy'.[12] As we have seen, the distinctive immutability of Iolo's oral tradition, existing as it does beyond the specifics of time and place, confers a kind of simultaneity on the process of literary history – a timelessness which effectively 'legitimize[s] the creative participation of one poet in one age with the work of a second in a later age'.[13]

In this intriguing *mise en abyme* of fraud, however, Iolo pushes the act of forgery back to 'some ancient Christian Bard'; in half-condoning the practice, he does not compromise his own editorial integrity. (By a nice irony, this was precisely the line taken for most of the nineteenth century by the many Welsh writers and scholars who were unwilling to impute inconsistencies and contradictions in the manuscripts to Iolo himself). But in a typically Iolo-esque manoeuvre, the essay then pulls back from its potentially dangerous position:

> Fraud however is in its own Nature of such pernicious tendency, that I will not venture to vindicate it on any occasion or pretence whatever, till some sound Casuist, keeping his arguments perfectly and demonstrably clear of every thing that borders upon sophistry, shall prove that it may safely, and with benign effects and consequences, continuing so to all eternity, be practiced in the propagation of truths, or in the production of effects of self-evident beneficence that could never otherwise be as well or as speedily effected, whilst at the same time the truths so propagated are independently of such pious frauds in themselves true to the clearest moral, if not mathematical demonstration.[14]

This cumbersome sentence can be readily paralleled elsewhere in Iolo's writings, often in similar contexts; though presumably aiming to persuade and reassure, his stylistic excess tends to betray a fundamental anxiety about the subject in hand. But its tortuous subjunctive mode and legalistic phrasing do help to dis-

[11] '[T]he monks were compelled to the pious fraud of forging them in Latin: and great numbers of these forged Latin charters, till lately supposed original, are still extant.' *Thomas Warton's History of English Poetry* (London, 1998 repr. of the 1774 edn.), I, p. 3 n. I am grateful to Nick Groom for this reference. For an excellent account of medieval forgeries, see Alfred Hiatt, *The Making of Medieval Forgeries: False Documents in Fifteenth-Century England* (London, 2004).

[12] Lewis, 'Eighteenth-Century Literary Forgeries', p. 228.

[13] Ibid., p. 231.

[14] NLW 13119B, p. 274 (several blank pages) and p. 287.

associate the writer from being directly implicated in the position advanced: here, Iolo can stand safely back and condemn all fraud as 'pernicious', while handing more daring thinking over to a theoretical third party, the casuist who can prove that the effects of fraud will be 'to all eternity' unequivocally 'benign'. What emerges most clearly here is a sense of truth as something solid, as unambiguous and 'demonstrable' as mathematics, and, crucially, detachable from the husk of the pious fraud which is the convenient medium of its transmission.

In another twist, Iolo then turns the negative associations of 'fraud' to his own advantage in arguing for the authenticity of Paul's authorship:

> For my own part rather than bring the charge of fraud against any one on this occasion, and let it be termed credulity or weakness, as the reader pleases, I would believe that these Triades were composed by, or from the dictates of St Paul. To me probability seems to lie on this side of the question, but who can be positive either for or against this opinion (or rather conjecture) on one side or the other.[15]

It would not merely be uncharitable, therefore, but almost immoral in the reader to *wish* to impute fraud to anyone, even an anonymous early Christian bard. Again, the assertion of authenticity is immediately qualified as a mere 'conjecture', and the reader is flatteringly allowed to take some responsibility in understanding the sheer complexity of deciding for or against the question. The next sentence is beautifully ironic: 'Divine Inspiration apart, there [it] seems to me that the composer, whoever he was, had as a writer, a thinker, and a pious man, abilities and qualities similar to those of St Paul.'[16] In other words, the author (sparing his blushes) is so much like St Paul that the positive identification of the 'real thing' ceases to matter.

It does not finish there. Iolo then finds another way of reprieving his putative author from the charge of fraud. This is the recasting or translation of an earlier work by a later writer, in which the work continues to be identified under the name of its originator. Again, his examples are religious: 'it would be obvious that he meant no more than that he had versified Pauls sentiments and doctrines, as we say the Psalms of David by Merrick, Ainsworth, Sternhold and Hopkins etc.'[17] Viewed as an act of translation, the process of putting another person's thoughts into new dress appears entirely legitimate (though it is hard to imagine him undertaking a similarly charitable rethinking of the 'Poems of Ossian by Macpherson'):

[15] Ibid., pp. 287–8.

[16] NLW 13119B, pp. 288–9.

[17] James Merrick (1720–1769) and Henry Ainsworth (1571–1622) produced metrical versions of the Psalms in 1765 and 1612 respectively; Thomas Sternhold and John Hopkins brought out *The Whole Book of Psalms* in 1633.

> on a quite similar idea, we may suppose that the old Welsh Bard, a Lolard possibly of the 14th Century (for such, as they were called, abounded then in Wales) put the doctrines of the New Testament into Triades to which he modestly prefered the fixing of Paul's name, those doctrines and sentiments being purely his, rather than his own, which would have bordered on presumption and would have also lessened the authority of the precepts.[18]

The potential author has now become a fourteenth-century Lollard, and his activity is exonerated, even applauded, as an act of modesty. Iolo here significantly invokes the idea of 'authority', a subject implicit in most forgery debates of the time. Against those who argued (as supporters of Ossian and Rowley did, and as Iolo does elsewhere) that no one gifted enough to mimic the language of a great writer would have 'the useless self-denial to deprive himself of the just fame to which his genius would be entitled',[19] comes the response that mere association with a Great Name from the past confers a weight, a glamour and authority that precedes any utterance whatsoever. The assumption of what Ruthven calls 'allonymity' ('whenever authors impute their own work to someone else in order to improve their chances of having it noticed')[20] enabled Macpherson to find himself, as Ossian, cited in the same breath as Milton and Homer; and, more extremely, gave the 'Shakespere' signature of William Henry Ireland the status of a holy relic.[21] In this instance, though, Iolo's pious Lollard is not portrayed as cynically 'buying in' to the St Paul brand-name, but rather as carrying that name forward in a reverential gesture of discipleship; the allonymous model is often religious.[22] But Iolo had literary precedents, too, particularly in the Welsh tradition of prophecy. Elsewhere, discussing the medieval practice of attributing prophetic verse to the great names of early Welsh tradition, such as Myrddin or Taliesin, Iolo shows some awareness of how fine a line may divide the invocation of authority from the fraudulent assumption of power.[23] The misleading attribution of poems to earlier poets had been raised as a critical problem by Evan Evans in his *Some Specimens of the Poetry of the Antient Welsh Bards* (1764), and was used by John Pinkerton (writing as 'Philistor' in the *Gentleman's Magazine* in August 1788) in an attempt to discredit Welsh tradition in general. Iolo's responses vary widely: in one place

[18] NLW 13119B, p. 290.

[19] NLW 13138A, pp. 88–9. The same point is made by Daniel Walters in relation to Chatterton in 1782: see Mary-Ann Constantine, '"Within a Door or Two": Iolo Morganwg, Chatterton and Bristol' in Heys (ed.), *From Gothic to Romantic*, p. 106.

[20] Ruthven, *Faking Literature*, p. 103.

[21] In 1795 the ailing James Boswell reputedly went down on his knees and kissed 'the invaluable relics of our bard', thanking God that he had lived to see them. He died a few weeks later. See Frank Brady, *James Boswell: The Later Years 1769–1795* (London, 1984), pp. 488, 578; Groom, *The Forger's Shadow*, pp. 217–18.

[22] Ruthven, *Faking Literature*, pp. 104–6.

[23] See NLW 13138A, p. 88.

he acknowledges that medieval poets could have hidden behind pseudonyms for politico-religious reasons, and in another, focused wholly on refuting Pinkerton, he is adamant that the 'simple Welsh' (who had, after all, naively accepted Geoffrey of Monmouth's fabrications for centuries) had 'never been acquainted with such a fashion, nor knew that such a species of imposture ever existed'.[24]

Another much shorter but equally intriguing piece has been called 'his most explicit statement about his work as a forger'.[25] It is a letter in Welsh in Iolo's hand, written as if from one Will Tabwr, a (fictitious) poet from the civil war period, to Iolo himself, here using his earlier bardic name, Iorwerth Morganwg. It is dated 1780. 'I hear', says Will, 'that you have been raising some of the Wise Old Welshmen from death to life.' He then says how much he would love to be resurrected for another visit to old Glamorgan, and launches into an attack on the current deplorable state of letters and morals in Wales, before ending:

> Da Iorwerth dywed y gair, ag allan o'r bedd y deuaf ar darawiad amrant. Mi ydwyf dy ddigrif a chellweirus wasanaethwr. Will Tabwr.
>
> O.S. mi a glywaf fod rhai yn dywedyd na fydd will tabwr fyth farw hyd y bot ti'n fyw Iorwerth. Llawer gwir a ddywedir mewn cellwair[26]

> (Good Iorwerth say the word and I'll be out of the grave in the blink of an eye. I am your droll and mischievous servant. Will Tabwr.
>
> P.S. I hear that some are saying Will Tabwr will never die while you are alive Iorwerth. Many a true word is spoken in jest.)

The postscript leaps out of the surrounding material like a confession. But on closer inspection, there is a problem with its 'explicitness'. In 1779 and 1780 Iolo was planning to set up a journal, to be called 'Dywenydd Morganwg' (The Delight of Glamorgan), and he seems to have got as far as thinking about subscriptions and print-runs (like many of his proposed publications, it did not get beyond the planning stage).[27] Another manuscript in a different volume makes it quite clear that the contents would include a regular series of 'characters', real and fictional, from Glamorgan's past. These characters would, in an entertaining manner, voice many of Iolo's own concerns and interests: poetry, morality, husbandry, and the need to keep the old traditional ways. Will Tabwr appears amongst them, and in a lively piece the editor 'Iorwerth' promises to resurrect him for some fun and games:

[24] NLW 13154A, p. 94 and NLW 21419E, no. 5. Both examples are discussed by Lewis, 'Eighteenth-Century Literary Forgeries', pp. 162–5.

[25] Lewis, 'Eighteenth-Century Literary Forgeries', p. 152.

[26] NLW 21414E, no. 5.

[27] For the planned *Dywenydd Morganwg*, see BL Add. 15024, ff. 188–9; NLW 21281E, Letter nos. 227 and 229, and NLW 13089B, pp. 34–7. See also Williams: *IM*, pp. 214, 363, 387–91. I am grateful to Cathryn Charnell-White for drawing this material to my attention.

> Hen gyfaill digri yw Will, a gobeithio bydd ei gyfeillach ef er lles inni oll, yn enwedig i benbyliaid Morganwg, un o ba rai ydwyf fy hun, fal y gwyr pawb o honoch.[28]
>
> Will is a merry old soul, and I hope his company will do us all good, especially the Glamorgan blockheads – of whom I myself am one, as you all know well.

If one reads the letter from Will Tabwr not as a private note from Iolo to himself, but rather as a draft of a piece to be published, with the raising of the dead to life as a primarily literary conceit, its status as personal revelation is altered and the 'real Iolo' once again slips away.

So much depends on context, on audience: in the letters accompanying various 'impositions' (the proverbs sent to Owain Myfyr, the Dafydd ap Gwilym poems sent to William Owen Pughe, or the Bewper Porch story sent to Sir Richard Colt Hoare), it is easy to agree with G. J. Williams and Geraint Phillips that Iolo's phrasing ranges from the disingenuous to the deceitful; in the manuscripts, where he often seems to be talking to himself, he appears much more self-deluded, wrapped up in his truth. There is, however, one unambiguously 'explicit' statement of forgery in the archive. This is a brusque, crowing note to his old adversary Edward Jones, Bardd y Brenin, whose own version of Welsh bardic tradition, popularized in several successful volumes from the 1780s onwards, did not follow the druido-bardic line of Iolo and William Owen Pughe, and whose politics were everything that Iolo was not.[29] The note, written in Oxford, must have been penned during the long journey on foot which took him from London to Birmingham and back down the Welsh borders to Merthyr Tydfil in the early summer of 1802.[30] It is very much in the style of his many manuscript rants against 'Humstrum' Jones: the presence of sealing wax, Jones's address and a postmark indicate, however, that it was actually sent:

> Oxford Coffee House monday noon.
> Jones,
> A Lady of my acquaintance has shown me the last book you have built. You open it, I find, with a second edition of Hardy-Cnute's monumental inscription. I have at last fairly caught the gudgeon. Three respectable Gentlemen were present about nine or ten years ago when I wrote the curious triads that you have printed on a quarto leaf of paper, imitating the old Manuscript hand writing. It was afterwards

[28] NLW 21414E, no. 5.

[29] Tecwyn Ellis, *Edward Jones, Bardd y Brenin (1752–1824)* (Caerdydd, 1957); for the antagonistic relations between Iolo and Jones, see idem, 'Bardd y Brenin, Iolo Morganwg a Derwyddiaeth', *NLWJ*, XIII (1963–4), 147–56, 224–34, 356–62; XIV (1965–6), 183–93, 321–9, 424–36; XV (1967–8), 177–96.

[30] NLW 21285E, Letter no. 867, Iolo Morganwg to Edward Jones, 24 May 1802. For the journey itself, see NLW 13174A.

> well smoked till quite of a dirty yellowish colour. It was then put into a book that was put in your way. You pocketed the leaf, knowing it not to be your own, but no matter for that little bit of theft. You did what was much better. You printed it as an ancient document, amongst your admirable rarities. I have, with those Gentlemen, spent a few hours in a most glorious laugh at your expense. You did well enough not to mention whence you had those Triads. The Public shall soon be informed whence you filched them, of what antiquity they are, and a number of other curious particulars relating to you and your Glewlwyd Gafaelfawr master of the ceremonies to King Arthur.
>
> Edward Williams

Here, it seems, is the 'laughter' of Gwyneth Lewis's poem, and it is not secret but disconcertingly public. That Iolo – who loathed Jones even before the latter gave him good reason to do so by informing on him and having him arrested for possible treason – should have wanted to make his rival look a fool is entirely plausible: but why, in 1793 or thereabouts, when he was thinking of presenting his own bardic triads to the world, would he have played such dangerous games in front of 'three respectable Gentlemen'? As Tecwyn Ellis shows, the forgeries, which were indeed published in the opening pages of Jones's *Bardic Museum* of 1802, follow the familiar pattern of blending genuine manuscript tradition with Iolo's own creations.[31] The many references to the high status of harpers and musicians (notably denigrated elsewhere in Iolo's bardic writings) were the bait with which Iolo astutely enough caught his gudgeon. This open demonstration of a talent for blending fact and fiction in the very genre he was busy evangelizing as the most perfect and reliable medium for the transmission of knowledge seems reckless in the extreme – unless, of course, those 'three Gentlemen' are themselves fictional, a mocking chorus to add to Jones's discomfiture. And there are other bizarre aspects to this short note. As we have seen, Iolo's great strength as a rewriter of the past was his subtle use of layered sources, the copies of copies of manuscripts which eluded easy verification; he mocks Chatterton and Ireland for their clumsy physical emulations of the 'original' – those 'appearances of colour, decay etc which art can never give at least has not been hitherto successful in attempting to do so'.[32] Yet here (and ten years after the event) he is as delighted with his own antique handwriting and the 'dirty yellowish colour' of his smoked quarto leaf as Chatterton must have been with his 'rolles' and 'explayneales'. The fact that Iolo is here effectively owning up to another 'Hardy-Cnute' (an

[31] Ellis, 'Bardd y Brenin, Iolo Morganwg a Derwyddiaeth', *NLWJ*, XIV (1965–6), 424–36. The triads appeared in Jones's *Bardic Museum* (1802), pp. 1–7. Iolo also sent Jones (in his usual, more circumspect fashion) a selection of traditional verses (*hen benillion*), some of which were also of his own devising. See Ellis, *Edward Jones*, pp. 111–12.

[32] NLW 13104B, p. 123.

earlier and long-running *cause célèbre* in the world of Scottish literary forgery, in which his other *bête noire*, John Pinkerton, became embroiled),[33] goes equally against the grain, given that his triads were designed to 'loudly testify against M.pherson the impositor the author of hardicnute its continuator and others of the same kidney'.[34] Indeed, all that holds this cluster of anomalies together is Iolo's well-documented hatred for Edward Jones: if the mask of 'honest Iolo' were ever going to slip, it would be in a malicious moment such as this. And yet, should anyone be tempted to take this as the last word on the subject, it is worth remembering that shortly after writing his triumphant note in the Oxford coffee house he would have visited the Rollright stone circle, where he experienced that profound, and deeply religious, sense of connection to the past that palpably lies behind so many of his re-creations. No one reading his pencilled journal entry on the stones could dismiss his forgeries as merely spiteful hoaxes.

But this book ends, improbably and appropriately enough, with an authentic forgery, a yellowed manuscript in mock-medieval script preserved among the papers of Edward Jones.[35] There is something very satisfying in the sight of it (and in touching it – relics still have their attraction, after all). Iolo's indignation at 'the present age of forgery' rings down through the centuries: he is furious at the insinuations of Owain Myfyr and the accusations of Edward Davies, dismissive of the efforts of Chatterton, scathing about Pinkerton, morally offended by the 'perjurer' Macpherson. This, apparently, is the only one of his inspired and misbegotten creations he ever acknowledged as his own.

[33] The supposedly ancient ballad, first published as a 'Fragment' in 1719, is usually (but not without controversy) attributed to Elizabeth Halket, Lady Wardlaw. Pinkerton published a lengthy continuation of the piece, with a detailed account of its 'genuine' provenance, in the second edition of his *Select Scottish Ballads* (London, 1783): see Mel Kersey, 'Ballads, Britishness and *Hardyknute*, 1719–1859', *Scottish Studies Review*, 5, no. 1 (2004), 40–56.

[34] NLW 13089E, p. 455.

[35] NLW 322E, pp. 115–16 (the relevant pages of the Edward Jones papers, though numbered correctly, have been bound out of order and are now situated in the middle). I am grateful to Geraint Phillips for helping to track them down.

Select Bibliography

Aaron, Jane, and Chris Williams (eds.), *Postcolonial Wales* (Cardiff, 2005).

Anderson, Benedict, *Imagined Communities: Reflections on the Origin and Spread of Nationalism* (London, 1983).

Astle, Thomas, *The Origin and Progress of Writing* (London, 1784).

Baines, Paul, *The House of Forgery in Eighteenth-Century Britain* (Aldershot, 1999).

Barrell, John, *The Idea of Landscape and the Sense of Place* (Cambridge, 1972).

Barrett, William, *The History and Antiquities of the City of Bristol* (Bristol, 1789).

Barry, Jonathan, 'The History and Antiquities of the City of Bristol: Chatterton in Bristol', *Angelaki*, 1, no. 2 (1994), 55–81.

Bassnett, Susan, *Translation Studies* (3rd edn., London, 2002).

—— and Harish Trivedi (eds.), *Post-Colonial Translation: Theory and Practice* (London, 1999).

Bate, Jonathan, *John Clare: A Biography* (London, 2003).

—— 'Shakespeare and Original Genius' in Penelope Murray (ed.), *Genius: The History of an Idea* (Oxford, 1989), pp. 76–97.

Beal, Joan C., 'Out in Left Field: Spelling Reformers of the Eighteenth Century', *Transactions of the Philological Society*, 100 (2002), 5–23.

Bendix, Regina, *In Search of Authenticity: The Formation of Folklore Studies* (London, 1997).

Benson, Larry D. (ed.), *The Riverside Chaucer* (3rd edn., Oxford, 1988).

Bentley, G. E., Jr., '"The Triumph of Owen"', *NLWJ*, XXXIV, no. 2 (1985), 248–61.

Blake, William, *A Descriptive Catalogue: 1809* (Oxford, 1990).

Blanchard, Nelly, 'Une fiction pour s'inventer: le *Barzaz-Breiz* (1839–1845–1867) dans le mouvement romantique' (unpublished University of Brest Ph.D. thesis, 2004).

Boidron, J.-J., *'Gousperoù Ar Raned' ha gourspered 'Ar Rannou': Les 'Vêpres des Grenouilles' ou 'Les Séries' des druides* (Rennes, 1993).

Boswell, James, *Life of Johnson*, ed. G. B. Hill, rev. L. F. Powell (6 vols., Oxford, 1934–64).

Bowen, D. J., 'Dafydd ap Gwilym a Morgannwg', *LlC*, V, no. 4 (1959), 164–73.

Brady, Frank, *James Boswell: The Later Years 1769–1795* (London, 1984).

Bredvold, Louis I., *The Contributions of John Wilkes to the 'Gazette Littéraire de l'Europe'* (Ann Arbor, Mich., 1950).

Bromwich, Rachel, 'The Mabinogion and Lady Charlotte Guest', *THSC* (1986), 127–41.

—— (ed.), *Selected Poems of Dafydd ap Gwilym* (2nd edn., Harmondsworth, 1985).

—— (ed.), *'Trioedd Ynys Prydain' in Welsh Literature and Scholarship* (Cardiff, 1969).

—— (ed.), *Trioedd Ynys Prydein: The Triads of the Island of Britain* (3rd edn., Cardiff, 2006).

Broudic, Fañch, *La pratique du breton de l'Ancien Régime à nos jours* (Rennes, 1995).

Bryant, Jacob, *Observations upon the Poems of Thomas Rowley: in which the authenticity of those poems is ascertained* (London, 1781).

Burgess, Thomas, *Christ, and not Saint Peter, the Rock of the Christian Church; and St Paul, the Founder of the Church in Britain* (Carmarthen, 1812).

Burke, Tim (ed.), *Eighteenth-Century English Labouring-Class Poets: Volume III, 1780–1800* (London, 2003).

Burns, Robert, *Poems, Chiefly in the Scottish Dialect* (Kilmarnock, 1786).

Carey, John (ed.), *John Milton: Complete Shorter Poems* (Harlow, 1968).

Carluer, Jean-Yves, 'Missionnaires gallois et protestants bretons, les réalités et les ambiguïtés d'une solidarité interceltique, 1832–1940', *TRIADE: Galles, Ecosse, Irlande* (1995), 47–67.

Carr, Glenda, 'An Uneasy Partnership: Iolo Morganwg and William Owen Pughe' in Jenkins (ed.), *Rattleskull Genius*, pp. 443–60.

Carruthers, Gerard, and Alan Rawes (eds.), *English Romanticism and the Celtic World* (Cambridge, 2003).

Carver, Jonathan, *Travels through the Interior Parts of North America, in the Years 1766, 1767 and 1768* (London, 1778).

Charnell-White, Cathryn, *Barbarism and Bardism: North Wales versus South Wales in the Bardic Vision of Iolo Morganwg* (Aberystwyth, 2004).

Child, Francis James, *English and Scottish Popular Ballads* (5 vols., 1882–98; repr. New York, 1965).

Christmas, William J., *The Lab'ring Muses: Work, Writing, and the Social Order in English Plebeian Poetry, 1730–1830* (London, 2001).

Clanchy, M. T., *From Memory to Written Record* (2nd edn., Oxford, 1993).

Colley, Linda, *Britons: Forging the Nation, 1707–1837* (Yale, 1992).

Conran, Tony, *Welsh Verse* (2nd edn., Bridgend, 1986).

Constantine, Mary-Ann, *Breton Ballads* (Aberystwyth, 1996).

—— *'Combustible Matter': Iolo Morganwg and the Bristol Volcano* (Aberystwyth, 2003).

—— 'Ballads Crossing Borders: La Villemarqué and the Breton *Lenore*', *Translation & Literature*, 8, no. 2 (1999), 197–216.

—— 'Iolo Morganwg, Coleridge, and the Bristol Lectures 1795', *Notes and Queries*, 52, no. 1 (2005), 42–4.

—— 'Neither Flesh nor Fowl: Merlin as Bird-man in Breton Folk Tradition', *Arthurian Literature*, XXI (2004), 95–114.

—— 'Ossian in Wales and Brittany' in Gaskill (ed.), *The Reception of Ossian in Europe*, pp. 67–90.

—— 'Prophecy and Pastiche in the Breton Ballads: *Groac'h Ahes* and *Gwenc'hlan*', *Cambrian Medieval Celtic Studies*, 30 (1995), 87–121.

—— '"Seeing daylight all the way"', *Planet*, 172 (2005), 55–61.

—— '"This Wildernessed Business of Publication": The Making of *Poems, Lyric and Pastoral* (1794)' in Jenkins (ed.), *Rattleskull Genius*, pp. 123–45.

—— '"Within a Door or Two": Iolo Morganwg, Chatterton and Bristol' in Heys (ed.), *From Gothic to Romantic*, pp. 104–15.

—— and Gerald Porter, *Fragments and Meaning in Traditional Song* (Oxford, 2003).

Cottle, Joseph, and Robert Southey (eds.), *The Works of Thomas Chatterton* (3 vols., London, 1803).

Crawford, Rachel, *Poetry, Enclosure and the Vernacular Landscape* (Cambridge, 2002).

Croker, Thomas Crofton, *Fairy Legends and Traditions of the South of Ireland* (3 vols., London, 1825–8).

Crowe, Richard M., 'Diddordebau Ieithyddol Iolo Morganwg' (unpublished University of Wales Ph.D. thesis, 1988).

—— 'Iolo Morganwg and the Dialects of Welsh' in Jenkins (ed.), *Rattleskull Genius*, pp. 315–31.

Cunningham, Bernadette, *The World of Geoffrey Keating: History, Myth and Religion in Seventeenth-Century Ireland* (Dublin, 2000).

Currie, James (ed.), *The Works of Robert Burns: With an Account of his Life, Criticism on his Writings, &c.* (new edn., 4 vols., London, 1819).

Davies, Brian, 'Archaeology and Ideology, or How Wales was Robbed of its Early History', *New Welsh Review*, 37 (1997), 38–51.

Davies, Caryl, *Adfeilion Babel: Agweddau ar Syniadaeth Ieithyddol y Ddeunawfed Ganrif* (Caerdydd, 2000).

Davies, D. Elwyn J., 'Astudiaeth o Feddwl a Chyfraniad Iolo Morganwg fel Rhesymolwr ac Undodwr' (unpublished University of Wales Ph.D. thesis, 1975).

Davies, Damian Walford, *Presences that Disturb: Models of Romantic Identity in the Literature and Culture of the 1790s* (Cardiff, 2002).

Davies, Edward, *Celtic Researches, on the Origin, Traditions & Language, of the Ancient Britons* (London, 1804).

—— *The Claims of Ossian Examined and Appreciated: An Essay on the Scottish and Irish Poems published under that name* (Swansea, 1825).

—— *The Mythology and Rites of the British Druids* (London, 1809).

Davies, Janet, 'Carnhuanawc', *Planet*, 65 (1987), 40–7.

Davies, John H. (ed.), *The Letters of Lewis, Richard, William and John Morris, of Anglesey (Morrisiaid Môn) 1728–1765* (2 vols., Aberystwyth, 1907–9).

Davies, Sioned, 'Cyfieithu'r Mabinogion' in J. E. Caerwyn Williams (ed.), *Ysgrifau Beirniadol XIII* (Dinbych, 1997), pp. 16–30.

Davis, John, *Life of Chatterton* (London, 1806).

Dearnley, Moira, '"Mad Ned" and the "Smatter-Dasher": Iolo Morganwg and Edward "Celtic" Davies' in Jenkins (ed.), *Rattleskull Genius*, pp. 425–42.

Doody, Margaret, *The Daring Muse* (Cambridge, 1985).

Duck, Stephen, *Poems on Several Occasions* (London, 1736).

Dujardin, Louis, *La Vie et les Oeuvres de Jean-François-Marie-Maurice-Agathe Le Gonidec, Grammairien et Lexicographe breton (1775–1838)* (Brest, 1949).

Eddy, Donald D., 'Dodsley's *Oeconomy of Human Life*, 1750–1751', *Modern Philology*, 85, no. 4 (1988), 460–79.

Edwards, Gavin, *Narrative Order 1789–1819* (Basingstoke, 2005).

Edwards, Huw Meirion, 'A Multitude of Voices: The Free-Metre Poetry of Iolo Morganwg' in Jenkins (ed.), *Rattleskull Genius*, pp. 95–121.

Ellis, R. J., 'Plodding Plowmen: Issues of Labour and Literacy in Gray's "Elegy"' in Goodridge (ed.), *The Independent Spirit*, pp. 27–43.

Ellis, Tecwyn, *Edward Jones, Bardd y Brenin (1752–1824)* (Caerdydd, 1957).
—— 'Bardd y Brenin, Iolo Morganwg a Derwyddiaeth', *NLWJ*, XIII, no. 2 (1963), 147–56, no. 3 (1964), 224–34; XIV, no. 2 (1965), 183–93, no. 3 (1966), 321–9, no. 4 (1966), 424–36; XV, no. 2 (1967), 177–96.
Evans, Evan, *Some Specimens of the Poetry of the Antient Welsh Bards* (London, 1764).
Evans, R. J. W., '"The Manuscripts": The Culture and Politics of Forgery in Central Europe' in Jenkins (ed.), *Rattleskull Genius*, pp. 51–68.
Fairer, David, *English Poetry of the Eighteenth Century 1700–1789* (London, 2003).
—— 'Chatterton's Poetic Afterlife, 1770–1794: A Context for Coleridge's *Monody*' in Groom (ed.), *Thomas Chatterton and Romantic Culture*, pp. 228–52.
—— 'Historical Criticism and the English Canon: A Spenserian Dispute in the 1750s', *Eighteenth-Century Life*, 24 (Spring, 2000), 43–64.
—— (ed.), *Thomas Warton's History of English Poetry* (4 vols., London, 1998).
Ferguson, Adam, *Essay on the History of Civil Society* (Edinburgh, 1767).
Ferguson, William, *The Identity of the Scottish Nation: An Historic Quest* (Edinburgh, 1998).
Fowler, Alastair (ed.), *John Milton: Paradise Lost* (Harlow, 1971).
Frank, Roberta, 'The Search for the Anglo-Saxon Oral Poet' in Donald Scragg (ed.), *Textual and Material Culture in Anglo-Saxon England: Thomas Northcote Toller and the Toller Memorial Lectures* (Cambridge, 2003), pp. 137–60.
Franklin, Caroline, 'The Welsh American Dream: Iolo Morganwg, Robert Southey and the Madoc Legend' in Carruthers and Rawes (eds.), *English Romanticism and the Celtic World*, pp. 69–84.
Fry, Edmund, *Pantographia* (London, 1799).
Fulford, Tim, *Landscape, Liberty and Authority* (Cambridge, 1996).
Gaskill, Howard, 'What Did James Macpherson Really Leave on Display at his Publisher's Shop in 1762?', *Scottish Gaelic Studies*, 16 (1990), 67–89.
—— (ed.), *James Macpherson: The Poems of Ossian and Related Works* (Edinburgh, 1996).
—— (ed.), *Ossian Revisited* (Edinburgh, 1991).
—— (ed.), *The Reception of Ossian in Europe* (London, 2004).
Goodridge, John, *Rural Life in Eighteenth-Century English Poetry* (Cambridge, 1995).
—— 'Clare Criticism, 1970–2000' in Kövesi and Goodridge (eds.), *John Clare: New Approaches*, pp. 202–50.
—— 'Identity, Authenticity, Class: John Clare and the Mask of Chatterton', *Angelaki*, 1, no. 2 (1994), 131–48.
—— (ed.), *The Independent Spirit: John Clare and the Self-Taught Tradition* (Helpston, 1994).
—— and J. C. Pellicer (eds.), *Cyder: A Poem in Two Books* (Cheltenham, 2001).
Gourvil, Francis, *Un centenaire: L'Eisteddfod d'Abergavenny (Septembre 1838) et les relations spirituelles Bretagne-Galles* (Morlaix, 1938).
—— *Théodore-Claude-Henri Hersart de la Villemarqué (1815–1895) et le 'Barzaz-Breiz' (1839–1845–1867)* (Rennes, 1960).
—— '"Voleur" sans le savoir: Prosper Mérimée et "Gwenc'hlan" en 1835', *Nouvelle revue de Bretagne* (March–August, 1949), 104–15, 211–22, 299–306.
Grafton, Anthony, *The Footnote* (London, 1997).
—— *Forgers and Critics: Creativity and Duplicity in Western Scholarship* (Princeton, NJ, 1990).
Gregory, G., *Lectures on the Sacred Poetry of the Hebrews* (2 vols., London, 1787).

Griggs, E. L. (ed.), *Collected Letters of Samuel Taylor Coleridge* (6 vols., Oxford, 1956–71).
Groom, Nick, *The Forger's Shadow* (London, 2002).
—— *The Making of Percy's 'Reliques'* (Oxford, 1999).
—— 'The Death of Chatterton' in Heys (ed.), *From Gothic to Romantic*, pp. 116–25.
—— (ed.), *Thomas Chatterton and Romantic Culture* (Basingstoke, 1999).
[Guest, Charlotte], *The Diaries of Lady Charlotte Guest: Extracts from her Journals 1833–1852, edited by her Grandson the Earl of Bessborough* (London, 1950).
Guest, Revel, and Angela V. John, *Lady Charlotte: A Biography of the Nineteenth Century* (London, 1989).
Guiomar, Jean-Yves, *Le bretonisme: les historiens bretons au XIXᵉ siècle* (Mayenne, 1987).
—— 'Le *Barzaz-Breiz* de Théodore Hersart de la Villemarqué' in Pierre Nora (ed.), *Les lieux de mémoire III. Les France* (7 vols., Paris, 1992), pp. 526–65.
—— 'Quand les bretonistes répudièrent la Gaule (1840–1850)' in Paul Viallaneix and Jean Ehrard (eds.), *Nos ancêtres les Gaulois* (Clermont-Ferrand, 1982), pp. 195–201.
Hardinge, George, *Rowley and Chatterton in the Shades* (London, 1782).
Harker, Dave, *Fakesong: The Manufacture of British 'folksong', 1700 to the Present Day* (Milton Keynes, 1985).
Haugen, Kristine Louise, 'Ossian and the Invention of Textual History', *Journal of the History of Ideas*, 59 (1998), 309–27.
Haycock, Marged, 'The Significance of the "Cad Goddau" Tree-List in the Book of Taliesin' in Martin J. Ball, James Fife, Erich Poppe and Jenny Rowland (eds.), *Celtic Linguistics: Readings in the Brythonic Languages. Festschrift for T. Arwyn Watkins* (Amsterdam/Philadelphia, 1990), pp. 297–331.
Haywood, Ian, *Faking It: Art and the Politics of Forgery* (Brighton, 1987).
—— *The Making of History: A Study of the Literary Forgeries of James Macpherson and Thomas Chatterton in relation to Eighteenth-Century Ideas of History and Fiction* (Rutherford, 1986).
Herron, Patrick, 'Ruthven's *Faking Literature*, Forging Literature and Faking Forged Literature', *Jacket*, 17 (2002) (http://jacketmagazine.com/17/herron.html).
Heys, Alistair (ed.), *From Gothic to Romantic: Chatterton's Bristol* (Bristol, 2005).
Hiatt, Alfred, *The Making of Medieval Forgeries: False Documents in Fifteenth-Century England* (London, 2004).
Higley, Sarah, *Between Languages: The Uncooperative Text in Early Welsh and Old English Nature Poetry* (University Park, Pa., 1992).
Hobsbawm, Eric, and Terence Ranger (eds.), *The Invention of Tradition* (Cambridge, 1983).
Holmes, Richard, 'Thomas Chatterton: the Case Re-opened', *Cornhill Magazine*, 178 (1970), 203–51.
Hudson, Nicholas, 'Oral Tradition: The Evolution of an Eighteenth-Century Concept' in S. J. Alvaro Ribeira and James G. Basker (eds.), *Tradition in Transition: Women Writers, Marginal Texts, and the Eighteenth-Century Canon* (Oxford, 1996), pp. 161–76.
Hume, David, *A Treatise of Human Nature* (3 vols., London, 1739–40).
Hutton, Ronald, 'William Stukeley's Religion', *Antiquaries Journal*, 85 (2005), 381–94.
Huws, Daniel, *Caneuon Llafar Gwlad ac Iolo a'i Fath* (Aberystwyth, 1993).
—— 'Iolo Morganwg and Traditional Music' in Jenkins (ed.), *Rattleskull Genius*, pp. 333–56.
Ifans, Rhiannon, *Gwaith Gruffudd Llwyd a'r Llygliwiaid Eraill* (Aberystwyth, 2000).

Inglis-Jones, Elisabeth, *Peacocks in Paradise* (London, 1950).

Jacquelot, C. de, 'L'Eisteddfod d'Abergavenny en 1838', *Le clocher breton* (1913), 2587–91, 2600–5.

Janowitz, Anne, *Lyric and Labour in the Romantic Tradition* (Cambridge, 1998).

Jenkins, Geraint H., *Literature, Religion and Society in Wales, 1660–1730* (Cardiff, 1978).

—— *'Perish Kings and Emperors, but Let the Bard of Liberty Live'* (Aberystwyth, 2006).

—— 'Historical Writing in the Eighteenth Century' in Branwen Jarvis (ed.), *A Guide to Welsh Literature, c.1700–1800* (Cardiff, 2000), pp. 23–44.

—— 'On the Trail of a "Rattleskull Genius"' in idem (ed.), *Rattleskull Genius*, pp. 1–26.

—— 'The Unitarian Firebrand, the Cambrian Society and the Eisteddfod' in idem (ed.), *Rattleskull Genius*, pp. 269–92.

—— 'The Urban Experiences of Iolo Morganwg', *WHR*, 22, no. 3 (2005), 463–98.

—— (ed.), *Language and Community in the Nineteenth Century* (Cardiff, 1998).

—— (ed.), *A Rattleskull Genius: The Many Faces of Iolo Morganwg* (Cardiff, 2005).

—— (ed.), *The Welsh Language before the Industrial Revolution* (Cardiff, 1997).

Jenkins, Philip, *The Making of a Ruling Class* (Cambridge, 1983).

Jenkins, R. T., 'Bardd a'i Gefndir', *THSC* (1946–7), 97–149.

Johnson, Samuel, *A Journey to the Western Isles of Scotland* (London, 1775).

—— *The Rambler* (6 vols., London, 1752).

Johnston, Arthur, 'William Blake and "The Ancient Britons"', *NLWJ*, XXII, no. 3 (1982), 304–20.

Jones, David Ceri, 'Iolo Morganwg and the Welsh Rural Landscape' in Jenkins (ed.), *Rattleskull Genius*, pp. 227–50.

Jones, David J. V., *The Last Rising: The Newport Insurrection of 1839* (Oxford, 1985).

Jones, Edward, *The Bardic Museum of Primitive British Literature* (London, 1802).

—— *Musical and Poetical Relicks of the Welsh Bards* (London, 1784).

Jones, Owen, Iolo Morganwg and William Owen Pughe, *The Myvyrian Archaiology of Wales* (3 vols., London, 1801–7).

Kaplan, Louise J., *The Family Romance of the Imposter-Poet: Thomas Chatterton* (Berkeley and Los Angeles, 1987).

Kaul, Suvir, *Poems of Nation, Anthems of Empire: English Verse in the Long Eighteenth Century* (London, 2000).

Kearney, Hugh, *The British Isles: A History of Four Nations* (Cambridge, 1989).

Keating, Geoffrey, *The General History of Ireland . . . collected by the learned Jeoffry Keating DD. Translated by Dermo'd O'Connor* (2 vols., London, 1723).

Keegan, Bridget, 'Boys, Marvellous Boys: John Clare's "Natural Genius"' in Kövesi and Goodridge (eds.), *John Clare: New Approaches*, pp. 65–76.

—— 'Nostalgic Chatterton: Fictions of Poetic Identity and the Forging of the Self-Taught Tradition' in Groom (ed.), *Thomas Chatterton and Romantic Culture*, pp. 210–27.

—— 'Rural Poetry and the Self-Taught Tradition' in Christine Gerrard (ed.), *A Companion to Eighteenth-Century Poetry* (Oxford, 2006), pp. 563–76.

Keevak, Michael, *The Pretended Asian: George Psalmanazar's Eighteenth-Century Formosan Hoax* (Detroit, Mich., 2004).

Kersey, Mel, 'Ballads, Britishness and *Hardyknute*, 1719–1859', *Scottish Studies Review*, 5, no. 1 (2004), 40–56.

Kinsley, James (ed.), *Burns: Poems and Songs* (Oxford, 1971).

Koch, John T., '*De Sancto Iudicaelo rege historia* and its implications for the Welsh Taliesin' in Joseph Falaky Nagy and Leslie Ellen Jones (eds.), *Heroic Poets and Poetic Heroes in Celtic Tradition: A Festschrift for Patrick K. Ford*, CSANA Yearbook, 3–4 (Dublin, 2005), pp. 247–62.

Korshin, Paul, 'Types of Eighteenth-Century Literary Patronage', *Eighteenth-Century Studies*, 7 (1974), 453–73.

Kövesi, Simon, and John Goodridge (eds.), *John Clare: New Approaches* (Helpston, 2000).

Kramnick, Jonathan Brody, *Making the English Canon: Print-Capitalism and the Cultural Past, 1700–1770* (Cambridge, 1998).

Kristmannsson, Gauti, *The Role of Translation in the Construction of National Literatures in Britain and Germany 1750–1830: Translation without an Original* (Frankfurt am Main, 2005).

La Rue, Gervais de, *Recherches sur les ouvrages des Bardes de la Bretagne armoricaine dans le Moyen âge* (Caen, 1815).

La Villemarqué, Pierre de, *La Villemarqué, sa vie, ses oeuvres* (Paris, 1926).

La Villemarqué, Théodore Hersart de, *Barzaz-Breiz: chants populaires de la Bretagne* (2 vols., Paris, 1839; 2 vols., Paris, 1845; 1867).

—— *Contes populaires des anciens bretons* (2 vols., Paris, 1842).

—— *Poèmes des bardes bretons du VIe siècle* (Paris and Vannes, 1850).

—— 'Les Bretons d'Angleterre et les Bretons de France', *Revue de Bretagne et de Vendée* (1867), 337–56.

—— 'La langue et la littérature de la Celtique sont-elles entrées comme élément dans la formation de la langue et de la littérature de la France?', ed. J.-Y. Guiomar, *BSAF*, CXVII (1988), 61–93.

—— 'Un rapport de M. de la Villemarqué', *Le clocher breton* (1906), 1096–9, 1109–12.

Landry, Donna, *The Muses of Resistance: Laboring-Class Women's Poetry in Britain 1739–1796* (Cambridge, 1990).

Laurent, Donatien, *Aux sources du Barzaz-Breiz: la mémoire d'un peuple* (Douarnenez, 1989).

—— 'Des antiquaires aux folkloristes: découverte et promotion des littératures orales' in Jean Balcou and Yves Le Gallo (eds.), *Histoire littéraire et culturelle de la Bretagne* (2 vols., Paris, 1987), II, pp. 335–54.

—— 'La *gwerz* de Skolan et la légende de Merlin', *Éthnologie française*, 1, 3–4 (1971), 19–54.

—— 'La Villemarqué, collecteur de chants populaires: étude des sources du premier *Barzaz-Breiz* à partir des originaux de collecte (1833–1840)' (unpublished University of Brest Ph.D. thesis, 1974).

—— 'Tradition and Innovation in Breton Oral Literature' in Glanmor Williams and Robert Owen Jones (eds.), *The Celts and the Renaissance: Tradition and Innovation* (Cardiff, 1990), pp. 91–9.

Le Disez, Jean-Yves, *Étrange Bretagne: récits des voyageurs britanniques en Bretagne (1830–1900)* (Rennes, 2002).

Le Gonidec, J.-F.-M.-M.-A., *Dictionnaire celto-breton ou breton-français* (Angoulême, 1821).

—— *Dictionnaire français–breton*, ed. Théodore Hersart de La Villemarqué (Saint-Brieuc, 1847).

—— *Grammaire celto-bretonne* (Paris, 1807).

Le Stum, Philippe, *Le néo-druidisme en Bretagne: origine, naissance, et développement, 1890–1914* (Rennes, 1998).

Leerssen, Joep, 'Celticism' in Terence Brown (ed.), *Celticism* (Amsterdam, 1990), pp. 1–20.

—— 'Ossian and the Rise of Literary Historicism' in Gaskill (ed.), *The Reception of Ossian*, pp. 109–25.

Lewis, Aneirin, 'Ieuan Fardd a'r Llenorion Saesneg', *LlC*, VII, nos. 3–4 (1963), 172–92.

—— (ed.), *The Correspondence of Thomas Percy and Evan Evans* (Louisiana, 1957).

Lewis, Gwyneth, 'Eighteenth-Century Literary Forgeries, with Special Reference to the Work of Iolo Morganwg' (unpublished University of Oxford D.Phil. thesis, 1991).

Lewis, Lionel Smithett, *St Joseph of Arimathea at Glastonbury* (Altrincham, 1955).

Llewellyn Jones, Howel, and Eurys Rolant (eds.), *Gwaith Iorwerth Fynglwyd* (Caerdydd, 1975).

Lloyd-Morgan, Ceridwen, 'French Texts, Welsh Translations' in Roger Ellis (ed.), *The Medieval Translator*, II (London, 1991), pp. 45–63.

Lord, Peter, *Words with Pictures: Welsh Images and Images of Wales in the Popular Press, 1640–1860* (Aberystwyth, 1995).

Lowth, Robert, *De Sacra Poesi Hebræorum Prælectiones Academicæ* (Oxford, 1753).

Lucas, John, 'Bloomfield and Clare' in Goodridge (ed.), *The Independent Spirit*, pp. 55–68.

Lynch, Jack, 'Forgery as Performance Art: The Strange Case of George Psalmanazar', *1650–1850: Ideas, Aesthetics and Inquiries in the Early Modern Era*, 11 (2005), 21–35.

McKenna, Catherine, 'Aspects of Tradition Formation in Eighteenth-Century Wales' in Joseph Falaky Nagy (ed.), *Memory and the Modern in Celtic Literatures*, CSANA Yearbook, 5 (Dublin, 2006), pp. 37–60.

Mackenzie, Henry, *Report . . . into the Nature and Authenticity of the Poems of Ossian* (Edinburgh, 1805).

Macpherson, James, *An Introduction to the History of Great Britain and Ireland* (London, 1771).

—— (trans.), *The Iliad of Homer, translated by James Macpherson Esq.* (London, 1773).

Makdisi, Saree, *William Blake and the Impossible History of the 1790s* (Chicago, 2003).

Malone, Edmond, *Cursory Observation on the Poems attributed to Thomas Chatterton* (London, 1782).

Manning, Susan, 'Henry Mackenzie and Ossian, or, the Emotional Value of Asterisks' in Stafford and Gaskill (eds.), *From Gaelic to Romantic*, pp. 136–52.

Mee, Jon, *Romanticism, Enthusiasm, and Regulation* (Oxford, 2003).

—— '"Images of Truth New Born": Iolo, William Blake and the Literary Radicalism of the 1790s' in Jenkins (ed.), *Rattleskull Genius*, pp. 173–93.

Meyerstein, E. H. W., *A Life of Thomas Chatterton* (London, 1930).

Milles, Jeremiah, *Poems . . . by Thomas Rowley* (London, 1782).

Milroy, James, and Lesley Milroy, *Authority in Language: Investigating Language Prescription and Standardization* (3rd edn., London, 1999).

Moore, Dafydd, *Enlightenment and Romance in James Macpherson's 'The Poems of Ossian': Myth, Genre and Cultural Change* (Aldershot, 2003).

—— 'The Reception of Ossian in England and Scotland' in Gaskill (ed.), *The Reception of Ossian*, pp. 21–39.

Morgan, Prys, *The Eighteenth Century Renaissance* (Llandybïe, 1981).

—— 'L'Abbé Pezron and the Celts', *THSC* (1965), 286–95.

—— 'From a Death to a View: The Hunt for the Welsh Past in the Romantic Period' in Hobsbawm and Ranger (eds.), *The Invention of Tradition*, pp. 43–100.

—— 'Thomas Price "Carnhuanawc" (1747–1848) et les Bretons', *TRIADE: Galles, Ecosse, Irlande* (1995), 5–13.

Morgan, R. W., *St Paul in Britain, or, The Origin of British as opposed to Papal Christianity* (Oxford, 1861).

Morris, Lewis, *Diddanwch Teuluaidd* (Llundain, 1763).

—— *Tlysau yr Hen Oesoedd* (Caergybi, 1735).

Nagy, Joseph Falaky, 'Observations on the Ossianesque in Medieval Irish Literature and Modern Irish Folklore', *Journal of American Folklore*, 114, no. 454 (2001), 436–46.

Newton, John, *Olney Hymns* (London, 1779).

Nicolas, Michel, *Le séparatisme en Bretagne* (Brasparts, 1986).

Nussbaum, Felicity A., *The Autobiographical Subject: Gender and Ideology in Eighteenth-Century England* (London, 1989).

Owen, A. S., *The Famous Druids: A Survey of Three Centuries of English Literature on Druids* (Oxford, 1962).

Owen, Hugh (ed.), *Additional Letters of the Morrises of Anglesey (1735–1786)* (2 vols., London, 1947–9).

Owen, William, *A Dictionary of the Welsh Language, Explained in English* (2 vols., London, 1793–1803).

—— *The Heroic Elegies and Other Pieces of Llywarç Hen* (London, 1792).

—— and Owen Jones (eds.), *Barddoniaeth Dafydd ab Gwilym* (London, 1789).

Owen Pughe, William, *A Grammar of the Welsh Language* (London, 1803).

Parfitt, Geoff (ed.), *The Complete Poems of Ben Jonson* (Harmondsworth, 1975).

Pedlar, Valerie, '"Written By Himself" – Edited by Others: The Autobiographical Writings of John Clare' in Kövesi and Goodridge (eds.), *John Clare: New Approaches*, pp. 17–31.

Pennant, Thomas, *Tour in Wales* (3 vols., London, 1778–83).

Pezron, Paul-Yves, *Antiquité de la nation et de la langue des Celtes* (Paris, 1703).

Phillips, Geraint, 'Forgery and Patronage: Iolo Morganwg and Owain Myfyr' in Jenkins (ed.), *Rattleskull Genius*, pp. 403–23.

—— 'Math o Wallgofrwydd: Iolo Morganwg, Opiwm a Thomas Chatterton', *NLWJ*, XXIX, no. 4 (1996), 391–410.

Pictet, Adolphe, *Le mystère des bardes de l'île de Bretagne: ou, La doctrine des bardes gallois du moyen âge sur Dieu, la vie future et la transmigration des âmes* (Geneva, 1856).

Pierce, Patricia, *The Great Shakespeare Fraud: The Strange, True Story of William-Henry Ireland* (Stroud, 2004).

Pinkerton, John, *Dissertation on the Origin and Progress of the Scythians or Goths* (London, 1787).

—— *Select Scotish Ballads* (2 vols., London, 1783).

Pittock, Murray G. H., *Celtic Identity and the British Image* (Manchester, 1999).
—— *Inventing and Resisting Britain: Cultural Identities in Britain and Ireland, 1685–1789* (New York, 1997).
—— 'Robert Burns and British Poetry', *PBA*, 121 (2002), 191–211.
Porter, James, 'Bring me the head of James Macpherson: The execution of Ossian and the wellsprings of Folkloristic Discourse', *Journal of American Folklore*, 114 (2001), 396–435.
Postic, Fañch, 'La Villemarqué et le Pays de Galles (1837–1838): deux lettres inédites de Thomas Price', *TRIADE: Galles, Ecosse, Irlande* (1995), 17–19.
—— 'Premiers échanges interceltiques: le voyage de La Villemarqué au Pays de Galles', *Armen*, 125 (2001), 39–40.
—— 'Propositions pour un enseignement bilingue en 1836: un mémoire inédit de Y.-M.-G. Laouénan', *BSAF*, CXXX (2001), 437–66.
Prescott, Sarah, '"Gray's Pale Spectre": Evan Evans, Thomas Gray and the Rise of Welsh Bardic Nationalism', *Modern Philology*, 104, no. 1 (2006), 72–95.
Rawson, Claude, 'Unparodying and Forgery: The Augustan Chatterton' in Groom (ed.), *Thomas Chatterton and Romantic Culture*, pp. 15–31.
Raynor, David, 'Ossian and Hume' in Gaskill (ed.), *Ossian Revisited*, pp. 147–63.
Rejhon, A. C., 'Hu Gadarn: Folklore and Fabrication' in Patrick K. Ford (ed.), *Celtic Folklore and Christianity: Studies in Memory of William W. Heist* (Santa Barbara, Calif., 1983), pp. 201–12.
Ritson, Joseph, *Scotish Songs* (2 vols., London, 1794).
Roberts, Brynley F. (ed.), *Breudwyt Maxen Wledic* (Dublin, 2005).
Robertson, J. L., 'Ossianic Heroic Poetry', *Transactions of the Gaelic Society of Inverness*, XXII (1897–8), 257–325.
Robinson, Douglas, *Western Translation Theory from Herodotus to Nietsche* (Manchester, 1997).
Robinson, Eric, and David Powell (eds.), *John Clare by Himself* (Ashington, 1996).
Roe, Nicholas, 'Authenticating Robert Burns', *Essays in Criticism*, 46 (1996), 195–218 (reprinted in Carol McGuirk (ed.), *Critical Essays on Robert Burns* (New York, 1998), pp. 208–24).
Rogers, Pat, 'Chatterton and the Club' in Groom (ed.), *Thomas Chatterton and Romantic Culture*, pp. 121–50.
Ross, Trevor, *The Making of the English Literary Canon: From the Middle Ages to the Late Eighteenth Century* (Montreal, 1998).
Rowland, Jenny (ed.), *Early Welsh Saga Poetry* (Cambridge, 1990).
Rubel, M. M., *Savage and Barbarian: Historical Attitudes in the Criticism of Homer and Ossian in Britain, 1760–1800* (Oxford, 1978).
Russett, Margaret, *Fictions and Fakes: Forging Romantic Authenticity, 1760–1845* (Cambridge, 2006).
Ruthven, K. K., *Faking Literature* (Cambridge, 2001).
Sales, Roger, *John Clare: A Literary Life* (Basingstoke, 2002).
Sher, Richard B., 'Percy, Shaw and the Ferguson "Cheat": National Prejudice in the Ossian Wars' in Gaskill (ed.), *Ossian Revisited*, pp. 207–45.

Shields, Anthea F., 'Thomas Spence and the English Language', *Transactions of the Philological Society* (1974), 33–64.

Smiles, Sam, *The Image of Antiquity: Ancient Britain and the Romantic Imagination* (London, 1994).

Smith, Olivia, *The Politics of Language, 1791–1818* (Oxford, 1984).

Southey, C. C. (ed.), *Life and Correspondence of Robert Southey* (6 vols., London, 1849–50).

Souvestre, Émile, *Les derniers bretons* (Paris, 1836).

Stafford, Fiona, *The Last of the Race: The Growth of a Myth from Milton to Darwin* (Oxford, 1994).

—— *The Sublime Savage: A Study of James Macpherson and the Poems of Ossian* (Edinburgh, 1988).

—— 'Dr Johnson and the Ruffian: New Evidence in the Dispute between Samuel Johnson and James Macpherson', *Notes and Queries*, new series, 36 (1989), 70–7.

—— and Howard Gaskill (eds.), *From Gaelic to Romantic: Ossianic Translations* (Amsterdam, 1998).

Stewart, Susan, 'Notes on Distressed Genres', *Journal of American Folklore*, 104, no. 411 (1991), 5–31.

—— 'Scandals of the Ballad' in eadem, *Crimes of Writing: Problems in the Containment of Representation* (Oxford, 1991), pp. 102–31.

Storey, Mark (ed.), *The Letters of John Clare* (Oxford, 1985).

Stott, Anne, *Hannah More: The First Victorian* (Oxford, 2003).

Suggett, Richard, 'Iolo Morganwg: Stonecutter, Builder, and Antiquary' in Jenkins (ed.), *Rattleskull Genius*, pp. 197–226.

Sven Myer, Gwenno, 'Y Cylchgrawn Llydaweg *Gwalarn* (1925–1944): Ei Amcanion, ei Iaith, ei Gyfraniad i Lenyddiaeth' (unpublished University of Wales MA thesis, 1998).

Sweet, Rosemary, *Antiquaries: The Discovery of the Past in Eighteenth-Century Britain* (London, 2004).

Tanguy, Bernard, *Aux origines du nationalisme breton: le renouveau des études bretonnes au XIXe siècle* (Paris, 1977).

—— 'L'Académie Celtique et le mouvement bretoniste devant la révolution française' in *La Révolution Française dans la conscience intellectuelle bretonne du XIXème siècle*, Cahiers de Bretagne Occidentale, 8 (Brest, 1988), pp. 127–44.

—— 'Des celtomanes aux bretonistes: les idées et les hommes' in Jean Balcou and Yves Le Gallo (eds.), *Histoire littéraire et culturelle de la Bretagne* (2 vols., Paris, 1987), II, pp. 293–334.

Taylor, Charles, *Sources of the Self: The Making of Modern Identity* (Cambridge, Mass., 1989).

Taylor, Donald S., *Thomas Chatterton's Art: Experiments in Imagined History* (Princeton, NJ, 1978).

—— (ed.), *The Complete Works of Thomas Chatterton: A Bicentenary Edition* (2 vols., Oxford, 1971).

Terry, Richard, *Poetry and the Making of the English Literary Past, 1660–1781* (Oxford, 2001).

Thiesse, Anne-Marie, *La création des identités nationales* (Paris, 1999).
Thomas, Einir Gwenllian, 'Astudiaeth Destunol o Statud Gruffudd ap Cynan' (unpublished University of Wales Ph.D. thesis, 2001).
Thomas, H. J., 'Iolo Morganwg Vindicated: Glamorgan's First Field Archaeologist', *Glamorgan–Gwent Archaeological Trust Annual Report*, 1983–4 (Swansea, 1985), pp. 149–57.
Thomas, M. Wynn, *Corresponding Cultures: The Two Literatures of Wales* (Cardiff, 1999).
Thomas, Mair Elvet, *Afiaith yng Ngwent: Hanes Cymdeithas Cymreigyddion y Fenni 1833–1854* (Caerdydd, 1978).
—— *The Welsh Spirit of Gwent* (Cardiff, 1988).
Thomson, D. S., *The Gaelic Sources of Macpherson's 'Ossian'* (Edinburgh, 1952).
Todd, Janet (ed.), *The Collected Letters of Mary Wollstonecraft* (London, 2003).
Treadwell, James, *Autobiographical Writing and British Literature 1783–1834* (Oxford, 2005).
Trumpener, Katie, *Bardic Nationalism: The Romantic Novel and the British Empire* (Princeton, NJ, 1997).
Turner, Sharon, *History of the Anglo-Saxons* (4 vols., London, 1799–1805).
—— *A Vindication of the Genuineness of the Ancient British Poems of Aneurin, Taliesin, Llywarch Hen, and Merdhin* (London, 1803).
Tyrwhitt, Thomas, *A Vindication of the Appendix to the Poems, called Rowley's* (London, 1782).
Walpole, Horace, *Anecdotes of Painting in England: with some Account of the Principal Artists, and Incidental Notes on Other Arts* (4 vols., Strawberry Hill, 1762–71).
Walters, John, *A Dissertation on the Welsh Language, pointing out its Antiquity, Copiousness, Grammatical Perfection* (Cowbridge, 1771).
Waring, Elijah, *Recollections and Anecdotes of Edward Williams* (London, 1850).
Warton, Thomas, *An Enquiry into the Authenticity of the Poems attributed to Thomas Rowley* (London, 1782).
—— *Five Pastoral Eclogues: The Scenes of which are suppos'd to lie among the Shepherds, oppress'd by the War in Germany* (London, 1745).
—— *The History of English Poetry, from the close of the eleventh to the commencement of the eighteenth century* (4 vols., London, 1774–81).
Weinbrot, Howard, *Britannia's Issue: The Rise of British Literature from Dryden to Ossian* (Cambridge, 1993).
Williams, D. Emrys, 'Rice Williams: The Contact between Thomas Percy and Evan Evans', *NLWJ*, XVII, no. 3 (1972), 287–98.
Williams, Edward, *Poems, Lyric and Pastoral* (2 vols., London, 1794).
Williams, G. J., *Edward Lhuyd ac Iolo Morganwg: Agweddau ar Hanes Astudiaethau Gwerin yng Nghymru* (Caerdydd, 1964).
—— *Iolo Morganwg – Y Gyfrol Gyntaf* (Caerdydd, 1956).
—— *Iolo Morganwg a Chywyddau'r Ychwanegiad* (Llundain, 1926).
—— *Traddodiad Llenyddol Morgannwg* (Caerdydd, 1948).
—— 'Cywyddau'r Chwanegiad', *LlC*, IV, no. 3 (1957), 229–30.
—— 'Leland a Bale a'r Traddodiad Derwyddol', *LlC*, IV, no. 1 (1956), 15–25.
—— 'Meddygon Myddfai', *LlC*, I, no. 3 (1951), 169–73.
—— 'Rhys Goch ap Rhiccert', *Y Beirniad*, VIII (1919), 211–26, 260.

Williams, Gwyn A., *Madoc: The Making of a Myth* (London, 1979).

Williams, Heather, 'Writing to Paris: Poets, Nobles and Savages in Nineteenth-Century Brittany', *French Studies*, 57 (2003), 475–90.

Williams, Ifor, 'Notes on Nennius', *BBCS*, VII, part 4 (1935), 380–8.

Williams, J., *La Basse Bretagne et le pays de Galles: quelques paroles simples et véridiques adressées a M. le Comte Hersart de la Villemarqué* (Paris, 1860).

Williams, Jane, *The Literary Remains of the Rev. Thomas Price, Carnhuanawc* (2 vols., Llandovery and London, 1855).

Williams, John (ab Ithel) (ed.), *Barddas* (2 vols., Llandovery, 1862, 1874).

Williams, Sian Rhiannon, *Oes y Byd i'r Iaith Gymraeg* (Caerdydd, 1992).

—— 'The Welsh Language in Industrial Monmouthshire *c.*1800–1901' in Jenkins (ed.), *Language and Community in the Nineteenth Century*, pp. 203–29.

Williams, Stephen J., 'Carnhuanawc, 1787–1848, Eisteddfodwr ac Ysgolhaig', *THSC* (1955), 18–30.

Williams, Taliesin (ed.), *Cyfrinach Beirdd Ynys Prydain: ys ef Llwybreiddiaeth ag Athrawiaeth ar y Farddoniaeth Gymraeg a'i Pherthynasau, yn ol Trefn a Dosparth y Prif Feirdd gynt ar y Gelfyddyd wrth Gerdd Dafod* (Abertawy, 1829).

—— *Iolo Manuscripts: A Selection of Ancient Welsh Manuscripts, in Prose and Verse, from the collection made by the late Edward Williams, Iolo Morganwg; for the Purpose of forming a continuation of the Myfyrian Archaiology; and Subsequently Proposed as Materials for a New History of Wales* (Llandovery, 1848).

Williams, Thomas, *Can-aouen Eisteddfod, written in the Breton language, for the Abergavenny Cymreigyddion Anniversary October 10th 1838* (Crickhowell, 1838).

Wood, Robert, *An Essay on the Original Genius and Writings of Homer: with a Comparative View of the Ancient and Present State of the Troade* (London, 1775).

Woodhouse, James, *Poems on Several Occasions: the second edition, corrected, with several additional pieces* (London, 1766).

Yearsley, Ann, *Poems, on Several Occasions* (4th edn., London, 1786).

Index